Persistent Poverty
in Rural America

RURAL STUDIES SERIES
of the
Rural Sociological Society

Series Editor

Forrest A. Deseran, *Louisiana State University*

Editorial Board

Rural Studies Series

Persistent Poverty in Rural America

Rural Sociological Society
Task Force on Persistent Rural Poverty

FOREWORD BY
Emery N. Castle

Westview Press

BOULDER · SAN FRANCISCO · OXFORD

Rural Sociological Society Business Office
Department of Sociology
Montana State University
Bozeman MT 59717

The project that is the subject of this report was approved by the Council of the Rural Sociological Society at its annual meeting in August 1990.

This report has been reviewed by three groups other than the authors: (1) the Task Force
Advisory Committee, (2) a panel of subject matter specialists, and (3) The Rural Sociological Society's Rural Studies Series Editorial Committee.

This project was supported by the W. K. Kellogg Foundation of Battle Creek, Michigan,
and the directors of the Regional Centers for Rural Development.

Rural Studies Series, Sponsored by the Rural Sociological Society

Published in 1993 in the United States of America by Westview Press, Inc., 5500 Central Avenue,
Boulder, Colorado 80301-2877, and in the United Kingdom by Westview Press, 36 Lonsdale Road,
Summertown, Oxford OX2 7EW

A CIP catalog record for this book is available from the Library of Congress.
ISBN 0-8133-8712-4

161698

Printed and bound in the United States of America

The paper used in this publication meets the requirements
of the American National Standard for Permanence of Paper
for Printed Library Materials Z39.48-1984.

10   9   8   7   6   5   4   3   2

AAX-5794

Contents

Foreword

To appreciate this volume, one needs to know how the Task Force on Persistent Rural Poverty came into being and how it was that Gene Summers became its director. This Foreword will provide some of this background and offer an opinion on the significance of the scholarship reported herein.

Gene Summers is a member and vice chairman of the National Rural Studies Committee. The NRSC is a multi-disciplinary group of scholars appointed for the purpose of encouraging those in higher education to give greater attention to the problems of rural America. It was made possible by a grant from the W. K. Kellogg Foundation to Oregon State University; its membership includes people from several disciplines, different regions of the Nation, and from both public and private academic institutions. The work of the Committee began in 1987 and will continue until 1995. I serve as its chair.

The Committee has attempted to inform itself about rural America in a number of ways, including meetings and field trips in the Pacific Northwest, the South, the Midwest, the Northeast, and Southwest. The meeting in the South was in the Mississippi Delta. While there, the Committee spent time with community leaders, residents of small towns, and workers in the catfish industry.

After the Mississippi meeting, some of the Committee members, including Gene Summers, wrote about their reactions to the meeting and field trip in the Delta. Gene's experience there triggered memories of his family and his childhood. His was a poor rural family from the same region of the nation. He related in a very personal way to the experiences of those with whom we talked and observed during the meetings and field trip. Those of us privileged to share in Gene's written observations were impressed with the way those childhood and family experiences have shaped the conceptual lens through which this sophisticated social scientist views the world. These experiences as well as his education as a sociologist provide motivation and permit observations not available to many others.

About the time of the Mississippi meeting Gene was also assuming the presidency of the Rural Sociological Society. He testifies that he was so affected by the Mississippi experience that he was moved to bring the matter of persistent rural poverty to the attention of the Council of the Society. The

Task Force on Persistent Rural Poverty of the Rural Sociological Society was the consequence, and it is its work which is reported in this volume. Professional disciplinary associations are more noted for their introversion than for their concern with the pressing problems of society. The leadership of Summers, as well as the general orientation of the Society, contributed to their willingness to undertake this major task.

I do not know a great deal about the Rural Sociological Society, although I have worked professionally with many of its members. It is significant that it chose to differentiate itself from the American Sociological Association by the adjective, "Rural." This is in contrast to those who established the Farm Economics Association, which later became the American Agricultural Economics Association. From the outset those sociologists concerned with people in the more sparsely populated areas adopted a commendable broad view. They recognized rural people were not always to be found on farms or engaged in agriculturally related pursuits. The myth that "rural" and "agriculture" are the same still stands in the way of a clear view of the countryside. It is to the credit of the rural sociologists that they recognized this early on and thereby acquired a broader research agenda than did the agricultural economists.

The many dimensions of poverty were used to organize the investigations of the numerous groups that constituted the Persistent Rural Poverty Task Force. The breadth of the Society and its self-assurance were again reflected in the multi-disciplinary nature of the undertaking. Academic disciplinary groups usually do not turn to other disciplines for help in analyzing social problems. It is to the credit of the Rural Sociological Society that it did so in this case. I am certain that the material reported in this volume has been improved by the participation of some non-sociologists.

Despite the severity of rural poverty issues and the multi-disciplinary nature of the undertaking, it was difficult for Summers to obtain funding for the effort. It is a tribute to his entrepreneurial and managerial skills that this product has been produced. Appreciation should also be expressed for the voluntary efforts of the numerous scholars who have contributed.

Each reader will bring their particular perspective to a work of this kind. For my part, it is easy to say what I have learned from this material. First, I have a much clearer notion of the severity and the extent of rural poverty than I did previously. Second, I have a deeper understanding of the underlying causes of rural poverty. Third, I have more insights, but not a blueprint, for the solution of this social pathology. I now know that much additional work is needed to produce a reliable conceptual base for the analysis of rural poverty.

Rural poverty is not one problem--it is many. Many Native Americans living in rural areas are poor, but their problems are very different from the poor in rural Appalachia. And the black people living in the Mississippi Delta have different issues to confront than do those in either of the other places. This is one facet of the fundamental, defining characteristic of rural America--its enormous diversity. In a policy context this diversity should challenge rather than paralyze us; people have fundamental needs regardless of location or social setting. The great domestic public policy challenge is to recognize differences while addressing fundamental human needs. As this is written, an attempt is being made to develop a health care program for this highly diverse nation. The information in this volume will be of value to those engaged in such activities; it will help them keep in mind that while many human needs are fundamental, the context in which those needs are satisfied varies enormously among social situations.

When people are arrayed according to their wealth and income, we label as "poverty" that category which is at the lowest extreme. The characteristics of this extreme category become important as we strive to understand poverty and decide what to do about it. Knowing more about rural poverty also informs us about rural economies and the income and wealth of rural people generally. While the welfare of the rural poor is a matter of legitimate concern, they do not constitute a large percentage of the total population; nevertheless, knowledge of their condition permits us to better understand the entire social, economic, and political system. Rural poverty, therefore, is a matter of general concern both because of the people in poverty and our own welfare and benefit.

Space and distance are the physical attributes which differentiate the countryside from the city and the suburbs. In a pure democracy, sparsely populated areas are at a disadvantage in obtaining political benefits. However, the United States has provided for spatial representation in its political system and some have argued that the sparsely populated areas are over-represented. It is my judgment that the political system of a predominantly urban nation fails to serve the countryside adequately for reasons other than political representation. As a nation becomes more urban, a smaller percentage of the population has knowledge of rural areas and rural people unless special effort is made to overcome this lack of knowledge. Inevitably this ignorance is reflected not only in the formulation but also in the execution of policies and programs. But if the political system fails to respond adequately to the needs of the countryside, what about the economic system? Can we not count on people to move to where the jobs are? Failing that, will industries not locate where wages are low and people are unemployed to obtain cheap and abundant labor? Any such general conclusion would represent a most naive application of the neo-classical economic model.

Despite recent developments in transportation and communication, space and distance remain important variables affecting rural public policy. Overcoming space still comes at a cost. People generally do not regard their place of residence as the precise equivalent of other places, so movement to places of possible employment does not occur immediately or without friction. Industries may well locate where wages are low and workers are available, but such industries are notoriously unstable and are not reliable means of alleviating low incomes. In the first place, these industries are vulnerable to even lower wage places abroad or elsewhere. Even if such employers remain in an area just because unskilled workers are available, wages are likely to remain low and the relative income position of the rural area may not change. Economics as a discipline does not offer unified explanation of why some nations remain poor relative to other nations or why some regions and areas within countries remain depressed over long periods of time.

All of this is to say that much needs to be done before social scientists will be able to offer policy makers a blueprint for action in bringing bypassed people and areas into the mainstream. From the work reported in this volume and from other scholarship that is emerging, some generalizations can, nevertheless, be drawn. First, the diversity of rural America should not be a reason for isolating such places and people from the mainstream activities of a predominantly urban society. Linkages and interactions need to be better understood and encouraged. Second, the solutions of most social problems are more easily obtained in the presence of a thriving economy than in its absence. It is understandable, even though it is unfortunate, that rural development has often been equated with rural economic development. It is unfortunate because the supply of rural places that could accommodate greater economic activity exceeds the demand for such places, and this often stimulates counterproductive competition among such places. Also, social conditions and obstacles may prevent some individuals, geographic areas, and groups from realizing their full potential for participation in mainstream social and economic activity. This volume is especially helpful in identifying and providing an understanding of these conditions and obstacles. I have referenced here the way race, ethnicity, gender, geographic place, and economic structure contribute to our understanding of the way things are and how they came to be that way. It is from such stuff that public policy is formulated.

Emery N. Castle
Corvallis, Oregon

Acknowledgments

The idea of a Task Force would never have been conceived were it not for Dr. Emery Castle and other members of the National Rural Studies Committee of the W. K. Kellogg Foundation. It was the experiences provided by a three-day visit of this Committee to the Mississippi Delta which prompted the president-elect of the Rural Sociological Society (Gene F. Summers) to approach the Council of the RSS with the proposal for the Task Force on Persistent Rural Poverty. The continued encouragement and support of Dr. Castle and the National Rural Studies Committee have been essential to the completion of this report.

To Dr. Gary King, program director at the W. K. Kellogg Foundation, we owe a very special debt of gratitude. When the proposal for the creation of the Task Force was merely an idea, Gary King stepped forward to provide guidance, encouragement, and his personal commitment to the goals of the Task Force. It was only through his wisdom and dedication that the Task Force became a reality.

Financial support for the work of the Task Force was provided by the W. K. Kellogg Foundation of Battle Creek, Michigan, and the directors of the Regional Centers for Rural Development, which are located on the campuses of Iowa State University, Mississippi State University, Oregon State University, and Pennsylvania State University.

In addition the departments, universities, and organizations with which Task Force members are affiliated have provided financial and in-kind support for the work of the Task Force. While there is no means for accounting the precise dollar value of these contributions, we are very much aware that without this support the work of the Task Force could not have been completed.

We wish also to acknowledge the contributions of many unnamed secretaries and students who provided assistance to the members of the Task Force. These are the colleagues whose ideas and labor are essential for an effort of this kind to be executed. We want to acknowledge our debt to them and to express our deep appreciation.

Nancy Carlisle and Bonnie Fabre are two of these skilled players whom we want to acknowledge. Nancy has been the force that has held together the communications and manuscript preparation processes and kept the Task Force chair from committing acts of violence against others and himself. Bonnie has kept us all out of jail with her skilled keeping of the financial records. Her cheerful handling of confused travelers and confusing expense accounts has been an inspiration for us all.

Finally comes Larry "The Big Guy" Meiller, who took crudely written sentences and turned them into prose with his magic editing pen. Everyone owes Larry a debt of gratitude, especially the readers of the Task Force report.

Gene F. Summers

Task Force on Persistent Rural Poverty

Chair, Gene F. Summers, University of Wisconsin-Madison
Staff, Nancy Carlisle, Bonnie Fabre
Editing, Larry Meiller
Statistical Consultant, Robert Hoppe

Working Group on Natural Resources
Craig R. Humphrey, **Chair**, The Pennsylvania State University
Matthew S. Carroll, Washington State University
Charles Geisler, Cornell University
Thomas G. Johnson, Virginia Polytechnic Institute and State University
Patrick C. West, University of Michigan
Gigi Berardi, Gettysburg College
Sally Fairfax, University of California-Berkeley
Louise Fortmann, University of California-Berkeley
Jonathan Kusel, University of California-Berkeley
Robert G. Lee, University of Washington
Seth Macinko, University of California-Berkeley
Nancy Lee Peluso, Yale University
Michael D. Schulman, North Carolina State University

Working Group on Spatial Location of Economic Activities
Thomas A. Lyson, **Co-Chair**, Cornell University
William W. Falk, **Co-Chair**, University of Maryland
Mark Henry, Clemson University
JoAnn Hickey, Western Carolina University
Mildred Warner, Cornell University

Working Group on Human Capital Investment
Daniel T. Lichter, **Chair**, Pennsylvania State University
Lionel J. Beaulieu, University of Florida
Jill L. Findeis, Pennsylvania State University
Ruy A. Teixeira, Economic Research Service, USDA

Working Group on Work Structures and Labor Market Dynamics
Leonard E. Bloomquist, Chair, Kansas State University
Christina Gringeri, University of Utah
H. L. Seyler, Kansas State University
Donald Tomaskovic-Devey, North Carolina State University
Cynthia Truelove, University of Wisconsin-Madison

Working Group on Racial and Ethnic Minorities
C. Matthew Snipp, Chair, University of Wisconsin-Madison
Hayward D. Horton, Iowa State University
Leif Jensen, Pennsylvania State University
Joane Nagel, University of Kansas
Refugio Rochin, University of California-Davis

Working Group on Rural Elderly
Nina Glasgow, Chair, Cornell University
Karen Holden, University of Wisconsin-Madison
Graham Rowles, University of Kentucky
Diane McLaughlin, Pennsylvania State University
Walter Davis, Mississippi State University

Working Group on Rural Women
Ann Tickamyer, Chair, University of Kentucky
Janet Bokemeier, Michigan State University
Shelley Feldman, Cornell University
John Paul Jones, University of Kentucky
DeeAnn Wenk, University of Oklahoma
Rosalind Harris, University of Kentucky

Working Group on the State and Rural Policy
Frederick Buttel, Chair, University of Wisconsin-Madison
William P. Browne, Central Michigan University
Susan Christopherson, Cornell University
John Gaventa, University of Tennessee-Knoxville
Donald Davis, University of Tennessee-Knoxville
David Freshwater, University of Kentucky
Philip McMichael, Cornell University
Philip Ehrensaft, University of Quebec-Montreal
Louis Swanson, University of Kentucky
Jess Gilbert, University of Wisconsin-Madison

Working Group on Children and Families
Patricia Garrett, **Chair**, University of North Carolina at Chapel Hill
Janet Fitchen, Ithaca College
Constance Hardesty, University of Oklahoma
Cynthia Johnson, North Carolina State University
Naurine Lennox, St. Olaf College
Maxine Thompson, North Carolina State University

Undergraduate Syllabus Project
Andre Hammonds, Indiana State University
Gene F. Summers, University of Wisconsin-Madison

Persistent Rural Poverty Report Reviewers

Advisory Committee
Sandra Batie, Virginia Tech and State University
Emery Castle, Oregon State University
Kenneth Deavers, Economic Research Service, U.S.D.A.
Janet Fitchen, Ithaca College
Barbara Stowe, Kansas State University
Julian Wolpert, Princeton University

Rural Sociological Society Rural Studies Series Editorial Committee
Forrest Deseran, **Chair**, Louisiana State University
Lionel J. Beaulieu, University of Florida
Lorna M. Butler, Washington State University
Linda Lobao, Ohio State University
Dudley L. Poston, Texas A&M University
C. Matthew Snipp, University of Wisconsin-Madison

Subject Matter Specialists
Sandra Batie, Virginia Tech & State University
E. M. Beck, Jr., University of Georgia
Steven Cornell, University of California-San Diego
Bonnie Thornton Dill, University of Maryland
Cynthia Duncan, University of New Hampshire
Greg Duncan, University of Michigan
Glenn Fuguitt, University of Wisconsin-Madison
Niles Hansen, University of Texas-Austin
Robert Hauser, University of Wisconsin-Madison
Susan Jenkins, University of Georgia
Joan Jensen, New Mexico State University

Jan Kodras, Florida State University
Linda Lobao, Ohio State University
Joe Molnar, Auburn University
Carolyn Sachs, Pennsylvania State University
Rogelio Saenz, Texas A&M University
William Serow, Florida State University
Doris Slesinger, University of Wisconsin-Madison
Jack Thigpen, Texas A&M University
Bruce Williams, University of Mississippi

Persistent Poverty
in Rural America

Introduction

For the past 25 years the United States has pursued a variety of programs and policies intended to alleviate poverty. In spite of these efforts, poverty persists. The past decade has ushered in a new round of debate about the extent and etiology of poverty in the United States (e.g., Wilson 1987; Murray 1984; Farley 1988). Much of this concern has centered on urban areas, where a highly visible poor population, segregated in poor inner-city neighborhoods, clearly needs our help. Because we live in an increasingly urban society, public perceptions of the social and economic problems of people burdened by poverty understandably have a clear urban orientation. Unfortunately, our reliance on national statistics, heavily weighted in favor of urban areas, often masks the extent of economic hardship in America's nonmetropolitan and rural areas. In fact, poverty rates in nonmetropolitan areas are higher than in metropolitan areas, and the demographic and economic foundations of nonmetropolitan poverty differ significantly from metropolitan areas and central cities (Duncan and Tickamyer 1988; O'Hare 1988).

In the post-World War II United States there have been three main phases of rural poverty. During the first phase, from 1945 until the 1960s consolidation of the "Great Society" programs, rural America was in a protracted phase of economic restructuring. These were years of rapid productivity increases, greater labor efficiency, and decanting of labor from the rural primary sectors-- agriculture, forestry, fisheries, mining. As a result, there was a slow, but steady deterioration in the economic bases of many rural regions and communities. Declining employment in rural primary industries led to a general pattern of net outmigration with pockets of poverty left behind. However, this also was a period of vigorous national economic growth, increased urban employment opportunities, occupational upgrading, and rising real wages in the larger economy. Thus, this first phase was marked by the generation and reinforcement of persistent rural poverty, and by an overall economic dynamism that enabled a fortunate minority of the rural poor to leave rural areas for higher-paying urban jobs.

During the second phase, the late 1960s and throughout the 1970s, growth and revitalization of rural communities and economies led to a general optimism about rural America's future. Communities experienced population growth where decline had been the trend. Manufacturing employment and service sector growth more than offset the continued decline in agricultural and other resource-based employment. There was talk of a rural renaissance.

But the experiences of the 1980s and early 1990s have brought about a third phase, one in which there has been a return to more pessimistic views. Downturns in many of the industries important to rural economies (agriculture, mining, energy, forestry, manufacturing) have resulted in near double-digit unemployment, a rise in business failures, fiscal crises in local government, declining public services and a renewal of the long-term trend of net outmigration and population declines. The turnaround of the 1970s appears to have turned around again.

The deteriorating social and economic well-being of rural society is reflected in a number of indicators of performance and conditions. Unemployment increased in rural labor markets from 1973 to 1988 despite the good record of job creation in the national economy (Brown et al. 1988; Parker 1989; U.S. Bureau of the Census, Current Population Surveys 1973-1988). Part-time and "informal" employment also have increased as a proportion of those employed in rural labor markets (Parker 1989). Earnings of rural workers are below those of urban workers and the situation is getting worse (see Chapter 1 in this volume). The "working poor" is a more common phenomenon in rural areas than in cities (Tickamyer 1992). Recent rural labor market studies reveal the existence of a clear and deep social division of labor which is manifest in various labor market experiences and outcomes (Summers et al. 1990). White women and racial and ethnic workers of both genders are most likely to have jobs with low earnings, little security and stability, and few advancement opportunities (Colclough 1988; Lichter 1989; Tickamyer 1992; Tickamyer and Bokemeier 1988). Racial and ethnic minorities, the elderly, and women in nonmetropolitan areas are particularly disadvantaged. Poverty persists in rural households and is becoming more prevalent in regions outside the South (Brown et al. 1988; Brown and Warner 1991). The existence and perpetuation of rural poverty are well documented by these trends and other indicators.

Past and present efforts to deal with rural poverty issues have focused on failures in the labor market as the source of problems. There seems to be a presumption that a smoothly functioning labor market would solve the problems of poverty. Give everyone a job and there would be no poverty. There is good reason, however, to question this view. The widespread existence of the "working poor" presents a reality inconsistent with the simple notion that merely providing jobs will solve poverty.

Even if labor markets functioned perfectly, some individuals and households would remain below the poverty threshold because certain groups are largely outside the labor market--the elderly, sick, disabled, and children. Moreover, others are only marginally linked to labor markets--racial and ethnic minorities, and many women. Why are the same groups of people living in poverty decade after decade, generation after generation? The reality of persistent poverty forces us to re-think the dynamics of labor markets and rural poverty, of the people and places left behind, the role of the state in intervening to minimize social and economic inequality especially for rural people and places.

Task Force Formation and Goals

In August, 1990 the Council of the Rural Sociological Society authorized the creation of a task force to provide conceptual clarification regarding the factors and dynamics of society which precipitate and perpetuate rural poverty. Earlier policy efforts assembled and implemented under the banner of the War on Poverty were guided by theoretical understandings which may be out of date or incorrect. Rural Americans are living in a changing global economy and shifting political arena which have significantly altered the conditions of the 1960s and 1970s.

In order to achieve this clarification, a task force consisting of nine working groups was organized. Each working group was to assess the theory and empirical knowledge in a definable area, to make a critical appraisal of the relevant concepts and evidence and to prepare a report assessing current thinking and offering corrections where appropriate.

The Task Force report consists of a statistical summary of poverty in rural America[1] and the reports of the nine working groups.

What the Report Is and Is Not

Since the announcement of the formation of the Task Force many requests have been received for information on the nature and extent of poverty in rural areas and for advice on what can be done to alleviate it. Clearly, there is a strong demand for this information, and in the long-run we expect the Task Force findings to contribute to the supply of available responses. However, the Task Force report is not an encyclopedia on the scope of rural poverty in America, nor is it a handbook for action programs to ameliorate rural poverty.

The Task Force report is a critical assessment of the theoretical explanations for persistent rural poverty. It is a review of these conceptual roadmaps undertaken with the explicit goal of identifying shortcomings in the theories, whatever their nature. In some instances the theories may be outdated by changes in the real world as evident in empirical studies. They might be flawed logically, or simply incomplete. In addition, there is the possibility that existing theoretical statements ignore some critical factors and perspectives needed to provide a fuller explanation of persistent rural poverty. Thus, the Task Force report consists of the findings and recommendations for theoretical renovations needed to provide a clearer and more complete understanding of the forces producing and perpetuating rural poverty. Our expectation is that these improvements in our understanding will make it possible to develop more appropriate and effective policies and actions.

Definitions

What Is Persistent Rural Poverty?

There are three questions posed: What is poverty? What is rural? and What is meant by persistent? On the face of it, these seem to be simple questions with simple answers. In reality, they are quite complex and have posed virtually intractable problems of definition that have occupied social scientists for years. In the end one is left with the necessity of making arbitrary decisions as to meanings for each of these critical terms.

"Poverty," as Ruggles says, "is ultimately a normative concept, not a statistical one" (Ruggles 1990:xv). One cannot define poverty without reference to social norms which change over time, and vary from place to place and among groups. However, the reference point in all instances is some minimum standard of living to which all society members should have access. While the elements that constitute a "standard of living" include cultural, political, and social considerations, it is most common to express them in terms of economic well-being.

The concept of a minimum standard of living, or poverty threshold, can be operationalized subjectively or objectively. The normative nature of poverty also can be viewed as a minimum below which no member of society should be allowed to suffer. This implies an "absolute" threshold that members of society regard as a minimal standard of living. The essence of this absolute threshold is basic needs, usually referring to material needs, and the measures are either the income or consumption required to achieve the threshold.

This approach to poverty has its origins around the turn of the century in the work of Rowntree in York, England (Rowntree 1901). Orshansky (1963, 1965) employed the same logic to establish a threshold of poverty in the United States during the War on Poverty. This remains the focus of most poverty measurement. The emphasis is on establishing "objective" thresholds of poverty for households of varying sizes and counting the numbers of persons and households "below the poverty line." More recently, there has been some interest in measuring the "depth of poverty."

Thus, researchers discuss the numbers of persons or households that are "below 125 percent of the poverty line" or "below 50 percent of the poverty line." This addition to the measurement of poverty is important because it permits one to examine the distribution of persons and households around the poverty line and to take into account the fact that a person earning only 50 percent of the poverty threshold is faced with much more serious circumstances than a person whose earnings are only one dollar below the poverty line.

Relative poverty introduces the normative concept again but in terms which reference a particular point in the income or consumption distribution. One could use the average of the income, earnings, or consumption distributions and calculate poverty relative to that point. For example, one might define relative poverty as household earnings 50 percent below the median earnings of all U.S. households of the same size. This avoids the task for defining absolute needs and places the emphasis on inequalities of income.

Subjective poverty focuses on the individual's or family's own definition of what is required to maintain what they consider to be a decent or minimally adequate level of living (Goedhart et al. 1977; Van Praag et al. 1980; Van Praag et al. 1982 and Hagenaar 1986). Subjective poverty has a certain appeal because it makes the normative nature of the concept quite explicit. In studies using subjective measurements it has been found that what is regarded as "minimal" does vary according to characteristics and circumstances of the respondent. For example, Goedhart et al. (1977) found that for each dollar of additional income, people raised their estimate of what was "just sufficient" income by 60 cents and Danziger et al. (1984) found this "income elasticity" to be 0.38. While such studies establish clearly the normative character of poverty, subjective poverty does not lend itself very well to public policy with the goal of raising persons and households to an acceptable standard of living.

When rural poverty is compared to urban poverty the spatial aspect of relative poverty is raised. Do income or earnings measures of economic poverty indicate accurately the threshold of poverty in both urban and rural settings? The answer is not entirely clear since rural residents are more likely to have access to subsistence activities such as hunting, fishing or gardening. Perhaps bartering is more common in rural communities. These and other non-monetary contributions to personal or household living standards are not accounted for in earnings-based measures of poverty and could lead one to infer that estimates of poverty in rural areas are too high. However, recent research by Ghelfi (1988) indicates that the costs of many basic needs are higher in rural areas. Thus, the issue is unresolved even though it is an empirical question that could and perhaps should be answered.

There are aspects of poverty which are non-economic in nature and, therefore, not accounted for in earnings- or income-based measures. Individuals, families, and groups--even entire communities--may be deprived of access to valued components of an acceptable living standard. Many rural residents are deprived of social services simply because these services are not available in their communities. Minority group members in particular may be deprived of access to labor markets, education, health care, and political participation because of discrimination. Cultural and institutional proscriptions may define gender roles in such a way that women are excluded from some labor markets or segments of them. These are important facets of poverty--rural and urban--that detract from individual and family well-being. In the literature on poverty, however, non-economic factors have been treated in a cursory fashion, if at all.

For the purposes of the Task Force another consideration was important. In order to assess the theoretical explanations of rural poverty, we had to accept the definition of poverty that was intrinsic to the theory being examined. Consequently, it was not possible for the Task Force to adopt a single definition of poverty and use it consistently throughout the Working Groups. Nevertheless, since most theories in question define poverty in economic terms and measure poverty as an absolute value--that is, these theories incorporate the federal poverty index as the operational definition of poverty--the official federal definition is the predominant meaning associated with the term "poverty" in the Task Force report. Where other meanings are employed, they are indicated by the authors.

What Is Rural? Throughout the report we have adopted the U.S. Bureau of the Census definitions of metropolitan and nonmetropolitan places. Also, we have taken license to substitute "rural" for nonmetropolitan. This is a linguistic choice and does not indicate a confusion on our part between nonmetropolitan places and rural places. We also make use of the Bureau of the Census distinction between the "central city" and the "suburbs" within metropolitan statistical areas. This division is significant both empirically and theoretically, as will become clear in the report.

Rural is a designation for the more sparsely populated areas of the nation. It is not a synonym for the economic base of these areas. Historically, rural areas were dominated by agricultural and other natural resource-based economic activities. But that is no longer true. Even though the mental images triggered by the word "rural" may still be those associated with the family farm, ranches, or mining and lumbering camps, most of rural America today is no longer dominated by such economic activities. The countryside may still be covered by fields of grain and forests, but most rural people earn a living in services and manufacturing. Even farm families gain well over one-half of their income from earnings off the farm. Moreover, small towns and their industries are no longer isolated. National and world events affect what goes on along Main Street, at the school, down at the Courthouse, and on the farm. The Task Force has been concerned with examining theoretical explanations of poverty within this changed context of rural places and people.

What Is Persistent? Persistent means to continue steadily and firmly in some state; especially in the face of opposition or remonstrance. When applied to rural poverty it refers to the continued existence of a substantial segment of the population with incomes below the poverty threshold in spite of ameliorative efforts. This meaning seems quite straightforward until one recognizes that poverty may persist even though some individuals and families may escape.

They may be replaced by others who fall into poverty; or those who escape may experience repeated spells of poverty; or certain places may persist in having high rates of poverty even though people come and go.

The Task Force has been concerned with the persistence of poverty among people and with the continuation of the aggregate or structural phenomenon of poverty, especially among people living in sparsely populated areas. However, persons theorizing about the existence and persistence of rural poverty usually adopt only one of the above perspectives, and thus we have people-oriented theories as well as place-oriented theories. The Task Force accepted these differences in perspective as a given and made its assessments of them in terms of their ability to account for the observed persistence of rural poverty as defined by the theory being examined.

Major Poverty Trends

Even though the Task Force goal is to provide an assessment of theoretical interpretations of poverty, an overview of major trends--overall rates, groups affected, geographic concentrations, and personal or family characteristics such as age, gender, marital status, race/ethnicity, education and labor market participation--is in order. Thus, using the latest available statistics, Chapter 1 of the report notes several important trends in rural poverty and compares them with urban experiences. These facts are worthy of mention because they are the empirical realities to which the various theories speak.

First, the gains in reducing poverty made during the late 1960s and 1970s were largely lost during the 1980s. The levels of rural poverty in the late 1980s were almost 20 percent.

Second, the poverty rate has been consistently highest in nonmetropolitan areas. Even when adjustments are made for in-kind payments and changing metropolitan-nonmetropolitan designations, poverty is proportionately a larger problem in rural American than in urban places.

Third, the rural-urban gap has been getting larger over the past 15 years.

Fourth, the rapid growth in poverty during the 1980s is not explained by the rise in female-headed families. While family composition is a factor in accounting for poverty, it alone does not account for the poverty increases of the past decade.

Fifth, the rural poverty rate is more sensitive to unemployment than is the rate of urban poverty. Nearly two-thirds of the variation in poverty rates between 1973 and 1989 is explained by the unemployment rate in nonmetropolitan areas, compared with only 22 percent in metro areas.

Sixth, there is a "suburban ridge" in the spatial distribution of income. Thus, poverty rates are much higher in the central cities and nonmetropolitan areas than in the suburbs of metropolitan areas. It is as though central cities are poverty craters surrounded by a ridge of high income beyond which lies a plain of poverty reaching to the next suburban ridge.

Seventh, black rural poverty is extremely concentrated in the South--97 percent of rural blacks with incomes below the poverty threshold live in the South. Moreover, the rate of poverty is significantly higher there (40.8%) than for blacks living in central cities (33.8%).

These are only some of the empirical realities to which social science theories speak. The ability of theories to interpret and explain the diversity of these conditions and trends is the ultimate criterion employed by the working groups of the Task Force in assessing their adequacy.

Major Existing Theories

Three theories were examined by nearly all of the Task Force Working Groups: culture of poverty theory, human capital theory, and economic organization theories. We turn to them first.

Culture of Poverty Theory. The culture of poverty theory does not adequately address poverty issues. However, the rejection of culture as an element in understanding poverty is unwarranted. Exclusion from participation in labor markets and the cash economy can create individual apathy, alienation, and deviant behaviors, as well as family and community disruptions and possibly disorganization (Lewis 1966). However, the subsequent appropriations of the theory by others to argue that poor people develop a "culture of poverty" which they internalize as their preferred way of life lacks empirical support. Unfortunately, rejection of the misappropriated use of cultural elements in relation to poverty has led to discrediting of cultural factors entirely.

We are concerned, as indicated in Chapter 8, that the persistently poor will become increasingly different from others, not because they share different values, but because they are exposed to different risks. Poor rural children are at considerable risk of developing conditions that will limit their ability to work as adults, either directly as in the case of handicapping conditions or indirectly as in the case of undereducation. What is called for is theoretical work that integrates cultural factors into explanations of how some children transcend the limitations imposed by a childhood lived in persistent poverty while intergenerational transmission of disadvantage occurs for others.

Recent work by scholars such as Fitchen (1981, 1991), Cornell and Kalt (1990), Gringeri (1990), and others, demonstrates that incorporating cultural elements into theory can enhance our understanding of poverty without "blaming the victims." Commitment to family and kin networks and to community as an enduring place may provide buffers from economic shocks and serve as a source of strength rather than weakness. Successful economic development projects on Indian reservations often involve cultural elements that are consistent with tribal values and behaviors. Moreover, cultural elements from the dominant society may preclude or constrain changes desired by the poor which could improve their economic status if permitted, as in the case of women seeking unsuccessfully to gain employment in the formal sector of production processes.

Human Capital Theory. The human capital theory appears to be robust and efficient as an explanation of earnings returns to human capital under certain circumstances. It provides explanations of earnings for individuals who are active in formal labor markets that reward labor productivity and have low unemployment rates. However, many of the rural poor are not active in formal labor markets which meet the necessary conditions for an appropriate application of human capital theory as an explanatory tool. Thus, there appears to be an excessive reliance on human capital theory as an explanation, a singularity of focus which ignores the diversity of people and places experiencing persistent poverty.

Some individuals are not expected to participate in labor markets--the disabled, children, the elderly. Some women and minorities are excluded by employer discrimination. Many are excluded, at least temporarily, because there are insufficient places of employment in the labor markets. Others are excluded from participation in those labor markets which reward labor productivity; especially women and minorities. Moreover, many rural areas simply do not have labor markets which yield high earnings for labor productivity.

There also is some empirical evidence that managers of production enterprises are shifting their management strategies from a primary concern with labor productivity to one emphasizing capital productivity. The evidence appears in two forms. First, returns to capital are being increased by shifting to labor intensive technologies which do not demand payment of high earnings for labor productivity, and thereby reducing labor costs. Second, capital is being made more mobile as investments are made wherever the highest short-term returns may be realized, thereby relinquishing a commitment to investments in places and people. To the extent this shift in management strategy occurs, the robustness and efficiency of the human capital theory as an explanation of earnings (and earnings-based measures of poverty) may be expected to erode.

Human capital theory is limited by its focus on individual decision making, and by its de-emphasis of structural and institutional constraints on economic opportunity, including the dynamics of power structures in the social relations of production. More attention needs to be given to the theoretical importance of family and community as units of analysis. These are the incubators of human capital and are important institutions which may facilitate or constrain its utilization.

This limitation is particularly noteworthy in the instances of racial and ethnic enclaves in rural America. The forces that maintain these enclaves, and that perpetuate the existence of dominant/minority social relations that characterize them, are not addressed by applications of human capital theory that assume the existence of a labor market in which, at worst, individual workers are discriminated against by individual employers. Such a truncated theory of poverty overlooks entirely the existence of multiple barriers surrounding minority communities which sometimes deny the whole community access to resources enjoyed by the dominant society.

Economic Organization Theories. These theories are concerned with how the structure of economic organizations influences work structures, performance outcomes, and earnings. The key concept is the organization of work, the interplay between technical and administrative imperatives on the one hand, and on the other, the relations among people, positions, and objects within workplace (Baron and Bielby 1980:738). Some analysts in this tradition have focused on the institutional level of economic organization, with their units of analysis being industrial sectors and/or labor market segments. Others have focused on the organizational level, taking firms as their units of analysis, and attending to internal labor markets and the growth of secondary ones. Still others have focused on "roles" within a work organization, with jobs being their units of analysis. All share the common premise that the outcomes of labor market experiences are structural constraints in the demand for labor more than they are characteristics of the labor supply. Therefore, these theories are proposed explicitly as an alternative to the human capital theory.

We find that these economic organization theories are useful in explaining labor market outcomes under some conditions, but are limited in several respects. They have very little, if anything, to say about informal work activities in either urban or rural settings. This silence can be attributed to a conceptual bias in the economic organization theories. They are concerned with conceptualizing how individuals or firms are insulated from market competition by the formal organization rules of economic institutions. The focus has been on isolating characteristics of economic institutions which insulate work structures from market competition. Consequently, informal work activities that generally are not insulated from competition are relegated to a residual category and assumed to conform to the principles of the market competition paradigm.

Another shortcoming of these theories concerns their contributors' view of historical change. Most have based their analyses of work organizations on the patterns of economic organization characteristic of the early post-World War II period in the United States. Even those contributors who have explicitly included historical change as part of their analysis view the development process as culminating in the organizational structures of "core" or "monopoly" firms. Beginning in the mid-1970s it became increasingly apparent that the organizational structures of these firms were changing rapidly as the United States and other industrialized nations began to experience industrial or capital "restructuring." The previously observed association of relatively higher earnings and job stability with employment in core or monopoly firms and/or other more privileged labor market segments began to weaken. This creates the need for alternative perspectives on the factors which affect the generation of earnings in labor markets, both formal and informal.

Summary. We find the Culture of Poverty Theory to be logically flawed and lacking support. Therefore, we recommend that cultural factors be reintroduced into theoretical work on poverty, but through more appropriate intellectual frameworks. We find Human Capital Theory and Economic Organization Theories to be incomplete as theories of poverty. Alone, they do not provide sufficient explanations for persistent rural poverty in its diverse forms.

Economic organization theory and human capital theory can provide complementary explanations of poverty, rather than contradictory ones. Each is appropriate at a different level of analysis, and the theoretical properties of each complement rather than contradict one another. Much theoretical work concerning poverty is organized around the framework of the supply of and demand for labor and is driven by moral assumptions such as the inherent value of work, legitimacy of access to consumption through work (except for children, disabled and the elderly), and just pay for honest toil. Human capital theory of earnings as a function of labor productivity is the principal conceptual scheme for addressing the supply side of this framework. The demand side of the framework is addressed largely by the economic organization theories. One body of theory emphasizes deficiencies of individuals as the source of poor earnings, and the other focuses on firm, sector, and market constraints on opportunities for earnings. These are inherently complementary rather than contradictory. Thus, the extended and rancorous debate of recent years is largely vacuous and counterproductive. Each theory provides useful, but limited, explanations of persistent rural poverty. It is time to end the debate and get on with building the potential benefits of complementary and cumulative explanations of persistent rural poverty.

New Directions

A major goal of the Task Force was to seek new directions in theory where shortcomings were found, and to go beyond that which exists. Thus, a great deal of the effort of the Working Groups was devoted to creating alternative explanations for persistent rural poverty. These are nascent theoretical statements that are innovative and challenging. It is these suggestions of new directions for theoretical exploration that we find exciting and worthy of attention by the entire social science community. Much of the creativity and promise, we believe, comes from the fact that each Working Group was a multi-disciplinary team collaborating in the construction of social science theory.

The paragraphs that follow provide only brief extractions from the new directions developed by the Working Groups. In some instances the proposals emerged simultaneously from several Working Groups; others are unique to a particular expression of persistent rural poverty. In any case, the reader must turn to the Working Groups' statements for a more complete discussion of proposed theoretical constructions.

Social Embeddedness Theory. Work structures can be meaningfully conceptualized as "embedded" in local social contexts. Work activities are purposive actions of individuals or groups, but their actions are embedded in a particular social context. As Granovetter (1985:487) puts it, "Actors do not behave or decide as atoms outside a social context, nor do they adhere slavishly to a script written for them by the particular intersection of social categories that they happen to occupy. Their attempts at purposive action are instead embedded in concrete, ongoing systems of social relations." The embeddedness argument is especially relevant to analysis of work activities in a market economy where economic action based on market exchanges is unfeasible outside of a context of established rules and regulations governing market exchanges.

However, work activities ought to be conceptualized more broadly than formal employment. Work includes all activities that contribute to the material survival of individuals and their households. It includes the jobs or businesses in which rural people are formally employed, and the work they do in the informal economy and/or self-provisioning activities. This broadened conception of work activities and their social embeddedness is particularly relevant to understanding the persistence of poverty among rural workers and communities. This is so because both formal and informal work activities are regulated, but by different types of regulatory systems. Formal work is regulated by the "institutions of society" (Castells and Portes 1989:12) while informal work activities are regulated by a network or networks of reciprocal social relations.

It is in this context that households, and individuals in them, construct survival strategies. Household members pool the earnings they receive from their formal and informal work with other resources (externally provided as well as internally produced) in order to reproduce the household. In this manner, the productive and reproductive processes co-exist and complement each other. The implication is that work activities need to be analyzed in the context of survival strategies. Thus, work activities are embedded in household structures (including an internal distribution of power) and these in turn are embedded in other networks of social relations, especially local ones. It is the exploration of these socially embedded relations that may hold the key to understanding class, gender, race, and ethnic "effects" in persistent rural poverty.

The Feminist Critique. In contrast to virtually every other approach to understanding poverty, feminist perspectives emphasize the extent to which women's economic opportunities are conditioned and shaped by their disadvantage in the wage labor market; by their disproportionate participation in informal and unpaid labor, both productive and reproductive; and by state policies toward women, work, and welfare. As demonstrated in Chapter 7, these factors can be integrated to produce a feminist perspective on rural women and poverty.

Scholarship on the rural economy has typically emphasized analyses of macro structures and processes such as the farm structure, the capitalization of agriculture, and the changing production and labor relations shaping the use of landed property. This orientation does not consider the roles of individuals and thus gender relations are ignored. This emphasis explains the relative neglect by rural sociologists, development economists, and rural policy analysts of women's contribution to the rural economy. Feminist theory provides the basic tools for constructing a theoretical model to apply to the problem of rural women's poverty. It focuses attention on gender, space, and the economy, relations of production and reproduction, and the ways these are embedded in social institutions.

It is an error to conceptualize women's rural poverty solely in terms of gender and the family. To do so only "tacks gender on" as an empirical apparatus, long after the theoretical issues concerning rural poverty have been decided. Such approaches may capture significant elements of women's role in the social reproduction of the family, but they fail to recognize the significance of women in the process of production.

In addition, conceptual claims made on behalf of the distinctiveness of the "rural" confound our ability to understand the web of social relations which connect all spaces, from the global metropolis to the rural farmstead. Rural poverty must be seen as an issue that cuts across all spaces, from urban to rural and from local to global. Finally, analyses which seek to understand poverty solely in economic terms, outside of either gender or spatial contexts, tend to so over-emphasize the role of waged labor such that questions regarding uncompensated work in the household are never asked; or they suffer from a spatial myopia which treats poverty as a monolithic phenomenon instead of one outcome of a geographically differentiated production system.

Biography and History. Personal biographies, or career trajectories, must be linked more explicitly with the historical context in which they are embedded (see especially Chapters 8 and 9). The macro/micro interface is an issue in social science because overly deterministic analyses at both the macro- and micro-levels have not successfully accounted for the diversity of human responses or human behavior contingencies. Theories of poverty need to be grounded in time as well as space. At the macro level, secular changes are captured by history. At the micro-level, structural realities are experienced in personal biographies. Together, history and biography provide potentially complementary insights into complex social processes.

Today's elders experienced the historical realities of World War I, the Great Depression, World War II, the Cold War and all the associated social changes of this period of history. Undoubtedly, they experienced different economic realities than will their daughters and sons. For example, the high rate of poverty among rural elderly widows surely has its origins in the facts of rural gendering of work during their lifetime, their husbands' occupations being excluded from Social Security, and the failure of rural employers to provide adequate retirement and death benefits. These are "period effects" which need to be combined with personal characteristics in accounting for poverty of people.

Both ethnographic research and quantitative analyses can be designed to be more comprehensive and to address issues at the macro-micro interface, as indicated in Chapter 8. That will require operationalizing concepts at different levels of analysis and integrating longitudinal data into studies. However, historical, macroeconomic data exist as well as longitudinal, microeconomic data. Consequently, it is possible to study biographies of poverty and link them with appropriate macro-level events and circumstances. Collaboration among social scientists, each skilled in analysis at macro- or micro-levels, and between social scientists and direct service providers are two tactics which could improve the relevance of theory to understanding persistent rural poverty. The experiences of the Task Force are evidence that such collaboration is feasible and potentially beneficial.

Community Theory. There is a general failure among contemporary theories of poverty to address the position of communities within the social, political and economic organization of society. The community perspective recognizes the deep commitments which rural workers and their families have for the social relations that are intrinsic to their local community. Often the sense of communion which binds these relations has its origin in "work as a way of life," as in the case of farming, lumbering, fishing, or mining. However, the social bonding may derive from other occupational networks, or from racial and ethnic identities. These commitments are not readily given up, even under conditions of deepening poverty and increasing restrictions on access to the resources that gave rise to the community, such as land, forests, ore, or fish. A community perspective on the matter of persistent rural poverty means going beyond the usual focus on market processes and worker outcomes that characterize of most poverty theory and research. A community perspective must deal with the internal dynamics of social relations within the community--race, ethnicity, gender, class--as well as the political, economic, and spatial context in which communities exist.

As a practical matter, it is easy to understand why politicians are reluctant to approach anti-poverty efforts from the community perspective. Politically, it is much more convenient to accept human deficiencies as the explanation for poverty. One can then introduce programs to remedy the shortcomings of human capital investments rather than entertain the explosive notion that political power structures themselves may be the source of persistent rural poverty, especially those dominating rural minorities. But the realities of practical politics are no excuse for social scientists to ignore the potential explanatory power of a community perspective in the matter of persistent rural poverty.

Institutional Theory. Theory which emphasizes the historical trajectory of institutions is necessary to explain persistent rural poverty. A clear example of this need appears in the continued oppression characteristic of rural minority-majority relations (see Chapter 6). African Americans, American Indians, and Hispanic Americans still live in the shadow of the institutions of slavery and sharecropping, reservations as concentration camps for conquered nations, and exploitative migrant labor markets and the associated colonias. Although the structures of these institutions have been modified, the contemporary versions have much the same effects on cultural, political, and social well-being of these rural minorities, with consequent continued economic impoverishment.

Rational Underinvestment. Human capital theory could be extended to account for "rational underinvestment" in human capital by individuals as potential workers and as community leaders. Elaborations of this idea will be found in Chapters 4, 5 and 8. The central argument is that people's attitudes and expectations with respect to education, occupational aspirations, and geographic mobility are first-order consequences of utility maximization, since people must weigh the short- and long-term consequences of their investments in human capital formation. These expectations lead to a second-order consequence, decision-making with respect to personal investment in education and acquiring technical, marketable skills. Johnson (1991) argues that these consequences of rational individual utility maximization do not operate uniformly in all communities.

Two important reasons for rational underinvestment in human capital are the shift from labor-intensive to capital-intensive production systems and the political power of local economic elites. Because the number of jobs is limited and declining, individuals find that the potential return on investment in their education is either too low or too uncertain to justify the sacrifice. The relatively high-paying jobs which require an education simply are not present in the community. At the same time local school boards and other governing bodies find the investment in educating their young often disappears when the graduates migrate to other communities for work.

The strategies and policies of the local economic elite may reinforce the disincentives of individuals to invest in human capital. Managers of rural industries often prefer a low-skilled, non-union labor force, and this preference has been underscored by "off-shore" movement of plants. Moreover, the absentee-ownership of firms does very little for developing interest in local issues such as public education. Thus, investment in the human capital of the current and future generation of workers by local leaders and workers is constrained by rational disincentives.

Dependency Theory. Dependency theory has salience for explaining poverty in extractive resource-dependent localities; especially where they are physically remote from population centers. Little theoretical attention is given in other theories to the transfer of wealth from rural communities and regions to urban areas. Nor has adequate attention been given to the limitations in the economic development potential of relatively remote extraction centers. Their dependency on metropolitan centers for trade and the lack of infrastructure for economic development within their boundaries make problems with plant closings and the shift from labor to capital intensive production especially difficult. Even though there are federal subsidies to rural based industries, especially agriculture, these funds are not distributed regionally and locally in ways which benefit low income people. This fact is generally known among social scientists concerned with rural poverty and among macro-theorists concerned with uneven development and theories of the state. Yet, theoretical work that explicitly addresses rural poverty and incorporates explanations of it has not been forthcoming.

Moral Exclusion Theory. Moral exclusion theory is an emergent explanation of how groups win or lose legitimacy in establishing rights of access to private and public goods. It promises to become increasingly powerful in explaining poverty among particular groups of people and places. Lack of political will is sometimes offered as an *ad hominem* explanation for why poverty is allowed to persist in a nation of great wealth. However, that merely raises the question of why the necessary political will is lacking. The theory of moral exclusion provides a framework for addressing that issue.

Social scientists would do well to turn their attention to the moral construction of poverty as has been done recently by Handler and Hasenfeld (1991) and Lee (1991). In doing so one would expect to gain insight into the ideological and moral foundations of the political apathy for anti-poverty measures. Racism and sexism are very probable "finds" when one takes up the moral construction of poverty, of who has rights to access private and public goods, the presumed bases of those rights, and who is excluded by application of those rules of access. Environmentalism or the "greening of America" may also play a role, inadvertently or otherwise, in constructing a moral exclusion of some rural workers by undermining traditional rural occupations and by limiting their access to natural resources.

By failing to address white middle-class urban American apathy toward the rural poor, and their antagonism toward minority populations (rural and urban) and all persons who deviate from middle-class norms of acceptable behavior, social scientists are collaborating with those who would do nothing about poverty. Our theoretical instruments of choice betray our commitment to a particular policy strategy--to reform the poor rather than the institutions and political structures which produce and sustain income inequality.

Global Economic Restructuring Theory. The dominant tradition in social theory, and the principal way in which poverty analysts have conceptualized research and application, has been to give priority to the nation-state and national society as the major units of analysis and policy formulation. Indeed, the real, though limited, progress made in the late 1960s and early 1970s in combatting persistent rural poverty occurred during the heyday of the nation-state economy. The post-War national political economy, in which there was substantial federal regulation of flows of capital, made possible many of the fiscal conditions and domestic policies that helped reduce rural and urban poverty levels, at least temporarily. Since that time "internationalizing forces" have become extremely important factors in the current phase of rural poverty. Chief among these internationalizing forces has been the creation of a virtual global market in money and credit, an accelerated pace of industrial relocation across increasingly unregulated nation-state borders, and the profound economic restructuring that has occurred as a result of economic liberalization. While rural America is not alone in being affected by global economic restructuring, these forces have had particularly pronounced effects on nonmetropolitan places and people.

The focus on restructuring increases our awareness that changes in work structures and other social structures in rural areas reflect an emergence of a new pattern of organizing work and related activities. Through an emphasis on the significance of structural and historical contexts provided by the theory, important insights are gained into the sources of variation in work structures. The conceptualization of regimes of accumulation and the institutional frameworks upon which they are constructed provide us with an approach for analyzing changes in, and variations among, rural work structures.

Nation-State Theories. While much of the progress achieved in the late 1960s and 1970s in combatting rural poverty originated in federal policy (especially social Keynesianism) and occurred when the American national-state and national economy still possessed a high degree of functional integrity, progress in combatting persistent rural poverty was mostly *unintended*. The U.S. national government has never had a meaningful rural policy. While the progress of the late 1960s and 1970s was substantial, the American national government has done little that really mattered in terms of eliminating the causes of *persistent* rural poverty, or persistent poverty generally for that matter. Indeed, there has been a near-total inability on the part of U.S. governing institutions to deal effectively and successfully with a wide range of rural needs. Much of this failure has had to do with the fact that rural policy has always been considered synonymous with farm or agricultural policy. After having been firmly institutionalized in the form of Depression-era farm programs, the farm policy "iron triangle"--of agency officials, Congressional committees, and commodity groups--has been very effective in defending their prerogatives. This has deflected any initiatives that would divert substantial agricultural commodity programs funding into agencies or programs dedicated to rural development and rural poverty alleviation. This situation will not likely be radically changed in the immediate future. Even if commodity programs are sharply reduced, the U.S. fiscal crisis and the lack of a coherent constituency for rural poverty alleviation make it improbable that there will be a meaningful rural policy anytime soon. In recent years, in fact, the most significant rural poverty policy innovations have tended to occur at the state or local governmental levels, typically prompted by citizens' movements or by public interest groups.

Conclusion

It is one thing to assess where we are in our theoretical work and to point out limitations. It is quite another to creatively construct the needed theoretical corrections. This is the challenge that lies ahead. As we take up that task, we offer the following criteria for judging the appropriateness of our theoretical adjustments (see Chapter 7 for further discussion). They attempt to call attention to gender, race, ethnicity, spatial location, and social embeddedness as critical factors which an adequate theory of poverty must address. With Tickamyer and her colleagues, we ask, does the theory recognize that:

1. Social reproduction and production are inseparable, necessary, and co-equal processes?
2. Gender, race, and ethnicity must be integrated into the theory rather than "tacked on?"
3. Individuals and social structures are mutually defined?
4. Social processes are embedded in time and space?
5. Local events and processes are linked to global ones?
6. The state is neither wholly subordinate to society nor independent of it?

Success in meeting these criteria will require that communications barriers among social science disciplines be dismantled and that segregation of work between urban and rural poverty be eliminated. The membership of the Task Force included anthropologists, economists, geographers, political scientists and social workers, as well as sociologists. Their accomplishments, as set forth in this report, are a testimony to the potential benefits of interdisciplinary collaboration. Likewise, the attention to comparative work by the Task Force demonstrates the necessity of painting all faces of poverty onto a single canvas. Urban and rural are no longer defensible as segregated analytical concepts. They are valuable as linked aspects of a common societal fabric.

Notes

This introduction was prepared by Gene F. Summers, University of Wisconsin-Madison; Leonard E. Bloomquist, Kansas State University; Frederick Buttel, University of Wisconsin-Madison; Patricia Garrett, University of North Carolina at Chapel Hill; Nina Glasgow, Cornell University; Craig Humphrey, Pennsylvania State University; Daniel

T. Lichter, Pennsylvania State University; Thomas Lyson, Cornell University; C. Matthew Snipp, University of Wisconsin-Madison and Ann Tickamyer, University of Kentucky.

1. The statistical summary was prepared by the Agriculture and Rural Economy Division, Economic Research Service, U.S. Department of Agriculture under the guidance of Robert Hoppe.

1

Poverty in Rural America: Trends and Demographic Characteristics

The American public generally perceives poverty as an urban problem. This probably stems from the fact that most people live in or near large cities and are likely to observe central city poverty. The rural poor are more dispersed and less visible. Statistics show, however, that poverty is as much a rural problem as an urban one.

Some argue that antipoverty policy has been aimed at the urban poor and has not fully served the rural poor (Institute for Research on Poverty 1980). If poor people living in rural America are to be helped, it is important to understand rural poverty and how it differs from urban poverty.

This chapter examines recent trends in rural poverty and discusses some of characteristics of the rural poor. Although I present some data for the South, the major focus is rural poverty in the nation as a whole, because many of the policy decisions regarding poverty are made at the national level.

Definitions

"Rural" is defined as nonmetropolitan (nonmetro) in this chapter. Similarly, "urban" is defined as metropolitan (metro). Counties lying within a metropolitan statistical area (MSA) are regarded as metro, while counties lying outside MSA's are nonmetro.[1] A county is part of a MSA if:

(1) it includes a city of at least 50,000, or (2) it includes a Census Bureau-defined urbanized area of at least 50,000 with a total metropolitan population of at least 100,000 (75,000 in New England). In addition to the county containing the main

city or urbanized area, an MSA may include other counties having strong commuting ties to the central county (U.S. Bureau of the Census 1991c:191).

Metro areas are divided into central cities and areas outside central cities. The largest city in a MSA is always considered a central city, but other cities in the MSA may be considered central cities if certain conditions indicating a central character are met. These conditions involve amount of commuting, size of population, and number of workers. (For more information, see the U.S. Federal Committee on Standard Metropolitan Statistical Areas 1979:39.)

Metro areas outside central cities are frequently treated as "suburbs" (U.S. Bureau of the Census 1991c:191). Following this convention, I also refer to areas outside central cities as suburban. This usage is not entirely accurate, however. Areas classified as suburban include some relatively sparsely settled areas at the edges of MSA's, some areas that are similar to central cities in character, and some areas that most people are likely to view as suburbs.

Metro-nonmetro designations are revised periodically to reflect the increasing urbanization of the Nation, and therefore may vary over time within a single data series. Three metro-nonmetro designations are used in the poverty data examined in this chapter. Metro-nonmetro designations based on the 1960 Census are used for the years 1967-70, and designations based on the 1970 Census are used for 1971-83. Designations announced on June 30, 1984, are used for 1985-90.[2] These changes in the metro-nonmetro designations cause a problem discussed in greater detail later.

The final term to define is "poverty." People are defined as living in poverty if their family money income is below the official poverty threshold appropriate for the size and type of their family. The Bureau of the Census uses 48 poverty thresholds to determine poverty status (U.S. Bureau of the Census 1991c:194-195). Different thresholds exist for elderly and nonelderly individuals, for two-person families with and without elderly householders, and for families with different numbers of children. The poverty threshold for a family of four with two children was $13,254 in 1990. The thresholds are adjusted annually by the Consumer Price Index to reflect inflation.

Data Sources

The poverty data in this chapter come from the income supplement to the Current Population Survey (CPS) conducted each March by the Bureau of the Census (U.S. Bureau of the Census 1991c:10-11). Income information is collected from a sample representing the population of the United States, excluding the institutionalized population and members of the Armed Forces living in barracks. All differences in poverty estimates between metro and nonmetro areas discussed in the text are significant at the 90 percent confidence level or more.   Personal income data prepared by the Bureau of Economic Analysis (BEA) are used to augment the poverty data.   Personal income is the income that people receive from all sources.   It is made up of wages and salaries, other labor income, self-employment income, property income, and transfer payments (U.S. Department of Commerce 1991b:M-30).

The BEA prepares personal income data for each county or county equivalent in the U.S., largely from administrative records and surveys or censuses conducted by other agencies (U.S. Department of Commerce 1991b:M-5). Unlike the CPS poverty data, the BEA data do not come from a single sample survey.   Therefore, statistical significance tests were not possible for the BEA data.

Poverty Trends

Considerable progress was made against nonmetro poverty during the late 1960s and early 1970s.   As shown in Figure 1.1, the nonmetro poverty rate declined from 20.2 percent in 1967 to 13.5 percent in 1978, interrupted by a noticeable increase during the 1973-75 recession.   Poverty rates in central cities, suburbs, and metro areas as a whole were more stable during the same period, fluctuating within fairly narrow ranges.

Not only did the nonmetro poverty rate decline in the early 1970s, but the gap between nonmetro and central city poverty rates also closed.   By the late 1970s, the central city poverty rate exceeded the nonmetro poverty rate.   This contrasts with the late 1960s, when the nonmetro poverty rate was higher.

Poverty increased sharply after 1979 in both metro and nonmetro areas.   By 1983, the official poverty rate reached 13.8 percent in metro areas as a whole, 19.8 percent in central cities, 9.6 percent in suburbs, and 18.3 percent in nonmetro areas.   After 1983, the metro poverty rates declined somewhat, but the nonmetro poverty rate stayed at about 18 percent through 1986.   The nonmetro poverty rate began to fall in 1987 and reached 15.7 percent by 1989. Note in Figure 1.1 that none of the poverty rates during the late 1980s fell as far as 1978 levels.

The poverty rates rose again in 1990, in response to the beginning of a recession.   However, the increase in the nonmetro poverty rate between 1989 and 1990 was not statistically significant.

The Reasons

The most striking feature of Figure 1.1 is the large increase in all poverty rates after 1979. Three major factors, listed more or less in chronological order, contributed to the increase in poverty rates from 1979 to 1983 (Getz and Hoppe 1983; U.S. Bureau of the Census 1983; Levitan 1985):

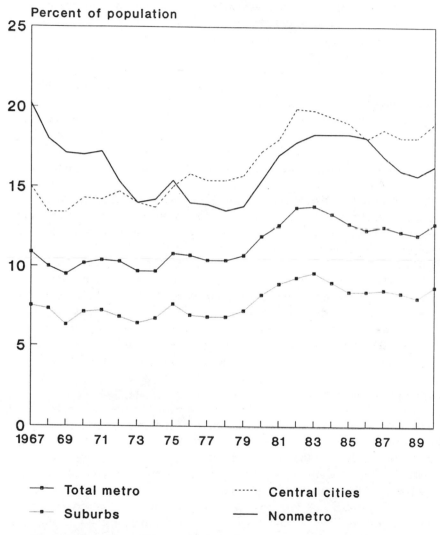

Figure 1.1 Poverty Rates by Residence, 1967-90

Percent of population

Legend:
- ■ Total metro
- ■ Suburbs
- ······ Central cities
- —— Nonmetro

Source: US Bureau of the Census, Current Population Survey, various years

1. Prices increased more rapidly than income in the late 1970s and early 1980s.[3] Because the poverty thresholds are adjusted for inflation, they increased as rapidly as prices. This caused people whose income was just marginally above the poverty level to fall into poverty if their income grew slower than prices and the poverty thresholds.
2. Economic downturns from 1980 to 1982 reduced the earnings of some people enough to make them poor.
3. Tightened eligibility requirements increased poverty by removing people from the welfare rolls or by reducing their benefits.

While some have suggested it, the increasing share of people living in families headed by a woman is not important in explaining the sharp increases in poverty rates between 1979 and 1983.[4] In fact, the growth in the percentage of the Nation's population in this group did not accelerate during the 1979-83 period (Figure 1.2).[5] Changes in the share of the population in this family type were fairly constant, never more than .6 percentage points per year, even during the 1979-83 period.

The gradual increase in the percentage of people in families headed by a woman was mirrored by a gradual decline in the percentage of people in other families, mostly married-couple families.[6] Steady changes like these cannot explain the sharp increases in poverty rates between 1979 and 1983 shown in Figure 1.1.

After the downturns ended and inflation abated, poverty rates declined in central cities, other metro areas, and metro areas as a whole. The recovery, however, seemed to have had a delayed effect on nonmetro poverty, as the nonmetro poverty rate did not begin to decline until 1987. The lag between the recovery and improving poverty rates may reflect relatively slow economic growth in nonmetro areas or revisions in the metro-nonmetro designations.

Slow Economic Growth

Nonmetro areas appear to have experienced slow income growth compared to metro areas in recent years, leading to a growing metro-nonmetro income gap that is not correlated with the national business cycle (Henry, Drabenstott, and Gibson 1987). This income gap can be measured by subtracting nonmetro per capita income from metro per capita income.

According to BEA personal income data, metro per capita income was about $3,100 higher in 1973, and the difference increased to $5,200 by 1989 (Figure 1.3). These differences are stated in real terms; they have been adjusted for inflation with the implicit price deflator for personal consumption expenditures. Stating the relationship between metro and nonmetro income slightly differently, nonmetro income fell from 78 percent of metro income in 1973 to 72 percent

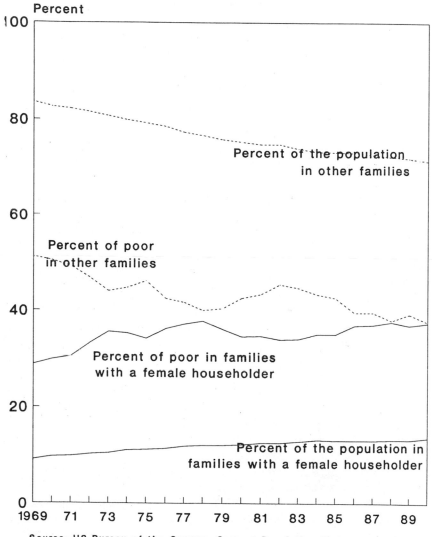

Figure 1.2 Distribution of U.S. Poor and Total Population by Family Type, 1969-90

Source: US Bureau of the Census, Current Population Survey, various years

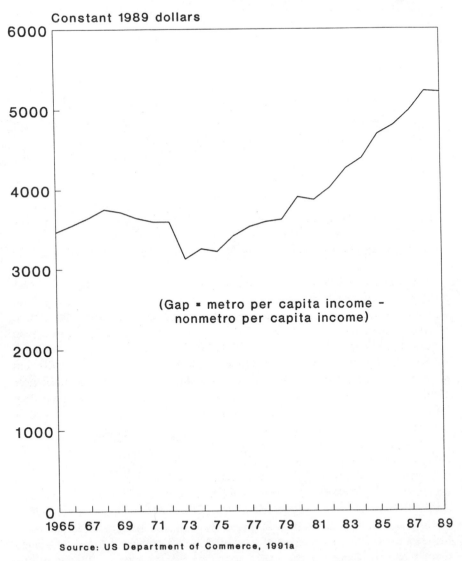

Figure 1.3 Nonmetro Per Capita Personal
Income Gap, 1969-89

Constant 1989 dollars

(Gap = metro per capita income –
nonmetro per capita income)

Source: US Department of Commerce, 1991a

in 1989 (Figure 1.4). Slower nonmetro income growth could be reflected in a stubbornly high rural poverty rate, even during recoveries.

In addition, the recessions of the early 1980s were particularly hard on rural areas. There was a greater rise in unemployment rates in nonmetro areas during the downturns at the beginning of the 1980s, and the nonmetro recovery was slower (Deavers, Hoppe, and Ross 1988).

The slowed recovery could help explain the delayed drop in the rural poverty rate, because nonmetro poverty appears to be particularly sensitive to unemployment. About 63 percent of the variation in the nonmetro poverty rate between 1973 and 1989 was explained by variation in the unemployment rate, compared with only 22 percent in metro areas (Hoppe 1991:16). The decline in the nonmetro poverty rate, when it finally did occur, was associated with a large drop in the unemployment rate. The 2.4 percentage point drop in the nonmetro poverty rate between 1986 and 1989 occurred at the same time as a 2.6 percentage point drop in the nonmetro unemployment rate.

Changes in Metro-Nonmetro Designations

A major change in metro-nonmetro designations used by the Bureau of the Census may also help explain why the nonmetro poverty rate remained so high from 1983 to 1986. Beginning with the 1985 poverty data, metro-nonmetro designations as of June 1984 were used rather than designations based on the 1970 Census.

This change decreased the nonmetro population by approximately 20.5 million or 28 percent. Nonmetro areas that were reclassified to metropolitan were more likely to be prosperous than the areas that remained nonmetro. The reclassification, therefore, would tend to raise the poverty rate of those who remained nonmetropolitan.

Nevertheless, the nonmetro poverty rate remained at 18 percent for two years *after* the new designations were introduced and did not begin dropping until after 1986. This suggests that the recovery did not help reduce nonmetro poverty much until after 1986, even if the analysis is limited to only the smaller nonmetro population included in the more recent designations.

The Census data are confirmed by BEA data. Unlike the Census poverty data, the BEA income data (Figures 1.3 and 1.4) use a constant metro-nonmetro designation. When the BEA releases its data each year, it uses the most current designations available for the entire time series. Both the BEA and Census data show the same general trend in the mid-1980s--nonmetro areas falling behind metro areas--despite differences in how metro and nonmetro areas are defined. In other words, the persistence of a high nonmetro poverty rate reflects much more than the change in the metro-nonmetro designations in Bureau of the Census data.

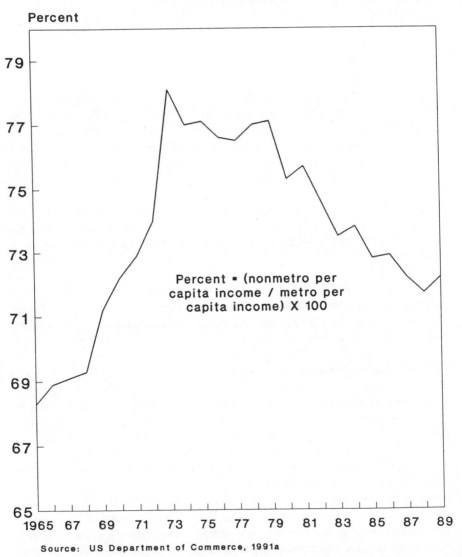

Figure 1.4 Nonmetro Per Capita Income as Percent
of Metro, 1969-89

Percent = (nonmetro per
capita income / metro per
capita income) X 100

Source: US Department of Commerce, 1991a

Do Poverty Statistics Overstate Rural Poverty?

Some argue that nonmetro poverty is not as severe as the poverty rates in Figure 1.1 indicate, because the official poverty statistics do not consider benefits received in kind rather than in cash, and because the poverty thresholds are not adjusted to reflect the supposedly lower living costs in nonmetro areas. Each of these criticisms of the official statistics are discussed below.

In-Kind Benefits

Benefits received as goods or services from such programs as Food Stamps, Medicare, and Medicaid are not counted as income when determining poverty status for the official poverty statistics. During the 1970s, conservative analysts argued that poverty would have been eliminated if both cash and in-kind benefits were included when measuring poverty (Anderson 1978; Browning 1975). To be fair, however, the poverty statistics should also be adjusted to reflect the payment of taxes, since the official poverty status is based on *pre-tax* cash income.

In the early 1980s, the Bureau of the Census embarked on a research program to explore the effects of a more complete concept of income that includes adjustments for taxes, capital gains, and noncash benefits from both employers and the government (U.S. Bureau of the Census 1991a:1). Making these adjustments does reduce the poverty rate in both metro and nonmetro areas (Figure 1.5). However, even after these adjustments, the nonmetro poverty rate remained higher each year. In 1990, for example, the nonmetro adjusted poverty rate was still three percentage points higher than the corresponding metro rate.

Cost-of-Living Differences[7]

Geographic differences in the cost of living are more difficult to address. Although nonmetro areas are generally perceived as having lower living costs, it is difficult to find systematic rural-urban differences in the cost of living (U.S. Department of Agriculture 1976; Ghelfi 1988).

Adjusting poverty statistics to reflect geographic differences in the cost of living would be a major undertaking. Developing a cost-of-living index with which to make the adjustments would be expensive and time-consuming (Hoppe 1979). Constructing the index would require large amounts of data and be complicated by geographic variations in the types and quality of goods available. And, using an inaccurate index might introduce more problems and inequities than not making any adjustments at all.

Despite proposed refinements in the definition and measurement of poverty to accommodate in-kind benefit and cost-of-living differentials, the current

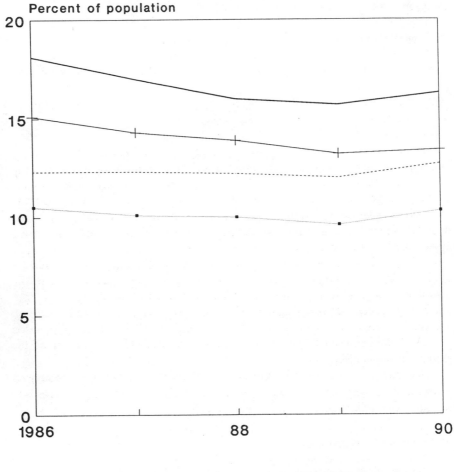

Figure 1.5 Poverty Rates by Residence,
Before and After Adjustments for In-Kind
Income and Taxes, 1986–90

Percent of population

----- Metro, unadjusted   —•— Metro, adjusted

—— Nonmetro, unadjusted   —+— Nonmetro, adjusted

Source: US Bureau of the Census, 1988, 1990a, 1990b, and 1991a

measures are adequate to indicate that the war on poverty, especially rural poverty, has not been won. We should not let technical arguments over poverty measurement hinder efforts to reduce rural poverty.

Characteristics of the Nonmetro Poor

It is important to compare the nonmetro poor with the metro poor in central cities and the suburbs. The three poor populations--nonmetro, central city and suburban--were large in 1990. The central city poor numbered 14 million, and the two other poor populations each included at least 9 million people (Table 1.1).

Poverty Rates

In general, poverty rates for specific population groups, such as people living in married-couple families, were higher in nonmetro areas than in metro areas as a whole (Table 1.1, Part A). However, poverty rates were similar for most population groups in central cities and nonmetro areas. There were few statistically significant differences between central cities and nonmetro areas. Unrelated individuals and blacks were the exceptions; their poverty rates were significantly higher in nonmetro areas.

Although none of the poverty rates for specific groups were significantly higher in central cities than in nonmetro areas, the poverty rate for the whole population was higher in central cities. This apparent contradiction results from the heavy concentration of families in central cities headed by women, a group with a very high poverty rate. About 20 percent of the central city population lived in families headed by a woman, compared with only 11 percent of the nonmetro population.

The situation was markedly different when the nonmetro poor were compared with the suburban poor. In these comparisons, each nonmetro poverty rate was substantially higher than its suburban counterpart.

Who Are the Nonmetro Poor?

The groups that made up the poor also differed among the three residential categories (Table 1.1, Part B). The nonmetro poor were much more likely to live in married-couple families. About 44 percent of the nonmetro poor lived in this type of family, compared with 37 percent of the suburban poor and only 27 percent of the central city poor. In contrast, about 45 percent of the central city poor lived in families headed by a woman, compared with about 30 percent of the suburban and nonmetro poor.

TABLE 1.1 Selected Characteristics of the Poor, by Residence, 1990

Item	United States Total	Metro Total	Metro Central Cities	Suburbs	Nonmetro
		--Thousands--			
Total poor	33,585	24,510	14,254	10,255	9,075
		--Percent--			
PART A: POVERTY RATES					
Poverty rate for total population	13.5*	12.7*	19.0*	8.7*	16.3
People in families with a female householder, no husband present[a]	37.2*	35.8*	43.9	26.6*	43.2
Related children	53.4	52.5	60.9	41.7*	56.8
Married-couple families[a]	6.9*	5.9*	9.1	4.4*	9.9
Related children	10.2*	9.1*	14.0	6.6*	14.0
Unrelated individuals[b]	20.7*	19.0*	21.8*	16.3*	27.7
Whites	10.7*	9.9*	14.3	7.6*	13.5
Blacks	31.9*	30.1*	33.8*	22.2*	40.8
Hispanics[c]	28.1	27.8	31.7	22.8**	32.0
Aged[d]	12.2*	10.8*	14.6	8.1*	16.1
Disabled[e]	35.9	34.8	43.6	25.8*	39.0
PART B: GROUPS MAKING UP THE POOR					
Poor who are:[f]					
People in families with a female householder, no husband present[a]	37.5*	40.1*	45.1*	33.2	30.3
Related children	21.9*	23.7*	26.7*	19.6	17.0
Married-couple families[a]	34.6*	31.0*	27.0*	36.7*	44.4
Related children	14.6*	13.5*	11.8*	15.9	17.6
Unrelated individuals[b]	22.2*	22.8*	22.6*	23.2*	20.4
Whites	66.5*	64.1*	53.8*	78.5*	72.9
Blacks	29.3*	31.4*	41.2*	17.8*	23.6
Hispanics[c]	17.9*	22.5*	24.7*	19.5*	5.4
Aged[d]	10.9*	9.8*	9.3*	10.4*	14.0
Disabled[e]	8.8	8.6	9.4	7.6	9.4

*Significantly different from the nonmetro estimate at the 95 percent confidence level.
**Significantly different from the nonmetro estimate at the 90 percent confidence level.
[a]The term "family refers to a group of two or more related persons how live together.
[b]Unrelated individuals living alone or with nonrelatives.
[c]Hispanics may be of any race.
[d]The aged are at least 65 years old. The aged and disabled are mutually exclusive.
[e]Age 16 to 64 with a "severe work disability." See U.S. Bureau of the census (1991c:198) for more information.
[f]the percentages in the grups sum to more than 100 percent because an individual may be in more than one group.
Source: U.S. Bureau of the Census, 1991c.

Nevertheless, poverty among families headed by a woman is a growing problem in rural areas. The share of the nonmetro poor living in such families has grown from 22 percent in 1969 to the current 30 percent (Figure 1.6). This growing share reflects a consistently high poverty rate for people in female-headed families plus a gradually increasing share of the total rural population living in that family type. The share of the total rural population living in female-headed families increased from 8.4 percent in 1969 to 11.5 percent in 1990, and the poverty rate for people in such families never fell below 37 percent during the past two decades.

Although gradual changes in family composition may not greatly affect the poverty rate during relatively short periods of time, they can affect the level of the poverty over longer periods. Between 1979 and 1989,[8] for example, the share of the nonmetro population who were unrelated individuals or who lived in families headed by a woman increased. These shifts meant that more of the population was living in poverty-prone groups in 1989 than in 1979. If the 1989 poverty rates for the various family types were weighted by 1979 family composition, the 1989 poverty rate would have been 14.8 percent in nonmetro areas. This is lower than the actual 1989 poverty rate (15.7 percent) but still higher than the 1979 poverty rate (13.7 percent). Thus, at least some of the difference in the poverty rate between the end of the 1970s and the end of the 1980s can be attributed to shifts in family composition.

Family composition can also affect participation in the labor market. Other studies have noted the greater attachment of the nonmetro poor to the labor market, whether measured by receipt of earned income, labor force participation by family heads, or number of workers per families (Jensen and McLaughlin 1992; Hoppe 1989). The greater prevalence of married-couple families among the nonmetro poor probably accounts for some of the nonmetro poor's greater attachment to the labor market. Married-couple families contain two potential adult workers, while families headed by a woman are more likely to contain only one potential worker. Even if one spouse in a married-couple family stays home to take care of children, the other spouse is free to participate in the labor market. The nonmetro poverty rate's greater sensitivity to the unemployment rate, which was discussed earlier, may also reflect the prevalence of married-couple families among the nonmetro poor.

Children made up between 34 and 38 percent of the poor in all three areas. Poor children in central cities, however, were more likely to live in families headed by a woman than their nonmetro or suburban counterparts. Over two-thirds of central city poor children lived in such families, compared with slightly less than half of nonmetro poor children and slightly more than half of suburban poor children.

Whites comprised a large share of the poor in nonmetro areas (73 percent) and in the suburbs (79 percent). In contrast, a much smaller share (54 percent) of the central city poor were white. A substantial minority of the nonmetro poor

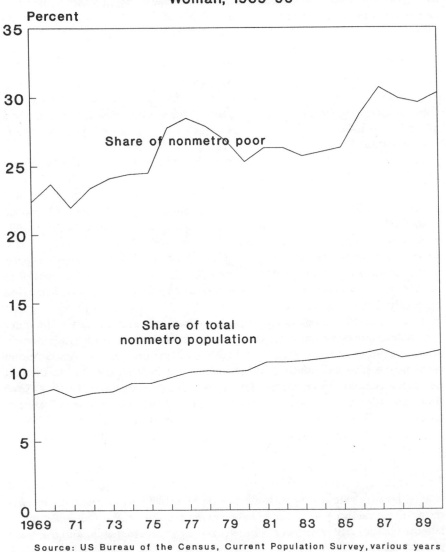

Figure 1.6 Share of Nonmetro Poor and Total Nonmetro Population in Families Headed by a Woman, 1969-90

Percent

Share of nonmetro poor

Share of total nonmetro population

Source: US Bureau of the Census, Current Population Survey, various years

(24 percent) was black, a smaller share than in central cities, but larger than in the suburbs. Only 5 percent of the nonmetro poor were Hispanic, a much smaller share than either central cities or the suburbs.

The aged formed a relatively small portion of the poor in all three areas. The elderly's share of the poor population, however, was higher in nonmetro and suburban areas than in central cities. Poverty among the elderly has decreased substantially since the early 1970s, due largely to changes in Social Security and the introduction of Supplemental Security Income (SSI) (Hoppe and Deavers 1992).

The disabled also made up a small share of the poor in all areas. There were no significant residential differences in the share of the poor who were disabled.

The farm population's share of the nonmetro poor should be mentioned, because many people still assume that most of the nonmetro or rural poor live on farms. In reality, less than one-tenth of the nonmetro poor are farm residents.

Geographic Concentration

Nonmetro poverty was concentrated in the South in 1990 (Table 1.2). About 55 percent of the nonmetro poor lived in the South, compared with only 30 percent of the central city poor and 41 percent of the suburban poor. Rural poverty among blacks was even more concentrated in the South. Nearly all poor nonmetro blacks (97 percent) lived in the South. Of course, nonmetro blacks were heavily concentrated in the South. About 95 percent of all nonmetro blacks lived in the South in 1990.

In an effort to further pinpoint poor or low-income rural areas, the U.S. Department of Agriculture conducted two county-level studies. One study identified nonmetro counties with high poverty rates in the 1980 Census (Morrissey 1985), and the other identified counties that have had chronically low per capita personal incomes over several decades (Bellamy and Ghelfi 1988).[9] Both the high-poverty and persistently low-income counties were heavily concentrated in the South.

Summary and Implications

The poverty rate has consistently been high in nonmetro areas. Even after considering benefits paid in kind and changing metro-nonmetro designations, it is clear that poverty is as much a rural problem as an urban one. Both Census poverty data and BEA personal income data show that nonmetro areas lagged behind metro areas in the 1980s.

The poverty rate for each population group is high in nonmetro areas, generally comparable to the corresponding central city rate. The exceptions are

TABLE 1.2 Selected Characteristics of the Poor, by Residence, 1990[a]

Race and Region	United States Total	Metro Total	Cities	Suburbs	Nonmetro
		--Thousand--			
Total poor, all regions	33,585	24,510	14,254	10,255	9,075
Poor in the South	13,456	8,437	4,237	4,200	5,019
		--Percent--			
Percent of total poor in the South	40.1*	34.4*	29.7*	41.0*	55.3
WHITE		--Thousand--			
Total white poor, all regions	22,326	15,711	7,664	8,047	6,615
White poor in South	7,708	4,827	1,982	2,845	2,881
		--Percent--			
Percent of white poor in the South	34.5*	30.7*	25.9*	35.4*	43.6
BLACK		--Thousand--			
Total black poor, all regions	9,837	7,696	5,870	1,826	2,141
Black poor in the South	5,538	3,465	2,183	1,282	2,073
		--Percent--			
Percent of black poor in the South	56.3*	45.0*	37.2*	70.2*	96.8

*Significantly different from the nonmetro estimate at the 95 percent confidence level.

[a]The South includes: Delaware, Maryland, District of Columbia, Virginia, West Virginia, North Carolina, South Carolina, Georgia, Florida, Kentucky, Tennessee, Alabama, Mississippi, Arkansas, Louisiana, Oklahoma, and Texas.

Source: U.S. Bureau of the Census, 1991c.

the poverty rates for unrelated individuals and blacks, which are higher in nonmetro areas than in the central cities.

The poor differ in metro and nonmetro areas. The nonmetro poor are more likely to live in married-couple families than either the central city or suburban poor. The nonmetro poor are also more heavily concentrated in the South than the poor living in central cities or suburbs. About 24 percent of the nonmetro poor are black, a smaller share than in central cities, but a larger share than in the suburbs. Nearly all nonmetro poor blacks live in the South, however. Finally, the level of nonmetro poverty seems to be more sensitive to unemployment than nonmetro poverty, which probably reflects the nonmetro poor's family structure.

Policy implications can be drawn from the information presented above. Because of the nonmetro poor's attachment to the labor market, issues such as the minimum wage, income taxes, the availability of jobs, job training, unemployment, and the strength of the economy, are important in any discussion of nonmetro poverty.

However, labor market strategies are not effective ways to reach the large share of nonmetro poor who cannot reasonably be expected to work. For example, the elderly and disabled make up 23 percent of nonmetro poor. The most effective way to reach these people is through income transfers. For example, increasing SSI benefits in selected states would help the elderly and disabled poor in nonmetro areas. About 60 percent of both the aged and the disabled poor live in the South, where state supplementation of SSI tends to be low (Hoppe and Deavers 1992).

Transfer programs are also important to poor children. Many poor children are currently helped through Aid to Families With Dependent Children (AFDC). However, AFDC historically has been a less effective antipoverty program in nonmetro areas, because a large share of the nonmetro poor live in states (largely southern) that have low AFDC benefits (Deavers et al. 1988).

In addition, a smaller portion of nonmetro poor children live in female-headed families, the main target group of AFDC. The recently passed Family Assistance Act could help the nonmetro poor by extending AFDC coverage to all poor married-couple families with an unemployed father (Rovner 1988:2,825-2,831). Before the FSA, only about half the states cover these families under AFDC. However, extension of the act to all states will have only a minor effect on the nonmetro poor (Jensen and McLaughlin 1992). Increasing benefits in low-benefit states would probably would have had a greater effect in rural areas.

Finally, where nonmetro poverty is concentrated, as in some parts of the South, state governments may be hard pressed to fund strategies to help the poor. Welfare reform proposals that seek to shift financial responsibility for antipoverty programs to the states must ensure that the states have enough revenue to accept their new responsibilities.

Notes

This chapter was written by Robert Hoppe from the Economic Research Service, USDA. It is a revised version of three earlier presentations; the first at a Congressional Research Service symposium (Hoppe 1988), the second at a Washington Statistical Society lecture (Hoppe and Bellamy 1989), and the third at Tuskegee University (Hoppe 1989). Parts of this paper also appeared in Deavers and Hoppe (1992).

1. Entire counties are the building blocks for MSA's, except in New England where cities and towns are used (U.S. Bureau of the Census, 1991c:191).

2. No residential poverty data were released for 1984. The 1984 residential data presented in this paper are averages of 1983 and 1985.

3. Income did not keep up with inflation from 1979 to 1982. During those years, growth in median family income averaged 7.4 percent per year, while growth in the consumer price index averaged 10.3 percent per year (U.S. Bureau of the Census 1991b:9).

4. The phrase "families headed by a woman" is used in the text rather than the more technically correct "families with a female householder, no husband present." The technically correct phrase is too long and awkward. The longer phrase is usually used in the tables and figures, however.

5. To make Figure 1.2 more readable, data for the metro and nonmetro populations were not presented. Similar trends occurred in nonmetro areas as in the nation as a whole, but at different levels.

6. "Other families" are largely married-couple families, but also include some families with a male householder, no wife present. Prior to 1988, the published data do not separate nonmetro people into married-couple families and families with a male householder, no wife present. People in families headed by a woman and people in other families do not sum to the total population because not all people are classified as part of a family. Some people who do not belong to families are "unrelated individuals" living alone or with nonrelatives. Others are members of "unrelated subfamilies," such as guests, lodgers, or resident employees and their families who live in a larger household, but are not related to the person or couple maintaining the household. For more details, see U.S. Bureau of the Census (1991c:196-197).

7. For more information about cost-of-living differentials and poverty measurement, see Hoppe (1992).

8. The years 1979 and 1989 were selected because they occurred at similar points in the business cycle.

9. Actually, the persistent low-income study was first conducted in the late 1970s (Davis 1979) and updated twice in the 1980s (Hoppe 1985; Bellamy and Ghelfi 1988).

2

Human Capital, Labor Supply, and Poverty in Rural America

We still understand very little about the basic causes of poverty--the extent to which it is a matter of genetic or cultural inheritance, a lack of human capital, a choice variable related to work and family decisions, a result of macroeconomic failures or of social stratification based on race, sex, or family background.
                                                                                    —Isabel Sawhill (1988)

Introduction

The emergence and growth of a highly visible underclass or ghetto poor population in U.S. cities has deflected attention away from the rural poor (e.g., Jencks and Peterson 1991; Katz 1989). The conventional wisdom is that poor people have become increasingly concentrated spatially, especially within large metropolitan central cities (Massey 1990). Indeed, some observers of urban poverty claim that geographic and social isolation from the economic and cultural mainstream has given impetus to a distinctive subculture that promotes and reinforces the cycle of poverty. To be sure, joblessness, welfare dependency, and nonmarital fertility may be borne of poverty and despair, but critics worry that a "way of life" has now emerged among the poor which fosters chronic economic deprivation and dependency from generation-to-generation (cf., Mead 1992; Jencks and Peterson 1991). It is not surprising then that much of the current policy debate is focused on welfare reform that encourages or even enforces more socially responsible behavior among those receiving public assistance (e.g., learnfare and wedfare programs).

The problem is that urban underclass research misrepresents the nature and causes of persistent poverty in rural areas. The perception of concentrated urban poverty is inconsistent with several facets of poverty in rural America. First, poverty rates are higher--not lower--in nonmetro than metro areas. In 1990, 16.3 percent of the nonmetro population were poor, compared with 12.7

percent in metro areas (U.S. Bureau of the Census 1991c). Second, regardless of race, a larger share of the nonmetro than metro poor are *chronically* poor. For example, 43 percent of nonmetro poor blacks experienced long-term poverty (over a 10-year period), compared with 30 percent of metro poor blacks (Adams and Duncan 1992). Third, compared with the urban poor, the rural poor are much less concentrated spatially. Among the nonmetro poor, for example, 38.7 percent reside in poor areas (minor civil divisions with poverty rates exceeding 20 percent). In contrast, 52 percent of the central city poor live in poor census tracks (U.S. Bureau of the Census 1991c). Fourth, the so-called behavioral poverty often associated with the concentration of low-income populations in urban neighborhoods is less apparent in rural areas. Rural areas have higher proportions of working poor, welfare dependence is lower, and family and kinship ties are often stronger (e.g., as measured by lower rates of nonmarital fertility and divorce) than in urban areas (Fuguitt, Brown, and Beale 1989).

The misunderstandings about rural poverty are not surprising. By its very nature, rural poverty is spatially dispersed and often invisible. The magnitude of the rural problem is nonetheless relatively large. In 1990, there were 9.1 million poor people living in nonmetro areas (U.S. Bureau of the Census 1991c). This contrasts with 9.8 million poor blacks, 6.0 million poor persons of Hispanic origin, 13.2 million poor children, and 3.4 million poor females heading families with children in the United States. Rural economic deprivation is a serious problem, but one hidden away in "forgotten places" like the Delta region or Appalachia or masked by the residential blending of poor and nonpoor people in rural areas. Chronic poverty in rural areas therefore is unlikely to foment the kind of social unrest associated with urban ghetto poverty. Rural poverty is "out of sight, out of mind" from a policy perspective.

Background and Specific Objectives

How can persistent poverty be explained in rural America? Why do rural people slip into poverty and how do they escape it? To be sure, much of the problem of poverty in rural America is systemic in nature. Rural poverty has historic (e.g., Appalachia or Delta poverty), economic (e.g., internationalization of the economy), and social (e.g., Jim Crow) origins that often have little to do with the behavior of the rural poor themselves (Duncan and Tickamyer 1988; Duncan 1992; Fitchen 1981).

Yet, public policy debates now increasingly center on individual deficiencies, especially on the lack of education and jobs skills or on maladaptive values and behavior like adolescent childbearing or drug use that may undermine investments in education and job skills (cf., Mead 1992; Katz 1989). This growing emphasis on behavioral poverty has an obvious practical and empirical basis. It is easier politically to remediate (and perhaps blame) individuals than societies, and education and training correlate positively with many indicators of labor market success. Education and other forms of human capital (general or firm-specific job training) continue to sort workers into good jobs and bad jobs, even in today's changing economy. And good jobs are the major route out of poverty.

The paradox is that despite significant increases in educational levels over recent decades, poverty and economic inequality remain high and persistent in rural America. As Shapiro (1989) reports, the average educational level of the nonmetro *poor* increased at a faster pace during 1978-87 than it did among the nonpoor. Education in the absence of adequate employment will not ameliorate poverty and its consequences. This is evident in the roughly 8.6 million rural underemployed workers today without full-time jobs that pay a decent living wage (Yetley 1988). But it is equally true that employment growth and industrial restructuring will not benefit the rural working poor if they lack the basic skills necessary to take advantage of new and better job opportunities. The critical question here is: Do poverty and unemployment result from a "skills gap" between rural workers and the jobs available to them? Or does poverty stem from the lack of good jobs available to rural workers? This is the classic debate.

Our goal is to evaluate the current emphasis on behaviorally-based poverty (i.e., the quantity and quality of rural labor), especially on the role of increased education and job skills in ameliorating persistent poverty--through work--in rural areas. Our specific objectives are:

1. To provide a brief overview of the dominant theoretical and policy perspective--*human capital theory*--that links personal human resources (e.g., especially education) with labor market outcomes and poverty.
2. To assess the evidence supporting (or failing to support) human capital explanations of persistent *rural* poverty. To what extent does rural poverty result from a lack of education and skills?
3. To evaluate the connection between human capital--especially education--and the poverty status and economic deprivation of rural Americans. Is the labor of rural workers, especially among the unskilled, being adequately rewarded?
4. To refocus attention on some of the major institutional (e.g., changing schools and families), demographic (e.g., rural out-migration), and economic (e.g., industrial restructuring) factors that diminish both the *production* of rural human capital and the economic *returns* to rural education and training.
5. To rethink specific research foci that will contribute to the poverty debate and to formulating effective social welfare policies and intervention strategies in rural areas.

Our understanding of the causes of rural poverty and welfare dependency pales in comparison to our current knowledge of the etiology and persistence of urban poverty (e.g., Wilson 1987; Jencks and Peterson 1991). In this chapter, our concern focuses primarily on the education and job skills of rural workers; we neither have all the answers nor have we necessarily raised all the right questions. We can conclude, however, that efforts to enhance rural human capital will not solve the rural poverty problem alone. Human resource development must be considered in concert with other poverty-reduction strategies, including welfare reform (e.g., expanded earned income credits) and economic development that creates *demand* for both low- and high-skill labor in rural areas. Rural America suffers primarily from a deficit of good jobs, not good workers.

Human Capital Theory

Human capital theory posits a relationship between a worker's human capital and the individual's labor market experiences. Workers with only weak skill levels due to lack of education or relevant experience are, according to human capital theory, less productive at work, and are therefore poorly rewarded in the labor market. Labor with low levels of human capital earn lower wages and experience more job instability, i.e., they are more likely to experience forms of underemployment that may result in poverty (Levitan, Mangum, and Marshall 1981; Thurow 1975).

Alternatively, more skillful or experienced workers are argued to be more productive employees. Labor with higher levels of human capital earn higher wages and experience more job stability (Thurow 1969). According to human capital theory, there is a direct relationship between skill (or human capital) acquisition and labor productivity. Further, the theory posits that investment by individuals in human capital will be rewarded in the labor market, since individuals are believed to be fairly compensated for their productivity at work.

To be sure, poverty is linked in fundamental ways to deficits in human capital; low schooling and inadequate general and job-specific training. As shown in Table 2.1, U.S. poverty rates in 1987 among those with less than 12 years of schooling were 22.2 percent, compared with 4.8 percent among those with some college (U.S. Bureau of the Census 1989). Although poverty rates were higher among women and blacks at each education level, additional education nonetheless was associated with reductions in poverty for each sex-race group.

It is no surprise that the high poverty rates among the least educated result, to a large degree, from the disadvantages they face in the labor market. Among 16-24 year olds in 1987, for example, the unemployment rate among high school dropouts was 20.5 percent, compared with 10.2 percent among high school

TABLE 2.1 Education and Percent in Poverty, Ages 15 and Older, United States, 1987

	Less than High School	High School	More than High School
Total	22.2%	9.3%	4.8%
White:			
Male	14.6	5.8	3.4
Female	21.3	8.6	4.7
Black:			
Male	33.4	17.7	9.6
Female	48.4	28.9	11.8

Source: U.S. Bureau of the Census, 1989. Poverty in the United States 1987. Current Population Reports, Series P-60, No. 163.

graduates with no additional schooling (U.S. Bureau of the Census 1989). Regardless of sex, race, or region, the least educated generally have the highest unemployment and underemployment rates. They also earn less, even if they work full-time, full-year. In 1990, for example, the median earnings of male high school graduates working year-round, full-time, was $25,891. Their counterparts with four years of college earned $41,106 (U.S. Bureau of the Census 1991b).

For working age adults, labor force nonparticipation and unemployment are the main pathways to poverty, while a steady job is the main avenue out. In 1989, the poverty rate was only 6.6 percent among family heads who worked *at any time during the year*, but 23.4 percent among those who did not work (Mead 1992). The obvious policy implication is that one can ameliorate poverty if the poor can be properly educated or trained--so that they can work. Employment encourages economic self-sufficiency and presumably lessens dependency on welfare or other kinds of public assistance. Children also benefit economically through greater parental attachment to the labor force; a working parent also serves as a role model that reinforces the work ethic in American society. One solution to poverty, then, resides in policies designed to upgrade the skills and training of workers so they can find a "good job" at decent wages.

Sawhill (1988) indicates that human capital theory and its theoretical derivatives provided the policy framework for fighting the War on Poverty during the 1960s. Programs such as Head Start (1965), Basic Education Opportunity Grants (1972), Job Corps (1964), the Manpower Development and

Training Act (1962), and Medicaid (1966) were aimed at enhancing, directly or indirectly, worker productivity. More recently, the 1988 Family Support Act included job training provisions and work requirements designed to help welfare mothers become self-sufficient.

Unfortunately, the chronic nature of poverty, both in urban and rural areas, suggests that these programs have only been partially successful, despite their well-meaning intentions. Evaluations of the effectiveness of compensatory education programs, employment and training programs, and health programs have produced mixed results, at best (Sawhill 1988). For many policy analysts, the problem is not with human capital theory, but rather with designing and implementing programs that work. Education and training programs continue to evolve programmatically and funding levels ebb and flow, but the fundamental assumptions, largely based on human capital theory, have changed relatively little since the 1960s.

Human Capital Explanations of Rural Poverty

Serious debate about the strengths and limitations of human capital theory is invariably mixed with conflicting ideologies about the root causes of low income and poverty. Human capital theory is frequently criticized for its emphasis on individual choices--choices to invest or not in schooling, training, or in work. The fundamental assumption of this perspective is that higher rural poverty simply reflects a less productive rural workforce, one without the requisite skills and education for today's changing rural labor market.

Critics of human capital theory emphasize instead the structural basis for human capital accumulation and poverty--essentially the demand side of the equation. It is a problem of not enough good jobs, rather than not enough skilled or motivated people. Surely, few individuals willingly choose to be poor. As Falk and Lyson (1988: 155) argue:

> The human capital thesis puts the burden for achieving economic success on the individual. This is as American as apple pie. It is also a myopic view of how people behave in the labor force. It is a cleverly succinct version of the 'work ethic': Hard work is supposed to pay off for everyone.... Human capital is only valuable to the degree that a line can actually be drawn to link investment and reward. [T]his line is more apparent for some than for others.

Their view, shared by many, is that investments in education and work often go unrewarded because of larger national (e.g., industrial restructuring or discrimination) and global economic forces (e.g., internationalization of the economy) over which rural workers have little control (Levy 1987; Bluestone

1990). The problem is that rural firms are unable or unwilling to pay higher wages, even for well-trained and skilled workers.

We cannot provide an exhaustive assessment here of these alternative and frequently competing views (Katz 1989). We can, however, evaluate the extent to which poverty in rural America is a product of: (1) deficits in the stock of human capital in rural areas--a skills gap, and (2) inadequate earnings "returns" to human capital in rural areas (i.e., that rural workers receive an unfavorable return on their educational investment). The two points are related. If rural workers are not adequately rewarded for skills and education--for whatever reason--it will affect individual incentives to make additional investments in human capital.

A Deficit of Human Capital in Rural America?

If measured crudely in terms of completed schooling, nonmetro areas continue to suffer a deficit of human capital compared with their metro counterparts. In 1988, for example, the mean educational level of workers aged 18-64 was 12.7 years in the nonmetro labor force, compared with a national average of 13.2 years (McGranahan and Ghelfi 1991). Rural-urban differences in the percentages completing college are even higher. Moreover, the high school dropout rate in nonmetro areas was 15.2 percent in 1985, compared with 13.9 percent in metro areas (Swaim and Teixeira 1991). This educational gap reflects, at least in part, metro-nonmetro differences in the age structure; rural areas have older workers who typically have below-average levels of education. But even among young adult workers aged 25-34 in 1988, the mean completed years of schooling in nonmetro areas was 12.8, compared with 13.5 years among their metro counterparts.

These educational disadvantages are especially high among nonmetro women and minorities (Swanson 1988). As shown in Table 2.2, 15.9 percent of white males (aged 25 and older) in nonmetro areas had four or more years of college, compared with 11.9 percent of white females, 6.0 percent of African Americans, and 4.9 of Hispanics. These data also indicate that educational achievement among women and minorities is substantially lower in nonmetro than in metro areas (Table 2.2).

The optimism implied by rising educational levels in the 1980s must be balanced by the pessimistic fact that educational attainment among young adults has increased very little. Among young adults aged 25-34 in the labor force, average years of completed schooling dropped in the 1980s by 0.6 percent, compared to an increase of 6.4 percent in the 1970s. The drop was even sharper (1.3 percent) in nonmetro areas (McGranahan and Ghelfi 1991). The result has been relatively slower overall growth in average education levels (18-64) in nonmetro areas than metro areas in the 1980s (2.3 percent compared to 2.9 percent in metro areas).

TABLE 2.2 High School and College Completion Rates, Ages 25 and Older, Nonmetropolitan and Metropolitan Area, 1989

	Metro		Nonmetro		Total	
	High School	College	High School	College	High School	College
Total:	78.8%	23.4%	70.2%	13.2%	76.9%	21.1%
Male	79.3	27.1	69.7	15.2	77.2	24.5
Female	78.3	20.0	70.6	11.5	76.6	18.1
White:	80.3	24.2	72.2	13.8	78.4	21.8
Male	82.1	31.6	71.7	15.9	80.7	28.3
Female	79.9	20.5	72.7	11.9	78.2	18.5
Black:	67.9	13.0	48.5	6.0	64.6	11.8
Male	67.5	12.9	48.0	5.5	64.2	11.7
Female	68.3	13.0	48.8	6.4	65.0	11.9
Hispanic:	51.5	10.3	43.7	4.9	50.9	9.9
Male	51.9	11.5	40.3	5.0	51.0	11.0
Female	51.0	9.1	47.3	4.9	50.7	8.8

Source: Robert Kominski. 1988. Educational Attainment in the United States: March 1989 and 1988. Current Population Reports, Series P-20, No. 451.

Trends in educational attainment in rural areas fail to tell the whole story about education and skill deficits. The so-called "skills gap" in rural areas is apparent on a number of other dimensions. For example, rural high school seniors take fewer science and mathematics courses than their urban counterparts (Swaim and Teixeira 1991), and they generally score lower on standardized mathematics achievement tests. Rural schools have a more difficult time attracting qualified teachers and often have poorer vocational training programs (Swaim and Teixeira 1991). A sizeable share of rural job applicants apparently lack basic skills in reading, writing, and computation (Tomaskovic-Devey 1991).

One manifestation of this fact is apparent in the comparative math and verbal Scholastic Aptitude Test (SATs) scores among students from schools located in different-sized communities (U.S. Department of Education 1990). As shown in Table 2.3, the median verbal and math scores of rural students were well below those of students from suburban, small city/town, and median-sized cities. For example, rural SAT verbal scores were 5.4 percent below those in suburban schools, and math scores were 6.7 percent lower. The problem of rural human

TABLE 2.3 Profile of Scholastic Aptitude Test Takers, by Location High School, 1988-89.

Location	Verbal Mean	Math Mean
TOTAL	427	476
Large city	417	467
Medium-sized city	429	476
Small city or town	428	473
Suburban	443	494
Rural	419	461

Source: United States Department of Education. 1990. Digest of Educational Statistics. Research and Improvement.

capital accumulation begins during childhood and, as we discuss later, is exacerbated by the exodus of the "brightest" rural students to colleges and jobs elsewhere.

Rural deficits in general and job-specific training are often more difficult to gauge. It is clear, however, that the early work experiences of youth are a potentially important part of the rural human capital story. Previous analyses have revealed that early labor market experiences (youth employment) are strongly associated with subsequent labor market success. Teen employment potentially provides valuable work experience that builds human capital and job skills. For example, Stevenson (1982), using data from the National Longitudinal Surveys, found that white male teenagers who were out of school and out of the labor force had significantly lower earnings four years later than did their similarly-aged but employed counterparts. Early success in the labor market culminates in later success, and one reason is because these workers acquire work experiences and training (however limited) on the job (Hamilton 1990). In nonmetro areas, unemployment rates among teens and young adults are higher than in metro areas. The unemployment rate of 16-24 year-olds in nonmetro areas was 11.8 percent in 1987, compared with 8.4 percent in metro areas (Bird 1990). The transition from schooling-to-work is more erratic in rural than in urban areas, which diminishes that short- and long-term labor market earnings of rural workers.

In sum, the evidence is clear: rural workers suffer deficits in education, cognitive skills, and work experience. Under these circumstances, it is not surprising that rural workers on average have higher rates of unemployment, underemployment, and poverty than their metro counterparts.

Diminished Returns to Human Capital in Rural Areas?

Explanations that emphasize rural human capital deficiencies alone are incomplete. The current deficit of rural human capital deflects attention from the fact that rural workers with *similar* skills (as measured by education) are rewarded differently from their urban counterparts (McGranahan and Ghelfi 1991). What is the evidence that employment and earnings "returns" to additional schooling are lower in rural areas?

We begin with the obvious: education and job skills are strongly linked to poverty, even in rural labor markets. Poverty rates are especially high among nonmetro household heads with less than a high school education. In 1987, for example, the nonmetro poverty rate was 19.9 percent for high school dropouts, and only 5.7 percent for those with one or more years of college (Shapiro 1989). While additional education also benefits rural minority groups (e.g., blacks), their poverty rates remain much higher than for whites at similar educational levels (Allen and Thompson 1990). For the most part, the beneficial effects of education on rural poverty operate through increased employment and labor market earnings. For example, Swaim (1990) has shown that a disproportionate share of nonmetro displaced workers have less than a high school education. Rural workers--like urban workers--experience positive economic returns to additional education and experience.

Recent studies also indicate that job skills and education are poorly rewarded in rural areas (Gorham 1992). For example, poverty rates at each level of education are higher in nonmetro than in metro areas (Shapiro 1989). Similar education levels produce dissimilar poverty rates in metro and nonmetro labor markets. Moreover, unemployment and various forms of underemployment--part-time work or low-paying jobs--are experienced in higher percentages in nonmetro than metro areas *at each level of education* (Lichter and Costanzo 1987). Nonmetro workers also are less likely to escape "bad jobs" or joblessness than metro workers, regardless of education, recent employment experiences, or occupation and industry of employment (Lichter and Landry 1991). Explanations of rural poverty *cannot* be reduced to compositional arguments that emphasize deficits in rural human capital.

Probably the most definitive evidence for this assertion comes from a recent study by McLaughlin and Perman (1991a). They found that differences in earnings returns to education and workplace experience accounted for the largest share of metro-nonmetro difference in earnings. In 1988, nonmetro-metro differences in returns to human capital (measured by education and years worked) accounted for about two-thirds of the metro/nonmetro earnings gap among white men. Human capital endowments apparently matter less than rural-urban differences in earnings returns for similarly-educated workers.

The problem of low earnings is particularly acute and growing in rural areas (McGranahan and Ghelfi 1991). Gorham (1992) has provided perhaps the most comprehensive study to date on the changing earnings of low-educated rural workers. She calculated the proportions of full-time, full-year rural workers with earnings below the poverty threshold (for a family of four). The trends between 1979 and 1987 were unmistakable; i.e., they indicate declining earnings in rural areas, especially for those with a high school education or less. For example, the proportion of rural high school dropouts with low earnings increased from 47.3 to 57.1 percent between 1979 and 1987. Among rural high school graduates, those with low earnings increased from 29.2 percent to 43.4 percent over this period.

These are disheartening numbers. The rural problem is magnified by the fact the declines in earnings among rural workers were much sharper than among their metro counterparts. The proportion of low-educated rural workers with low earnings was smaller than that of their metro counterparts in 1979, but it was larger in 1987 (Gorham 1992). Moreover, among rural college graduates, the proportion with low earnings was 26 percent greater than urban college graduates in 1979. By 1987, the proportion was 57 percent higher. The earnings of rural, low-educated workers have deteriorated in both absolute and relative terms in comparison to similarly-educated metro workers. Equally disquieting is the evidence that earnings returns to a college education have *declined* especially rapidly in rural areas during the 1980s (McGranahan and Ghelfi 1991).

The lesson is clear: Rural workers receive fewer economic rewards from work and education than do their urban counterparts.

Rural Human Capital: Creating It and Making It Pay

Rural social policy must focus on two questions: (1) *why* is there a persistent deficit of human capital in rural areas, and (2) *why* is human capital--especially education--poorly rewarded in rural areas? The answers provide a basis, at least in part, for intervention strategies that ameliorate persistent poverty in rural areas.

Promoting Rural Human Capital

How can a deficit of rural human capital be reduced or eliminated? Our aim here is to identify specific points of emphasis among many competing concerns related to rural human capital formation. Specifically, our discussion focuses on: (1) children and youth, (2) displaced workers, women, and minorities, and (3) the rural "brain drain."

Refocusing on Rural Children and Youth. If our goal as a society is to improve the human capital and job skills of the next generation, we must start with today's children. Underinvestment or misinvestments in children today will become the human capital and poverty problems of tomorrow (Fuchs and Reklis 1992). No children should be poor, regardless of their current living arrangements or whether or not their parents work. This is a human resource policy, not a maintenance policy.

In our view, addressing the current deficit of rural human capital must therefore begin with our basic institutions--our families, schools, and communities (Coleman 1988; Beaulieu 1989; Hobbs 1991). At the extreme, some say the problem is a product of dysfunctional families and communities (Murray 1984; Mead 1992). A familiar theme is that family poverty and isolation from the economic mainstream breeds a "culture" (e.g., low value placed on education) that reinforces the disadvantaged position of poor people. While this argument may be less relevant in rural areas (Fuguitt et al. 1989), it nevertheless is clear that rural families are changing rapidly and the potential economic toll may indeed be large for the next generation of rural adults (Lichter and Eggebeen 1992).

Given recent U.S. trends, over 60 percent of first marriages are expected to end in divorce or separation (Martin and Bumpass 1989), over one-quarter of all births occur outside of wedlock, and about half of all American children can expect to spend time during childhood in a single-parent family. Rural children have not been immune to these trends (Heaton 1991). Because females face the poorest job opportunities in rural economies, female headship is often associated with poverty that potentially undermines human capital formation and contributes to the reproduction of poverty from generation to generation. In nonmetro areas, almost 60 percent of the 1980-1990 increase in child poverty rates was attributable to children's changing living arrangements (Lichter and Eggebeen 1992). Nearly one-in-four rural children today lives in poverty--a rate higher than that experienced in metro areas.

Rural poverty in the next generation will not be eliminated unless we reduce poverty among children today or design programs that mitigate its negative consequences for human capital formation (Huston 1991). Sum and Fogg (1991) have shown, using a national sample, that poor adolescents are four times as likely as the nonpoor to be poor as young adults. Children from one-parent families receive lower grades and test scores than those from two-parent families (Mulkey, Crain, and Harrington 1992). In rural areas, Wenk and Hardesty (1992) found that youth living in two-parent households were substantially more likely to complete high school than their counterparts living in single-parent families. This family effect persisted even when the poverty status of these children was controlled. The low academic achievement of single-parent children cannot be reduced to a matter of family economic resources (Huston 1991).

It is clear that family policy must therefore address the apparent educationally debilitating effects of single parenthood and low income (Schorr 1989; Entwisle and Alexander 1992). Building human capital in rural areas must begin with policies that *strengthen the family*--married-couple and lone-parent families alike. Proposed policy initiatives now center on child support insurance, refundable child tax credits, expanded earned income credits, federally-subsidized child care, family leave provisions, and child or family allowances (Ellwood 1988; Garfinkel and McLanahan 1986).

In debating these family policies, we must be especially sensitive to rural America's unique labor market circumstances. Children in rural female-headed families are especially "at risk;" their poverty rates exceed those of their urban counterparts (Lichter and Eggebeen 1992). The problems of isolation, inadequate social service delivery systems, and too few job opportunities have a large impact on rural workers and their families (Bokemeier and Garkovich 1991). Rural single mothers, in particular, face severe problems in the labor market, have access to limited childcare, and receive welfare benefits that are typically lower than those for urban mothers (Rank and Hirschl 1988; Edin and Jencks 1991). In the final analysis, the most effective family policy may be one that strengthens the economic foundations of families through good jobs (Fitchen 1992).

Our focus on strengthening rural families provides needed balance to the current tendency to blame schools for the failure of many children to meet minimal academic standards. To some extent, the blame is misplaced; "school effects" have historically been quite small in comparison to "family effects" (Jencks et al. 1972). There is room for improvement, however. A recent William T. Grant Foundation (1988) report claims that our educational institutions have not responded well to the changing economic and family environments experienced by today's children.

Our view is that rural schools must increasingly recognize and adapt to the needs of low- and middle-income children in order to meet their basic education needs (Huston 1991; Schorr 1989). Given ongoing family change, rural schools and communities may be required to play a larger role in reducing or eliminating the ties that bind poverty between parental and filial generations. Project Head Start and Chapter 1 programs remain as perhaps the best examples of successful efforts to promote early cognitive development and educational achievement among poor children (Children's Defense Fund 1991; Katz 1989). Compensatory education programs, continued through the primary education years, may solve part of the problem of low educational achievement among low income children. Education should be a mechanism that reduces the ascriptive effects of a disadvantaged family socioeconomic background--but this is frequently not the case.

This is an especially important issue in rural schools; many are currently not serving the educational needs of poor children. In a case study of poor rural families in upstate New York, Fitchen (1991:214) states that "the myth that education is the key to escaping poverty should be questioned." She argues that rural schools have failed to lift people out of poverty, indeed that schools do not provide "magic carpets out of poverty." Her view is that our educational institutions fail to level opportunities across social classes, but rather perpetuate class differences from generation to generation. One problem, according to Fitchen (1981), is that rural teachers and administrators have low expectations about the academic potential of poor children. These children are stigmatized and blamed for their low economic status. Jencks et al. (1972) have similarly argued that schools serve primarily as certification and selection agencies that create greater inequality. Elementary and secondary schools simply reinforce the ascriptive constraints of social class background, gender, and race.

The problems of inadequate rural education are also acute at the post-secondary level. The emphasis on low educational aspirations and achievement diverts attention from economic questions that often shape later educational decision-making. What does higher education cost and what are the benefits? Human capital theory implies that the education demanded by individuals responds in part to variations in the costs of schooling, both direct and indirect, and to anticipated "returns" to additional years of schooling (Blaug 1976). During the past decade or so, the cost of a college education has soared while the funding available to finance education has declined (Swaim and Teixeira 1991). Between 1975 and 1985, the total average annual cost to attend a four-year university increased from $2,917 to $5,914.

This may explain, at least in part, why the children of low-income parents have lower educational achievement levels than middle-income parents' children. It may also explain the stagnation in rural educational levels in the 1980s (McGranahan and Ghelfi 1991). Rural youth may suffer doubly. Not only are they disproportionately poor, but the direct and indirect education costs may be higher because rural youth typically lack access to community or junior colleges that ease the transition to post-secondary schooling. This is compounded by the fact that economic incentives for additional schooling are arguably lower for these youth, especially if they plan to return to economically-depressed rural areas (McLaughlin and Perman 1991a). Can rural youth be expected to invest in additional schooling if jobs, especially high-skill jobs requiring many years of schooling, are unavailable in rural areas (Shapiro 1989)?

To be sure, a college education is not the answer for all rural youth. Many lack the aptitude or motivation. The "Forgotten Half"--the roughly 20 million 16-24 year olds nationwide who are unlikely to attend college--also need some assurance of a bright future. This is the group that suffered the most economically in the 1980s, especially in rural areas (Gorham 1992; McGranahan and Ghelfi 1991). The William Grant Foundation (1989) proposed four solutions: (1) promote better adult-child relationships by encouraging businesses and schools to be more responsive to working parents and family life, (2) develop community-based activities that address the developmental needs of children through service and youth organizations that involve youth and community activities, (3) extend employment and training opportunities aimed at the Forgotten Half, and (4) provide better education programs through access to financial aid, counseling, and academic support. Bipartisan political support is also apparently growing for an extended apprenticeship program targeted at the Forgotten Half. It should be a national goal that every young adult--rural or urban, rich or poor, college-bound or not--acquires the basic skills necessary to insure a successful transition from school to a good job.

The Situation of Displaced Workers, Women, and Minorities. The distinction continues to be made between the deserving and undeserving poor (Ellwood 1988; Katz 1989; Mead 1992). A substantial share of rural workers, through no fault of their own, have lost their jobs and have been unable to find another at a decent wage. Swaim (1990) has reported that 10.1 million workers were displaced from full-time jobs during 1981-86 alone. About 2.5 million of these lived in nonmetro areas. Of this number, roughly 40 percent were jobless for more than six months, and about one-third reported reductions in earnings of 25 percent or more upon reentry into the labor force. Downward occupational mobility increasingly typified nonmetro workers in the 1980s.

Those affected were often workers who came of labor-force age when the lure of high-paying, factory assembly line jobs was difficult to resist. The availability of higher wage jobs in manufacturing, to some extent, created a disincentive for pursuing additional education. But the current transformation of the rural economy means that this segment of the rural labor force is now paying a high price in unemployment, low earnings, and poverty. These adult workers invested in job skills that were appropriate for yesterday's economy, but inappropriate for today's.

In our increasingly global economy, it may well be in the national interest to facilitate the restructuring of the economy from older, slow-growth production industries to new high growth, high tech industries. Short-term employment dislocations are an "unavoidable cost" for sustained economic growth in the long term (Swaim 1990). The problem is that displaced rural workers often lack the skills or education necessary to command a high paying job in the new economy. Indeed, young males are at greatest risk of displacement (Swaim 1989). Policy responses to the rural human capital problem must therefore be reactive in part, targeted in the short-run at chronically unemployed rural adults and designed to foster greater economic self-sufficiency and adaptability in the ever-changing rural and national economy. Adult literacy programs, job training, and adult education programs are current policy responses to the problem. Tickamyer and Duncan (1991) also argue for a new rural initiative that emphasizes public service employment (perhaps even including WPA-type programs of the depression era). Public sector employment pays better than other rural jobs, it is more stable, and it does not compete with jobs in the private sector.

To date, however, funding for such efforts has been woefully inadequate (Jencks 1992). Indeed, Shapiro (1989) has shown that inflation-adjusted federal funding for employment and training programs decreased by 57 percent between 1981 and 1989. The political will to invest additional resources in retraining or adult education has been weak, in part because the demonstrated payoffs have been modest (Sawhill 1988; Jencks 1991).

Without intervention the economic future is bleak for today's rural displaced workers and their families. But is it the responsibility of government to assist displaced workers in making the transition to a new economy? If so, how do we create incentives for rural businesses to invest in the general and job-specific training of workers? How do we become a nation of life-long learners rather than a nation of "throw-away" workers? In addressing these questions, it is important to remember that the rural demographic group achieving the largest reductions in poverty over the last 20 years was the elderly. This country's greatest success in reducing poverty had little to do with policies that rested on the assumptions of human capital theory. And it may be why policy initiatives designed to *guarantee* a liveable wage (i.e., through combinations of jobs programs, minimum wage legislation, and earned income credits) are now being discussed in policy circles (Ellwood 1988; Greenstein and Shapiro 1992).

The current problem of worker displacement is exacerbated by impending changes in the *demography* of the labor force. Labor force projections indicate that women and minorities will comprise a growing share of the future labor force (Fullerton 1989). These historically disadvantaged groups continue to suffer disproportionately high rates of unemployment, underemployment, and low earnings (Lichter 1989; Swanson 1988). Women and blacks have higher rates of poverty because of their lower human capital (e.g., post-secondary education; Table 2.2) and because returns to human capital are lower than for white males (Findeis 1992). Current labor force projections clearly warn us of *built-in* upward demographic pressure for future increases in rural poverty.

The policy implication is that, at a minimum, education and retraining programs must be sensitive to the issues of labor force diversity. What educational barriers faced by rural minority groups and women limit their integration into the labor force? How can women and minorities obtain the job-related experiences necessary to compete successfully in the rural labor market? Without seriously addressing these human capital questions, impending shifts in the racial and gender composition of the rural labor force necessarily imply an increasingly impoverished and underemployed rural labor force. The overall employment situation for rural America will get worse before it gets better. In a society where the economic pie is arguably getting smaller (or not expanding as rapidly as in the past), concerns about equity can only grow.

The equity issue is especially relevant in predominantly black public schools in the South, which have had a history of inadequate funding and weaker academic performance. In some cases, local elites have failed to promote public school development so as to ensure a steady source of agricultural labor (Molnar and Traxler 1991). Jensen (1991) has argued that funding for these schools must be supplemented with federal monies, that adult education programs should be implemented, and that affirmative action educational programs should be developed. At the same time, implementing preferential programs for disadvantaged minorities is a difficult undertaking politically (Wilson 1987; Jensen 1991). An alternative strategy is to target poor schools for additional federal monies, regardless of racial or ethnic makeup. In practice, this would disproportionately benefit predominantly black schools, while also meeting the needs of poor rural schools comprised mostly of white students.

Finally, we return to the family. Discussions of the rural human capital problem cannot be separated from the fact that minorities and women have been affected most by family change (Eggebeen and Lichter 1991; McLaughlin and Sachs 1988; Caplan, Choy, and Witemore 1992). Nearly two-thirds of African-American children are born outside of wedlock, and a disproportionate share of black women head one-parent families with children. Poverty rates in female-headed, black families with children are very high (about 60 percent), especially in rural areas (U.S. Bureau of the Census 1989; Dill and Williams 1992). In the absence of generous increases in welfare benefits or greater stability in minority families, the future promises more--not less--racial inequality. High rates of rural poverty among the current generation of rural black children will give impetus to unacceptably high rates of poverty as they age. We cannot solve the problem of racial and gender inequality without building policies that support the economic viability of minority (and all) families.

The Rural Brain Drain. Historically, the stock of human resources in rural areas has been diminished by substantial out-migration (Fuguitt et al. 1989). Debates about the effectiveness of rural schools and retraining programs are largely intellectual exercises if rural communities continue to export their "best and brightest" to urban areas. This rural exodus affects rural community incentives to invest in educational and training programs because other places, especially urban employment centers, often benefit the most. Indeed, rural states have educated their young people only to see many of the most talented and skilled leave for better employment opportunities elsewhere.

Current educational deficits in rural areas are clearly linked to ongoing migration trends (Lichter, McLaughlin, and Cornwell 1992; Swanson and Butler 1988). During the 1985-86 period, for example, nonmetro areas experienced an annual net *outmigration* rate of -2.60 per 100 among college-educated persons, and a net *inmigration* rate of .17 among those with less than a high school degree. Nonmetro areas are clearly exchanging their best educated for less educated people from metro areas. The out-migration of the "best and brightest" has exacerbated the deficit of human capital in nonmetro areas.

More troubling is that this depletion of rural human capital *accelerated* during the post-turnaround period, when nonmetro areas experienced substantial net outmigration (Lichter et al. 1992). As shown in Figure 2.1, over 50,000 individuals with 13 or more years of completed schooling migrated from metro-to-nonmetro than from nonmetro-to-metro areas at the peak nonmetropolitan population "turnaround" (1975-76). By 1987-88, the exodus of the highly educated from nonmetro areas accelerated. Fitchen (1991) claims that rural areas, at least in upstate New York, may now be importing poor people from urban areas, many of whom have low education, unstable family relationships, and are dependent on public assistance.

If confirmed at a national level, this pattern represents a historic reversal of trends of the early 20th century when cities served as magnets of the rural unskilled and uneducated. The apparent influx of poor people to rural areas has interesting implications. One is that the newly-arrived poor may find it easier to "get by" (e.g., lower housing costs) in rural areas (Fitchen 1991). Another is that the poor may be increasingly isolated in declining rural labor markets. Indeed, the apparent lack of good job opportunities for the least educated and skilled is apparent *everywhere*, which means that labor immobility may increasingly characterize the nonmetro poor (Lichter 1992). Unfortunately, we currently have only limited information about whether rural poverty is becoming more spatially concentrated, i.e., whether rural ghettos are forming.

Much of the recent outmigration from rural areas is highly selective of young adults, a clear message that the employment situation of young adults is especially bleak in rural areas. Nonmetro areas, on balance, exported over 200,000 individuals aged 18-29 during 1987-88 (Lichter et al. 1992). At the peak of the nonmetro turnaround (1975-76), rural areas lost only about 10,000 young adults to metro areas. From a rural policy standpoint, there is an obvious need to focus on rural transitions from schooling to full-time, full-year work. What happens to rural youth after high school? What determines whether these young adults stay in rural areas to work, leave for job opportunities elsewhere, or continue in post-secondary schooling? These are basic policy questions that should be addressed (Hauser 1991).

Finally, migration patterns raise serious and longstanding concerns about the equity of current funding practices for education. The selective out-migration of skilled workers from rural areas and states argues for a broader federal and state role in rural educational funding. Local funding for education places a large burden on rural school districts while the community as a whole may see only limited economic benefits. Whether the funding of primary and secondary education is accomplished best at the state and local level is an increasingly important rural policy question (McGranahan 1991). Education is a public good that benefits society as a whole. Many rural communities are making educational investments only to see their young adults leave for the city. It is hardly surprising then that local education funding is a contentious issue, one that sometimes pits families with children against those without children.

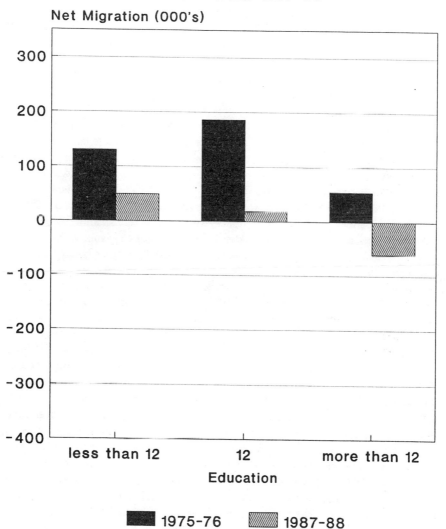

Figure 2.1 Nonmetro Net Migration, by Education
1975-76 and 1987-88

Net Migration (000's)

Education

■ 1975-76   ▨ 1987-88

Source: 1976 and 1988 March CPS machine-readable files

Rewarding Work and Education in Rural Areas

Why are rural workers--both skilled and unskilled--poorly rewarded for their labor? This is an important question because efforts to increase the education and skills of rural youth and older workers are often sabotaged from the start by perceptions, real or imagined, of limited job opportunities in rural labor markets (Bickel and Papagiannis 1988). How can programs aimed at reducing drop-out rates in rural high schools succeed, for example, if current labor market conditions offer little guarantee of finding a good job at graduation? In this section, we explore various explanations for the comparatively low earnings returns to education in rural areas, a situation that ultimately undermines human capital investments. Our discussion focuses primarily on: (1) problems of measurement and selectivity, (2) individual and family-related constraints, and (3) local, national, and global economic changes.

Measurement and Selectivity Issues. One argument is that the observed low earnings returns to education in rural areas is artifactual. Does a year of education mean something different in rural and urban areas (Marshall and Briggs 1989)? The low earnings returns to education in rural areas may simply reflect the inadequacy of rural schools--their ineffectiveness in successfully preparing students for the jobs available in rural areas. This is the "school quality" issue. Although empirical evidence is limited, this argument implies that rural workers receive less remuneration for each additional year of education than their urban counterparts because similarly-educated rural workers are simply less productive or less skilled. We need studies that compare the earnings or poverty rates of urban workers educated in rural schools with urban workers educated in urban schools. Do rural "school effects" adversely effect labor market outcomes?

A related issue is whether assessments of returns are distorted by problems of selectivity, especially patterns of selective out-migration. It is well-known, for example, that individual investments in migration can enhance (or diminish) returns to human capital. Simply, education is poorly rewarded in rural areas because out-migration has already depleted the most talented and ambitious. Left behind may be similarly-educated workers--if measured crudely by years of schooling--but less motivated, less capable, or less productive workers. These differences are then reflected in wage disparities between rural and urban workers with similar levels of measured education and skills. This view implies that low earnings returns reside primarily in the failure of rural workers to optimize their productive resources (e.g., education). Some people, for a variety of reasons, choose not to move or cannot move from rural areas, despite available work elsewhere that is commensurate with education or skill levels.

The policy implications here are two-fold. If returns to education are lower because rural schools are ineffective, then policy must be directed toward improving primary and secondary education in rural areas. One argument is that school-business partnerships must be formed to educate school leaders about the unique needs of rural industry (Beaulieu 1989). The kinds of educational and vocational opportunities available to rural students must be brought up to the standards of wealthier suburban schools. It should be a priority to insure that a year of education means the same thing, whether the child lives in a rural or urban school district and regardless of race or gender. Unfortunately, current political realities (e.g., local funding for schools) and different community educational standards make this a difficult if not impossible task.

Conversely, if the lower employment and earnings returns reflect a rural worker's *choice* to remain in rural areas, then the policy implications are different. If immobility is voluntary, then it is difficult to argue that government is obligated to address the "poor returns" problem in rural areas. On the other hand, if immobility is involuntary due to constraints or to the limited information about job alternatives, policy that minimizes these constraints to rural labor mobility (e.g., tax credits, relocation assistance, rural job banks) must be considered. The goal should be to optimize the matching of rural workers to jobs, *whether in rural or urban areas*.

Individual Limitations and Family Constraints. The diminished relationship between education (and other skills) and labor market rewards in rural areas also has a basis in other individual or family-related constraints. Rural labor may be underutilized. For example, rural areas contain a disproportionate share of the nation's occupationally disabled (Fuguitt et al. 1989). In 1990, 11.2 percent of nonmetro people aged 16-64 reported a work-related disability. The comparable figure in metro areas was 8.7 percent (U.S. Bureau of the Census 1991c). The disabled experience very high poverty rates. In nonmetro areas, 30.7 percent were below official poverty thresholds. Human capital will not be rewarded if it cannot be "put to work."

Institutionalized family patterns in rural areas may potentially affect returns to personal resources, especially among women. Indeed, it can be argued that access to child care is a serious constraint on employment, especially for those women heading households with young children (see discussion in Mead 1992). In rural areas, the lack of good and affordable child care presumably depresses female labor-force participation rates, the ability to supply labor to the labor market (e.g., rural women are more likely to work part-time), and earnings. It also means that rural women may reap a smaller return on their investments in human capital.

Traditional family values and gender roles in rural areas further imply that marriage itself can be an impediment to women's employment. In married-couple families, for example, the "secondary earner strategy" has been one way to augment family income and escape poverty. But, from a normative standpoint, this strategy may be less available in rural areas (Jensen and Tienda 1989). Indeed, in addition to limited job opportunities (Lichter 1989), the socialization experiences of young rural women often discourage them from additional human capital investment and work-related activities. In a study of education and occupation aspirations among rural youth, Cosby and Steven (1979) found that the future plans of young girls typically focused on family and marriage, while young boys focused on work plans.

It is not surprising then that rural women have higher poverty rates and lower earnings than similarly-educated women in urban areas (McLaughlin and Sachs 1988). Economic underemployment rates, measured using the Labor Utilization Framework, are also higher for nonmetro women than for men at each level of education (Findeis 1992). In 1988, 44 percent of high school-educated nonmetro women were either "discouraged," unemployed, involuntarily part-time employed, or working at a low-wage job. The rate among their nonmetro male counterparts was 30 percent. Findeis (1992) also reported large gender differences in returns to work experience; continuous work experience was less strongly associated with earnings among women than among men. You cannot reward education and skills if they are not used, and female labor is seriously underutilized in rural areas.

The main problem is that few rural women have access to "good jobs," regardless of education. In 1988, only 7 percent of women employed in rural services earned wages exceeding $10.00/hour (roughly $20,000 annually, if full-time employed), compared to 24 percent of rural men (Findeis 1992). In manufacturing, 5 percent of women but 28 percent men exceeded this wage. Most rural women are concentrated in low-wage, low-status occupations and industries (Bloomquist 1990; Bokemeier and Tickamyer 1985). Simply removing the educational barriers to women will not solve the poverty problem. Unless policies encourage creating and maintaining "good jobs," and eliminating existing barriers like discrimination and child care constraints, women will likely remain concentrated in the worst jobs. Development efforts to diversify the industrial and occupational structure of rural labor market areas will likely help women by broadening their employment choices.

Clearly, we need to evaluate the extent to which diminished returns to human capital among rural women reflect inequalities in the home and in the labor market. Our understanding of *why* female labor is underutilized and poorly compensated in rural areas is limited. This is unfortunate because women's employment potentially is a key pathway out of poverty for single mothers and for families with low-earning husbands. Poverty in rural areas will be difficult to eliminate without first addressing the issue of gender inequality in economic rewards from employment.

Labor Market Factors and Low Demand. While most observers agree that job opportunities and earnings for those with a high school diploma or less have declined since the mid-1970s, there is much less agreement about why. Two viewpoints are prevalent (Jencks 1991; Bluestone 1990). One argument is that the poor earnings returns to low-educated workers simply reflect the declining demand for low-skill labor in the production sector. Deindustrialization and the sectoral restructuring of the economy have affected primarily the least educated. This has been especially true in rural areas (Falk and Lyson 1988). Exporting low-skill factory jobs overseas has gone hand-in-hand with weakening demand for low-skill and semi-skilled labor at home. High-paying union jobs are being replaced with low-wage service jobs, and many production industries are forcing wage and benefit concessions. Low-skill workers have been on the front line of labor force change and they have suffered heavy casualties.

A second view is that the declining earnings for the poorly educated reflects shifts in the composition of demand; a growing share of workers presumably are ill-prepared for the jobs currently available. Low earnings do not reside in low demand, but in the human capital and skill deficiencies of today's workers.

A common complaint is that employers, even in rural areas, cannot find enough workers with the literacy and computational skills they need (Tomaskovic-Devey 1991). But recent studies indicate that this so-called "skills gap" alone cannot explain the stagnant real earnings in the 1980s (cf., Johnston and Packer 1987; Mishel and Teixeira 1991). To be sure, the least educated have been hit hardest by recent labor force changes, but the most skilled and educated young workers have also had minimal growth in real earnings during the past decade (Jencks 1991). Mishel and Teixeira (1991) have shown that real wages declined for the large majority of the workforce in the 1980s. Shortages of highly skilled and educated workers should have increased the wages of these workers, but this was not the case.

The problem is that the economic fortunes of all rural workers are inextricably tied to serious structural disadvantages embedded in rural labor markets. For example, the geographic isolation associated with rural labor markets reduces the labor power of rural residents (McGranahan 1991; Molnar and Traxler 1991). The strength of the association between human capital and labor market rewards depends on the range of employment opportunities available to rural workers--where prospective employers must "compete" for labor (Falk and Lyson 1988). Earnings returns in rural labor markets are adversely affected by the lack of diversity in employment opportunities, a situation that is difficult to change from a rural policy standpoint.

Workers in specific micro-regions with high minority concentrations also receive limited economic benefits from additional education. The physical and social isolation in Appalachia, in the Delta region, and on Indian reservations amplify the disadvantaged position of poor people, especially poor minorities (Duncan 1992; Summers 1991). In such cases, more education will not help. As Summers (1991:180) poignantly states, "An educated labor force without jobs is an educated, unemployed labor force." There can be no return on additional schooling unless there are efforts to create greater demand for labor--more good jobs (Levy and Michel 1991).

Compared to their urban counterparts, the rural workers' earnings also suffer from low rates of worker unionization and from high levels of occupational and industrial segregation by race and gender.   Low and declining rates of unionization diminish worker power, while contributing to the low earnings returns to low-skill workers (McLaughlin and Perman 1991a). The "crowding" implied by high rural rates of occupational and industrial segregation by race and gender also potentially reduces earnings returns to human capital (Bloomquist 1990). Furthermore, returns to human capital are limited by the small size of many rural businesses. Previous research has shown that returns to education increase with firm size (Stolzenburg 1978).

Clearly, the structure of rural labor markets is different from urban labor markets in ways that adversely affect returns to human capital.   A disproportionate share of rural workers, especially women and minorities, are located in the periphery or competitive industrial sector, and earnings returns to human capital typically are lower in the periphery than in the core industrial sector (Bokemeier and Tickamyer 1985). Using a regression switching model, Sakamoto and Chen (1991) found that the effect of an additional year of schooling or experience had a larger effect on log-earnings in the core than in the periphery industrial sector. Similarly, in evaluating labor force transitions, Lichter and Landry (1991) showed that periphery-sector workers were much less likely to shift from a marginal, low paying job to an adequate job over the one-year period considered. Rural workers face built-in labor market constraints that seriously compromise their ability to find jobs commensurate with skill levels.

But the lack of *high-skill* jobs that utilize the skills or education of rural workers also is partly to blame (McGranahan and Ghelfi 1991). In metro areas, manufacturing has moved since 1979 from simpler to more complex industries that demand higher skilled labor (U.S. Department of Agriculture 1990/91). However, during the 1979-86 period, the ratio of routine to complex industrial employment in nonmetro areas remained low (roughly .45) and relatively constant. As a result, nonmetro areas experienced low growth rates of jobs that require a college education. From 1980-88, growth in jobs requiring a college education increased by only about 5 percent in rural areas, in contrast to nearly a 40 percent increase in high education jobs in metro areas (McGranahan and Ghelfi 1991; U.S. Department of Agriculture 1990/91).

There can be little doubt that the slow growth in high-skill jobs in rural areas has contributed to the rural exodus of educated labor (McGranahan and Ghelfi 1991). Teixeira (1991), for example, has reported that rural areas in the 1980s experienced a slowdown in skill level growth--less than one-fifth the rate observed in the previous decade. In contrast, skill growth slowed only modestly in metro areas. For example, growth in handling data skills (DOT measure) in rural areas fell from a ten-year rate of 4.69 percent in the 1970s to .62 percent in the 1980s, verbal aptitude growth from 2.82 percent to .40 percent, and GED growth from 2.20 percent to just .20 percent. For these same indicators, the skill growth rates in urban areas declined only slightly between the 1970s and

1980s from 3.50 percent to 3.16 percent; from 1.69 to 1.49 percent; and from 1.94 to 1.51 percent, respectively (Teixeira and Michel 1991).

Under such circumstances, it is not surprising that earnings returns to additional education--even at high education levels--in nonmetro areas lag those found in metro areas. One serious implication is that rural workers may be *over-educated* for the kinds of work currently available in rural areas. Roughly 11 percent of the nonmetro labor force are experiencing an education-occupation "mismatch" (Lichter 1987). These workers have educational levels well in excess of the levels typical for their occupation. Rural workers apparently are not compensated for this additional (presumably unneeded) education (Shockey 1989).

In our view, the unique character of rural labor markets is also responsible for the limited effectiveness of past and present rural job retraining programs (often designed with urban clients in mind). Summarizing previous studies, Whitener (1991) notes that rural funding levels are inequitable, training facilities are limited, and the training itself is not often linked to jobs. The Job Training and Partnership Act (JTPA) has met with more success, but the results are still discouraging. In nonmetro areas, one-third of JTPA participants were unemployed 13 weeks after completing training, and over half of those finding jobs were paid a wage of less than $5.00 per hour (Redman 1990). These nonmetro workers are being retrained for low-skill, low-paying jobs. It is not surprising then that unemployment and underemployment rates have been only marginally affected by current programs.

This discussion implies that efforts to eradicate rural poverty will not succeed simply by increasing the human capital (e.g., education, job training) of rural workers. The problem is that rural workers are not being adequately rewarded for their work efforts (Brown and Deavers 1987; Tickamyer and Duncan 1991). The paradox today is that some conservative poverty analysts now say that part of the poverty problem is motivational (Mead 1992); jobs are available but workers simply are not taking them. Although empirical evidence is generally lacking for rural areas, this argument would appear to have only limited applicability for rural America, where a high proportion of poor families have a least one working adult (Greenstein and Shapiro 1992; Morrissey 1991b).

To address the rural poverty problem, we need jobs that pay a decent wage. Moreover, there is little evidence that upgrading the educational levels alone will spark local rural economies (Teixeira and Swaim 1991). A recent U.S. Department of Agriculture report has as the central conclusion "that the low education levels of local workforces were not significant contributors to the economic problems of rural areas in the 1980's" (McGranahan 1991:10). They instead locate the rural economic problem in the lack of demand for high-skill and high-education labor. The policy options to increase demand include designating rural enterprise zones, creating modern rural infrastructures, and providing tax incentives to rural entrepreneurs and businesses.

At the same time, we must recognize that workers at the bottom of the income distribution are not often the main beneficiaries of rural economic development (Larson 1989). Public policy should therefore seek to match rural people with jobs, *wherever they are*. Rural job banks, relocation assistance, tax credits, mortgage buyouts, etc., may be potentially useful mechanisms for unharnessing the productive potential of rural workers. We also need to seriously consider changes in minimum wage legislation or in the tax code (e.g., family allowances) that support rural people who work, even if it is at a low-paying job (Jencks 1992; Ellwood 1988). During the 1980s, the minimum wage failed to keep pace with inflation (Greenstein and Shapiro 1992). In a society that values the "work ethic," it is difficult to justify punitive wages for people working full-time at bad jobs. They should be rewarded, not discouraged.

Rethinking Policy Research on Human Capital and Poverty

There is no clear blue-print of policy solutions to the problems of rural poverty and human resource development. We do know, however, that poverty comes in many forms, that it has many causes, and that there are many solutions. In this chapter, we have focused on one strategy: Enhancing rural human capital through additional education and job skills. Our focus on human capital has been designed to evaluate the historic and contemporary role of education and skills in the economic stratification process in rural areas.

Poverty in rural America is different--different from the past and from urban poverty. As we have seen, rural workers experience rates of unemployment and underemployment that exceed their urban counterparts, *even at similar levels of education*. It is clear that solving the rural problem of poverty will require something more than simply providing rural people with additional education or training. *The fundamental problem resides in the low wages and inadequate employment opportunities found in rural America, especially among young adults, minorities, women, and the least educated.* Low rural wages compound the rural poverty problem by reducing incentives to invest in additional education and job training, which ultimately reinforces their disadvantaged position. Low income and low human capital are thus inseparable and self-reinforcing in rural areas.

Future policy research on human capital and rural poverty must overcome some entrenched assumptions and conceptual barriers that sometimes limit our ability to identify the causes and develop solutions to the problem. *First*, it is fashionable today among liberal social scientists to denigrate human capital theory, to hold it up as a foil for presenting other approaches to the rural poverty problem. We are told that human capital theorists make unrealistic assumptions about the competitiveness of labor markets. They "blame the victim" for poverty. They ignore or minimize gender and racial discrimination. To some extent, these charges are true. But this does not diminish the fact that education and training remain the best pathway to a good job *somewhere*--and a good job is still the best way to avoid poverty.

Second, the tendency for ad hominem thinking often causes us to disregard family demographic change as a potentially important mechanism producing low human capital in rural areas and elsewhere. The rural family is the "crucible for the reproduction of poverty" (Molnar and Traxler 1991: 80), but such sentiment is still construed, even in the 1990s, to mean that the family is "to blame" for the rise of poverty (Baca Zinn 1989). This is a legacy of the 1960s War on Poverty, of discredited culture-of-poverty theories, and of the controversial Moynihan Report, which implicated the breakdown of the family for the disadvantaged circumstances of black Americans (Katz 1989). We need to refocus on family change as both cause and consequence of rural poverty. But this should be done without making the family a scapegoat or deflecting attention from other equally or more important causes of rural poverty, such as too few jobs.

Third, education and job skills make slips into poverty a poverty with hope; it is usually of a short-term nature. The poverty of despair--long term or chronic poverty--is more intractable and it is naive to think that more education is the only or main solution. Rural ghetto poverty--in Appalachia, in the lower Rio Grande, in the rural black belt--is deep-seated and resilient to change. We need to know more about the extent and etiology of chronic or long-term poverty in rural areas (Summers 1991; Adams and Duncan 1991). Is there a rural "underclass" and what are its manifestations (O'Hare and Curry-White 1991)?

Fourth, we cannot expect educational achievement and performance to improve in rural areas without it being rewarded in the labor market. Rural youngsters will not be motivated, work hard, or excel in school if their achievements are not recognized with a good job. Businesses, secondary schools, and vocational schools must work together to ensure that rural students, *especially those who do not attend a four-year college*, have the opportunity for a good job upon graduation. For minorities and women, there must be some assurance that they will not face discrimination or other barriers like child care in the rural labor market (Jensen 1991). We have only a very rudimentary understanding of differences between rural areas and large cities in the manifestations of overt and subtle job discrimination.

Fifth, while the lack of good jobs is a problem, a serious conceptual barrier is the past and current emphasis among social scientists (especially sociologists) on the structural causes of rural poverty, often to the exclusion of behavioral ones. For this reason, Katz (1989) argues that sociologists and anthropologists lost much of their influence in public policy circles following the War on Poverty. To be sure, rural poverty *is* a product of built-in inequities in our competitive market economy. But in the absence of radical changes in our economic, political, and welfare systems, poverty solutions will continue to focus on modifying individual behavior. There is a continuing need, therefore, to identify specific behaviors--dropping-out of school, drug use, out-of-wedlock childbearing--that affect rural human capital formation and perpetuate chronic poverty from parental to filial generations. We know virtually nothing about the factors contributing to the reproduction of *rural* poverty from generation to generation.

Sixth, we also cannot ignore the political basis for existing economic inequality. Indeed, O'Connor (1992) argues that the greatest barriers to rural poverty are not cultural or economic, but political. Efforts to empower poor communities in the past have had some success (e.g., farm cooperatives, credit unions, etc.), but until the poor and nonpoor share democratic control over our basic institutions, poverty will be difficult to eliminate (Suitts 1992). In what ways do institutionalized sexism and racism work to the disadvantage of historically oppressed rural groups?

Seventh, we need to rethink and reassess the widely-held notion that improving rural human capital is a necessary *precondition* for economic growth. There is little evidence that upgrading worker skills by itself will "jump-start" the rural economy. Teixeira and Mishel (1991) call this an "education-based, supply-push" theory of human development, but support for it as a development strategy is generally lacking (McGranahan 1991). The implication is that education benefits for rural places may be limited given short-term projected changes in the skill demands in rural areas. *We need to emphasize public and private sector job creation that benefits the indigenous and poor population.* Job creation that largely benefits new residents serves only to hide the employment problems of the chronically poor in a thicket of improving rural employment statistics.

Eighth, we need to think of human capital more broadly. It is not simply a set of skills. It is not only knowledge derived from experiences in school. Rather, it must include other basic character traits that we all share as one society--the work ethic, personal responsibility, and integrity. A recent survey by the Commission on the Skills of the American Workforce indicated that the primary concern of 80 percent of employers was finding workers with a good work ethic and social skills. These traits are built from our relationships in groups--families and communities--and these traits lay the foundation for later educational and occupational achievement. We need to develop strong, supportive groups--social capital--for rural children and young working adults. Social capital builds human capital (Coleman 1988; Beaulieu, Israel, and Smith 1990).

Conclusion

The decade of the 1980s was a watershed period for rural America. A competitive global economy, the early 1980s recession and subsequent stagnant rural job growth, the lingering farm crisis, the changing family, and the current corporate restructuring of industry have taken a toll on the rural community and its people. In many ways, the demographic and economic forces currently underway nationally and in rural areas suggest that poverty and stagnant income growth are not likely to abate in the foreseeable future.

The problem is that after literally thousands of studies, we still have only a rudimentary understanding of poverty and its causes (Sawhill 1988). The etiology of poverty is even more of a mystery in rural areas. As we have described here, explanations that emphasize behavioral causes of rural poverty, especially low education and inadequate job skills, are incomplete. Clearly, the rural human capital deficit cannot be ignored, but perhaps a more fundamental problem is the lack of jobs in rural America that pay a living wage. Education and job creation must go hand-in-hand. Unfortunately, debates about welfare reform and anti-poverty legislation now center on the urban underclass, while the chronic employment problems of a silent and invisible rural poor population go virtually ignored. It is time to shift the nature of the debate.

Notes

This chapter was written by Daniel T. Lichter, Pennsylvania State University; Lionel J. Beaulieu, University of Florida; Jill L. Findeis, Pennsylvania State University and Ruy A. Teixeira, Economic Research Service, USDA.

3

Work Structures and Rural Poverty

Introduction

Perhaps one of the most challenging aspects of rural poverty is the fact that so many of the rural poor are "working poor." Indeed, Deavers and Hoppe (1992) report that in 1987, 64.6 percent of poor families in nonmetro areas had a family member working in formal employment (compared to only 54.1 percent of metro poor families). Moreover, 42.1 percent of all rural workers earned less than $11,611 in 1987, the official poverty line for a family of four persons in that year (compared to only 28.9 percent in metropolitan areas (Gorham 1992). It seems, therefore, that much of the explanation for persistent rural poverty lies in the nature of work structures in rural areas. The purpose of this chapter is to review different theoretical perspectives on work structures. Our intent is not to provide a comprehensive review of perspectives on work structures, but to draw insights from them concerning the relationship between work structures and rural poverty. We begin by noting some premises which will guide our review.

The first premise is that we need to understand not only the types of work the "working poor" do, but more fundamentally, what it is about **work structures** in rural areas that generates such relatively poor remuneration. The relationship between work structures and rural poverty should be viewed as an outcome of how all work activities are organized in rural areas, not just those of the working poor. We will apply our conceptual framework to an analysis of the relationship between work structures and rural poverty, but it could be used to analyze the relationship between work structures and other aspects of rural areas as well (or for that matter, aspects of nonrural areas).

Another premise is that work activities need to be conceptualized more broadly than formal employment. We agree with Mingione's claim that work should include all types of formal employment, but also a variety of irregular, temporary or occasional activities undertaken to raise cash and various activities that produce use values, goods and services for direct consumption either by the individual and his/her household or by other individuals and households, which are more or less necessary for the survival of individuals as distributed in different houschold structures (Mingione 1991:74).

In short, we regard work as including all activities that contribute to the material survival of individuals and their households. Our analysis consequently will consider the jobs or businesses in which rural people are formally employed, and the work they do in the informal economy and/or self-provisioning activities.[1]

Informal work activities (including self-provisioning) are distinguished from work in the formal economy by the latter's regulation by "institutions of society" (Castells and Portes 1989:12). Mingione (1991:97) specifically mentions institutions such as the state, business corporations and trade unions, which are the major components of what he calls the "associative regulatory system." That is not to say that informal work activities are unregulated. They are regulated, but by a network of reciprocal relations rather than by formal institutions (Mingione 1991:95). Thus, both formal and informal work activities are regulated, but by different types of regulatory systems.

A final premise is that work structures need to be conceptualized as "embedded" in local social contexts. In making this "embeddedness argument" (cf., Granovetter 1985; Mingione 1991) we claim that work activities are purposive actions of individuals or groups, but these actions are embedded in a particular social context. As Granovetter (1985:487) puts it, "Actors do not behave or decide as atoms outside a social context, nor do they adhere slavishly to a script written for them by the particular intersection of social categories that they happen to occupy. Their attempts at purposive action are instead embedded in concrete, ongoing systems of social relations."

The embeddedness argument is especially relevant to an analysis of work activities in a market economy. Economic action based on market exchange is unfeasible outside of a context of established rules and regulations which govern market exchanges.

It cannot reasonably be supposed that atomized social actors will come to a "market" compromise for reasons of natural "morality" or because they already foresee that the outcome will be a compromise acceptable to both parties. Atomized market behaviour is an abstract model without rules. In reality, *market behaviour occurs according to rules that are set not by the market itself but by the socio-regulatory contexts.* Concrete action is not, therefore, individualistic/ atomized but conditioned by these contexts (Mingione 1991:8).

The implication is that much of the explanation for the relationship between work structures and rural poverty lies in the way in which rural work structures are embedded in other social relations systems.

Two dimensions of rural work structures' embeddedness will be considered. The first concerns the embeddedness of work structures in systems of economic relations (or social relations of production). The key consideration in this regard will be the extent to which we can attribute low earnings among rural workers to the structure of the economic organizations in which their work activities are embedded. The second dimension concerns the embeddedness of work structures in other social relations in the local social context. We agree with Mingione (1991) that a new paradigm is necessary in order to fully understand this aspect of the embeddedness of work structures. It requires a new conceptual lens; one that views work structures as embedded in complex mixes of associative and reciprocal structures of regulation. The key consideration from this perspective is the socio-regulatory context of rural work structures.

Theoretical Perspectives on Work Structures

To begin, a few general comments are in order. First, the theoretical perspectives on work structures we review generally do not focus on rural work structures in the United States. We believe it is possible, however, to deduce how each perspective would analyze the relationship between work structures and rural poverty in the United States. To the extent possible we will provide evidence consistent with a particular deduction and note how that evidence would be interpreted by its proponents. Second, most perspectives on work structures focus exclusively on work organization in formal employment. Thus, most of the discussion in this section will be on work structures in the formal economy. We will close each subsection by noting what each perspective's explanation of the role of informal work activities and self-provisioning in rural social contexts would seem to be, but that part of our discussion will be largely conjectural. Finally, the implicit ordering of the literature review is from theoretical perspectives formulated within what Mingione (1991) calls the "market paradigm" (that is, perspectives which view work structures as organized and regulated by competitive market behaviors) to those that are more consistent with his "embeddedness paradigm" (perspectives which view work structures as organized and regulated by systems of other social relations in which they are embedded). We consequently will end this section with a review of Mingione's own perspective on work structures.

Human Ecology Perspective

From the human ecology perspective, work structures are viewed as the organization of work (or what ecologists call sustenance activities) into a "sustenance complex" (cf., Gibbs and Martin 1959; Hawley 1950). The structure of a sustenance complex results from the interplay between supply and demand factors of a competitive market on the one hand and demographic, environmental, and technological factors on the other. The latter are seen as constraints on competitive market behavior, but competition is "the master process" underlying the organization of sustenance activities (Lyon 1987).[2]

A major concern of the ecological perspective is the extent to which sustenance organization varies among different types of social contexts. Indeed, as Gibbs and Martin (1959:30) put it, "It is in this variability in the characteristics of sustenance organization among populations that human ecology finds its fundamental problem." The variability in sustenance organization is seen has having internal and external dimensions, which in combination define the parameters of the division of labor (cf., Clemente and Sturgis 1972; Gibbs and Martin 1975; Hawley 1984). The internal division of labor refers to the differentiation of sustenance activities within a social context (or in ecological terms, a population) and their "functional interdependence" (Gibbs and Martin 1975). The external, or spatial division of labor refers to the differentiation of places or local areas according to the dominant type of sustenance activity (generally measured as industry types) and the interdependence of the dominant "functions" of different social contexts within a regional or national system (Berry and Kasarda 1977; Duncan and Lieberson 1970).[3]

Research on the division of labor within local social contexts has tended to focus on the relative advantages of industrial diversity for the stability and economic well-being of the local population (Brewer 1985; Killian and Hady 1988; Kort 1981). Consistent with the market paradigm, the relationship is usually conceptualized as the effect of industrial diversity in an ecological area on its "economic performance." While most research on this relationship examines either metropolitan areas or larger regions, a few studies have focused on rural areas. In a study of the economic performance of rural labor market areas (LMAs) between 1969 and 1984,[4] Killian and Hady (1988) report that the performance of rural LMAs with a diversified industrial structure was second only to those specializing in public administration and education. More directly related to our focus on rural poverty, a recent study by Tickamyer (1992) found that the proportion of poor households in rural LMAs in the southeastern region of the United States was lowest in areas with a "nonconcentrated" industrial structure. In fact, the average poverty rate in the rural "nonconcentrated" LMAs was not substantially higher than the poverty rates in urban LMAs in the same region (14.5 percent compared to 13.9 percent, respectively; the poverty rates for southern rural LMAs with an industrial specialization averaged 18.7 percent and higher [see Tickamyer 1992:47-48]).

It seems, therefore, that a rural work structure characterized by industrial diversity contributes to a social context in which poverty rates are relatively low, at least compared to rural labor markets with a high degree of industrial specialization.[5] However, one should not overemphasize the strength of the relationship between industrial diversity and rural poverty. Poverty rates are based on an official poverty threshold which is extremely low. When a broader definition of poverty is used, industrial diversity does not appear to be as effective at reducing rural poverty as the above findings suggest. As Tickamyer (1992:45) notes, "the percentage of the population near poverty (1.5 times the poverty level) does not vary across [southern] rural labor markets...This suggests that the diverse rural labor markets offer only a fairly small rise in income compared to nondiversified ones."

Human ecologists conceptualize the spatial division of labor as the functional interdependence of local sustenance organizations within urban or regional systems (cf., Berry and Kasarda 1977; Duncan and Lieberson 1970; Pred 1966). The functional interdependence of places within a system is viewed as a "hierarchic pattern of relationships...A hierarchy [which] is clearly a power gradient; power inherent in functions diminishes with degree of removal from the role at the apex" (Hawley 1984:911). The hierarchy is often referred to as the urban hierarchy, with the "hierarchic pattern of relationships" being strongly related to the population size of the areas in the system (Berry and Kasarda 1977, Chapter 15).

The urban hierarchy concept is derived from central place theory, which claims that certain places constitute a central node in a network of exchanges of economic resources (Christaller 1966; Losch 1954). The urban hierarchy is conceptualized as hierarchical levels of central places and their surrounding areas, with each higher level characterized by greater population size and density and a broader range of economic (or sustenance) activities (Bloomquist 1990; Horan and Tolbert 1984; Stanback and Knight 1970). Central places in higher levels of the urban hierarchy also exercise considerable dominance over their surrounding areas and over places in lower levels of the hierarchy. The primary source of this power, according to most human ecologists, is the large urban centers' role as "impulses of economic change," with economic changes occurring through a general pattern of "hierarchical diffusion" (Berry and Kasarda 1977:390).

The urban hierarchy concept implies an awareness of the embeddedness of local sustenance organizations in larger geographic systems. However, the continued influence of the market paradigm is evident in most human ecologists' research on the urban hierarchy's relationship to the spatial division of labor (but see Lincoln 1978). The focus generally is on the competitive advantages of different-sized places for the location of particular sustenance activities, or industries (cf., Blackley 1986; Goldstein and Gronberg 1984; Kale and Lonsdale 1979; McGranahan 1988). The key advantage for large places near the apex of the urban hierarchy is the "agglomerative advantages" tied to their large, diversified economies (Blackley 1986:479; see also Goldstein and Gronberg 1984). Because of these agglomerative advantages, "industries and firms dealing with volatile or unestablished markets, rapid technological change, or other conditions requiring innovative responses will favor metropolitan locations, where they have ready access to information, specialized skills, and professional expertise" (McGranahan 1988:31).

The chief advantages for rural areas from the ecological perspective are the relatively low cost for land and cheap labor availability (Kale and Lonsdale 1977; McGranahan 1988). Another advantage for some rural areas would be the access to natural resources they afford to industries, plus possible "rural amenities" (Bloomquist 1988; McGranahan 1988). Generally, however, rural areas in the spatial division of labor serve as the sites for routine, low-skilled work activities. And, as McGranahan (1988) shows convincingly, the rural/urban division of labor also effects job distribution. Within most industries routine production jobs are located disproportionately in rural areas while managerial and professional-technical jobs are concentrated in large metropolitan areas.

The human ecologists' analysis of the spatial division of labor has two implications for the relationship between work structures and rural poverty. First, routine production jobs generally pay low wages because the limited skills required to perform them do not garner a high market price. The high incidence of "working poor" in rural areas is due, in part at least, to the prevalence of low-skilled jobs in rural areas, jobs which are paid poorly in a competitive labor market. Second, the concentration of innovative work activities in urban areas "suggests that rural industries will tend to be less innovative and less able to adapt to new conditions than urban industries" (McGranahan 1988:31). The persistence of rural poverty would likely be tied to the limited adaptability of rural industries and the stagnant demand for their products or services.

Researchers influenced by the human ecology perspective have also investigated the role of regions in the spatial division of labor (see Weinstein et al. 1985 for a comprehensive analysis). This has been especially true for studies of the manufacturing sector (Blackley 1986; Bloomquist 1988). These and similar studies have distinguished the South, and the rural South in particular, as the region in which routine, low-wage manufacturing jobs are concentrated. Consistent with the competitive market paradigm, Blackley (1986:476) attributes the South's distinction to it being "a relatively labor abundant region with a more favorable labor market climate" for employers; consequently, areas in the region with low wage rates (which apparently would include most rural areas) are especially attractive to firms employing labor-intensive technologies (Blackley 1986:479; Bloomquist 1988:61).

To our knowledge, no human ecologists have investigated the role of informal work activities and self-provisioning in the "sustenance complex" of an area. However, these types of activities could be analyzed from the ecological perspective. Indeed, Gibbs and Martin (1959:Figure 1, p. 31) explicitly note such activities in their examples of different types of sustenance organization. They do not discuss the ecological conditions which would make their examples of informally organized sustenance activities more or less prevalent, however. Their examples include such things as a "Farmers' mutual aid harvesting crew...producing for own use" or an "Individual mining coal for his own use."

Based on the general perspective, though, it seems the role of informal work activities and self-provisioning would be governed by the competitive process of "selective survival" (Gibbs and Martin 1959:33). That is, individuals in a population choose among competing modes of sustenance organization in order to enhance their survival. Under some conditions, incorporating informal work activities and self-provisioning into a population's sustenance organization could greatly enhance its members' survival capabilities. Human ecologists, therefore, would view informal work activities in a rural social context as an adaptation to conditions which determine the local population's survival. Human ecologists would investigate possible competitive advantages for individuals in that context to informally access particular goods or services. They would not rely on formal exchange mechanisms (such as market exchange in the formal economy and/or government programs).

Researchers influenced by the human ecology perspective have uncovered significant patterns in the relationship between work structures and rural poverty that are consistent with major ecological concepts. The reliance on competition as the "master process" which determines the type of work located in rural social contexts and the remuneration received for the performance of that work ignores the influence of organizational relations, however. Lincoln (1978:222) stresses, for example, that "metropolitan dominance" is not simply a matter of large metropolitan areas' competitive advantages over smaller places; it also involves metropolis-based economic organizations "having the administrative authority to literally control the operations of units central to the functioning of smaller subordinate communities." He also argues that such organizational connections imply a different set of social relations than those implied by a focus on competitive advantages. While he does not develop his argument further, we suggest that an extension of his argument would be a consideration of how work structures are influenced by characteristics of the economic organizations in which work activities are embedded. That is the focus of the next perspective to be reviewed.

Economic Organization Perspective

From the economic organization perspective, work structures are embedded in firms and other economic organizations. The concern is with how the structure of economic organizations influences work structures. The key conceptual notion for this perspective is the *"organization of work*--that is, the interplay between technical and administrative imperatives on the one hand, and relations among people, positions, and objects within the workplace on the other" (Baron and Bielby 1980:738). Competitive market behaviors continue to play an important role in the organization of work for many analysts with this perspective. However, they are either relegated to particular industrial sectors and/or labor market segments (Doeringer and Piore 1971; Edwards 1979; O'Connor 1973; Thurow 1975) or conceptualized as potential firm-level behaviors (Averitt 1968; Shepherd 1975; Williamson 1975).[6]

Baron and Bielby (1980:747) note that contributors to the economic organization perspective (they call it the "new structuralist" perspective) often differ in the level of social organization and the corresponding unit of analysis upon which they focus.[7] Some analysts have focused on the institutional level of economic organization, with their units of analysis being industrial sectors and/or labor market segments (Beck et al., 1978; Harrison 1974; O'Connor 1973; Piore 1975). Others have focused on the organizational level, taking firms as their units of analysis (Averitt 1968; Shepherd 1975; Williamson 1975). Still others have focused on the level of "roles" within a work organization, with jobs being their units of analysis (Sorensen and Kalleberg 1981; Thurow 1975). Baron and Bielby's (1980:748) preference is for the organizational level, because "analyses of the structure of work and how it changes over time embody some assumptions (most often implicit ones) about *who* decides how work will be organized and what *criteria* are employed in making those choices...on behalf of the firm." We share this preference, but believe nonetheless that much can be learned about rural work structures from a review of analyses which have focused on the other levels of social organization.

Institutional Level. Beginning with economic organization at the institutional level, most analysts have conceptualized economic organization in terms of a "segmented economy," usually consisting of two segments or sectors (Beck et al. 1978; Bluestone et al. 1973; Doeringer and Piore 1971; Harrison 1974) but occasionally consisting of three or more segments (Freedman 1976; Hodson 1978; Kaufman et al. 1981; O'Connor 1973; Piore 1975). However many segments are specified, a common theme is that segments are differentiated according to the organization of work within the segments. At least one segment is distinguished by its work structures being insulated in some way from market competition (cf., Beck et al. 1978; Freedman 1976; Kaufman et al. 1981; O'Connor 1973).

While contributors to the "segmented economy" literature generally agree about the structural differentiation of work activities at the institutional level, they differ in how they conceptualize the segments. Some analyze industrial segmentation while others analyze labor market segmentation.[8] Industrial sectors[9] are conceptualized "as structural entities which derive from the nature of modern industrial capitalism" (Beck et al. 1978:706). The structural differentiation of industries into sectors is linked to the emergence during the late nineteenth and early twentieth centuries of large corporate enterprises which gained monopoly or oligopolistic control over their respective industries--and sometimes over other industries as well (cf., Chandler 1962; Galbraith 1967; O'Connor 1973). This did not occur in all industries, however, and industries became differentiated by the extent to which competition was restricted by the concentration of market power in a few firms.

O'Connor, who characterizes concentrated industries as the monopoly sector, discusses the implications of the organization of production in these industries by "monopoly capital" for wages, prices and profits:

> In the monopoly sector market forces are not the main determinants of wages, prices, and profits. Monopolistic corporations have substantial market power. Prices are administered, and in comparative terms price movements are sealed off from market forces...If labor costs rise, monopolistic corporations will attempt to protect planned profit targets by increasing prices (O'Connor 1973:19-20).

The relative insulation of firms in the monopoly, or core, sector from market competition allows them to pass on increased labor costs. They raise their prices without jeopardizing their profit margins because potential competitors will also increase their prices, due to the administration of prices by the firms with oligopolistic power. Firms in the monopoly sector thus have greater flexibility to acquiesce to workers' demands for higher wages and benefits, which results in relatively high earnings--at least when compared to earnings in more competitive industries where wage and price competition predominate.

Earnings comparisons in the two major industrial sectors at the national level have consistently found significant differences between the average earnings of workers employed in concentrated and competitive industries (Beck et al. 1978; Hodson 1978; Tolbert et al. 1980). The differences are significant net of the effects of various worker characteristics such as formal education, work experience, gender and race. Moreover, Beck et al. (1978) report that the probability of being paid poverty-level earnings is much greater in the competitive, or periphery, sector than in the monopoly, or core, sector.

Analysts of the industrial structure of local economies report similar findings. For example, Bloomquist and Summers (1982) found that growth in competitive sector employment in nonmetropolitan counties contributes to an increase in the proportion of low-income families, while growth in concentrated sector employment contributes to an increase in middle-income families. Similarly, Lobao (1990) reports that for all counties in the 48 contiguous States, higher proportions of competitive sector employment is associated with lower median incomes.

There is compelling evidence that part of the explanation for the relationship between rural work structures and rural poverty may lie in rural areas' specialization in competitive sector employment. McGranahan (1983:173) analyzed the spatial distribution of "core" and "periphery" manufacturing employment in counties classified by their rural/urban status, and found that the more "rural" a county, the greater the specialization in periphery manufacturing. Specifically, in the most "rural" of counties (nonmetropolitan counties which are not adjacent to a metropolitan area), 79 percent of manufacturing jobs in 1979 were in periphery manufacturing industries. By contrast, in the same year less than 20 percent of manufacturing jobs in the largest metropolitan areas (over 1 million population) were in the periphery sector. In general, the proportion of periphery manufacturing jobs increases monotonically as the comparison progresses through categories of smaller and less densely populated counties.

Labor market segments are conceptualized as distinct markets, or arenas, in which workers exchange their labor power for wages, status, and other job rewards. The structural differentiation of labor markets is attributed to the development of institutional barriers which limit workers' mobility between labor market segments (Althauser and Kalleberg 1981; Kerr 1954). The barriers shelter workers in a more privileged labor market segment from competition with workers outside that segment (Freedman 1976). Institutional barriers may arise from various sources, but labor market segmentation analysts have tended to focus on three interrelated aspects of the organization of work: (1) establishment of an internal labor market in economic organizations, "within which the pricing and allocation of labor is governed by a set of administrative rules and procedures" (Doeringer and Piore 1971:1-2), (2) skill-specific work activities performed in economic organizations and the limited transferability of those skills to other organizations (Freedman 1976), and (3) workers' power to influence the organization of work through unionization and other collective actions (Stolzenberg 1975).

Market competition plays a role in the more privileged labor market segments, but only in allocating workers to entry-level positions. Once a worker gains access to one of these positions his/her mobility to other positions is governed by administrative rules of the economic organization, acquisition of specialized skills through on-the-job training, and/or terms of the labor contract negotiated between management and union representatives. The benefits of work organizations which shelter workers from market competition include "jobs with relatively high wages, good working conditions, chances of advancement, equity and due process in the administration of work rules, and, above all, employment stability" (Piore 1975: 126).

Analysts of labor market segmentation contrast work in the more privileged labor market segments with work in the so-called secondary labor market, which is characterized by low-wage jobs with little advancement opportunity. The most important contrast, though, is the very low employment stability associated with jobs in the secondary labor market. Indeed, Piore (1975:126) claims that the other characteristics which differentiate labor market segments are "derivatives" of the relative stability of employment in them. Employment instability in the secondary labor market is attributed to the economic organization's need for "flexibility" in its labor demands (Freedman 1976:114) as well as to "behavioral traits" of the workers' themselves that contribute to a high labor turnover (Doeringer and Piore 1971:Chapter 8). Both factors lead to a primary role for market competition in the mobility of workers among jobs within the secondary labor market.

Another characteristic of the secondary labor market that is commonly emphasized is the "highly personalized relationship between workers and supervisors which leaves wide latitude for favoritism and is conducive to harsh and capricious work discipline" (Piore 1975:126; see also Rosenberg 1975). While this aspect of the organization of work is an important feature of jobs in the secondary labor market, it should not be viewed as a "derivative" of the instability of work in this segment. Rather, highly personalized relationships between workers and supervisors should be understood as a characteristic of work organizations in secondary labor markets that may or may not contribute to work instability. The latitude for favoritism which such relationships produce could actually enhance work stability for the boss' favorite(s). Moreover, as will be discussed in more detail below, highly personalized relationships actually could prove conducive to smooth and reliable work discipline.

Analysts have estimated the effects on earnings of individuals working in an occupation with one or more of the above institutional barriers to market competition. The results have largely been consistent with the predictions of the labor market segmentation perspective. Specifically, workers employed in occupations with institutional barriers to mobility (such as a high degree of training required for performing work activities and a high degree of unionization) have significantly higher annual earnings than workers who lack these shelters from market competition (cf., Alexander 1974; Bibb and Form 1977; Freedman 1976; Kalleberg et al. 1981; Stolzenberg 1975).[10]

Kalleberg et al. (1981) interpret these and similar institutional barriers as indicators of workers' relative power in the employment relationship. For them, worker power refers "to those attributes acquired by workers *after* entry into the labor force that enhance their monetary benefits" (Kalleberg et al. 1981:656-657, emphasis in original).[11] Although other analysts may make slightly different interpretations, the general agreement is that working in labor markets which are sheltered from direct market competition enhances the ability of individuals in the privileged labor markets to bargain for higher wages and better working conditions (either individually or collectively).

Unfortunately, none of the studies just cited focused on the impacts of their indicators of labor market segmentation within rural social contexts. Assuming that the impacts of institutional barriers on earnings do not vary systematically across urban and rural contexts (admittedly a debatable assumption), then part of the explanation could be attributed to the tendency for rural areas to specialize in routine work activities (recall the discussion above of the spatial division of labor) and for the low unionization rates among rural workers. From this perspective, then, low earnings in rural labor markets stem in large part from rural workers not having sufficient power to shelter themselves from market competition.

A limitation of the labor market segmentation studies discussed above is that they did not directly measure what many consider the key institutional barrier for labor market segments: the existence of an internal labor market.[12] Some analysts use a firm characteristic, establishment size, as an indicator of the firm's organizational capacity to develop an internal labor market (Kalleberg et al. 1981; Stolzenberg 1978).[13] Kalleberg et al. (1981) do find that establishment size is positively related to earnings, as is employer tenure--a likely outcome of the existence of an internal labor market. They are surprised, however, to find that "employer tenure interacts only weakly with establishment size, our closest indicator of (firm) internal labor markets" (Kalleberg et al. 1981:677). The finding also could suggest that establishment size is not a close indicator of internal labor markets.

We argue that internal labor markets should be measured more directly. Internal labor markets should be conceptualized at the firm level of analysis and not at the institutional level. The administrative rules and procedures that govern job mobility within an internal labor market are aspects of a firm's "governance structure" (Williamson 1975). More broadly, the firm or workplace is the organizational context in which the structure of each labor market segment is established. As Edwards (1979:178) argues, the fundamental basis for dividing workers into distinct segments "is to be found in the workplace, not in the labor market." He argues further that "a distinct system of control inside the firm underlies each of the...market segments" (Edwards 1979:178).

Firm Level. The latter argument brings us to another problem with the conceptualization of internal labor markets (and of labor market segmentation in general): labor market segments should be conceptualized as distinct work organizations embedded in the social relations of a firm or workplace and not simply as clusters of market-related characteristics of individual workers. Following Edwards (1979), the approach to analyzing labor market segments should focus on the system of control which organizes work in each segment.

The system-of-control approach leads to a somewhat different understanding of the role of job skills, schooling, on-the-job training, experience, and other technical characteristics of labor. These characteristics are usually thought to create different types of labor (and so they do), and therefore to be the basis themselves of different treatment in the labor market. The relevance of these technical attributes, even their preeminence in certain cases, cannot be denied. However,...it is the system of control that creates the context within which experience, training, schooling, skills, and other attributes assume their importance (Edwards 1979:179).

Edwards (1979:19) defines the system of control as the social relations of production within the firm which enable employers and/or their supervisors to provide direction for work activities, evaluate workers' performance in those activities and to reward and discipline workers. He identifies three types of control systems: (1) simple control, which refers to the exercise of control solely through interpersonal relations between workers and their supervisor(s), (2) technical control, which refers to the exercise of control through the design of machines and the industrial architecture of the workplace, and (3) bureaucratic control, which refers to the exercise of control through formal rules and procedures. Edwards (1979:20) claims the latter two types are "structural" systems of control, meaning they are "embedded in either the physical structure of the labor process (producing 'technical' control) or in its social structure (producing 'bureaucratic' control)."

While Edwards' conceptualization is consistent with the embeddedness paradigm, we argue that all three types must be conceptualized as embedded, not just the two "structural" types. The simple system of control is embedded in the structure of personal relationships between the boss and worker(s), such as kinship ties, personal loyalties and other interpersonal relations which could influence the organization of work. The technical and bureaucratic systems of control do not differ from the simple system of control in their embeddedness but in the type of structure in which they are embedded (which also is the basis for the difference between them).

Edwards' contrast is appropriate, however, because the simple system of control is embedded in a fundamentally different type of structure than the other two types. It is embedded in a structure of *personal* relationships among individuals while the technical and bureaucratic control systems are embedded in the formal organizational structure of the firm. Edwards' (1979:145) description of the institutionalization of power under the bureaucratic system highlights the contrast between this type of control and simple control:[14] "Hierarchical relations...[are] transformed from relations between (unequally powerful) people to relations between jobholders or relations between jobs themselves, abstracted from the specific people or the concrete work tasks involved."

The key firm characteristic which underlies the transformation of work organizations from a simple system of control to a bureaucratic system is organizational size (cf., Averitt 1968; Baron 1984; Granovetter 1984; Hodson 1983; Stolzenberg 1978). Simple control requires employee numbers to be small enough that virtually all workers have personal relationships with the employer (Edwards 1979:26). Moreover, large-scale organizations are more likely to have complex and highly specialized production systems that require on-the-job training (Baron 1984; Hodson 1983). The consequence for the organization of work is that large workplaces are more likely than smaller ones to have internal labor markets (Stolzenberg 1978; Granovetter 1984:332).

Significantly for our purposes, researchers have consistently found that large work organizations have the resources to afford higher wage rates among their workers (Hodson 1983; Kalleberg et al. 1981; Masters 1969; Stolzenberg 1978). The relatively low earnings of rural workers could, therefore, be due to the disproportionate share of small firms in rural areas. Phillips and Miller (1992:65) report, for example, that in 1986, 60.8 percent of employees in nonmetropolitan counties in the Midwest worked in small and medium-size firms (those with less than 500 employees), compared to only 48.5 percent of employees in metropolitan counties in that region. We are not aware of a study that provides direct, systematic evidence on the effect of rural firms' small size on their workers' earnings, but presumably the findings for national-level data would hold in both rural and urban areas.

One case study provides important insights about how small rural firms which do pay low wages organize work activities through a system of simple control. Doeringer (1984) conducted case studies in two rural areas in Maine. He describes the workers in the small firms in those areas as follows:

> The picture that emerges in small rural firms is...one of a work force that receives pay, fringe benefits, and working conditions comparable to those provided by the least attractive employers in urban labor markets but exhibits attitudes and behavior like those found in the most attractive jobs in urban labor markets. Instead of high alienation and high turnover, employees of small firms showed a dedication and commitment to their employers that is most characteristic of employees of high-wage nonunion firms that cultivate and encourage workers to identify with the goals of the firms (Doeringer 1984:279).

Doeringer's explanation is consistent with the embeddedness paradigm. He argues that workers in rural firms are highly committed because work activities are embedded in a structure of interpersonal relationships. Doeringer (1984:281) specifically emphasizes the role of paternalism in the work organizations of small rural firms:

> Paternalism assumes a number of benign forms in the firms studied. Management knows each worker by his or her first name; there is a generally

relaxed atmosphere about social relations in the plant; relatives are given special consideration in employment, and there is often an attempt to tailor job assignments and working hours to the needs of individual workers.

Doeringer (1984:281-2) also notes various "fringelike" benefits which workers receive through the paternalistic organization of work, such as personal loans for home improvements, for automobile purchases, or to meet a sudden financial crisis. In addition, workers may be able to borrow tools or use company equipment for personal projects. The employer also has an implicit commitment to give hiring preferences to the children of employees and possibly to other relatives as well.

Doeringer stresses that while the paternalism which he describes implies reciprocal social relations between employers and loyal workers, the structure of interpersonal relationships involves unequal exchanges. "Managers and employers control both jobs and discretionary benefits. As a result they set the terms of the exchange, and it is to be expected to run in their favor, even if the exchange is conducted in the most benign of ways" (Doeringer 1984:284). Moreover, workers who quit their jobs generally have difficulty finding reemployment in the area because quitting is seen as evidence of a disloyal, and hence unreliable, worker. Thus, workers in small rural firms may derive some "fringelike" benefits to compensate for their low earnings, but those benefits are only provided at the discretion of the paternalistic employer. They are not entitlements which can be "claimed" as a matter of legal right.

Doeringer (1984:276) also notes "widespread opportunities for informal employment" in the rural areas he studied. And he implies that informal work is more prevalent in rural than urban areas. While some of the informal work he observed was "quite remunerative," Doeringer claims most of the informal work in the areas "is a form of low-wage earnings that supplements income from other sources" (Doeringer 1984:276). Doeringer claims the low level of remuneration for most informal work results because the products of such work are sold in highly competitive markets marked by uncertain demand.

Job Level. The final level of social organization analyzed by contributors to the organizational perspective is the level of work "roles" or jobs (Sorensen and Kalleberg 1981; Spilerman 1977; Thurow 1975). Analysts who take jobs as their unit of analysis generally adopt some variation of Thurow's "job-competition model" to describe the organization of work activities into job structures (usually conceptualized as promotion ladders internal to a firm). The model is formulated as an alternative to the "wage-determination model" of the neoclassical economics perspective. As Thurow (1975:75) puts it, "instead of competing against one another based on the wages that they are willing to accept, individuals compete against one another for job opportunities based on their relative costs of being trained to fill whatever job is being considered." Moreover, people's earnings depend on the marginal productivity of the job they acquire and not directly on their personal characteristics. Thurow (1975:86-97) does not deny the importance of personal characteristics; rather, education, innate abilities, ascriptive characteristics, etc., are "background characteristics" which influence individuals' relative ranking in the "labor queue" used by employers in their hiring decisions.

From the perspective of the embeddedness paradigm, a limitation of Thurow's job-competition model is that he simply displaces the mechanism through which labor markets regulate themselves from individuals' competition over wages to competition over individuals' position in labor queues.[15] Position in labor queues is not determined solely by competition over who is the most qualified for a job, however. It also is influenced by the structure of other social relations in which work organizations are embedded. For example, Doeringer's (1984) claim that paternalistic practices in small rural firms carry an implied commitment by the employer to give hiring preferences to relatives of "loyal" workers suggests that the labor queues for such firms are embedded in a structure of kinship relations. Position in the labor queue for those firms is influenced by a person's relatives and not just their own characteristics.

Sorensen and Kalleberg (1981) argue that workers' ability to control access to their jobs enhances their bargaining power *vis-a-vis* management, which could alter the relationship between a job's productivity and its wage rate. To the extent that workers are able to control access to their jobs, the earnings they receive are determined not by the marginal productivity of their jobs but by their bargaining power (with the marginal productivity of workers' jobs being a contributing factor to their bargaining power). Sorensen and Kalleberg (1981) offer a more sophisticated account of how workers' earnings are tied to characteristics of their jobs than does Thurow (1975). They also rely on a notion of individual competition to describe the process through which job vacancies are filled. Indeed, Sorensen and Kalleberg's description of "vacancy competition" also refers to the ranking of job-seekers in a labor queue. Sorensen and Kalleberg (1981:66) do broaden the characteristics which determine individuals' relative ranking in the labor queue to "characteristics deemed relevant by employers." However, they still view people's ranking as the consequence of how their characteristics compare to those of competitors, not by the relationships in which they and the employer are embedded.[16]

Spilerman's (1977) conceptualization of job structures as "career lines" or "job trajectories" moves us closer to the embeddedness paradigm. First, Spilerman views career lines as embedded in time; that is, he is concerned with career lines as the work histories of individuals and with how job rewards vary across time. His primary concern is with conceptualizing work histories as a life-cycle phenomenon (although he also notes the influence of the historical dimension of time). Thus, most of Spilerman's (1977:573-5) discussion of the time dimension focuses on how workers' capacity to remain in a job trajectory may be vulnerable to their aging. Significantly for our purposes, he points out that jobs which require exhausting physical work (such as farm labor, mining, etc.) are especially age-vulnerable in their career lines and are often located in small, rural communities which offer few alternatives to older workers who may need to switch jobs (Spilerman 1977:575).

Spilerman identifies other ways in which career lines can be viewed as embedded (although he does not use the term):

> Career lines are shaped by the nature of industry structures (e.g., occupational distribution, mode of recruiting into upper status slots such as promotion from below vs. hiring from outside the firm) and by the institutional demography of the labor market (e.g., mix of industry types, which ones are expanding and which ones are contracting). The latter consideration is important because job trajectories often cross firm and industry boundaries instead of remaining entirely within them (Spilerman 1977:552).

For Spilerman (1977:586), career lines constitute intermediary structures that relate the characteristics and life-history of individual workers to the structure and history of the work organizations in which they hold their jobs. He also stresses that individuals enter a career line early in their working lives that profoundly influences their future jobs and earnings. Thus, determinants of career-line entrance "loom large" in his analysis, for "entrance is tantamount to launching an individual on earnings and status trajectories...." (Spilerman 1977:586).

Spilerman discusses two determinants of career-line entrance, both of which are consistent with the embeddedness paradigm. The first is community of residence. He notes that many cities have a limited range of industries, and, "because career-line features are to a large degree a consequence of industry organization, a limited variety of career-line structures" (Spilerman 1977:586). The second determinant of career-line entrance discussed by Spilerman is the role of kinship and friendship networks in obtaining jobs (cf., Granovetter 1974; Greico 1987). Spilerman (1977:589) argues that interpersonal networks are especially important for obtaining "low-status" jobs, particularly blue-collar jobs, but Granovetter (1974) shows how personal contacts play an important role in white-collar workers' careers as well.

Few empirical studies have assessed the validity of Spilerman's career-line model of job structures, partly due to the complex research design required to do such an assessment.[17] Two studies that have assessed Spilerman's model provide strong evidence in support of his reasoning (Kaufman and Spilerman 1982; Spenner et al. 1982).[18] Spenner and his colleagues conducted an intricate analysis of distinct career lines among individuals grouped by major occupational groups, labor market segments and gender. They identified important features of career lines such as earnings potential over lifespan and the variability in the number and age-width of career lines' entry and exit portals.

The most important features of career lines for analyzing the relationship between work structures and rural poverty are their earnings potential over workers' life span and the diffuseness of their "exit portals." The significance of the former should be obvious; the significance of the latter is related to the extent to which workers who enter a career line in rural areas find themselves locked into that career line.

Unfortunately, Spenner and his colleagues do not investigate the effects of career-line structures in local social contexts, but we can make some inferences about rural work structures from their findings. First, the earnings profiles for individuals in various occupation groups indicate that work in occupations disproportionately located in rural areas results in lower earnings potential than work in more urban occupations (Spenner et al. 1982:61-62). The most obvious "rural" occupation is of course farming, and it is significant that the farm occupation group has the least earnings potential among both men and women. Two other occupation groups with low earnings profiles, service and semi-skilled manual jobs (operatives and laborers), also are disproportionately located in rural areas. Thus, the persistence of rural poverty seems partially due to the prevalence of career lines in rural areas with limited earnings potential.

With respect to the diffuseness of career lines' exit portals, farming occupations again are distinctive for being the most disadvantaged career line. Spenner et al. (1982:56) report that individuals who had exited a farm occupation had a much lower number of "destinations" than individuals who exited from other occupation groups. Moreover, the number of destinations drops precipitously for individuals who have not exited farm occupations by their mid-thirties. A similar life-cycle pattern was found for exits from service occupations, although the average number of destinations is greater for this occupation group than for the farm occupation group. For rural workers employed in either farm or service occupations, the option to switch careers in order to improve their earnings potential becomes more limited as they get older. Rural workers in semi-skilled manual jobs may have more flexibility, as the pattern for semi-skilled manual occupations is medium-range in the diffuseness of exit portals throughout the lifespan.

An implication of the career-line model of job structures for rural poverty is that the low poverty of many rural workers results from limitations in the earnings potential and exit portals of their career lines. A promising research strategy would be to incorporate measures related to Spilerman's (1977) insights about the importance of local job structures (conceptualized as career lines) and of interpersonal networks for gaining entrance to a particular career line into an analysis similar to Spenner et al's (1982). Measures of local job structures could include indices derived from contributors to the human ecology and economic organization perspectives reviewed above, but they would need to be supplemented with information on career-line properties. Measures of the role of interpersonal networks could build on Doeringer's (1984) observations, possibly incorporating network analysis and sociometric techniques for describing the networks (see Greico 1987). The purpose would be to describe the interpersonal networks, and to ascertain the extent to which those networks funnel certain kinds of individuals into career lines with low earnings potential and whether they also serve as obstacles to the working poor exiting from their low-paying jobs.

With the exception of Doeringer's (1984:276) observations, contributors to the economic organization perspective have had very little to say about informal work activities--in rural or urban areas. This silence can be attributed to a conceptual bias in the economic organization perspective; that is, the primary concern has been the conceptualization of how individuals or firms are insulated from market competition by the formal organization of economic institutions. The focus, therefore, has been on characteristics of economic institutions *as formal organizations* which insulate work structures from market competition. Informal work activities which are not insulated from competition generally are relegated to a residual category (to be contrasted with work in "core" or "primary" economic organizations), but are usually underdeveloped as a theoretical construct. If anything, the organization of work in the residual category is assumed to conform to principles of the market competition paradigm (cf., Averitt 1968; Edwards 1979; O'Connor 1973; Thurow 1975).

Another problem with the economic organization perspective concerns its contributors' view of historical change (and in particular, of capitalist development). Most contributors have based their analyses of work organizations on what Osterman (1988) calls the "postwar labor market model"-- a model based on the patterns of economic organization characteristics of the early post-World War II period in the United States. Even those contributors who have explicitly included historical change as part of their analysis view the development process as culminating in the organizational structures of "core" or "monopoly" firms (cf., Averitt 1968; Edwards 1979). Beginning in the mid-1970's, however, it became increasingly apparent that the organizational structures of these firms were unravelling as the U. S. and other capitalist economies began to experience industrial or capital "restructuring" (cf., Massey 1984; Piore and Sabel 1984; Urry 1984). The association of relatively high earnings and job stability with work in core or monopoly firms and/or the more privileged labor market segments was attenuated. This created a need for an alternative perspective on the organization of work in capitalist societies. We turn now to a review of contributors to this alternative perspective, which we have labelled the "Economic Restructuring" perspective.

Economic Restructuring Perspective

For most contributors to this perspective, the economic restructuring that has occurred in recent decades is the result of the increased interdependence of national economies within the capitalist world economy. The latter could be understood as a gradual process, constituted by the global diffusion of capital, labor and technology (Galston 1988; Summers et al. 1990:138-9). But for most analysts of economic restructuring, the focus is on the restructuring that occurred during and after the economic crisis of the seventies, when there was widespread de-stabilization of national economies, including the U. S. economy (cf., Bowles et al. 1983; De Vroey 1984; Piore and Sabel 1984).

Analysts of economic restructuring usually see the worldwide economic crisis of the early seventies as a systemic crisis, one that was made highly probable if not inevitable by contradictions in the national economies of the industrialized countries (De Vroey 1984:60). However, there also is general agreement that the crisis was precipitated by two international events of 1973-- the Arab oil embargo and the Soviet wheat deal. Both events "increased the instability of national economic systems that were predicated on rigid wages and prices and hence vulnerable to shortages in basic inputs and raw materials" (Piore and Sabel 1984:175). The consequence of these events was the virtual elimination of oil and wheat surpluses which had been amassed in order to buffer their prices from variations in demand. With the buffers for these commodities removed, their prices rose substantially throughout the world.

> Given the rigid wages and prices central to the system of macroeconomic regulation, price increases in these crucial markets levered all wages and prices upward. This rise set off an unprecedented wave of inflation in virtually all the industrial countries. Everything that made for stability in times of plenty increased instability in times of want (Piore and Sabel 1984:176).

Although not all wages in the U. S. were levered upward during the seventies as Piore and Sabel suggest (Levy 1987), the national economy certainly experienced an unprecedented wave of inflation. In addition, the regulatory system of the postwar labor market model proved ill-suited to resolve the crisis. More significant for economic restructuring than the instability caused by the aforementioned "supply shocks", however, was the transformation of the regulatory system itself. In the U. S. this transformation included governmental "deregulation" as well as the suspension of the wage determination rules central to the regulatory system.[19] Piore and Sabel (1984:183) claim the consequence was the turning of a crisis of *supply* into a crisis of *demand*. The symptoms of this crisis of demand, still very much evident in the U. S. and other national economies, include slow economic growth, low productivity gains, and high unemployment.

Piore and Sabel's (1984) analysis of the proximate causes of the economic crisis of the seventies and the economic restructuring it unleashed is insightful in many ways. But they fail to develop an adequate conceptualization of the underlying dynamic that produced the economic restructuring (Noel 1987;

Truelove 1989). To suggest that the outcome of this process "depends on a thousand imponderables" (Piore and Sabel 1984:281) is particularly unsatisfying. "Such a statement denies that anything systematic can be said about the historical development of capitalism. In fact, choices are made within specific constraints and according to a certain logic" (Noel 1987:311). That logic, according to Noel, is the logic of capital accumulation, which refers to the process by which capitalism is reproduced and expanded over time (Marx 1967).

The concept of capital accumulation specifies the transformation of social relations as part of the historical process--not just of social relations in non-capitalist societies but also of established social structures in capitalist societies. Capital accumulation is a dialectical process involving the successive construction and destruction of social structures, with the latter occurring during major economic crises (Noel 1987; Schumpeter 1942). Building on this concept of capital accumulation, members of the French "Regulation Theory" school analyze the crisis of the seventies as a structural crisis of capital accumulation (Aglietta 1979, 1982; De Vroey 1984; Lipeitz 1986).[20] Noel (1987:311) provides a nice summary of the approach taken by regulationists:

> The regulationists, like Schumpeter, see capitalist development as a succession of periods, each period having a specific institutional framework with corresponding social norms. These frameworks are called "regimes of accumulation." ...[A] regime of accumulation is a social structure that connects the individual decisions of producers and the socially determined effective demand they must confront (Noel 1987:311).

The regulationists conceptualize the institutional framework undergirding the postwar labor market model as a regime of intensive accumulation. The institutional framework of this regime includes the wage determination rules of the regulatory system referred to above (see note 20), a relatively uncontrolled money supply and an active, interventionist state. The corresponding social norm is that of mass consumption (Aglietta 1979; De Vroey 1984). Regulationists often refer to specific institutionalized arrangements such as the wage determination rules or the Bretton Woods international monetary system as components of the framework constructed for the intensive accumulation. However, we agree with De Vroey (1984:47) that the regime of intensive accumulation should be conceptualized at a broader level, essentially as an ideal type. It refers to the typical "gestalt" of the postwar stage of capitalist development, where the institutional framework and corresponding social norms of the regime of intensive accumulation have coexisted with elements of a regime of extensive accumulation,[21] plus other institutional frameworks and their respective norms, although the regime of intensive accumulation is viewed as dominant.

The regime of intensive accumulation is often identified as a "fordist" regime, in reference to the double, concomitant changes generally associated with the production of Henry Ford's "Model T": (1) technical changes in production that led to the mass production of standardized commodities and (2) changes in the way of life that facilitated the mass consumption of those commodities (De Vroey 1984:52-3). In order for mass consumption to occur the real wages of a large proportion of workers had to increase enough to allow them to purchase the commodities. Thus, under fordism "[w]ages are not just a cost but also an outlet for capitalist production. Therefore, while wage decreases might benefit capitalists by increasing profit margins, they have the negative counter-effect of restricting demand" (De Vroey 1984:53).

The cornerstone of the fordist regime of intensive accumulation was the sustained generalized increase in labor productivity--and the implicit linkage of (many) workers' wage increases to improvements in productivity (De Vroey 1984; Noel 1987). When the rate of productivity growth began to decline in the late sixties, however, the foundation for the regime of intensive accumulation was eroded (Aglietta 1982). Wage increases could no longer be accommodated by intensifying production. Owners and managers of economic organizations reacted by increasingly regarding wages more as a production cost than as a means to increase demand for commodities. Such reactions further undermined the foundation for intensive accumulation by restricting demand. The result was a highly unstable institutional framework which was ripe for restructuring. To the regulationists, then, it was only because the foundation of the regime of intensive accumulation was already shaken that the oil and wheat "supply shocks" were catalysts for the economic restructuring of the U. S. and other national economies (De Vroey 1984; Noel 1987).

The regulationists' view of economic restructuring as an aspect of a crisis of capital accumulation places their approach firmly within the embeddedness paradigm. First, the regime of accumulation concept specifies economic organizations as embedded in an institutional framework. According to this conceptualization, work activities are organized and wages are determined within an institutional framework or structural context. This includes not only economic organizations, but also government agencies, international organizations and other formal organizations, as well as norms about appropriate behavior. Second, regulationists view regimes of accumulation as historically contingent (De Vroey 1984). The reproduction of the institutional framework for a regime of accumulation is not automatic but is contingent upon conflict resolution in a given historical context over the control and distribution of the products of work activities. In sum, regulationists regard work activities as embedded within a regime of accumulation which in turn is embedded within a historical context.

Analyzing rural work structures from the economic restructuring perspective provides valuable insights about the persistence of rural poverty. Following the regulation approach implies a twin focus on the structural and historical contexts of rural work structures. Focus on the structural context implies a consideration of how rural areas' work structures fit into the institutional framework of the regime of intensive accumulation. It also includes other frameworks such as a regime of extensive accumulation or perhaps even an institutional framework for "flexible specialization" as opposed to mass production (Piore and Sabel 1984:258-76; Harvey 1988). Focus on the historical context implies consideration of how rural work structures have been shaped by previous "rounds of accumulation" (Truelove 1989; Massey 1984; Rees 1984).

To illustrate the insights that can be gained from adopting an economic restructuring perspective on the relationship between work structures and rural poverty, we will discuss how the restructuring of the U. S. farm system could be analyzed from this perspective. The farm system has experienced restructuring throughout the twentieth century, driven by the interrelated processes of farm mechanization and farm consolidation (Fite 1981; Lobao 1990). But the pace of change associated with those processes accelerated after World War II, which regulationists say happened because agricultural production was incorporated into the regime of intensive accumulation (Friedmann 1987; Kenney et al. 1989).[22] The integration of agriculture into the institutional framework of U. S. Fordism did not come without costs for rural areas, however. The number of farms declined by over 60 percent between 1940 and 1980 (Lobao 1990:34). Displaced farmers and farm laborers either sought work elsewhere or had to be absorbed by the local economy. Most migrated, resulting in substantial population loss for many rural areas, which in turn contributed to a decline in economic and social institutions dependent on the local population (Buttel 1980).

Especially significant for a focus on the structural context of rural work structures is that most of the decrease in farms occurred among medium-size family farms, which historically were the mainstay of American agriculture (Lobao 1990; Stockdale 1982). Moreover, researchers have found that economic vitality of the rural community is enhanced by the presence of medium-size family farms (Flora and Flora 1986; Lobao 1990; see also Skees and Swanson 1986). Moreover, family-operated farms tend to purchase farm inputs and consumption goods locally, thereby helping to sustain local retailers (Murdock and Leistritz 1988). The implication is that not only have millions of farmers and farm laborers been displaced by the restructuring of the farm sector, but the pattern of that restructuring also has undermined an important source of economic vitality for the nonfarm sector in rural economies.

The impact of economic restructuring on socioeconomic conditions in rural areas also depends on their historical context. Crucial from the regulation perspective is how restructuring is mediated by a local context which is already structured by previous rounds of accumulation (Truelove 1989), or what Massey (1984) refers to as "rounds of investment":

> At any point in time the geographical pattern of economic activity which is associated with...new spatial structures is overlaid on and combined with the pattern produced in previous periods. And each new combination of successive layers produces, or may produce, a new form and a new distribution of inequality, which in turn is the geographical basis for the next round of investment (Massey 1984:123).

The influence of previous rounds of accumulation is reflected not only in the multi-layered pattern of economic activities within a local social context, but also in the social and political institutions which constituted the local framework for capital accumulation in previous rounds (Truelove 1989). Indeed, local social and political institutions are central to the mediation of the impacts of economic restructuring.

Continuing with the analysis of the impact of farm restructuring on local socioeconomic conditions, it seems the historical context of the Midwest region contributed to the amelioration of the effects of industrialized farming on local economic well-being in that region: "The Midwest context of protection of family farming, state regulation of corporate farming, and history of agrarian populism may [have] offset any deleterious impacts of industrialized farming" (Lobao 1990:191)--at least in the context of a strong farm economy.[23] In contrast, the historical context of the South, and of the old Cotton Belt in particular, seems to have exacerbated the negative effects of industrialized farming. Lobao notes her findings for counties in that region are consistent with Skees and Swanson's (1988) claim that the old Cotton Belt, with its long history of coercive treatment of agrarian labor and the more recent history of local states highly supportive of the interests of capital (see Falk and Lyson 1988; Wood 1986), is particularly susceptible to the adverse effects of industrialized farming.

With respect to informal work activities, especially significant from the economic restructuring perspective is the expansion in the role that informal work activities have played in the U. S. economy (as well as in other industrialized economies) since the economic crisis of the seventies (see Kolko 1988; Portes et al., 1989). Indeed, the increased informalization in the organization of work is seen as part of the response to the crisis. It is viewed as a strategy for reducing labor costs, not only in terms of wages paid but also in terms of benefit packages, maintenance of health and safety standards and other production costs related to state regulation of economic organizations (Castells and Portes 1989). Other analysts of informalization from the economic restructuring perspective link it with the growth of the service sector in national economies (Gershuny 1978,1988; Sassen-Koob 1986). While analysts differ on the implications of informalization for the people involved in informal work activities,[24] there is a general agreement within the perspective that the trend toward informalization is "a response to a fundamental and global process of economic restructuring" (Summers et al. 1990).

Few analysts of informal work activities from the economic restructuring perspective have focused on rural social contexts in the U.S. (but see Gringeri 1990a). Especially important for rural work structures is the resurgence of "homework," where economic organizations contract households to perform work activities in their residence. Homework usually is paid by the piece or unit of production rather than by labor-time, and is characterized by limited or no fringe benefits or job security (Leidner 1987; Gringeri 1990a). Rural social contexts would seem to be fertile ground for employers to contract homework activities: "family farms have a long history of casual, cash-based activities, such as 'egg money', which sets the foundation for the acceptance and entrance of informal labour-like homework" (Summers et al. 1990:153). Moreover, some local governments in rural areas have included the attraction of companies that rely on homeworking as part of their overall economic development strategy (Gringeri 1990a). The prevalence of such activities in rural social contexts could be interpreted from the economic restructuring perspective as the persistence of the regime of extensive accumulation. To the extent that rural work structures are organized under the regime of extensive accumulation, then workers must reproduce themselves outside of the formal wage relation (De Vroey 1984:Table 1).

The contribution of the economic restructuring perspective to our understanding of the relationship between work structures and rural poverty is threefold. First, the focus on restructuring increases our awareness (of the possibility at least) that changes in work structures and other social structures in rural areas reflect an emergence of a new pattern for organizing work and other activities. Second, the emphasis on the significance of structural and historical contexts provides important clues about the sources of variation in work structures among rural social contexts. Finally, the conceptualization of regimes of accumulation and the institutional frameworks upon which they are constructed provides us with an approach for analyzing changes in, and variations among, rural work structures.

The economic restructuring perspective is not without limitations, however. The most important limitations, for our purposes, concern (1) causal explanations of restructuring that are either too general (the regulationists) or too ad hoc (Piore and Sabel), and (2) inadequate conceptualization of the role that individual choices and actions play in the construction and destruction of regimes of accumulation (Noel 1987:330-3). Both limitations stem from contributors to the economic restructuring perspective failing to develop fully a conceptualization of how work activities are regulated by the social relations in which they are embedded. We believe that one of Mingione's (1991) major contributions to economic sociology is the development of such a conceptualization. We close our review of theoretical perspectives on work structures, therefore, with a discussion of Mingione's perspective.

Mingione's Social Embeddedness Perspective

Mingione's (1991) pathbreaking reformulation of the sociology of economic life offers a critical new lens for analyzing the relationship between work structures and rural poverty. While he shares with the regulationists a vision of work structures embedded in a system of social regulation, the focal point for Mingione is the regulatory structure based on reciprocity. He does not deny the significance of what he calls the "associative regulatory process."

> Interest groups, trade unions, cartels, etc., directly or through the state, and even the state itself, bring into being the institutional regulations needed to prevent, at different times and in different social contexts, competitive market tensions from undermining the social order and, thereby, also the very possibility for capitalism itself. In my view, this is only part of the picture and by itself cannot fully explain the various regulatory processes (Mingione 1991:107-8).

Mingione's aim is to illuminate the rest of the picture with a conceptualization of social regulation in the reciprocal realm. He stresses that the reciprocal regulatory process should not be idealized; "reciprocal systems are by definition systems of power" (Mingione 1991:27). The fundamental distinction between the two regulatory processes is the priority of group interest over the immediate interests of individuals in reciprocal organizations. Both aspects of reciprocal organizations need to be kept in mind in the following discussion.

Mingione's accomplishment is not just an illumination of an aspect of the regulatory process which has been obscured by others, however. He portrays the social contexts in which work structures are embedded as complex mixes of associative and reciprocal kinds of relationships organized to regulate the tensions produced by competitive market behaviors. Following Polanyi (1957), Mingione (1991:3) contends that competitive market behaviors constitute one of the three basic forms of exchange relations, the other two being reciprocity and redistribution. He also notes a crucial difference between market exchange relations and the other two forms.

> Reciprocity is a form of exchange based...on eventual restitution, or on restitution to somebody different from the actual donor. For these reasons, actions of reciprocal exchange depend on a set of established relations and rules as to who gives and who receives, and what is given and at what time. Similarly, redistributive exchange does not make sense beyond the existence of established relations and rules that determine what resources are taken from the direct producers for redistribution, to who[m] they are allocated and in what

ratios, and also who does the taking and for what reasons. Market exchange, on the contrary, makes sense as an abstract concept only if it is perceived as a finished transaction taking place between as many actors as possible who are unaffected by other kinds of established social relations (Mingione 1991:3).

For Mingione (1991:4), then, market transactions occur "within historically established conditions of social organization, shaped by complex mixes of reciprocity and redistribution." He further argues that market relations produce tensions which the two socio-organizational systems must attempt to accommodate. Tensions arise from the fact that market exchange is based on divergent interests and therefore on competition. This is true for all market exchanges, in that the buyer wishes to sell a commodity at the highest possible price whereas the seller wants to buy it at the lowest price (Mingione 1991:7-8). The tensions inherent in market exchanges are exacerbated in labor market transactions because the key "commodity" being exchanged, labor power, is what Polanyi (1957) calls a "fictitious" commodity.[25] Labor power "cannot be shoved about, used indiscriminately, or even left unused, without affecting also the human individual who happens to be the bearer of this peculiar commodity" (Polanyi 1957:73). Thus, not only do the buyers and sellers of labor power have divergent interests, the social regulation of labor market transactions have implications far beyond the "price" of labor. At stake is the social reproduction of workers and their households.

Mingione identifies two "crucial moments" in the general regulatory process during the industrial age, moments he claims can be traced in specific social contexts. The first concerns the regulatory potential of reciprocal networks. The potential has developed along two lines: "the limiting of market tensions beyond the confines established by the associative regulatory structure and the absorption of market tensions in ways which are either prohibited or not properly taken into account by the associative regulatory system" (Mingione 1991:108). The second crucial moment concerns the associative regulatory process, which also has developed along two lines: "the setting of limits to the devastating penetration of destructive market tensions into community networks and, at the same time, the reshaping of social organization based on reciprocity in order to make it compatible with industrial development" (Mingione 1991:109).

The regulatory process needs to be understood, therefore, as the simultaneous, and often contradictory, regulation of market tensions by reciprocal and associative forms of social organization. And in the process these two forms of social organization may transform each other. Mingione acknowledges that the associative regulatory structure has been dominant during the industrial age. Indeed, industrial development could be characterized as the increasing importance of associative systems in the regulatory process. But regulations and limitations rooted in the reciprocal realm remain important, though often "hidden." Moreover, Mingione (1991:32) contends that the "fragmented societies" which have emerged in the present era of economic restructuring "are characterized by the increasing importance of reciprocal contexts" that interfere with regulations and limitations rooted in the associative realm.

Another of Mingione's points concerns the worldwide nature of the regulatory process. He notes that if social regulation was completely effective at imposing limitations on competitive tensions then it would suffocate industrial economic growth. "For both regulation and growth to be possible at the same time, the process of industrial development has to find ways of diverting competitive tensions to areas where they can be absorbed, rather than merely setting up barriers to social chaos" (Mingione 1991:116). Thus, Mingione characterizes industrial development as a highly uneven process involving two contradictory trends: increasing associative regulation and high rates of industrial growth in advanced capitalist countries accompanied by "an aggressive destruction of community-based social shelters in the periphery, in the sense of both underdeveloped countries and marginalized and deprived groups" (Mingione 1991:116). This uneven process generates periodic crises in industrial development, crises that he believes stem from an inadequate transformation of regulatory structures based on reciprocity. Either reciprocal organizations in the periphery cannot absorb competitive tensions or they effectively resist attempts to reshape them by the associative regulatory system.

Mingione argues that tracing the general regulatory process in specific social contexts requires one to consider reciprocal forms of social organization present in those contexts. For him, the household is the most basic form of reciprocal organization. He defines the household as "a set of changing social relations which establish a set of mutual obligations...aimed at helping its members survive....[S]urvival is not only intended in a strict sense but also includes strategies for promoting welfare and possibly social mobility, both within generations and from one to the next" (Mingione 1991:132). Diversity in households' survival strategies is seen as an important source of heterogeneity among social contexts.

Mingione's analysis of patterns in household survival strategies provides important insights on the role of workers' earnings in those strategies. He notes that the structure of household strategies

> can be considered in terms of different configurations of monetary consumption in relation to needs which are satisfied by unpaid domestic work or activities directed at immediate household consumption of resources contributed from outside the household, such as redistribution from the state and various contributions deriving from different reciprocal networks (Mingione 1991:140).

The implication for work activities is that they must be analyzed in the context of an overall survival strategy. This strategy involves household members pooling the earnings they receive for their work with other resources (externally provided as well as internally produced) in order to reproduce the household. From Mingione's perspective, therefore, the important question is how the low earnings that many rural workers receive are incorporated into their households' reproductive strategies.

Mingione's conceptualization of work activities as a component of households' reproductive strategies deepens our understanding of the embeddedness paradigm:

> Within the household as a unit of social reproduction, embedded in different supportive reciprocal networks, decisions are taken according to the varying and changing internal distribution of power on which is the best possible allocation of available resources to meet subsistence needs, given the existing relations between work opportunities and income and the parallel possibilities of saving subsistence spending through...self-provisioning and/or given the existence of other reciprocal or redistributive resources. In this sense, the complex structure of reproduction expresses, among other processes, the formation of the labour supply at given conditions of labour demand and of overall work opportunities (Mingione 1991:141).

Work activities are embedded in household structures (including an internal distribution of power). These in turn are embedded in other reciprocal networks and in associative structures of redistribution. This multi-layered conceptualization of the embeddedness of work activities requires one to consider not only how work opportunities are organized in a particular social context, but also how household members organize their work activities in the context of the overall reproductive strategy.

The implication for the relationship between work structures and rural poverty is that it should be viewed as the consequence of the articulation of work structures and household strategies in rural social contexts.

> The interconnection between the complex specific structure of demand and the complex specific patterns of social reproduction will result in a wage/income structure and in a specific capacity of monetary expenditure on subsistence goods and services produced and sold within the market system (commodification) (Mingione 1991:128).

Rural poverty would be high, therefore, in those social contexts in which rural households face a wage/income structure that affords them low earnings and in which they have limited external resources to improve their financial situation.[26]

While consideration of alternative sources of income that rural households could use to supplement their low earnings is important, Mingione's embeddedness perspective leads us to additional considerations. The first concerns whether the external resources are obtained from the associative or the reciprocal realm. If resources are obtained from the associative realm (most notably various state restributive programs) then the focus would be on the extent to which those resources help limit the devastation of the commodification process on the working poor--by which we mean an increased reliance on goods and services that require monetary expenditures in conjunction with low earnings from their work activities (informal as well as formal). A related issue would be whether rural households' access to external resources from the associative realm contributes to a reshaping of reciprocal organizations in order to make them more compatible to industrial development. If resources are obtained from the reciprocal realm (such as gifts or charity from relatives, friends and/or community organizations, inherited wealth, etc.) then the focus would shift to a concern with the potential of these reciprocal networks to limit and/or absorb market tensions that have escaped regulation by the associative regulatory system. The second set of concerns is related to the process of uneven development as characterized by Mingione. Of particular concern in this regard would be how poverty in rural social contexts is related to the diversion of market tensions into rural peripheral areas and marginalized rural households.

Mingione's perspective has yet to have had a great influence on researchers studying rural poverty. Two recently published case studies of rural poverty do report evidence which can be interpreted with Mingione's conceptual framework, however (Dill and Williams 1992; Fitchen 1992). The fact that they were conducted in two different regions (the rural South and Northeast, respectively) also permits some tentative conjectures about variations in the impacts of the socio-regulatory context on poor rural households' reproductive strategies.

Fitchen studied poor families in rural New York State and described household strategies that included complex mixes of work activities, welfare payments, Food Stamps, reliance on Medicaid for health care, and reciprocal networks with relatives and friends. Many of the rural households she studied needed to supplement their earnings with other resources in order to survive. Fitchen (1992:189) points out, for example, that AFDC cases decreased in the late eighties, "as women who had been on welfare have taken jobs. But this decrease has been accompanied by an increase in Food Stamps and Medicaid for people not on public assistance, as these jobs have left them still near or even below the poverty line and still eligible for--and desperately in need of--these programs." State redistributive programs such as Food Stamps and Medicaid do, therefore, help many rural households meet very basic subsistence needs, but the eligibility requirements limit their availability to destitute poor.

Moreover, the other major state redistributive program, AFDC (which technically provides rural women an alternative to working at a low-paying job), is administered such that welfare recipients find themselves in an "employment-welfare bind." Fitchen (1992:190) illustrates this bind with the case of a young woman who was the sole provider for herself and her child.

> The Welfare Department wanted her to get a job and she herself desperately wanted off welfare. The only job she could get was a thirty-hour-a-week job in a supermarket in town at $3.75 an hour, which yielded an income well below the poverty level.... She can retain Medicaid, Food Stamps, and partial assistance for a while, but when that runs out she expects to be much worse off than when she had full public assistance. But if she were to quit her supermarket job, she would be "sanctioned" by the Welfare Department, which would require her to wait thirty days before applying again for any benefits.

With regard to the potential of reciprocal networks to absorb market tensions, Fitchen gives evidence of an increasing instability of the rural poor's reciprocal networks. She notes, first of all, that the incidence of female-headed households among the rural poor had increased dramatically in her study counties since her previous research in the seventies, which is consistent with national trends (Deavers and Hoppe 1992:13). Fitchen (1992:195) also claims that extended family networks are less developed and less available for poor families now than in the seventies. For the poor households she studied, therefore, their reciprocal networks anchored among relatives have a diminished potential for absorbing the tensions created by low incomes. Fitchen (1992:195) does note that some poor households rely on networks of peers for assistance, but she claims such networks often lack "the stability, permanence and resources of the old family-based network, economically impoverished as it may have been."

Fitchen (1992:186) also gives evidence relevant to the process of uneven development. She contends that much of the growth in low-income residents in the counties she studied was due to in-migration. Some of the in-migrants were young adults who returned to their home counties after they lost their jobs in the "Sunbelt" and elsewhere. But Fitchen also found a sizeable number of in-migrants who were "nonlocals," many of whom had migrated from large urban areas. The primary motivation for the urban low-income families to move to rural villages was to find cheaper housing. Increase in both types of low-income migrants can be interpreted as due to market tensions, whether they be tied to stagnating regional economies or to escalating housing costs in the urban core, being diverted to the rural social contexts studied by Fitchen.

Dill and Williams (1992) report preliminary findings from their study of a segment of the rural poor which clearly has been marginalized by the process of uneven development--African American single mothers in the rural South. They contend that for the women they interviewed

> survival is a process of constantly struggling to acquire resources from three primary sources--work, welfare, and kin...[and although they] use different strategies, make different arrangements, and have different needs,...it is clear that without their kinship networks they would be extremely hard pressed to provide for themselves and their children (Dill and Williams 1992:106).

The authors' description of strong family-based networks is in contrast with Fitchen's description of reciprocal networks in the rural Northeast. A conclusion should not be drawn from this contrast, given the preliminary nature of both studies and their different foci. However, it does suggest a topic for further research on rural poverty: the possibility of regional and/or ethnic variations in the role that reciprocal networks play in rural households' reproductive strategies.

Dill and Williams (1992:103-4) also address the role of the local/regional associative structure at restricting the work opportunities for African American women in the formal economy. They note that the women they interviewed who are employed are concentrated in the worst-paying jobs in the local economy, and the "the Delta and Black Belt economies, as they exist today, are the conscious construction of the rural White elite" (Dill and Williams 1992:104; see also Brown and Warner 1989; Tomaskovic-Devey 1990). Thus, local white elites in the rural South use their control over the local associative regulatory system to restrict the work opportunities for African Americans (men as well as women) to jobs with extremely low pay, often only part-time, and with few, if any, fringe benefits. Researchers studying work structures in other rural social contexts also need to investigate the extent to which the work opportunities for poor households are consciously restricted by local elites. And there is some cursory evidence of such actions in other contexts. Fitchen (1992:191) notes, for example, that long-term unemployed people in rural New York are frequently labeled "unemployable" by employers and employment personnel. Similarly, recall Doeringer's (1984:282-3) claim that quitting a job in rural Maine could result in a worker being regarded as "disloyal" by other local employers. In both contexts, the local work opportunities for people labeled negatively are greatly restricted, if not nonexistent.

We hope that examination of the two case studies has given some indication of the contributions which Mingione's embeddedness perspective can make to our understanding of the relationship between work structures and rural poverty. Analyzing the relationship from his perspective requires a concern not only with the type of jobs available in an area, or with how rural work structures are embedded in a structural and historical context, but also with how the work activities which constitute those structures are themselves embedded in households' reproductive strategies. Mingione's conceptual framework allows for what we believe are valuable interpretations of evidence reported by Fitchen (1992) and Dill and Williams (1992). It also alerted us to additional issues which need to be addressed. One such issue is the role of informal work activities in the reproductive strategies of rural households. We close our review of Mingione's perspective with a discussion of his view of informal activities.

Mingione (1991:97) maintains that "informal activities cannot be understood unless they are seen in relation to the question of social regulation." For him, the starting point for answering this question is to address the role of reciprocal networks in the regulation of informal work activities. He contends that

> although such activities differ greatly in diverse social contexts, they are usually accompanied by some sort of network with reciprocal features. The informational aspect is the most evident and recurrent of these features. By definition, informal activities are not officially recorded and publicized even when they are not illegal and are tolerated by the authorities. Economic operators and customers are involved in a network of information which is based on a certain degree of reciprocal trust. The network opens up or remains closed depending partly on the extent to which the informal activity is able to expand, and partly on how many people it can involve before becoming too risky or economically inconvenient (Mingione 1991:95-6).

Thus, a reciprocal network of information and trust is crucial to the organization of many informal work activities. The social regulation of such activities involves complex structures of reciprocal organizations. "Family, community, sometimes regional and ethnic solidarity, a wide informational/trust network are all involved to a certain extent in making possible the diverse livelihood arrangements found in the informal sector" (Mingione 1991:96).

Mingione also points to important sources of variation in the extent to which rural households' rely on informal work activities in their reproductive strategies. Noting that the income-to-working-time ratio for informal activities generally is low, Mingione (1991:171) contends that "active involvement in the informal sector is easier for relatively large households and for those which are socially and geographically stable." Stability is necessary because it would be difficult to establish reciprocal networks where there is a high turnover among potential members. Stability also is an important condition for the spread of informal activities within a social context, according to Mingione. The advantages of local contexts with population stability for the organization of such activities include "the possibility of recourse to large and compact kinship networks, [and] the persistence and continuity of neighborhoods and community solidarity and co-operation" (Mingione 1991:178).

From Mingione's perspective, then, informal work activities are regulated by the reciprocal networks in which households are embedded. His emphasis on the importance of information exchange and trust to many such networks suggests that researchers studying informal activities among the rural poor need to investigate these important aspects of social regulation in the informal sector. In addition, his claim that the effectiveness of informal work activities at generating income and other resources is facilitated by large household size and stability (of the household as well as in the local social context) could serve as hypotheses concerning the variation in rural households' reliance on informal networks in their reproductive strategies. Research informed by these and other insights about informal activities which Mingione (1991) offers could, we believe, greatly improve our understanding of the social organization of informal work activities in rural social contexts.

Conclusion

We began this chapter by noting the significance of work structures in rural areas to the persistence of rural poverty. We argued that to fully understand the relationship between work structures and rural poverty, we need to expand our focus beyond the types of jobs in which the rural poor are employed to include the structure of all work activities in rural areas (informal work activities as well as formal employment). We also advocated a shift in our paradigmatic assumptions about how work structures are organized. Of paramount importance to this shift is the abandonment of the model of a self-regulating market as the basis for the social organization of work activities. The organization of work activities needs to be viewed as the consequence of work activities' embeddedness in other systems of social relations, not as the outcome of an "invisible hand" which regulates competitive market behaviors. Following Mingione (1991), we have argued further that the other systems of social relations are best conceptualized as the "socio-regulatory context" in which household members organize their work activities.

While our review of theoretical perspectives on work structures reflects our theoretical agenda, we have been respectful of the insights about the relationship between work structures and rural poverty which can be culled from perspectives rooted in the market paradigm. We hope that readers who feel more comfortable working within the market paradigm will find our discussions of those perspectives helpful in their formulation of a research agenda concerning the impact of work structures on rural poverty. But we also hope we have been provocative (in the positive meaning of the term). Our aim has been to demonstrate the value of formulating a research agenda consistent with the embeddedness paradigm. It should involve not only a broader view of what constitutes work structures, but also the adoption of a new conceptual lens for analyzing them. The research objective from the perspective of the embeddedness paradigm is to understand the socio-regulatory contexts in which rural poverty persists. The structure of work activities could remain the focus, but it needs to be conceptualized in terms of its embeddedness in other social relations which constitute the socio-regulatory context.

Notes

This chapter was written by Leonard E. Bloomquist, Kansas State University; Christina Gringeri, University of Utah; Donald Tomaskovic-Devey, North Carolina State University; and Cynthia Truelove, University of Wisconsin-Madison. The discussion to follow has benefitted from the participation of Paul Swaim and H. L. Seyler in early meetings of our working group. We also would like to thank Richard Goe and James Miley for helpful suggestions on relevant literature to review. Elizabeth Keller provided valuable assistance in the collation and typing of the References section.

1. Self-provisioning activities are especially pertinent for an analysis of rural poverty, because historically rural **farm** households provided for some of their material needs by consuming their own farm products and managing extensive gardens (but see Fite 1981 on the decline of self-provisioning activities among farm households in the decades following World War II) At least that was the rationale for establishing a lower poverty threshold for farm families in the official definition of poverty status (Orshansky 1963).

2. Lyon (1987) actually uses this phrase to characterize Park's (1952) theory of human ecology, but competition plays an equally significant role in the general perspective as well. Among later ecological theorists the regulatory role of competition is often an implicit assumption, but without this assumption their conceptualization of how sustenance activities are organized for purposes of "adaptation" (Hawley 1950, 1984) or "selective survival" (Gibbs and Martin 1959) would not be intelligible (cf., Logan and Molotch 1987; Miley 1980).

3. See Clark (1981) and Massey (1984) for alternative conceptualizations of the spatial division of labor.

4. They measure economic performance in terms of the income and unemployment levels of the local population, plus the growth and stability of income and employment in the area.

5. The reference point for Killian and Hady's (1988) analysis of rural LMAs is the economic performance of metropolitan LMAs. With regard to rural LMAs specializing in public administration and education having the highest overall performance rating, they had lower income levels and a slower income growth than diversified LMAs. It was the former's better performance on employment measures that gave them a slightly higher overall performance rating than diversified LMAs.

6. Williamson (1975) argues that competitive market behavior is only one "rational" approach which firms can take to organizing production. Hierarchical approaches such as vertical integration, oligopolistic control and internal labor markets can also be "rational," depending on a firm's organizational environment.

7. The highest level of social organization, according to Baron and Bielby (1980), is the societal level, with the corresponding unit of analysis being the (national) economy. Since we are developing a conceptual framework for analyzing work

structures in a particular society (or more appropriately, a nation-state [see Tilly 1984:20-26]), we will not discuss analysts who have focused at this level.

8. Snipp and Bloomquist (1989:5) note that the two conceptualizations are consistent with the Marxian and Weberian traditions within sociology, respectively: "Industrial segmentation parallels Marxist ideas about the organization of capital, while labor market segmentation resonates with Weberian notions about the organization of labor."

9. For purposes of clarification, we will refer to the industrial segments as "sectors," reserving the "segments" label for labor market segments.

10. Alexander (1974) is an exception to the rule regarding analysts of labor market segmentation in that he delineates labor markets using industry categories. The underlying dynamic to the segmentation process is the same though: construction of barriers to workers' mobility between "segments."

11. Kalleberg et al. (1981:657) emphasize *after* entry into the labor force in order to distinguish these attributes from so-called "human capital" attributes such as education and intelligence.

12. As Freedman (1976:174) puts it: "The concept of an internal labor market in its simplest form is the antithesis of a classically defined labor market." It is no coincidence, we suggest, that for many analysts of labor market segmentation "primary" labor markets are often referred to as internal labor markets (e.g., Doeringer and Piore 1971).

13. Kalleberg et al. (1981:665) note that technically establishment size is not a firm characteristic, since firms often have more than one establishment. Following Stolzenberg (1978), however, they argue that establishment size is a reasonable proxy for firm size because "small employer [read: firm] size is a sufficient condition for small establishment size and large establishment size is sufficient for large employer size."

14. Edwards (1979:128-9) views technical control as an intermediate type of control, with respect to the contrast between "rule by supervisory command" under simple control and "rule of law" under bureaucratic control as well as in the historical development of systems of control under U.S. capitalism.

15. Moreover, Thurow relies exclusively on training costs as the criterion which determines an individual's relative position in a labor queue. As he puts it, "Basically, employers use background characteristics to indicate expected training costs and then attempt to rank and hire their potential labor force from those with the lowest training costs to those with the highest training costs" (Thurow 1975:91).

16. See Tomaskovic-Devey 1990 for a conceptualization of labor queues and job queues as socially organized, rather than the outcome of competitive market behaviors.

17. Ideally one would need a large panel data set containing information on individuals' work histories throughout their working lives. Use of synthetic cohorts to approximate work histories is a strategy that Spilerman (1977) and others (Kaufman and Spilerman 1982; Spenner et al. 1982) have used for illustrative purposes, but it requires strong assumptions (see Spenner et al. 1982:11-13 for an excellent discussion).

18. It also should be noted that Spenner et al. (1982) provide strong support for the vacancy competition model as initially formulated by Sorensen (1977). Their specification of the model does not rely on the notion of individuals competing for relative positions in a labor queue, however. They acknowledge the role that individual characteristics play in gaining access to vacant jobs, but they stress that the vacancies individuals have access to are largely determined by the career-line structure of which they are a part (Spenner et al. 1982:162).

19. Two basic rules governed the wage determination system of the postwar labor market model: (a) wage increases for workers in the "core" or "monopoly" sector were tied to productivity increases plus increases in the cost of living and (b) and "pattern bargaining" by workers in this sector *vis-a-vis* workers in other "core" industries (Piore and Sabel 1984:79-82; O'Connor 1973; and Osterman 1988). The wages of workers in the "periphery" or "competitive" sector, on the other hand, were determined by market forces: the demand for labor relative to its supply (O'Connor 1973:21). The result, according to O'Connor (1973:27) was the relative impoverishment of workers in the competitive sector.

20. De Vroey (1984:55) characterizes the present historical conjuncture as a structural crisis, by which he means the specific institutions and social processes created for the purpose of capital accumulation in the early postwar period have become dysfunctional to capital accumulation in the present historical context.

21. The regime of extensive accumulation was dominant until World War I, according to the regulationists. Capital accumulation under this regime involves little productivity growth and stable consumption patterns. Capital accumulation is accomplished through the expansion of capitalist organizations into "new sectors, new areas, and new countries" (Noel 1987:312). Components of the ideal-typical institutional framework of extensive accumulation includes wages determined through market competition, tight control over the money supply and a noninterventionist state (De Vroey 1984; Noel 1987). The regime of extensive accumulation lost its dominance to the regime of intensive accumulation during the long transition between the two world wars. That is not to say, however, that the institutional framework constructed for extensive accumulation has completely disappeared. One could analyze the organization of work in the competitive or periphery sector, for example, as reflecting elements of the regime of extensive accumulation.

22. Actually, changes in the farm sector prior to World War II is a good illustration of how the expansion of capitalist organizations into new areas under the regime of extensive accumulation often create the conditions for their integration into a regime of intensive accumulation. Not only did farm mechanization during the first half of the twentieth century help create new markets for Ford and other manufacturers (the "Fordson" was an early competitor among gas-powered farm tractors), it also increased farmers' dependence on money for the purchase of farm inputs and other commodities. As a result, the conditions were established for transforming agricultural production itself into a system of capitalistic enterprises struggling to maintain profitability in the grips of a "cost-price squeeze" (see Williams 1987 for an illuminating history of the farm tractor in the U.S.).

23. Lobao cautions, however, that her finding of a positive effect of industrialized farming on economic well-being within the Midwest only holds for a 1980 cross-sectional analysis--just before the farm financial crisis hit the Midwestern farm economy. She emphasizes that "the long-term implications for industrialized farming are clear:...[it] tends to limit future economic potential wherever it is found" (Lobao 1990:192).

24. For example, Gershuny and Sassen-Koob differ on the implications of the informalization in the service sector for the quality of working conditions. Gershuny (1988) stresses the positive aspects, such as the increased importance of innovative self-service activities based on the use of advanced technologies. Sassen-Koob (1986), on the other hand, stresses the negative aspects, noting that urban areas which have had rapid growth in informal work have experienced a downgrading in their manufacturing base combined with a sharp decline in unionization (or perhaps those areas undergoing deindustrialization which have a history of nonunionized labor).

25. Polanyi (1957:72-3) also claims land and money are fictitious commodities. Land "is only another name for nature" while money "is merely a token of purchasing power." They, along with labor power, are distinguished from genuine commodities in that the "fictitious" commodities are not produced for sale. We limit our discussion to the fictitiousness of labor power because of our focus on work activities. We do not discount, however, the importance of regulating tensions created by the treatment of nature or money as a commodity. (The 1992 "Earth Summit" is illustrative of the former.)

26. This expectation is based on the assumption that rural households' reproductive strategies are sufficiently embedded in the commodification process for them to rely on goods and service which require monetary expenditures. To the extent that rural households are able to shelter themselves from the commodification process through reciprocal networks of exchange and/or self-provisioning activities, then their need for monetary expenditures would be reduced and the impact of relatively impoverished wage/income structure on their livelihood would be ameliorated. As noted in the previous subsection, however, the commodification process has penetrated most rural social contexts, making farm as well as nonfarm rural households increasingly dependent on goods and services distributed through the market system.

4

Spatial Location of Economic
Activities, Uneven Development,
and Rural Poverty

Theoretical Background

Economic growth and development are inherently uneven. They vary across time and territory. Most of the classical social theorists recognized and incorporated both time and space dimensions in their writings about economic change. In distinguishing between place poverty and person poverty, contemporary theorists have focused on explanations of uneven development across space.

Virtually all rural and regional development theories are shaped by a common set of assumptions about the spatial distribution of poverty. First, most conceptual frameworks account for the fact that rural poverty is found in all regions of the country. Second, there are particular regions where the incidence of rural poverty is greater. For example, the economy lags in regions such as Appalachia, the Black Belt and the Lower Rio Grande Valley. Third, every region of the country has its own 'history.' History is critical to understanding how a region will develop, because historical circumstance serves as a constraint to economic development. And, fourth, regional and local opportunity structures are configured by cultural, political, social and economic forces both inside and outside a region.

While the emphasis placed on different factors in explaining uneven development varies across theoretical perspectives, all theories assume that in capitalist societies the patterning of economic activities across space is ever changing. Current configurations of socioeconomic conditions, including industries, occupations and measures of economic well-being can be understood as the outcome of economic forces and historical, political, cultural and technological circumstances. Storper and Walker (1989:10) summarize common threads among theories when they note that not only are capitalist societies spatially expansionist in the same sense that they are economically expansionist, but regional economic configurations tend to be unstable over time. Consequently, "...as industries localize, cluster, disperse and shift, they do so in a manner that continually differentiates territorial economies, in terms of output, employment, income, rate of growth, and a host of concrete qualities of local economic, political and social structures."

Viewed from these perspectives, rural poverty is one manifestation of particular development processes that allocate economic opportunities across space (and time). Because industrial development and expansion are inherently uneven, at any particular point in time some areas will expand and grow while other places will stagnate and decline (cf. Markusen 1985; Scott and Storper 1988; Weinstein, Gross and Rees 1985). To the extent that economic growth is related to economic well-being, poverty will be unevenly distributed over the territorial landscape.

Below we examine several schools of thought within two broadly defined theoretical traditions related to the spatial location of economic activities, uneven development and rural poverty. The first set of theories is derived mainly from work by neoclassical economists and regional scientists and includes the neoclassical paradigm as well as central place theory. The second set of theories is more sociologically oriented and includes Marxist and world systems perspectives as well as the new institutionalism.

Economic Theories

Neoclassical Economics and Spatial Patterns of Well-Being

Neoclassical economics in its most generic sense has focused on the spatial implications of economic growth by positing that labor and capital are mobile and will tend to move to areas with highest return, thus equalizing returns to production factors (i.e., labor and capital). When uneven development persists, it is attributed to differential resource endowments, other locational attributes and to the product cycle and its implications for production organization in lagging regions.

Neoclassical arguments regarding convergence of return rates to economic resources over space are well known (cf. Borts and Stein 1964; Baumol 1986; Rasmussen and Zuehlke 1988). These models suggest a "catch-up" hypothesis between leading and lagging regions. Nardinelli, Wallace and Warner (1987:204) note that "the basic assumption of the catch-up hypothesis is that transfer of technology and resources will cause per capita incomes to converge as resources move to areas where return rates are maximized. While convergence is taking place, states or regions with low initial levels of income per capita will grow more rapidly than states or nations with high initial levels of income per capita."

One counterpoint to the neoclassical equilibrium view expressed by Kaldor (1972) is a growth model of cumulative causation that yields divergence in per capita well-being over time as some places build on initial advantages. In recent years, Krugman (1991a) and Arthur (1990) have proposed growth theories that explain differential regional growth by building on two major themes: increasing returns in the production function and the role of chance or fortuitous circumstance in explaining regional growth differentials.

The concentration of an industry in a particular region follows from the "localization" economies of Marshall. For example, new firms in an industry are attracted to a region that has a labor pool with experience and skills needed by those firms. In addition, specialized services and material inputs may be cheaper and more widely available in regions with a core of firms in the industry; and information flows regarding new technologies, resource availability, and the like may be superior in regions where other firms in an industry are located (Krugman 1991b:484-485).

However, studies by regional economists (for example, Hoover 1948) have tended to look at individual industries and why they locate in particular regions. In a broader view of regional economics, Krugman explains "why manufacturing in general might end up concentrated in one of a few regions of the country, with the remaining regions playing the 'peripheral' role of agricultural suppliers to the manufacturing 'core'" (Krugman 1991b:485).

Krugman explains the tendency for firms to cluster in selected regions as follows: With increasing returns in the production process, economies of scale exist that yield incentives for firms to produce from a single location for a national market. To minimize transportation costs, firms locate where there is a large local demand--but there is a large local demand where firms tend to locate. This interaction among increasing returns, transportation costs and area concentration of demand tends to keep firms clustered where production began. And the initial production location may be determined by geographical/historical happenstance--a natural resource endowment or political treaty that yields some initial reason to locate production in an area. Krugman (1991a:10-15) illustrates this model for the manufacturing belt in the U.S.

There may be an important role for random disturbances to both rural and urban places that yield initial advantages to some places (Arthur 1990). Increasing returns suggests that dynamic processes are influenced by random events that give initial advantages to regions. These regions are able to achieve sustained growth advantages over other regions until the next stochastic shock changes the course of events along a new path. Arthur believes these processes can be modelled and probability statements made about the occurrence of alternative solutions--say to the spatial distribution of rural and urban economic activity.

This view of the dynamics of rural/urban economies is less tidy than the neoclassical convergence solution. Because the economic backbone of rural America is no longer farming and mining as it was in the time of Marshall's *Principles*, manufacturing and services take on added importance in nonmetropolitan areas. In Krugman's paradigm, manufacturing is characterized by increasing returns to scale (Krugman 1991b:485). Thus, the economies of rural areas may be more subject to the positive feedbacks of the cumulative causation processes than when farming dominated rural America. If so, some rural areas will prosper due to fortuitous circumstance but if market forces alone dictate the outcomes there may be little reason to believe in a general convergence in well-being across economic space.

Current critiques of neoclassical growth models also suggest that one can attribute only about 50 percent of growth differentials to the growth of capital and labor inputs. Technological progress accounts for the remaining sources of growth. This requires analyzing how new knowledge is formed and how it enters the production function (Romer 1990). Some empirical research supports the view that it is a lack of human capital investment rather than lagging machinery and equipment investment that retards growth in developing countries (The Economist 1992:18). A focus on human capital disparities among regions may also largely explain regional growth differentials.

Central Place Theory and Spatial Patterns of Well-Being

Central Place Theory is a second body of theory that can shed light on the structure of spatial economic activity. The system of urban/rural places is the subject matter of central place theory. The classic location theory associated with Losch and Christaller involves the assumption of a homogeneous plain. But it allows for more than one urban place. The economic geography that results is a spatial pattern of trade areas around the various urban places that are hexagonal, uniform, and geographically pervasive.

A hierarchy of hexagonal trade areas emerges around various cities. There is a different trade area for each product or service, depending upon: (1) transfer costs, (2) market density (i.e., buying power and effective demand per unit of physical space), and (3) the importance of scale, or other agglomeration economies (Hoover 1971:127). In an economy of many goods and services, trade areas of many sizes will emerge, all centered on particular urban places. From this perspective, every rural site becomes part of the hinterland of urban places (Braudel 1982:20-88).

Central place theory provides an explanation for the spatial distribution of cities and rural hinterlands and it may also yield insight into the level of well-being that results in each place in the hierarchy. Two competing theories of interregional wage differentials have garnered the most attention. First, following Farber and Newman (1986:1-3), the structural variation argument emphasizes the role of heterogeneous area labor markets. The wage expected by a worker with a given set of skills, education, etc. would differ by area because labor markets across regions value these characteristics differently. For example, worker productivity for a physician may be higher in a large urban medical center than in a clinic in a low order village of the central place system. If productivity is higher in the higher order place for a given type of worker, then wage rates would also be higher, all else the same.

The second view is that wage differences across regions represent compensating differentials that counter regional differences in living costs and nonmonetary regional attributes (e.g., environmental amenities). In this view, the wage expected by a worker with a given set of characteristics would be the same in all regions, after adjusting for living costs and environmental differences across regions.

This view is also consistent with some regions obtaining large differences in the level of some worker characteristics (Farber and Newman 1986). For example, large urban complexes may have greater shares of workers with high levels of academic and technical training. If so, worker characteristic prices may indeed converge but the levels obtained in urban versus remote regions may be vastly different. Thus, per capita income convergence is unlikely, even after accounting for cost-of-living and non-monetary regional differences. The remote location of some rural regions may generate the differences in demands for characteristic levels between these disadvantaged regions and other areas more favorably located within the system of central places. For example, higher order central place medical centers may have a large staff of specialized surgeons, while low order place hospitals may have only a few general surgeons.

One might also suggest that the interregional flows of labor (with embodied characteristics) required to reach spatial price convergence encounter significant barriers. These barriers are likely to be associated with the concept of economic distance. Economic distance incorporates all the costs of overcoming the friction of distance--travel costs, travel time costs, and costs of disrupting personal linkages to an area. The greater the economic distance between an advantaged and a disadvantaged region, the greater the costs of obtaining information about opportunities available by migrating and the greater the costs of making the physical move. So the more remote the disadvantaged region, the less likely the possibility that migration will eliminate the lower real income that is, itself, the result of remoteness.

Furthermore, the out-migration may not be a random cross-section of the disadvantaged region's population. Migration is a risky undertaking and those who migrate may be more prone to taking risks, thus depriving the region they leave of a sizeable part of those in the native population who are most likely to become entrepreneurs. Migrants may also be disproportionately made up of the better educated, higher skilled, and younger persons in the population because they are apt to be better informed of potential opportunities in other regions (Hoover 1971). The state can help redress spatial differences through investments in technology, infrastructure, and human resources to expand productive capacities and markets of lagging regions (Edwards 1981).

Sociological Theories

Sociologically oriented theories also attempt to bring 'space' or locality into studies of economic well-being and welfare. These theories have been developed in response to the perceived deficiencies of neoclassical approaches. What unites more sociologically oriented perspectives is a concern with factors and conditions outside of the market (i.e., norms, social structure, etc.) that bear on socioeconomic well-being (Young and Lyson forthcoming, 1993).

Marxist Theories

Marxist approaches to the spatial patterning of economic development, in contrast to Neoclassical or Central Place theory, insist that uneven development reflects the fundamental contradictions of capitalism. Capitalists are constantly seeking ways to enhance profits. One way they can do this is to move their production facilities (e.g., factories) from areas where labor costs are high to areas where they are low. From a Marxist perspective, the deindustrialization of parts of the Northeast and Midwest and the concomitant growth of manufacturing jobs in the rural South can be read as a deliberate attempt by large corporations to increase profits by shedding high wage, unionized workers for lower wage, unorganized workers (Harvey 1985; Falk and Lyson 1988).

The local state plays an important role in this process. It encourages firms to relocate by offering lucrative business incentive packages. These state-based industrial policies implicitly rest on the notion that economic development is a contest that pits one locality against another. The 'prize' is a new industry or firm and the jobs it brings with it. Much like a high stakes poker game, one community's incentives are bid against another community's incentives in an effort to 'win' a new employer. In this game, however, there are no real winners. Communities that offer incentive packages and fail to attract new jobs are losers. Likewise, communities that become caught-up in this process may find that they have bartered away their ability to improve the lot of their most needy residents. Rural communities, small towns, and less affluent regions are the most disadvantaged in this game, because they have less to offer prospective employers. These places are trapped at the bottom of a system they unwittingly helped to create (Lyson 1989).

Some regions, of course, are able to maintain an economically and politically dominant position for long periods of time. These places are known in the literature as 'core' areas. Their built-in advantage results from an ability to 'exploit' the natural resources and labor in less-favored 'peripheral' regions (Wadley 1986). Over the long run, historically prosperous regions like New England move through growth and decline cycles. However, these places maintain their dominant positions in the U.S. economy because they are able to draw and build upon their comparative advantage in terms of skilled, highly educated labor, well-developed infrastructure and indigenous sources of venture capital.

World Systems Theory

A more historical approach to uneven development than that presented by the Marxists is World Systems theory. The World Systems approach focuses on the historical dynamics of the evolving world economic system and its implications for nation states. The deterministic focus of the Marxist/dependency theorists is replaced by the possibility of upward or downward mobility of core, periphery, and semi-periphery areas in the world economy (So 1990). Semi-peripheral areas provide dynamism between core (high tech, high income) economies and peripheral (low tech, low income) economies by providing a mix of both. Over time, the relative position of states in the world economy changes. A single world market is mediated regionally by each state's political and cultural systems and its relationship to the world economy. The national economy is no longer the sole building block of the world economy. The global market for production and distribution creates a radically new context for the role of firms, states, labor and capital markets (Knox and Agnew 1989). The state's role under this theoretical scenario is limited by these new structural realties and implications for regional policy are uncertain.

The disorganized capitalism reflected in the world systems perspective reflects a restructuring of social, economic, cultural and political relationships. Flexible organizational forms for production decrease the state's power and the ability of national level labor movements to negotiate with capital. New technologies increase worker productivity but also the threat of capital substitution for labor. The 'deconcentration' of capital--separating finance from industry in national markets--limits the state's ability to control investment flows in the economy (Lash and Urry 1987). The 'time-space' compression introduced by these changes allows exploitation of relatively small differences between places and an "acceleration of shifts in the patterning of uneven development on the basis of particular local mixes of skills and resources...." (Knox and Agnew 1989:181).

Institutional Theory

Institutional theory represents an alternative to the Neoclassical, Central Place, Marxist, or World Systems perspectives. Rather than emphasize market forces, class interests, or both as the driving forces behind the spatial distribution of economic activities, institutionalists give more consideration to other social factors. Piore and Sabel (1984), for example, see municipally supported, flexibly specialized, craft-oriented enterprises as the engines of regional development in advanced industrial societies. A region in which this type of activity takes hold is presumed to offer a better living standard and higher quality of life to its residents than a region dependent upon mass-production enterprises. Piore and Sable offer the Third Italy as a prime example of this type of institutional development, while Hansen (1990;1991) has addressed this phenomenon elsewhere in Europe. More recently, Harrison (1992) has articulated the fundamental importance of trust and embeddedness of economic relations as the cornerstones leading to the development of industrial districts and to improved socioeconomic conditions in a region.

Mingione (1991) argues that economic development scholars make artificial distinctions between formal and informal economic activities. According to Mingione, post-industrial society is increasingly fragmented, socially, economically and politically. With fragmentation, however, comes the opportunity for new lines of political action and economic organization that can directly affect the level and distribution of poverty in an area. Other institutionalists have examined the role of small-scale enterprises (Whatmore, Lowe, and Marsden 1991), values (Berry 1989), and informal economic relations (Portes, Castells, and Benton 1989) as explanations for regional growth and development.

Research Questions

Drawing on the insights from economic and sociological theories, four sets of questions related to uneven regional economic development and socioeconomic well-being can be raised. Each question taps a salient dimension within one or more of the theoretical traditions noted above and serves as the focus for a considerable body of scholarship.

First, is economic growth related to the incidence of poverty? If so, under what conditions does economic growth alleviate poverty? Second, how important is indigenous development in reducing poverty? Stated differently, can small-scale manufacturing enterprises enhance local socioeconomic well-being? Third, to what degree is economic space configured by outside forces? More specifically, how is the location of decision making related to poverty? And fourth, how is migration related to poverty? That is, why do people remain in lagging rural regions rather than move to nearby growth centers? In the sections below we address each set of questions. The common focus to addressing each question set lies in the linkages among territory, economic development processes and socioeconomic well-being as they are articulated in the theories noted above.

Can Economic Growth Alleviate Poverty?

Three important themes found in the poverty literature help clarify the relationship between economic growth and the incidence of poverty. The first theme is centered in neoclassical economics and states that human capital investments such as education are important to solving the poverty problem (cf. Deaton 1988; Sawhill 1988). The second theme is that transfer payments can reduce absolute poverty if they can be made in such a way as to minimize adverse work incentives (Sawhill 1988). Thus, for example, transfer payments in the form of social security, medicaid and the like helped greatly reduce elderly poverty over the past 30 years. The third theme is that economic growth can pull all people up the income ladder absolutely and thus reduce poverty most effectively for those individuals who manifest the greatest attachment to the labor force (e.g., household heads). However, an unanswered question is whether economic growth alone can reduce rural poverty in those regions/places characterized by unfavorable occupational and industrial mixes. The "new economic geography" of Krugman (1991a) and Arthur (1990) suggests that cumulative causation forces will be strong and lagging regions will be interspersed between growth areas, even during boom periods.

Harry Johnson (1965) emphasized the growth solution to the poverty problem during the early debates over the role government should play in the War on Poverty.

> The point is that most of the sources of poverty will gradually dissolve under the pressure of a high demand for labor. This point is extremely relevant to the problem of poverty in the United States, and to the whole antipoverty program...it implies that the really effective solution to the problem of poverty lies in raising the level of demand for goods and services--and, therefore for labor--to the point where poverty, instead of being part of the natural order of things, becomes a signal of economic waste that it will pay someone to take steps to eliminate. The key to the solution of the poverty problem, therefore is not simply to try to educate and train the poor up to the point where someone will find them employable at a decent wage, but to raise demand so as to make labor scarce enough for it to be privately profitable to find a way of making the poor employable at a decent wage (Johnson 1965:169).

Growth and Poverty: What Do the Data Suggest?

Empirical evidence on the effectiveness of growth as a way out of poverty is inconclusive. Sawhill (1988) recently noted that the incidence of poverty fell from about 22 percent in 1960 to about 12 percent in 1970. During the 1970's, the poverty rate varied between 11 and 13 percent, while in the 1980's it has risen into the 13-14 percent range. The Institute for Research on Poverty recently released estimates of state poverty rates for the 1986-1988 period. Table 4.1 lists these estimates and the annual personal income growth rate for each state from 1983 to 1988. Simple linear regressions of state poverty rates on state personal income growth rates indicate that poverty rates decline as a state's income growth rate increases. While this suggests a link between poverty reduction and economic growth, we need more research on the links between small area growth rates and the impact on the poverty incidence in subpopulation groups.

Morrissey (1991b) examined metro and nonmetro poverty rates for 1987 and found nonmetro workers almost twice as likely to be in poverty as metro workers. Again, the local labor market was important in explaining the higher incidence of poverty in nonmetro areas. Nonmetro workers had fewer jobs to choose from, wages in rural areas were lower and full-time opportunities less likely in rural areas than in metro places. Lower educational levels in rural areas were an important reason that the incidence of poverty exceeded that in metro areas.

Lerman and Mikesell (1989) provided a more geographically detailed description of the incidence of poverty. They found 1983 poverty rates higher in the central city area of metro places (with more than two million persons) than in rural areas. However, poverty rates were higher in rural areas than in all other urban areas. In addition, it didn't matter whether the income-based poverty measure or a wealth-adjusted measure was used. The rural area poverty rate exceeded that of all but the largest central city areas (Lerman and Mikesell 1989:9).

Clarifying the relationship between economic growth and poverty, Robert Solow (1991) recently noted that the incidence of poverty is disproportionately high among the old, the uneducated, among female headed families, rural people, those in low paying occupations and industries, and among those with a weak attachment to the labor market. This suggests that demographic change in rural counties may interact with economic growth to influence the incidence of poverty. It has been shown that blacks and Hispanics have poverty rates that are about three times the rates of white households. More dramatically, the incidence of poverty for white children who live in households with a single parent is four times that for white children living in households with two parents. Almost two-thirds of all black and Hispanic children living in single parent households are poor. Finally, persons living in households headed by

TABLE 4.1 State Poverty Rates 1986-88 and Personal Income Growth

State		All	1986-88[a] Poverty Rates White	1983-88[b] Annual Income Growth
1	Alabama	21.6	12.9	7.28
2	Alaska	11.0	7.3	2.70
3	Arizona	13.6	9.3	9.79
4	Arkansas	21.8	14.7	6.70
5	California	12.7	7.4	8.54
6	Colorado	12.7	8.8	5.52
7	Connecticut	6.3	4.2	8.92
8	Delaware	9.8	6.3	8.61
9	District of Columbia	13.2	4.0	6.57
10	Florida	12.5	7.5	9.41
11	Georgia	14.4	6.1	9.60
12	Hawaii	9.7	10.8	7.40
13	Idaho	15.4	14.2	5.37
14	Illinois	13.0	7.2	6.67
15	Indiana	11.2	9.3	7.03
16	Iowa	12.8	12.5	5.50
17	Kansas	9.7	7.5	5.94
18	Kentucky	17.8	16.5	6.22
19	Louisiana	22.5	10.8	3.12
20	Maine	11.6	11.6	9.10
21	Maryland	8.3	4.5	8.96
22	Massachusetts	8.9	6.1	9.07
23	Michigan	12.9	8.9	7.32
24	Minnesota	11.4	9.9	7.50
25	Mississippi	25.8	11.4	6.33
26	Missouri	14.5	12.1	6.83
27	Montana	16.8	14.9	4.01
28	Nebraska	12.5	11.1	5.65
29	Nevada	9.1	6.7	9.74
30	New Hampshire	4.6	4.6	11.46
31	New Jersey	8.1	4.3	8.58
32	New Mexico	20.6	11.6	6.40
33	New York	13.6	7.5	7.58
34	North Carolina	13.7	8.8	8.86
35	North Dakota	12.3	11.3	3.06
36	Ohio	12.9	10.2	6.35

(continued)

TABLE 4.1 (continued)

State	All	1986-88[a] Poverty Rates White	1983-88[b] Annual Income Growth
37 Oklahoma	16.6	12.7	3.19
38 Oregon	11.8	10.4	6.53
39 Pennsylvania	10.2	8.1	6.50
40 Rhode Island	8.8	6.7	7.91
41 South Carolina	16.0	6.9	8.14
42 South Dakota	15.9	13.6	6.11
43 Tennessee	18.4	14.1	8.22
44 Texas	17.7	7.9	5.40
45 Utah	10.8	10.1	6.56
46 Vermont	10.2	10.2	8.82
47 Virginia	10.4	6.4	8.93
48 Washington	11.3	9.4	7.01
49 West Virginia	21.6	20.9	4.23
50 Wisconsin	8.6	6.3	6.49
51 Wyoming	11.8	11.8	1.31

Sources: [a]Focus, Institute for Research on Poverty, Spring, 1991.
            [b]Survey of Current Business, August, 1989.

women aged 18-64 are about three to four times as likely to be living in poverty as persons residing in households headed by males aged 18-64.

Since poverty rates have declined substantially since World War II, a key concern is how much of the change in poverty rates is attributable to economic growth and how much to demographic change? Gottschalk and Danziger (1985) provided some reliable estimates of a small but significant reduction in poverty rates from secular (long-term) growth. However, they noted that small secular effects are often swamped by cyclical impacts on the poor who suffer more during recessionary periods.

While Gottschalk and Danziger found that transfer payments have been the primary force behind reducing poverty among the elderly, for working-age, male heads of households, the ability to earn income in the marketplace is the key to reducing poverty. However, the ability to hold a job is sensitive to the business cycle. During the expansion years in the 1967-79 period, the incidence of poverty declined, while poverty rates increased during the 1979-82 recessionary period.

For the 1973-1987 period, Shapiro (1989:26) found that 71 percent of the yearly variation in nonmetro poverty rates was associated with the nonmetro unemployment rate. This same association in metro places suggests that we can attribute only 37 percent of the poverty rate variation to unemployment rate change. This result suggests that rural poverty is more sensitive to the business cycle than is poverty in metro places. Since most nonmetro places are less diverse than metro places, they tend to have larger spikes--up and down--in local unemployment rates. This means that reductions in the incidence of rural poverty may be more responsive to economic growth but subject to wider cyclical swings than in metropolitan places.

Northrup (1990) found that the sectoral composition of growth in the labor market will affect the demographic composition of the incidence of poverty. During periods of rapid growth in U.S. manufacturing, male headed households enjoyed greater reductions in the incidence of poverty than female headed households. However, during recessionary periods, female headed households fared better than others because the service sectors were less likely to eliminate jobs than manufacturing sectors. Since many service sectors employ large shares of females, these households tended to ride out recessionary periods better than other households (Northrup 1990:157).

Should We Expect Growth to Reduce the Incidence of Rural Poverty?

Many analysts are skeptical that market forces alone can generate the kind of growth in lagging rural regions needed to reduce the incidence of poverty. Simply put, why doesn't 'trickle-down' work as a cure for rural poverty?

One answer to this puzzle comes from Sawhill (1988) who noted that poverty and unemployment of household heads are closely intertwined. Thus, the question for lagging rural areas is why, when economic growth washes over these regions as it did in the South during the 1970's and 1980's, has it failed to reduce unemployment and underemployment sufficiently to reduce the incidence of poverty? Trickle-down economics suggests that industrialization will create job vacancies in lower paying jobs that have been left by those moving up to positions in new industries. These open positions will then be available to new job entrants or reentrants as a first rung on the employment ladder. Here, basic job skills are learned and experience gained prior to movement up the ladder.

There are a number of possible pitfalls in this scenario, however. From a dual labor market perspective (see Bulow and Summers 1986, for a general overview), trickle down fails because many new entrants to the labor force in lagging rural regions may be only able to obtain low-wage jobs in the secondary sector. Secondary sector jobs tend to have no job ladders and little chance for escape into the primary sector, where high wages and advancement ladders prevail. It seems likely that much of the high and persistent incidence of poverty for female household heads in the rural South is a consequence of a dual labor market structure.

In addition, rural workers who lose jobs when plants close are not necessarily willing to take secondary sector jobs that seem so readily available in the growing, but low-paying, service and trade sectors of the economy. Some may prefer unemployment and the increased likelihood of falling below the poverty line. Part of the reason may be from a person's unwillingness to take the relatively low-status position of a secondary job when friends and relatives are working at a local plant. Even in the rural South the wage differential between a textile job and one in local fast food or hotel housekeeping is likely to be substantial. A person may prefer to stay unemployed than take a "bad" job if they have strong preferences for the relative income position they once occupied (see Blinder 1988, for an explanation of the mechanics of this relative income hypothesis). These people may comprise the "new poor" in contrast to the families who endured poverty conditions for generations.

The United States is entering an era in which eight of 10 new entrants to the labor force will be women or minorities. This is also likely to be occurring in a period of labor shortages (Broder 1989). If this is indeed the future, the policy prescription for reducing working-age poverty may be as Johnson proposed--let the market bid up the wages of scarce labor. The demographics may be such that black female heads of households will be lifted out of poverty by these demand-side forces. At the minimum, the next 20 years promise to be a period where if the market is going to deliver on poverty reduction, it should be most able to achieve this goal. Still, there will be geographical barriers to overcome. The spatial mismatch between where new jobs are located and where the unemployed reside is often thought of as a metropolitan area issue. However, the rural poor may be much less likely than urban poor to know about opportunities in the growing urban fringes. Both formal labor market information flows--job training centers, etc.--and informal networks--family and friends--may be weaker between rural and urban places than within a metro complex.

Optimism for a growth solution to poverty is tempered by the realization that the strong economic growth between 1983 and 1989 did very little to reduce overall poverty rates, especially in lagging rural regions. In fact, poverty increased in many of these areas during the period (Lyson 1989). Moreover, cyclical downturns seem to impact the poorest most severely. And the portent of a growing dual labor market structure is gaining serious discussion. It might be that the dual labor market paradigm works to achieve lower poverty incidences in places like the rural South, but at levels far below those possible with primary sector jobs.

Small-Scale Production and Poverty

There is a growing body of empirical evidence from Europe and the United States suggesting that regions with strong small business sectors, especially small, flexibly specialized manufacturing enterprises, manifest higher levels of socioeconomic well-being and less poverty than regions where the economy depends on large, absentee owned firms (Piore and Sabel 1984; Harrison 1992). Based in part on these findings, small business development, especially small manufacturing, has been a focus of rural development policy in the 1980's and 1990's as a means to diversify the rural economy. This sector has been lauded as a source of entrepreneurship and local leadership in rural areas.

The conceptual rationale for expecting small manufacturing enterprises to enhance socioeconomic welfare rests on a theory of industrial districts (Harrison 1992; Piore and Sabel 1984). Industrial districts represent a form of regional industrial organization that does not conform to neoclassical assumptions about agglomeration economies (Perroux 1955), but rather rests on "....a very strong form of embedding of economic (business) relations into a deeper social fabric, providing a force powerful enough to provide for the reproduction of even so paradoxical a practice as cooperative competition" (Harrison 1992:in press).

The precursor to this line of contemporary theoretical development dates back to 1946 when two government-sponsored research reports were published. Both reports focused on the relationship between the concentration of economic power at the community level and the general welfare of local residents (Goldschmidt 1946; Mills and Ulmer 1946). The thesis advanced in these studies was that communities in which the economic base was composed of many small, locally-owned firms would manifest higher levels of social, economic and political welfare than communities where the economic base was dominated by a few, large, absentee-owned firms.

Goldschmidt looked at agricultural communities in the Central Valley of California. One community, Dinuba, was supported by relatively small, family farms, while the other, Arvin, was surrounded by large, corporate-run enterprises. These communities were "...selected for their divergence in scale of farm operations". However, they were also very similar in "... most fundamental economic and geographic factors, particularly richness of potential resources, agricultural production, relationship to other communities, and the more general techniques and institutional patterns of production." Using a broad array of data collection and analysis techniques, Goldschmidt concluded that "the community surrounded by large-scale farm operations offered the poorer social environment according to every test made" (Goldschmidt 1978:420).

The Mills and Ulmer study was similar in design to the Goldschmidt study. However, Mills and Ulmer focused on manufacturing rather than agricultural communities. Their findings were consonant with those of Goldschmidt. According to Mills and Ulmer (1970:124):

1. Small-business cities provided their residents a considerably more balanced economic life than did big business cities;
2. The general level of civic welfare was appreciably higher in the small-business cities;
3. These differences between city life in big- and small-business cities were in the cases studied due largely to differences in industrial organization--that is, specifically to the dominance of big business on the one hand and the prevalence of small business on the other.

Over the past 45 years both studies have been replicated several times (see Lobao 1990, for a comprehensive review; also Lyson 1991; Fowler 1964) and most support the basic findings reported in 1946. The effects of small manufacturing on socioeconomic welfare have taken on added importance in recent years as the economic base in the United States has been undergoing a significant structural transformation. The number of large manufacturing establishments in many regions of the country has decreased, as production facilities have either succumbed to competition from Third World countries or have themselves moved off-shore. A simple tally of manufacturing enterprises by size from the County Business Patterns shows that between 1980 and 1988, the number of large manufacturing establishments employing 250 or more workers decreased by 1,719 or 10.8 percent. At the same time, the number of relatively small manufacturing concerns in the U.S. has risen. The number of small manufacturing establishments employing fewer than 20 workers increased by 40,524 or 20.9 percent between 1980 and 1988. Reindustrialization and restructuring are two terms that have been coined to describe American adjustments to a new global economy (Lobao 1990; Peet 1991; Storper and Walker 1989).

Many who have examined these structural shifts have indicated the shifts represent a new and favorable economic order. The conceptual underpinnings of an economic production system in which large-scale manufacturers give way to smaller, flexibly specialized enterprises was set forth by Piore and Sabel (1984) and has recently been elaborated upon by Harrison (1992). Piore and Sabel contrast two modes of economic organization: large-scale, standardized, mass forms of production and smaller-scale, municipally supported craft forms of production.

As mass production gained prominence over craft-based enterprises throughout the manufacturing spectrum during the later 19th and early 20th centuries, advanced industrial nations like the U.S. passed over the 'first' industrial divide. The need for large quantities of cheap, standardized products manifested itself in the development of large-scale, technologically specialized, organizationally homogeneous and regionally concentrated production units. In contrast, small-scale, heterogeneous, dispersed forms of economic organization came to be seen as technically inferior, economically unprofitable and unable to meet the needs of a growing and modernizing population.

The guiding principles behind conventional mass production are that production should be concentrated into fewer units, machinery should be substituted for labor whenever possible, and jobs should be routinized to the point where workers become interchangeable. The consequences of this type of economic organization for American communities and workers was the subject of the Mills and Ulmer study 45 years ago.

Piore and Sabel provide an interesting explanation for how mass production techniques came to be viewed as the sine quo non of the modern economy. They note that at certain times in history, technological branching points push industrial development along divergent paths. These branching points mark "...the consolidation of new visions of efficient production--new technological paradigms, or trajectories (Piore and Sabel 1984:44). The sheer material success of mass production techniques have made these techniques irresistible as a production paradigm. Piore and Sabel (1984:47) conclude that "...mass production won out in the realm of ideas as it won out in the realm of practice."

Despite what appears to be the compelling logic undergirding the spread of mass production processes in manufacturing, Piore and Sabel (1984) provide a structural rationale for the reemergence of smaller-scale production units. They note that when mass production techniques diffuse over the economic landscape, some small-scale older forms of craft production remain in place because they are able to provide luxury goods, experimental products, and the standardized goods for which the demand is too unstable for large organizations to dedicate their resources. Modern craft production remains an enduring category of economic organization by taking up markets rejected by mass production (Piore and Sabel 1984:206-207).

While some small-scale, craft-based units of economic production are able to survive by clinging to simple techniques, seeking out niche markets, and maximizing family labor, another scenario puts this form of economic production on a more competitive footing with large-scale mass production. The key to the survival and growth of "modern" craft forms of production lies not in taking up markets rejected by mass producers, but in shifting toward flexible production techniques, technological sophistication and an active role by local/regional government in sustaining this type of production. Using textiles, machine tools, and steel mills as exemplars, Piore and Sabel (1984:207) note:

> As firms have faced the need to redesign products and methods to address rising
> costs and growing competition, they have found ways to cut the costs of
> customized production....[and]....draw customers away from formerly cheaper
> mass produced goods. Technological dynamism has thus allowed a shift from

a purely reactive strategy, aimed at survival, to an expansive strategy which has threatened to cut ground away from mass production. In short, craft has challenged mass production as the paradigm.

The Second Industrial Divide, then, refers to the reemergence of a small-scale, modern craft form of production as a significant source of goods and services in advanced industrial societies.

Undergirding a move toward small-scale, flexibly specialized enterprises is a political and economic culture that rests on trust and the embeddedness of economic relations within communities and households. According to Harrison (1992:in press "...proximity promotes the 'digestion' of experience which leads to trust which promotes recontracting (and the sharing of common support services), which ultimately enhances regional growth...." In this model, manufacturing firms compete on quality and technique and less on price. Cast in somewhat different terms, Piore and Sabel (1984) suggest that the state can play an important role in nurturing "yeoman democracy." According to Piore and Sabel (1984:305): "Yeoman democracy presumes that the state must guarantee that market transactions do not permanently advantage one group of traders--and thus undermine the balance of wealth and power that makes possible a community of producers."

In recent years, attention has been directed at enumerating both the benefits and costs of small business development as an engine of rural and regional economic growth (Allen and Hayward 1990; Andre 1989; Birch 1987; Lin, Buss and Popovich 1990). Most studies, however, have either been small case studies or have dealt with employment issues such as wages, job creation, job benefits, and the like. Virtually no one has examined the effects of small manufacturing on the incidence of rural poverty.

Can a regional development strategy centered on small-scale manufacturing help alleviate poverty? There are both theoretical and empirical suggestions that it can (Piore and Sabel 1984; Mills and Ulmer 1946/1970; Goldschmidt 1946/1978; Harrison 1992). However, considerably more research is needed to begin to identify the salient dimensions of this problem. It may be that flexible specialization represents one pathway to a viable small-scale manufacturing base. Furthermore, issues of control of decision making in local areas are especially troublesome with respect to indigenous economic development. We deal with these issues in the next section.

Beyond this, however, mainstream sociological and economic research has typically identified small manufacturing with the 'periphery' (see Jacobs 1982 for a summary of many of these studies). In virtually all models, employment in small enterprises is assumed to be less desirable than employment in large-scale or 'core' enterprises. However, it is worth noting that most of these models rarely take into account local social and economic contexts.

How Does the Location of Economic Decision Making
Relate to Rural Poverty?

According to neoclassical theory, opportunity for economic development in lagging regions is based on a) comparative advantage (in labor costs, access to raw materials or markets, or through a preferential policy environment), b) investment in human capital, physical infrastructure or market expansion, or c) new technology or product development (Edwards 1981). By exploring the dimensions of territory and power relations in economic development of lagging regions through the work of neoclassical, institutionalist and Marxist scholars, one can more critically assess prospects for economic development. It appears that restructuring the domestic economy in response to globalization of production may have exacerbated the spatial disadvantage of rural areas.

This section suggests that there has been a relative decline in the participation and power of local economic decision makers (in production, finance and policy formation) and that this may limit options for rural economic development and poverty alleviation. Four general areas are addressed: the organization of production, the emergence of the global corporation and capital markets, the role of the state, and local development options.

First, the organization of more complex production networks has reduced the locational stability and independence of rural producers, including small manufacturers. Second, emergence of the global corporation and the international integration of capital markets have created opportunities for locational mobility of capital to the detriment of rural areas. Third, increasing state interest in international economics creates a policy environment with limited emphasis on regional welfare, thus undermining the decision-making power of rural actors. Finally, within the context of this complex international economic network, options for regaining local control exist but may be limited in their impact on poverty alleviation.

Production Organization

With respect to the organization of production, communications and transport innovations have reduced circulation costs and allowed production separation into skilled and unskilled parts which can be reassembled in a global production system (Knox and Agnew 1989). These new locational and organizational possibilities may have important implications for the competitiveness of rural areas in a more locationally flexible world economy (Scott and Storper 1988).

Traditionally rural areas have competed on the basis of cost reduction to entice branch manufacturing plants through low wages, low taxes and subsidies. This strategy has had limited impact on alleviating poverty and holds even less promise for the future. First, shorter product life cycles and quickening obsolescence of mature products is reducing options for branch plant diffusion to rural areas (Glasmeier 1990). Second, competition in a global market puts downward pressure on the social wage due to lower production costs in developing nations. Third, the lack of innovative decision-making activities in branch plants moves such regions to the periphery of economic life and results in production of lower quality jobs (Malecki 1988). While branch plants have been an important source of employment in rural economies, they have provided second-class status because of their emphasis on bottom-of-cycle manufacturing processes, lower wages, and lack of a multi-tiered employment structure for occupational mobility (Bloomquist 1988). Although the shift of manufacturing plants to rural areas helped fuel the 'rural renaissance' of the 1970s, especially in the South, by the 1980s they were shifting in record numbers to the lower cost labor markets in the developing world. Speaking to the implications for poor people of this type of development, Moen (1989:42) noted:

> During the 1980s rural manufacturers who had relied on low wage labor began to modernize as domestic and foreign competition made cost reduction urgent. Employment levels of unskilled workers dropped, although the demand for skilled workers to operate these new machines has remained strong. In these rural manufacturing counties, technological change has adversely affected the poor and unskilled in each of the last two generations.

Limited backward linkages in the local economy due to preexisting supplier relationships (Susman and Schutz 1983) and failure to invest in the most remote, rural locations or those with high minority populations (Rosenfeld, Bergman and Rubin 1985) demonstrate limited development potential, even at the height of manufacturing plant diffusion. While more complex manufacturing in urban areas dramatically increased educational requirements of jobs, rural dependence on routine manufacturing has resulted in flat demand for education, lower wages and out migration of skilled workers at two-and-a-half times the rate of unskilled workers (Reid and Frederick 1990).

In a global economic system, competition through product and process innovation holds much greater development potential. However, higher technology firms are unlikely to favor rural locations. The amenity values required by research and development talent, the demand for skilled labor and the increasing rate of technology change are demands best met by urban markets (Glasmeier 1990; Markusen 1987).

The locational competitiveness of rural areas is similarly diminished in services and retailing. Retail and service firms have dropped by more than four percent in the 1970s and 1980s while rural population increased (Johansen and Fuguitt 1990). Centralized regional retail firms have experienced phenomenal growth in the same time period, undercutting local firms through cheaper goods, larger variety and extensive use of part-time employees to cut labor costs (Flora and Flora 1988). Although telecommunications were expected to enhance the competitiveness of rural services (Reich 1988), investment in telecommunications has favored urban areas and undermined the competitiveness of some rural businesses (Parker, Hudson, Dillman and Roscoe 1989; O.T.A. 1990). Complex services seem to require spatial proximity similar to that of complex manufacturing. This is evidenced by the increasing concentration of producer services in metropolitan areas (Glasmeier 1990; Reid and Frederick 1990; Cook 1991).

While the growth in small manufacturing described in the previous section offers an alternative to branch plant manufacturing, it is critical that we examine the characteristics of such small firms to determine if they have the same attributes as the ones described by Mills and Ulmer or Piore and Sabel. The growth of at least some small manufacturing firms in rural areas can be attributed to the need of large firms for flexibility in production supply. The independence of small firms (a critical component of the Mills and Ulmer and Piore and Sabel arguments) is challenged by the web of interrelationships which connect them to parent, "core," companies. Often, a single parent firm provides financial support, technology and markets (Young and Francis 1989). The parent firm may also provide inputs, thus limiting the multiplier effect within the local economy (Knox and Agnew 1989). In addition, the parent firm may guarantee a market, assistance in securing raw materials, and technical and managerial support. However, the relationship with the subcontracting firm is one of unequal power. Under this scenario, the subcontractor is used to smooth production over cyclical demand, to speed up production of first-run products after prototype development, or to decrease costs later in the production cycle (Holmes 1986). While the parent firm achieves greater flexibility, the subcontractor absorbs the risk.

Unlike the idealized, inter-dependent small firm networks of the industrial district school, subcontracting networks between small firms and dominant core firms have strengthened small firm access to capital, markets and new technology, but have maintained relations of unequal power (Young and Francis 1991; Amin and Robins 1990). One must determine whether flexibility is achieved through dynamism among "cooperatively competitive" small firm networks or as a result of exploitation (Harrison 1992). For example, subcontractors often absorb the risk of unstable demand without the benefits of higher wage employment. Small firms are known to offer poorer wages, working conditions and benefits than larger firms. This may lead to an increase in socioeconomic inequality and a general lowering of the living standard for American workers and communities (Bluestone and Harrison 1988; Glasmeier 1990). Nor do small firms provide diversified insurance against cyclical market downturns. Their heavy reliance on single market outlets for their goods links their fate to that of the parent firm. Despite local entrepreneurship, real control is not local. Care in distinguishing characteristics of small firm contracting networks is required if local economic development is to be realistically assessed.

The declining ability of rural areas to retain significant decision-making roles in manufacturing, retail and services, limits the diversity, skill and wage levels of rural economies and undermines the basis for future competitiveness. Exacerbating this picture is the emergence of the global corporation as a new actor on the economic development scene.

Global Corporation and International Integration of Capital Markets

In an economy with global production and capital markets, multinational corporations become the primary economic actors. The ability of national government policy or locally-based firms to affect these global actors is limited (Amin and Robins 1990). Three characteristics of the global corporation have critical implications for its impact on local economic development. The global corporation is characterized by product diversity, locational mobility, and a financial orientation. Since most conglomerate multinationals focus on many product lines (across different sectors), corporate decisions may not reflect interest in performance of a particular product or plant, but rather in the financial performance of the firm as a whole. Increased emphasis on the financial aspects of global corporations has lead to a process of 'locational rationalization' where the fixed capital or production of each plant, remunerative by its own standards, is checked continuously against more profitable employment elsewhere (Taylor and Thrift 1982).

Profitability of a local subsidiary is no longer sufficient justification to ensure its continued relevance to the parent firm. The search for the most profitable capital investment has increased the speed with which fixed capital in one location can be abandoned for another. Since the locational switching of multinationals may have more to do with profits in another sector of currency differentials than profitability of the local plant, local managers have less power to ensure their plant's survival (Taylor and Thrift 1982).

With the increased importance of debt management, the role of investment bankers and other financial analysts in corporate circles has created a new management class, quite removed from the day-to-day realities of production (Urry 1988). Decisions made at such a distance (both experiential and locational) from production results in a disenfranchisement of local management in long-term corporate planning. The role of banks and insurance companies in undermining conservation practices of farms over which they have a substantial financial interest is an example of the effect of such external control (Strange 1988; Green 1984). Concern with local socioeconomic well-being is reduced as commitment to ventures in any one location has become more transitory.

Financial markets have the potential to be key factors in building economic space and in controlling the development of regions (Harvey 1985). The 'hypermobility' of capital, facilitated by the highly articulated international financial system, creates pressure for national economies to shape themselves according to international conditions, since the performance of each national economy is evaluated on the basis of the "most spatially and temporally mobile form of capital--money itself" (Scott and Storper 1988:6). The state's control over global capital is constrained because the "spatial scale within which the state exercises sovereign power does not conform to the spatial scale of transnational corporation decision making" (Johnson 1989:277). The state is forced to focus on the national crisis and regional policy becomes at best a luxury and at worst irrelevant (Johnston 1988; Agnew 1988). Susman and Schultz (1983:175-76) summarize this perspective:

> Changes in the world economy have rendered all regions, including the old industrial regions, vulnerable to decisions made in remote centers of capital control and subject to a hypermobility of capital that defeats any serious local planning....Under global capitalism, regions are more dependent on, and sensitive to, not only the movement of capital, but capital that moves more rapidly.

State Policy

Although the state's power to influence the global market is limited, the importance of global competitiveness shifts state concern from addressing regional inequality (the basis for much rural development policy of the past) to efforts to create an attractive environment for capital. This is achieved by creating more locational flexibility through such mechanisms as deregulation and non-enforcement of anti-trust laws (Christopherson 1990). These mechanisms secure national competitiveness within the international system, but they undermine the viability of local economies by favoring capital at the expense of community (Gunn and Gunn 1991).

Flora and Flora (1988) have outlined a number of areas where the state's response has contributed to the disadvantageous position of rural areas. These include: (1) relaxation of anti-trust laws which has allowed consolidation, purchase of local profitable firms which are merged with unprofitable firms elsewhere and shut down; (2) tax laws favoring capital intensive urban development; (3) cuts in public works, social programs and revenue sharing; (4) shifts from formula to competitive funding, which puts rural areas at a disadvantage; (5) inappropriate cost estimates of providing services in rural areas, which leads to inadequate funding (e.g., medicaid); and (6) deregulation, which has increased costs and decreased access to capital, transportation and communications services in rural areas.

Deregulation in banking provides an example of how state policy has created a more favorable environment for capital at the expense of community. Some of the implications of deregulation for rural communities include: (1) increasing interest rates, which give an incentive to lend to more profitable and hence risky projects to cover the costs of capital, (2) lifting geographic restrictions, which shifts control over loan decisions away from local communities toward rational technical criteria of money market centers, and (3) emphasis on more lucrative products and geographic markets, which limits capital availability for loans in the local service area (Green 1984; Christopherson 1990).

There has been considerable debate about whether deregulation of the U.S. banking industry has reduced rural access to credit. Some studies suggest deregulation could result in wider choice for rural customers (Milkove and Sullivan 1989), and attribute the reduction in the rural loan growth rate in the 1980s to a weak business climate in general (Morris and Drabenstott 1991). However, Markley (nd) has found that rural New England businesses suffered greater credit problems in markets dominated by large affiliated banks than in those dominated by independent banks or a mixed market. While small banks reported greater flexibility in loan decisions, large bank lenders found they were losing autonomy as lending decisions were increasingly made at regional headquarters.

In short, deregulation enables short-term attention to profits over an ever widening geographical space, thus reducing the role banks once played in supporting investment in productive infrastructure over the long term for specific localities and regions. Not only are rural areas less attractive locations for action in the new international credit system, the financial institutions remaining in rural areas have less autonomy in decision making due to increased control from distant financial centers.

As the state fights to preserve its place within the world economy, it no longer can afford the luxury of regional policy, and regional issues such as poverty no longer attract policy makers' attention. Under the industrial capitalism regime (from the end of WW-II to 1970), mass production for a mass market encouraged state investment in regional development and other forms of social Keynesianism to build a broad national market. Under the current regime of global capitalism, uneven regional development does not seriously impede production and marketing (Christopherson 1990). Not only are old-form regional policies expensive, they no longer engage with economic reality. The rate of subsidy on fixed and variable capital is minimal compared to the cost differentials associated with the new international labor division (Johnson 1988). In addition, the new localized pattern of spatial economic inequality reflects specific production relationships in specific industries, not regional competition as previously understood (Agnew 1988).

An alternative model of state investments to create industrial districts has been outlined by Piore and Sabel in Italy. In the United States, the federal government has played an important role through military contracts in developing such districts as Route 128 in Massachusetts and the Silicon Valley in California. The suburban bias of U.S. government investment and the dislocations caused by recent reductions in military spending raise questions about the prospects of such industrial district development in depressed rural areas, however (Buttel and Gillespie 1991; Harrison 1992). Not only has government funding favored suburban areas, state support for deregulation in communications, transportation and banking has further undermined rural areas' ability to compete in a mass production or a flexibly specialized economy.

In addition, one should temper enthusiasm for such flexibly specialized industrial districts by critically assessing the key characteristics of such districts. While the trust relations and social embeddedness implicit in industrial districts are the key to their success, these features also require culture homogeneity and serve to facilitate discrimination and continued minority group exploitation, even in the third Italy itself (Harrison 1992). The lack of cultural homogeneity in many rural poor regions of the United States and the effectiveness of embedded social relations in preventing economic development which benefits minority groups should be a serious caution to the faith placed in the 'progressive' features of the industrial district notion (Brown and Warner 1991).

Options for Local Control

While the organization of production and work is fundamental to the structuring of economic space, the specifics of history and human agency play a significant role in molding the local impact of those forces (Lipietz 1986; Hudson and Sadler 1988; Scott and Storper 1988). There exist examples of alternatives which promote local control despite an unfavorable macroeconomic and political climate (Flora and Flora 1988; Davis and Gaventa 1991). Indeed, some scholars feel the global issue is overplayed and underestimates the role played by local capital and businesses in contributing to underdevelopment or counteracting it. The 'growth from within' strategy becomes the only effective development approach in an environment where rural areas have little comparative advantage (Tomaskovic-Devey 1991). Gunn and Gunn (1991) explore how communities might take more control over capital and social surplus distribution across geography and class. They identify alternative institutions such as credit unions, community development loan funds, community development corporations, land trusts and health cooperatives. These institutions are competitive in the larger political and economic context and more responsive to community needs. Flora, Chriss, Gale, Green, Schmidt and Flora (1991) describe a number of self development projects which have generated jobs and income in rural communities through local initiative, local resource investment, and retention of local control. However, while local control often results in retention of greater linkage effects (Coffey 1990), and creation of more skilled jobs preserved for local workers, such development has not benefitted the poor any more than industrial recruitment strategies. Benefits accrue primarily to the middle class (Green, Flora, Flora and Schmidt 1990).

Even if local control is effective in generating development there is no guarantee it will be applied to alleviating poverty. In high poverty areas such as the South, placing hope in the ability of progressive local economic structures is unwise, given the historical effectiveness of local political, cultural and economic structures as a brake on development (Brown and Warner 1991). In low poverty areas such as the rural Northeast, increasing heterogeneity (in terms of race, class, length of residence and relationship to community as work place or residence) has led to a crisis in rural identity and an unwillingness to acknowledge worsening local poverty as a community problem (Fitchen 1991).

Why Do Poor People Stay in Economically Lagging Rural Regions?

Under the neoclassical assumption of perfect mobility for the factors of production, the location of poverty would be expected to shift from one locale to another in the wake of significant capital and labor movements. In addition, the assumed tendency for these production forces to seek out areas which will yield the largest return on investment infers that poverty within a given locale should not last long. Research identifying pockets of poverty, persistently low-income counties, and places left behind, however, suggests that some areas have been unequal participants in this network of production flows. Thus, poverty researchers inevitably confront the question of why people choose to remain in economically lagging regions rather than move to nearby growth centers.

While the outmigration question has been addressed from both macro and micro levels, it is the interaction of these levels of analysis which best explains the lack of mobility (both chosen and forced) for populations within areas of persistent poverty. For example, although low wages or low levels of human capital may be seen as individual characteristics (micro) or characteristics of the population as a whole (macro), motivations to migrate, such as upward social mobility, are generally assessed at the micro level. Since an individual calculation of the potential for upward mobility would include people's assessment of the costs and benefits of remaining or leaving, their decision takes into account both individual (e.g., change in job title) and collective (e.g., status of occupation within the community) factors. Although statistical concerns regarding problems of aggregation must be properly addressed, the need to consider both the macro and the micro dimensions of migration appears warranted. Remaining at the macro level will allow for a description of general patterns among those who remain. However, one can best understand the decision-making process at the micro level. Thus, the following conceptual and analytical review of migration will include both analysis levels.

Undergirding most economic migration theories has been the singular concern with "....differences in net economic advantages, chiefly differences in wages, (as) the main cause of migration" (Hicks el al. 1932:76). Economists stress the importance of utility maximization in the migration decision-making process. Inherent in these calculations are the beliefs that labor is able to move freely and that potential migrants have complete information on which to base their decision. Thus, it is assumed that the individual fully knows the economic advantage of relocating to an infinite number of open markets. At the macro level, the interest is on variables which reflect labor market differentials (e.g., wages, unemployment, labor market structure) and state intervention (e.g., various types of public assistance). At the micro level, human capital maximization (e.g., education, training, work experience) is generally considered the most important determinant of migration. In general, economic migration theories "start with the assumption that migration is based largely on rational economic calculations by the potential migrant" (De Jong and Fawcett 1981:23) and that a "person chooses to migrate if he or she believes the benefits will exceed the costs" (DeVanzo 1981:92).

Although some economic models consider noneconomic factors, the tendency is to emphasize objective rather than subjective variables (e.g., consumption levels of various goods and services versus happiness or satisfaction with goods and services, or geographic distance to relatives versus perceived importance of family ties) (Goodman 1981:133). Most economic migration theories would blame a lack of outmigration from poverty areas on deficient human capital. That is, those with adequate levels of education, training, and experience seek out areas to maximize on these investments, leaving behind a labor pool which presumably receives compensation appropriate to their level of human capital. While those with higher human capital levels tend to migrate, this relationship is far from perfect. Recent studies on the rural South (Beaulieu 1988; Hickey 1992) demonstrate that those who remain in nonmetropolitan areas continue to experience negative returns on human capital investment. Thus, the combination of human capital and market forces within these areas does not provide sufficient motivation to induce outmigration for all who would benefit from such a move. Some say this lack of fit between economic theory and behavior is due to the heavy emphasis on market forces and relative neglect of social and political forces (Brown and Warner 1991; Evensky 1991).

While sociodemographic theories acknowledge the importance of expected economic returns as one motivation for migration, these models also address the importance of nonpecuniary determinants in the decision-making process. The most commonly used noneconomic factors include motivations for migration (e.g., economic returns or social mobility) and the influence of mediating structures (e.g., community attachment, satisfaction, and norms regarding migration). Each of these indicators, when linked with particular demographic characteristics (e.g., age, sex, marital status, race, etc.) has been shown to affect migration decision-making (cf. DeJong and Gardner 1981; Garkovich 1989; Greenwood 1975; Ritchey 1976; Price and Sikes 1975).

Models constructed to explain migration decision-making are often complex. Three dimensions are generally included which serve to (1) describe the individual, (2) the motivations for migration, and (3) the conditions which facilitate or mitigate against a decision to migrate. The first consists of identifying the population of interest. In this step, the researcher selects a target population based on a consideration of demographic characteristics such as age, sex, race, or marital status. Since each of these characteristics has a well-established relationship to migration patterns, controlling for sample demographics enhances some of the explanatory power of migration models. For example, some of the lack of migration from areas of persistent rural poverty can be accounted for by the higher proportion of elderly, concentration of minorities, and lower educational levels among the population. The second set of factors consists of the reported reasons or motivations to migrate (e.g., social mobility, career aspirations, economic return). A third set of factors may be introduced as intervening variables (these are referred to as mediating structures). By controlling on mediating structures, a researcher is able to specify the conditions under which a particular study population will perceive a benefit attached to migration.

The inclusion of mediating structures in migration models is predicated on the assumption that the social context in which individuals reside can either facilitate or mitigate against migration over and above the effects of individual demographic characteristics. This would appear to be particularly important in the context of decisions to remain in depressed rural areas. As Uhlenberg notes (1973:309):

> When migration is viewed within a social structure, dependence upon the local community and assimilation elsewhere appear as critical determinants of whether motivation for migration becomes actual movement. Those with (1) deep roots in the community; (2) strong kinship ties in the local areas; (3) large investments in the community; and (4) an inability to assimilate easily into a new social environment are likely to resist migration.

An assessment of community attachment, community satisfaction, and community norms provides a lens through which individuals view "opportunities" in areas outside their own community. Among the potential factors in the community attachment dimension are kin, friendship and associational ties to the community along with length of residence. Indices of community satisfaction are generally composed of items which assess the perceived extent to which household members' needs are being met in the local community. Satisfaction with the immediate household environment, along with local services, markets, institutions, and amenities are included in this dimension.

Finally, community norms must be taken into account. The propensity for racial and ethnic enclaves in rural areas, along with regional cultural variations, suggests the need to control for the presence of collective conscience regarding extra-local migration and the assimilation of majority values. Research on the reasons for return migration by selected groups in rural areas emphasizes the importance of factors such as an unwillingness to embrace mainstream values, a preference for raising their family in a rural area, and employment in industries locating in the rural area subsequent to their outmigration (Price and Sikes 1975:30-31).

The answer to the question of why people stay in lagging rural areas rather than migrate to nearby growth centers may elude simple quantification, but it is actually quite straightforward and understandable. Despite the economic hardship and limited social mobility opportunities in areas of persistent rural poverty, the local rural community appears to provide residents with feelings of security and stability, along with strong ties to family and friends. These noneconomic assets, which have allowed rural residents to weather changes in the structure of agriculture and limited employment opportunities in peripheral manufacturing enterprises have been defined as the few things which endure.

The homogeneity of culture, typical of many rural areas, becomes the foundation upon which ties to family and friends are built. When residence in the rural area has been of long duration, the impact of local culture defines each resident's place in the subsociety, thereby providing a set of norms and values which are reinforced through interaction within his or her own group. While a 'rational' outsider might question the attractiveness of the social 'place' occupied by the majority who live in depressed areas, rural residents whose value orientations are steeped in the local culture take both pride and comfort in the stability gained through such an identification. A knowledge of who you are interacting with and their status relative to yours provides a sense of continuity and security that mere wages or a job cannot convey. Ownership of a parcel of land or a house, regardless of their market value, allows the rural resident to hold on to a measure of independence which would likely be forfeited if one moved to a more metropolitan area. Although it would be foolish to suggest that day-to-day living in a depressed rural area is either romantic or nostalgic, the significance of the attachments to the people and the land in these areas should not be discounted.

Territory, Economic Development, and Poverty

In dynamic capitalist societies economic development, by definition, will be uneven. Because space or territory is not 'frictionless', ensembles of economic activities and employment opportunities tend to cluster geographically. This territorial 'lumpiness' of economic life means that rural poverty is best viewed as one outcome of uneven development processes. Over time, the economic development process reshapes the territorial configuration of economic life, including the configuration of poverty. On the one hand, this process of economic formation and reformation offers hope that poverty can be alleviated as new opportunities wash over lagging economic regions. On the other hand, however, history has shown us that in the ebb and flow of economic opportunities some regions improve, while others decline. In other words, in a capitalist society like the United States, poverty is embedded in the process of regional/rural economic development.

To Conclude

There is little in the existing social science literature that speaks directly to the relationships among territory, economic development processes and poverty. The New Industrial/Economic Geography (cf. Storper and Walker 1989; Scott and Storper 1984; Knox and Agnew 1989; Markusen 1987; Krugman 1991a), the New Rural Sociology (cf. Lobao 1990; Buttel, Larson and Gillespie 1990; Lyson and Falk 1992), and the New Institutional Economics (cf. Piore and Sabel 1984; Mingione 1991) have begun to take space or locality into their theories of economic development. This work offers insights into how economic activities are dispersed over the geographical landscape.

The material we reviewed and presented in this chapter is a first step toward integrating poverty into these newly established lines of research. The renewed attention being paid to rural poverty, coupled with the emergence of several new lines of social science research dealing with territory and development, offers new opportunities for creative and productive thinking on poverty. The challenge, of course, in not only to understand rural poverty, but to alleviate it.

Notes

This chapter was written by Thomas A. Lyson, Cornell University; William W. Falk, University of Maryland; Mark Henry, Clemson University; JoAnn Hickey, Western Carolina University; and Mildred Warner, Cornell University.

5

Theories in the Study of Natural Resource-Dependent Communities and Persistent Rural Poverty in the United States

Introduction

This chapter focuses on the relationship between natural resource-dependence and persistent poverty in communities or regions within the United States. These places have or traditionally had a significant part of their local economy based upon resource extraction activities such as farming, mining, timber harvesting, commercial fishing, or grazing. The activities just mentioned receive the most attention in the discussion, but the theories included in our analysis broadly apply to other resource domains as well. We also recognize that as the United States increasingly takes on the structure of a service economy, some resource-based communities/regions experience economic growth due to commercial tourism and recreation because of their rural amenities (Burch n.d.; Hester 1985; Kusel 1991). While such growth does not necessarily alleviate poverty, the dynamics of this important shift in the economic base of these areas and its relationship to the problem of rural poverty cannot be covered here. We therefore invite others with interest in this important facet of poverty in resource-dependent communities and regions to carry on where we finish.

Poverty (defined as the household income level below which people are unable to purchase weekly food requirements with one-third of their income) has been increasing in the United States since the end of the Great Society programs in the late 1970s. Eighteen percent of the residents in nonmetropolitan counties now live in poverty, and this condition now exceeds the twelve percent of metropolitan residents who live in poverty (Hoppe 1989). This gap began widening between 1985 and 1989 (Lobao 1990:49). In addition, ten percent of all nonmetropolitan counties have records of persistent poverty going back at least two decades (Bender et al. 1985; Brown and Warner 1991).

A number of studies suggest that resource-dependent communities are among the poorest places in the United States both in terms of the rate and persistence of poverty (Brown and Warner 1991). Research on forest dependent communities east and west of the Mississippi divide indicates relatively high levels of unemployment, low median income, and substantial amounts of substandard housing (Drielsma 1984; Weeks 1990). The oil-dependent economy of Alaska has, to date, been unable to arrest the growth of exceptionally high rural poverty levels (Berardi 1991). In Alaska and elsewhere, rural poverty has a startling connection with high rates of suicide, homicide, tuberculosis, alcoholism and infant mortality.

How is it that communities in close proximity to natural resources, which by definition play an essential role in the nation's development and prosperity, harbor relatively large numbers of impoverished persons and households? What is the systematic relationship between wealth generation and the impoverization of rural people? These questions are central issues in the study of persistent poverty in natural resource-dependent communities.

It is important to note at the onset of this discussion that scholars in the field of natural resources are not of one mind about what causes impoverishment in natural resource-dependent communities. There are, in fact, numerous theoretical models which are now being developed to explain rural poverty. We have identified four theories in the social sciences with applicability to this problem: (1) the neoclassical economic theory of human capital; (2) a power-based theory of natural resource bureaucracy; (3) structural theories with emphasis on rural restructuring; and (4) a theory of the social construction of nature. These theories and their underlying social and economic processes are the subject of this discussion.

We hasten to add that the four selected models do not represent all theoretical work in the field of poverty and natural resources. They are, however, central to the independent, ongoing research of the Working Group responsible for developing this chapter. Since our group was selected to include representative scholars in the field, covering a broad range of extractive activities, we argue that the theories are important ones, but by no means an exhaustive set.

Before presenting these selected theories, the discussion will focus on two preliminary considerations. First, we discuss the concept of poverty itself, a primary focus in the work of several members of the Working Group. Throughout the discussion readers will see that our focus has been on social and economic processes to accentuate social inequality and limit rural people's capabilities and options, including low income rural people. Thus, our focus is a broader one than explaining rates of poverty as defined by income levels.

We then offer a general overview of some social forces at work in resource-dependent rural communities and regions which lead to the creation of relative and/or absolute poverty. These forces are recognized in the theoretical and more policy-oriented writing by members of the Working Group. However, even the most theoretical efforts only identify some of the major trends now at work in these communities and regions, since each theory has its own particular domain and conceptual properties of individuals and groups relevant to its particular focus. Thus, a brief overview of the processes which the theories explicitly or implicitly identify as working to limit community and personal development in these rural areas will serve to better integrate the discussion.

The Concept of Poverty

Poverty can be defined as both a relative and an absolute state. In absolute terms it is material deprivation to such an extent that one's physical well-being is at risk. Extreme material deprivation leads not only to physical degradation but mental despair. Material deprivation is first a consequence and subsequently a cause of malnutrition, high infant mortality, and, often, violent crime (Chambers 1983; Shkilnyk 1985; Berardi 1991). Poverty usually entails the unjust loss of choice in one's culture or functional lifestyle.

Relative poverty is structural, amounting to a social position in which income, compared to that of others, is insufficient to meet basic needs and personal dignity. Relative poverty derives from one's position in a social stratification system, and the relative impotence one experiences because of that strata. It also derives from the nature of local community or regional conditions such as the availability and quality of basic services like education and health care facilities (Townsend 1979; Schulman 1992).

Both absolute and relative poverty are linked to powerlessness or the inability to change one's circumstances, to control one's life, or to handle the pressures and contingencies of everyday life (Chambers 1983:103; Brown and Ingram 1987:6). Powerlessness is also a relative condition related to one's class position within a stratification system or one's status as a member of a particular racial or ethnic group. Often these two conditions are combined into one (Gaventa 1980; Knowlton 1972; West 1982, 1992; Chambers 1983; Schulman 1992). Absolute poverty may be alleviated without changing relative poverty. The latter is rooted in the distribution of goods, services and resources in society and requires structural change rather than individual initiative to alter.

While it may be possible to establish some absolute standard defining what poverty is in terms of nutrition or housing, poverty tends to be socially defined, often by those not living in poverty. The point is best illustrated with a comparison of the poverty threshold as estimated by the U.S. Social Security Administration's Orshansky Index for a family of four in contrast with the threshold defined by participants of a national Gallup poll within the United States (1989).[1] In 1988, using the Orshansky Index, a family of four was "poor" at or below a combined income of $12,092. Gallup poll respondents a year later defined the threshold at $15,017, or twenty-four percent higher (Wilson 1991). Thus, poverty has a subjective component and is socially (and politically) defined (Orshansky 1963; 1978).

While poverty often means sub-standard levels of food, shelter and clothing, it also involves important limitations on individuals' social well-being (Kusel 1991; Sen 1985a,b). By social well-being we mean the capabilities and opportunities available to individuals in a community. In this sense, the concept of poverty goes beyond its pernicious material dimensions. It includes limitations in humans' abilities to develop their social beings. The human self provides a sense of both personal identity and relatedness to those in the surrounding community. Thus, as poverty spreads, it thwarts the development of reciprocal and interdependent relationships among members of a community or locale (Bellah, Madsen et al. 1985; Selznick 1987).

Persistent poverty may be more likely where the social well-being of a relatively large number of people is impoverished. Labor markets, schools, local government, and daily community relations in general lose vitality because of poverty. Consequently, people in poverty lose some of their effectiveness in improving their well-being. Poverty is a condition which affects individual and household well-being. But the condition also implicates entire communities as they encounter financial and social limitations because so many people are unable or unwilling to participate in local activities (Young and Newton 1980). One of the more important limitations placed on communities because of poverty involves the weakening of efforts to organize local residents for purposes of economic development, since places with significant levels of poverty obviously need a more engaging local economy (Kusel 1991b). As already mentioned, one of the more important paths for research on resource-dependent areas is to conduct comparative analyses of impoverished communities and regions more and less successful in mobilizing people for economic development purposes.

Impoverization and Resource Dependency: General Social Forces

At least five general social forces emerge from the individual projects upon which this discussion is based. The first is rural deindustrialization and what may be an inevitable decline in the demand for skilled and semi-skilled workers in relatively specialized, resource-based economies, and the challenge this trend presents for rural communities. Not to be confused with the long-term trend in agriculture and other resource-dependent activities where capital is substituted for labor (Kenney et al. 1989; Commins 1990), deindustrialization involves plant closings, employment cutbacks, and wage concessions in rural areas. Manufacturing has been an important source of economic growth in rural areas during the 1960s and 1970s (Summers, et al. 1976; Summers and Branch 1984). To a limited extent rural manufacturing absorbed workers displaced by mechanization in farming and other extractive activities and served as an important source of off-farm income. The restructuring of U.S. manufacturing in the wake of the oil embargo in 1974 and increased foreign competition since then is am important trend not only for rural America, but the entire United States (Drucker 1986). Surprisingly, the extent to which this trend limits economic development and serves as a source of poverty in rural and urban areas has not been adequately addressed in the literature.

A second process involves the ability of resource extraction firms to hold considerable economic and political power in rural regions. While this power may be an inevitable result of the competitiveness of natural resource extraction and production and the large firms which historically have developed in the process, the impact of this economic and political power can be very problematic for rural regions and communities. While they depend upon the firms because of the specialized and often remote locations of resource extraction activities, the power of the firm, as we will show, can lead to rational underinvestment in human capital. This problem can lead to the development of young workers poorly prepared for volatile, rapidly changing skill requirements in contemporary labor markets. This problem is similar to the one identified in the first process discussed above.

The third process is closely related to the second and involves the tendency of natural resource bureaucracies, important agencies in rural regions with abundant resources, to voluntarily or involuntarily become controlled by their most powerful clients. This process of co-optation or domination, in turn, means that less powerful clients, including small farmers, family-based logging contractors, and small-scale fishing enterprises may not gain access to resources controlled by the bureaucratic agency. This can lead to relative or absolute poverty. The large firm's use of the natural resource may reduce the environment's value for other users, as when mining operations pollute rivers and streams or oil drilling adversely affects the ability of Native Alaskans to practice subsistence hunting and fishing.

In some instances, even large resource-extraction firms may be pre-empted from access to public lands and resources because of growing interest in environmental preservation in the United States. Many social scientists argue that the United States is undergoing fundamental changes in basic values, including a shift from viewing nature as a resource to be exploited to a view of nature as a diversity of living forms worthy of care and preservation (Hays 1987; Nash 1989; Inglehart 1990). With the completion of the Interstate Highway System, more and more post-world War II suburban children have unprecedented exposure to the spectacular natural sites of the United States because of their affluence and access to state and national parks. As these people mature, public officials responsible for managing public lands encounter more and more environmental clients. The implications this trend has for developing some resource extraction regions is an important part of the discussion.

A final process evident from the projects of the Working Group is the development of segmented labor markets and core-periphery relations. Here, rural areas become sites for resource extraction and employment opportunities with low pay and few fringe benefits. This process is both spatial and organizational. It is spatial to the extent that resource extraction occurs in remote locations in the case of some commodities. For reasons to be explained in the discussion, these sites are not conducive to processing and finishing the natural resource or building equipment necessary for doing so. It is an organizational phenomena because resource extraction firms often gain control of large amounts of land in an effort to remain competitive through the control of future supplies of a natural resource. This pre-empts other land uses in the community or region.

Can people mobilize local resources and create viable local economic development efforts, particularly in the presence of rapid changes associated with resource depletion, automation, and capital flight associated with increasingly global economic competition? This is a key question emerging from our work. The nature of development in resource-dependent communities and regions will be shaped by the nature of alliances among workers in resource extraction firms, corporate decision-makers, and state actors. Environmental groups increasingly also play roles in shaping the development process in rural areas. Reactions by these groups to the social processes identified here, especially their entrepreneurial activities, political alliances, and power in public and private decision-making will play a vital role in determining trajectories for the development of resource-dependent extractive communities and their levels of poverty.

Selected Theoretical Models for Explaining Poverty in Resource-Dependent Communities

The four theoretical models included in this discussion are presented in analytical form in Table 5.1. While these models are prevalent in social science literature, they do not share equal weight with respect to logical adequacy, conceptual clarity, or empirical verification. In addition, their implicit assumptions differ concerning how individuals and groups interact and affect one another.

Human capital theory and its application to resource-dependent communities is among the more prevalent, but even here scholars note that empirically-based work related to these theories is sparse. Work on the structural perspective, especially as it has been applied to the study of agriculture, also has an extensive

TABLE 5.1 Selected Theoretical Models in the Study of Natural Resource Dependence and Rural Poverty

	Major scholarly contribution(s)	Basic casual force	First-order consequence	Second-order consequence
Human capital theory	Theodore Schultze (1961); Gary Becker (1962)	Rational individual utility maximization.	Decisions about mobility and personal investment in education, health and skills.	Rational under-investment in human capital and depressed local economic opportunity.
Power theory of natural resource bureaucracy	Philip Selznick (1949); Clark Knowlton (1970, 1972); William Burch (1971)	Continued efforts on the part of groups to gain and hold power and authority in bureaucracies.	Use of external sanctions, infiltration, and ideological beliefs and values.	Accumulation of differential opportunities for life chances by different classes and status groups.
The social construction of nature	Berger and Luckmann (1966); Tuchman (1968)	Intergroup difference in cultural values and ethical beliefs about moral behavior.	Myth management and the formation of icons.	Social inequality in the attribution of value to nature.
Structural analysis and rural restructuring	Kautsky (1899); Doeringer and Piore (1971); Markusen, (1985, 1987)	Formation of monopolies and oligopolies in the development of sectors within an economy.	Dual or segmented labor markets; spatial separation of core and peripheral economies.	Profit-cycles leading to capital flight.

literature. However, that work also takes on a new form when combined with the literature on economic restructuring. Power-based theories of bureaucracy have received considerable attention in the literature. Other work discussed in this section centers on the social construction of nature.

Poverty and Human Capital Investment

It has been argued that persistent and growing rural poverty may be an outcome of rational under-investment in human capital within rural areas generally, including resource-dependent communities and regions. Underinvestment is rational from the perspective of the individual and the rural community rather than from the perspective of society as a whole (Smith 1988a, 1988b; Stallmann et al. 1991; Johnson 1991; Johnson and Broomhall 1991; Broomhall 1991). This argument is based upon human capital theory (Schultz 1961, 1979; Becker 1962).

As suggested in Table 5.1, human capital theory rests on the strategic assumption that individuals seek to maximize utility over the course of their lives. Thus, they must choose between enjoying current consumption or foregoing it to increase their income, and thus future consumption. The theory suggests that individuals will forego current consumption if the utility they would gain from the consumption of income, personal satisfaction and, perhaps, social recognition is less than the discounted utility from consumption later in time.

A key concept in the theory is the building of human capital through education, job experience, acquired skills, improved health, and the exercise of geographic mobility. Foregone current consumption is the sum of the direct costs of the investment such as schooling and moving costs. Added to these costs is the opportunity cost of time spent acquiring human capital in school or job training programs. It may also include nonmonetary costs such as the displeasure received from schooling, and the emotional costs of leaving friends, co-workers, and family to get a job.

Extending the Theory. People's attitudes and expectations with respect to education, occupational aspirations, and geographic mobility are first-order consequences of utility maximization, since people must weigh the short- and long-term consequences of their investments in human capital formation. These expectations lead to two second-order consequences: (1) decision-making with respect to personal investment in education and the acquisition of technical, marketable skills; and (2) community decision-making about municipal tax rates and expenditures on basic services, including education. Johnson (1991) argues that the first- and second-order consequences of rational individual utility maximization do not operate uniformly in different communities. This observation leads to the use of human capital theory in explaining persistent rural poverty in resource-dependent places.

Poverty in Resource Extraction Communities. An important part of Johnson's argument centers on the structure of extractive economies, especially the role played by large, absentee-owned firms. Natural resource-based economies are often dominated by large, absentee-owned firms. These firms are often large mining or lumber companies, pulp and paper companies, or energy companies.[2] As large firms come to dominate a resource-dependent community, they tend to increase production levels while decreasing employment, shifting from labor-intensive to capital-intensive technology (Friedland et al. 1981).

In many resource-dependent communities, the extractive industry can exert considerable influence on the local land market and government. By purchasing a considerable portion of vacant rural land, an extractive industry gains control of the future flow of natural resources. It also creates a dual market for land--a small, highly priced market for residential, commercial and small farm uses, and a large market for low-priced natural resource land. Thus, the extractive industry is able to shift the tax burden to other residents while limiting their access to such lands.[3] Furthermore, the vast amounts of land that industry owns gives them substantial leverage in local politics, especially with respect to the assessment and taxation of land designated for extraction process.

Two important reasons for rational underinvestment in human capital are the shift from labor-intensive to capital-intensive natural resource extraction and the political power of large firms in often highly specialized resource-dependent communities. Because the number of jobs are limited and declining, individuals find that the potential return on investment in their education is either too low or too uncertain to justify the sacrifice. The relatively high-paying jobs which require an education simply are not there. At the same time local school boards and other governing bodies find the investment in educating their youth often disappears when the graduates migrate to other communities for work.

Even where local economies are not dominated by large extractive industries, the rational underinvestment in human capital is likely to persist, especially in relatively isolated resource-dependent communities. Consider the economic development strategies of most communities. According to Johnson (1991), these strategies reinforce the decisions of individuals. Community leaders have little appreciation for the role that new employers will play in human capital decisions. They neglect how wage levels, environmental and social issues, or job certainty affect human capital investment incentives, recruiting almost any form of outside capital for economic development. This process, at best, creates short-run employment growth and long-term deficits in human capital investment.

The strategies and policies of the predominant industries in rural areas either overtly, or inadvertently, reinforce the incentives facing individuals. Industries need a low-skilled, docile labor force, and this need has increased recently with intensified foreign competition in products such as crude petroleum, wood pulp, and agricultural products. In addition, the absentee-ownership of the firms does very little for the development of interest in local issues such as public education.

Unions, while ostensibly the countervailing power to and antagonist of large firms, have similar incentive systems. Unions are monopolistic sellers of labor. Entrepreneurs and individualists are their competitors. General education may erode the membership and support for the union because it creates alternatives for people. Furthermore, individualism and solidarity are not always compatible at negotiation time.

Moreover, the class and tax structures of resource-dependent communities are such that local officials would be hard pressed to improve public education, even if they were so inclined. By shifting the tax burden for services such as schools onto small land owners whose incomes already are low, officials contribute to an environment which is not at all conducive to a diverse public infrastructure. Thus, in a system where the education of the next generation is dependent upon the taxable wealth in a community, the potential for persistent poverty is great, especially where large, absentee-owned extraction companies are able to shift the tax burden to other residents.

Empirical Evidence. There is surprisingly little empirical evidence related to hypotheses about the rational underinvestment in human capital within resource-dependent communities. Johnson, Kraybill, and Deaton (1989) measured the relationship between income level, stability, and certainty and human capital investment in Virginia, comparing counties dependent on natural resource extraction activities with those having other economic bases. The authors found low income had a more negative effect on human capital investment in natural resource-dependent counties than in others. They also found natural resource-dependent counties were adversely affected by income instability, a property which negatively influenced ten indicators of human capital investment. In addition, they found that income inequality in the resource-dependent counties was positively associated with levels of per capita investment in human capital.

In a related endeavor Stallmann, et al. (1991) estimated the relationship between two measures of human capital investment, the school dropout rate and the percent of graduating seniors continuing on to college, and various aspects of the local labor market. They found that greater opportunities in the managerial fields and higher unemployment rates in the local area encourage investment in education, while more opportunities in the lower skilled service industries discourage investment in education.

Broomhall (1991) conducted an extensive survey of graduating seniors in three school districts in Appalachian Virginia and one in Appalachian Kentucky, asking an extensive list of questions about attitudes, perceptions, and educational performance of students, dropouts, and their parents. Broomhall's work suggests that (1) those who are more willing to move to obtain employment tend to place a higher value on education; (2) those who perceive education as more valuable perform better in school; and (3) those who perceive education as being more valuable have higher educational and occupational aspirations.

Each of these studies lends at least some support for various aspects of the human capital theory of educational investment. They also directly or indirectly support the hypotheses about the influence of natural resource industries in individuals' decisions to invest in education. Individual poverty in many natural resource economies is, in turn, attributed to lower mobility, health, productivity, educational attainment, and bargaining power in the labor market. And the persistence of these conditions is blamed on the nature of natural resource industries, the continuous out-migration from rural areas of the most talented, the intergenerational process of attitude formation, and the short-run nature of economic development strategies.

Comments. Critical questions can be raised about both the empirical work cited above as well as the hypotheses implicit in the theory. Vail (1992), for example, points out that the empirical work by Johnson, Broomhall, Stallmann and others really is only preliminary. He also suggests that we need rigorous empirical tests based upon hypotheses which are explicitly derived from human capital theory. In addition, Vail (1992) argues that rural youth may not continue undervaluing the benefits of a high school diploma in the foreseeable future. This important argument is based upon at least two premises. First, nearly all young people from impoverished rural areas now realize they must leave their home communities if they are to have adequate employment, and that a high school diploma is essential for obtaining employment with adequate pay. Second, while school boards and governments in resource-dependent communities and regions may persist in minimizing services such as education, states have other interests. Realizing that state economic development requires demonstrable evidence that their labor force has the human capital investment needed by newly emerging, internationally competitive manufacturing or service-oriented firms, state-level incentives may change the priorities and practices of local government, especially with regard to education and vocational training.

Vail (1989) and Marchak (1983) also point out that the technology now being used in some resource extraction activities is considerably more sophisticated than in the past. In logging, for example, state-of-the-art technology includes a "multipurpose base vehicle." "The operator uses hand controls designed for fighter aircraft and a computer-controlled processing unit, programmed with current market prices so each stem can be bucked (cut) into the most valuable assortment of parts" (Vail 1989:368). Modern paper production also requires a highly trained workforce. "The modern pulpmill has workers tending automatic control panels, reading computer printouts on the adequacy of chemical mixtures, temperatures of pulp in each stage of production, and other conditions of production" (Marchak 1983:168). Drip irrigation systems in agriculture and the technological complexities of modern ocean-going commercial fishing craft also exemplify the growing need for a highly trained workforce within the extractive sector. Thus, international competition and opportunities may shift employment demand in rural areas from a semi-skilled workforce to one which is more skilled.

Other scholars would argue that the theory has strengths and fundamental weaknesses. Its strength is the social psychological linkages which it identifies between attitudes and expectations with respect to human capital investment and institutions such as government, schools, and absentee-owned extraction firms. It recognizes the centrality of political decision-making, class structure, the control of capital investment and wages by absentee-owned firms for underinvestment in human capital and therefore potential impoverishment. However, it is a weak theory because it focuses on individual decision-making as the basic unit of analysis. Thus, the basic causal mechanisms limiting people's ability to pay taxes because of the political and economic dominance of resource extraction firms is treated as an important but marginal phenomenon. Since other theories in the discussion each implicitly contain unique views about the strengths and weaknesses of human capital theory as well as other theories, we can address these limitation as the discussion unfolds.

Power, Domination, and Natural Resource Bureaucracy

Another explanation for persistent poverty are theories that explain impoverishment in terms of differential access to scarce natural resources controlled by private or public bureaucracies. At least five concepts are central to this theory. Power refers to the ability of an individual or group to impose their will on others, even in the face of opposition. Domination "...implies a more consistent, patterned structure of control than mere power that must be exerted each time to gain and hold control" (Weber 1968:lxxxiii). Constituencies are groups or individuals to whom a bureaucratic agency is accountable (Selznick 1966:145). While constituencies can gain the ability to dominate a bureaucracy through a common economic class position, status groups sharing a common lifestyle are also a source of domination. The concept of a social class refers to people within a common economic stratum sharing relatively comparable abilities to operate or influence impersonal markets as consumers or producers. Status groups share similar social recognition or prestige based upon ethnicity, occupation or some other lifestyle characteristic. Through their influence on bureaucracies, both classes and status groups can act as suppressors of the poor.

While relationships between the poor and either private or public bureaucracies are germane to power-based theories, a considerable literature has developed around public bureaucracies having the legal authority and implementation capacity to open the access to common property, including the nation's air and water.[4] A common theme underscores the influence of power constituencies on natural resource bureaucracy policy which in turn discriminate against the poor and near poor. As one observer notes, "The brute fact (that) the 'lion gets the lion's share' has made these bureaucracies the instruments that have kept the poor, and kept them from paths of rural development that would have lessened ... rural poverty within their sphere of influence (West 1992:5)." At least five paths to domination and persistent rural poverty are identified in this literature that fall into two basic types, power-based domination and domination through resource control.

Power-based Domination. This form of domination involves the exertion of external power resources by a constituency, usually via threats, and then, as necessary, carrying out the threats.[5] These threats or potential threats often create a stable form of domination in which threats are unneeded and domination flows evenly and automatically, leading to the control of internal social relations within a bureaucracy. When the large ranchers in the 1930's threatened the U.S. Forest Service with supporting transfer of the Forest Service to the Department of Interior, the Forest Service buckled under and the distribution rights that had protected small grazers were destroyed with immediate and lasting consequences for Arizona homesteaders and small farmers in western Montana.

Sometimes domination does not involve overt detectable threats but rather the application of constant behind-the-scenes political pressure. In this way the large canning companies ensured that the Bureau of Fisheries let them monopolize the declining fish stocks and eliminate the Native American fishermen from the fishery (Cooley 1963; Burch 1971; West 1982a:100-101).

More generally in Indian affairs, the Bureau of Indian Affairs (BIA) has been constantly barraged by large-scale resource development interests intent on gaining access to Indian resources and profits and denying Indian sovereignty. This effort effectively limits the chances for self determination and development of Indian natural resources, on their own terms, to escape from harsh reservation poverty (Danzinger 1974; Philp 1977; Cahn 1969; Kickingbird and Ducheneaux 1973; McNickle 1975). Here the multiplicity of interests exerted a common domination through external sanctions to uphold the right of white corporate power to take Indian resources at will. A telling case from Aberle (1970) showed that when the Navajo tried to develop their own coal resources in partnership with a small outside firm, large coal companies lobbied heavily with the BIA and killed the threat to their own exclusive access to reservation coal resources (West 1982b). Now the coal companies offer to make video tapes of the sacred sites the native-Americans will lose when their coal is strip mined, all with approval of the BIA. In the Social Impact Assessment (SIA) trade, these are called "mitigation measures." In the context of power theories of bureaucracy, the actions of the BIA and coal companies are indicators of domination with negative consequences for both culture and rural poverty on Indian reservations.

Various forms of co-optation are another variant of power-based domination (Selznick 1966; West 1982a). Here, an agency grants real power to a powerful external constituency without the formal recognition of responsibility. That is, unacknowledged authority operates within the authority structure of an agency. The consequences of informal co-optation are well documented in Selznick's (1966) *TVA and the Grass Roots*, where large agricultural interests dominated and shaped Tennessee Valley Authority programs and land use planning. Fertilizer production programs and dam relocation helped more prosperous farmers and did not help the rural poor, including black southern farmers.

When Selznick formulated his classic concept of informal co-optation, sharing power but not responsibility, he contrasted it with "formal co-optation," or the sharing of responsibility but not power. However, there is a third category important for power-based theory of domination over resource bureaucracies. This form involves both the sharing of formal power and the formal recognition of responsibility for this authority. West (1982a:59) calls this "power sharing formal co-optation."

The decentralization of the Soil Conservation Service is a classic example of power sharing formal co-optation. Most power for allocating resources is vested in decentralized boards dominated by local (usually large) farmers. Small farmers who need the soil conservation assistance and are losing soil fertility on small farms are left with the least federal assistance as a result of this form of domination (Hardin 1952, 1967; Burch 1971; West 1982a). In this instance domination was a result of social inequality in land tenure, providing large-scale farmers with the opportunity to exert more political influence over Soil Conservation officials.

Domination Through Constellation of Interests. No external threats or the exercise of power sanctions are involved in this form of domination. Instead, a constituency dominates an agency because it has some resource or capacity which the agency needs, so the agency acts on behalf of the constituent. During the 1950s, for example, large cattle ranchers were losing their political influence with the U.S. Forest Service; yet, the Forest Service increased the number of grazing permits issued to large ranchers. In this instance, the U.S. Forest Service wanted to increase beef production to meet a growing demand nationwide. Large ranchers had the resources to help the Forest Service increase meat production by financing range improvements on national forest grazing lands. Many rural poor around the national forests suffered, especially Spanish Americans of northern New Mexico. Their access to Forest Service grazing land was substantially reduced, leading to increased malnutrition among Spanish American children for lack of milk protein (Knowlton 1970; West 1982a).

A second example is the recent conflict between Michigan Indians and sports fishing groups. The Michigan Department of Natural Resources (DNR) sided with the sports group, even though Indians' fishing rights are guaranteed through the Treaty of 1836. In this case the bureaucratic capacity of the DNR Fisheries Division relies on sport fishing license sales for its budget. Because of this dependency, it is in the interest of the DNR to protect the sport fishery (West 1985).[6]

Cooperative Domination. Biases among bureaucratic officials themselves can result in what appears to be domination. Where the ideology of the key bureaucrats and the interests of powerful constituencies are at odds, the kinds of external domination described above are more difficult and contentious. Where the ideology of agency bureaucrats agrees with powerful external constituents, there is no need for external domination. Rather, a voluntary coalition between the state and other private or public groups develops.

Structures of power create cooperative domination, and more senior officials recruit new bureaucratic actors to maintain it. Thus we can expect a pattern of selective promotion in which ideological soulmates are promoted to the highest power positions in the bureaucracy. In addition, organizational socialization helps to create "correct" thinking. Thus, the coincidence of interests and ideologies between bureaucrats and key constituents is no coincidence, but rather a deliberate act of power relations.

While the conflict between Michigan sport fishers and Native-Americans serves as an example of domination through constellation of interests, it also contains evidence for cooperative domination. Agency records and interviews conducted by West (1992:17) indicated what he called "...true commitment to the sport fishery in opposition to the Indian fishing right claim." This commitment was evident in joint coalition strategy sessions in MUCC offices; the selection by the state of an attorney sympathetic to sport fishers; and direct efforts by one DNR official to organize tourism and sport fishing groups against the Indian fishing right claims.

Had this system of cooperative domination been allowed to proceed unchecked, the Native American fishing rights would have been dashed and the one traditional base of their meager economy would have been dismantled. Already high rates of relative and absolute rural poverty would have increased markedly. In this case, however, a court ruling leveled an uneven balance of power between the contending groups, and the Native Americans negotiated a less than ideal, but very favorable settlement (West 1985). The power resource of the Native American Rights Fund was critical to this settlement, providing skilled, committed lawyers to the tribes at no charge.[7]

Comments. The domination of natural resource bureaucracies by groups using external sanctions, domination through a constellation of interests and bureaucratic bias can serve as powerful causal mechanisms in the creation of rural poverty. Power and domination are especially important sources of poverty under conditions where the poor depend upon natural resources controlled by a public or private bureaucracy. In many instances these conditions also involve an uneven distribution of power, either because of the immense financial and political resources of extraction industry firms such as oil companies or because of the growing strength of status groups such as sport fishers or environmentalists.

What is theoretically important about some of the cases identified is not that domination can lead to poverty, but that in some cases such as the native-Americans in Michigan, poor people have been able to overcome at least some of the suppression which is causing their poverty. Their ability to do so is an important anomaly for this literature, suggesting that groups assumed to be powerless can wield power. What causes people to either remain quiescent or to rebel, given the kinds of natural and human resource policy which a public or private bureaucracy practices in a community or region? This is an important issue raised in Gaventa's (1980) work on the mobilization of southern coal miners, in Levine's (1982) writing on working class families living near the Love Canal, a toxic waste dump in suburban Niagara Falls, N.Y., and most recently work by Peluso (1991) on impoverished households in rural Indonesia. How do impoverished groups come to challenge the natural resource policies of groups such as the Forest Service or a state regulatory agency? What outcomes result from such challenges?

Comparative community research represents one promising way to extend the literature, since much of it involves single qualitative case studies and therefore suffers from even more empirical limitations than human capital theory.[8] The relative ability of small landholders and resource extraction workers to realize their interests through coalitions which interact more effectively with private and public resource bureaucrats would be the focal point in this potentially fruitful avenue of research. Vail (1989) provides exemplary work by comparing the well-being of small private nonindustrial forest landowners in Maine and Sweden. The deep sense of individualism among Maine's forest landowners creates an opportunity for corporate timber buyers to monopolize markets for raw logs, devaluing the holdings of the forest landowners. Swedish farmers engage in collective bargaining with lumber buyers and operate their own cooperative mills. Thus, cooperative organization enables Swedish land owners to realize more value from their forests.

This comparative research could benefit from an integration of the literature on power with work on resource mobilization developed in the study of social movements. Resource mobilization theory directs attention to social movement organizations (SMOs) with professional staff serving to extend an organized effort on behalf of a social cause into new groups. The Native American Rights Fund, mentioned above, may have played such a mobilizing role in the dispute between Native Americans and the Michigan DNR. A number of natural resource SMOs exist. The Forest Trust (1991), a national organization designed to enhance the efforts of for-profit and not-for-profit rural economic development groups, identifies twenty local organizations working to improve resource-dependent communities in the South and West. One group cited by the

Trust is the Mountain Association for Community Development, a group working to help communities in eastern Kentucky make the transition from coal mining to the development of forest-based industries (Miller 1990). Another is the Federation of Southern Cooperatives, an interstate organizing and coordinating body for fifty-five black farm cooperatives and fifteen thousand small-scale black farmers.[9] Scholarly work on the effectiveness of these and similar groups could advance the study of power and domination of resource bureaucracies in a substantial way.

Whether patterns of bureaucratic domination are stable or dynamic over periods as long as several decades is an equally important issue for the advancement of this literature. To the extent that patterns of domination change in time, the causal mechanisms leading to change in the interest groups controlling a resource bureaucracy, especially the mobilization and strategies of the insurgent groups, would be theoretically important. Recent historical work on the U.S. Department of Agriculture, for example, indicates that between 1948 and 1953 it went from being a bureaucratic agency controlling a substantial part of the federal budget with considerable interest in small farmers who were poor to an agency with declining resources and an interest in protecting large farmers (Hooks 1990, 1991; James 1986). We also have evidence of dramatic changes in the policies of the Environmental Protection Agency between 1980 and 1985 because of growing public fear of health impairments caused by hazardous chemical wastes, sometimes undetected in residential neighborhoods (Szasz 1992). Natural resource bureaucracies can come under the influence of their constituents by a variety of mechanisms. However, that influence is fluid, dynamic, and at times elusive or unpredictable. Gaining an even better picture of this dynamic quality and its significance for rural poverty is a challenge of the day.

The Structural Perspective and Rural Restructuring

Power-based theories of resource dependency and poverty emphasize the relationship between groups and the state. However, other structural theories identify the nature of local and regional economies and their linkages with even larger trade networks as the basic causal force in causing poverty. Well-being or poverty is a consequence of competitive market forces and the resulting structure of local economies, the relative power of labor, and spatial characteristics. People in a given locality share a common fate because they reside in a place having unique advantages and disadvantages as sites for capital investment. These characteristics are reflected in the spatial distribution of poverty and well-being. Individual characteristics such as race and gender are important for the allocation of poverty, but poverty rates within a locality are primarily due to the structure of economic activity (Hodge and Laslett 1980; Tomaskovic-Devey 1988).

Table 5.1 depicts the structural perspective. As firms emerge in a given sector they go through profit cycles which include four unique stages: (1)innovation, superprofits, and agglomeration; (2) standardization, normal profits, and geographic dispersion of plants and firms; (3) domination of the sector by oligopolies; and (4) market decline, profit squeezes, and plant closings. The linkages between phases three and four are especially important. The declining competitiveness of oligopolized sectors can lead to price squeezes wherein the ability of firms to continue with the capital accumulation process becomes problematic. This brings about plant closings and capital flight into other regions here and abroad with lower wage rates, more state subsidies for capital, and lower taxes (Markusen 1987; Gottdiener 1985). The nature of these stages or profit cycles and their social significance for poverty and the changing structure of localities and regions is the subject of this section.

Economic Segmentation. Studies of industrial segmentation constitute one of the major components of the structural perspective. Industrial segmentation theorists argue that the economy of advanced industrial societies consists of distinct sectors (Doeringer and Piore 1971; O'Connor 1973; Edwards 1979; Gordon et al. 1982). Here economic concentration is identified with at least some advantages for communities and workers. The core, also known as the oligopoly or monopoly sector, consists of large-scale bureaucratic firms which dominate their product markets. Positions within core sector firms are highly sought after jobs: income from employment is high and many fringe benefits such as health insurance, paid vacations, and retirement programs are part of the returns for workers. The peripheral or competitive sector consists of many small-scale, informally organized firms that generate lower paid and lower quality positions than core firms (Edwards 1979). A third sector, the state, provides collective or public goods such as roads and schools necessary for the continued operation of the other sectors. Earnings in the state sector tend to fall between the core and the periphery (Hodson 1978; Marchak 1983).

Industrial segmentation research has tended to concentrate on the difference in job outcomes such as earnings and benefits among the different sectors (Beck et al. 1978; Hodson 1983; Marchak 1983; Tigges 1988). Accordingly, poverty in a locality is the consequence of the organization of the economy, particularly the extent to which peripheral firms which create low quality positions dominate a locality. However, it also can be linked to the core, since monopolies are prone to capital flight, as suggested by Markusen (1987).

Contemporary studies of industrial segmentation with implications for rural poverty include work on rural restructuring or the crisis and reorganization of capitalism in its later or advanced stages of development (Kenney et al. 1989; Noel 1987). Research documents shifts in national economic structure and their impact on rural areas including a decreased dependence on farming and other extraction activities, the decline of rural industries, and the rise of the service sector as the dominant form of rural employment (Falk and Lyson 1988).

Restructuring also involves labor's declining ability to advance its interests due to rising industrial unemployment and a contraction of state social welfare programs (Bluestone and Harrison 1982; Wilson 1987). In this process the restructuring of rural regions occurs unevenly. Major regional changes in the organization of manufacturing and resource extraction due to globalization and the increased mobility of capital has made economic well-being ephemeral, with poverty and prosperity alternating among different regions and localities (Markusen 1987).

State policies to assist capital accumulation and reorganization decrease the relative power of labor, but contribute to the overall pattern of rural restructuring. At the heart of these policies is a concerted effort to provide the public infrastructure for private capital investment in industrial agriculture, forestry, and manufacturing in the developing nations. Reynolds (1985) characterizes the 1950s and 1960s as a foreign-aid boom in which the NATO countries competed with the now independent Soviet bloc for the allegiance of the nonaligned, natural resource-rich developing nations. Others argue that Western interest in the economic development of the southern hemisphere reflected national leaders' aversion to the depressed pre-World War II economies of Europe and the United States (Oliver 1971).

Payer (1982) finds that lending patterns of the Bank shifted in time from very large infrastructure programs for transnational roads and hydroelectric facilities in the 1950s to institutional facilities including universities, hospitals and research laboratories in the 1960s. Under the direction of Robert McNamara between 1968 and 1980, the Bank turned to smaller-scale projects in an effort to reach the poorest forty percent of the world's people. Given the massive scale and cost of many early projects, the infrastructure of roads, port facilities, and electrical generating capacity would not be in place until the late 1960s, and it would take additional time before private investors began shifting industrial capital from Europe and the United States to agricultural enterprises and industrial assembly facilities in the now newly industrializing countries.

The dramatic restructuring of the American economy now taking place because of the globalization of industrial agriculture and manufacturing involves changes in the quality and quantity of employment opportunities for U.S. workers, regional shifts in population distribution, and most recently, rising levels of poverty. While the scholarly literature has accomplished much in unraveling the historic roots of the restructuring process (Harrison 1984; Mollenkopf 1983; Bluestone and Harrison 1982) as well as its consequences for interregional growth and change (Markusen 1987; Sternlieb and Hughes 1975), many important questions remain. The restructuring process has involved a shift in employment from manufacturing to services, a change having especially dramatic effects on localities in the old industrial belt, including the East North Central, Mid-Atlantic, and New England states. The Office of Technology Assessment (1986) estimated that in the period of 1979-1985 alone, the United

States lost 11.5 million jobs because of plant closings, relocation, automation, or shrinking industrial output. Moreover, a disproportionate share of the job losses occurred in the old manufacturing belt, a region from the Great Lakes east to New York and Boston. Rural-urban differences in the impact of restructuring have not, as yet, been well documented in the literature, and the magnitude of the problem in terms of increasing rural poverty in general or poverty in resource-dependent communities in particular, has yet to be determined.

Segmentation, Dependency, and Extraction. Some scholars argue that natural resource extraction is a unique activity, one that cannot even be compared to other industrial processing such as primary or secondary manufacturing (Bunker 1989; Marchak 1983). Mining and oil drilling, for example, remove the thermodynamic and material wealth of a region. Thus, they can deplete the resource base of rural localities, possibly even limiting future growth. Moreover, these localities tend to be in geographically isolated areas dependent upon core regions where there is a concentration of population, industry, and administrative centers for corporations and government. When natural resources are extracted from one region and transferred to another (where they are transformed into industrial or consumer products), rural areas lose value-added potential which would stimulate economic development. Poverty is generated as resource extraction produces unequal exchange between dependent regions and core areas and as resources are depleted.

The increasingly remote character of natural resources, at least in the case of some commodities, means that the movements of core capital into the periphery and the exportation of the resource to core processing centers involves relatively high transportation costs. This characteristic of some resource-dependent communities, perhaps more than others, makes them different because it reduces the possibility of incremental growth in other sectors within a given peripheral community or region. It simply is more rational to invest capital where roads, workers, housing, suppliers and other forms of infrastructure already exist, rather than in underdeveloped peripheries, even those with an abundance of natural resources (Marchak 1983; Bunker 1989). As resources become increasingly inaccessible, only large firms can afford the capital necessary to find, reach, and procure the resource. Consequently, the likelihood of a resource-dependent areas being both highly specialized and dependent upon a large, absentee-owned extraction firm becomes greater in time (Freudenburg 1991).[10]

When one extractive firm dominates a locality, household and community structures become dominated by the workplace. In the absence of self-sustaining and autonomous local production systems, no base for local opposition or resistance to power domination from the outside can develop. In company town situations, even the income of workers goes back to the dominant firm because it controls the flow of nearly all goods and services needed by workers and their families (Caudill 1962). Thus, the relative power of labor in natural resource extractive localities tends to be low (Young and Newton 1980).

The above reasoning is one way of showing why resource-dependent communities often remain economically specialized, vulnerable to economic crises linked with the volatility of international commodity markets and competition, and economically unstable. It also suggests that much of the value created from processing of natural resources occurs in the core, locking the periphery into an economically inferior position.

Dependency theory also has been applied to the structure of agriculture. Agriculture involves not just farming, but also large-scale agribusiness input and output corporations (de Janvry and LeVeen 1986; Havens 1986; Friedland et al. 1981). Many of these corporations are divisions of multinational firms in the core sector that are vertically integrated into agricultural production. As a consequence, control in agriculture has shifted away from the farm. While agribusiness corporations in the core sector generate high quality positions, farming is left in the periphery.

In addition, farming itself is not a homogeneous sub-sector. Work in agrarian political economy analyzes the shape and structure of farming under late capitalism. Several theorists argue that the penetration of capital into the farm economy creates a segmented structure similar to that of industry (Kautsky 1988; deJanvry and LeVeen 1986). Small, often part-time farms, persist in the periphery of the agricultural structure, while large-scale industrial farms dependent on hired labor dominate the sector's core. Studies emphasize the diversity within farming and the restructuring of agriculture towards fewer farms, larger farms, and the growth of capital-intensive technologies. At one end of the farm structure are large-scale farms which employ large numbers of wage laborers. At the other end are small-scale units dependent upon off-farm work. The middle-sized units provide their own labor and management, but are dependent upon off-farm markets in land and capital. State policies, despite the rhetoric of saving the family farm, facilitate these changes by subsidizing land, labor, capital, water, and technology costs of large-scale farms (Albrecht and Murdock 1988; Lobao 1990).[11]

Segmentation and Stratification. The impact of these trends in the structure of extraction activities on poverty and well-being are an important part of this literature. This is especially the case in work on agrarian political economy because of the important work by Walter Goldschmidt (1947) who evaluated the structure of agriculture and its relationship to community well-being. Goldschmidt found that an increase in the concentration of land and other forms of capital within the farm sector led to a decline in rural economic and social well-being.[12] Goldschmidt noted that in contrast to a community surrounded by large farms, a community surrounded by small farms had a higher percentage of self-employment and white collar workers; a lower percentage of farm wage laborers; more business and retail trade; more schools, parks, civic and social organization, newspapers, and churches; better developed infrastructure and more local decision-making. The dimensions of well-being that were most affected were living conditions and income.

The extensive literature stemming from this classic work now suggests that farm structures generate different types and quality of farm jobs and farm households (Lobao 1990; Lobao and Schulman 1991). Large-scale industrial type farms generate many poorly paid temporary wage labor positions. Small-scale type farms generate poor farm households because their smallness translates into a lack of control over resources and high degrees of self-exploitation in order to survive. Medium scale family farms generate owner-operator households with higher incomes, more control over resources, and more involvement in the local community than other types of farm structures. However, because they lack the market power of large-scale farms and the diversity of income sources of small-scale units, medium-scale family units are particularly vulnerable to the fluctuations in the farm economy. Overall, the structure of agriculture is changing towards a bimodal distribution with many large-scale and small-scale units as medium-scale units disappear (Albrecht and Murdock 1988; Buttel 1983).

Labor Market Inequality. Studies of labor market inequality constitute the third component of the structural perspective. Labor markets are localities within which exchange relations between labor and capital occur. Local labor markets are determined by the structure of industry, including the number of firms, the types of employment positions, and the structure of the labor force, including their skill levels and degree of unionization. Characteristics of the labor force, the extent of employment competition, labor organizations, and non-market labor guarantees such as welfare influence the bargaining power of labor. Labor markets characterized by a higher relative power of labor tend to have lower poverty levels (Lobao 1990; Lobao and Schulman 1992). Labor markets dominated by high wage core industries result in better local socioeconomic conditions such as higher income and lower poverty. In the case of timber-dependent communities, this kind of labor market is also less influenced by the volatility of markets for commodities such as paper or dimensional lumber, since the industries are capable of producing diverse products (Marchak 1983). Labor market inequality is also influenced by state policies involving accumulation and reproduction. State policies which support private capital accumulation or which subsidize the reproduction costs of labor power influence the structure of jobs and the relative power of labor with a local labor market.[13]

Comments. In summary, the structural perspective contains a basic set of questions that researchers must ask if they are to understand the forces that cause poverty in a rural locality, including places with extractive economies. The first set of questions focus upon the overall economic structure. What is the nature of the extractive economy? What types of industries and firms dominate the local industrial structure? What types of positions are generated by resource extraction firms, related manufacturing or processing firms, and state employment? The second set of questions deal with the balance of the relationships between capital and labor in the local labor market. What are the characteristics of the labor force? How much competition exists in the local labor market? What organizations such as labor unions or state programs exist which improve the relative power of labor? The third set of questions highlight the spatial characteristics of the rural locality. Where is it located relative to urban communities with more diverse employment opportunities? What is its natural resource and land tenure base? What is the historical pattern of uneven development? Finally, a fourth set of questions concern the wider sociopolitical conditions influencing a resource-dependent community. What is the nature of the accumulation process? How have changes such as globalization and restructuring influenced the organization of local forces within the particular rural locality under study? How do state policies and programs effect the overall industrial structure, the relative power of labor, and the geographical unevenness of development?

Of the theoretical models discussed so far, the structural perspective clearly has its closest affinity and compatibility with the power-based theory. In fact, the relative power of labor to influence wages through negotiation with private firms and public agencies reflects a power-based phenomenon. While the structuralist perspective may seem overly deterministic to students of power or human capital theory, it nonetheless introduces important notions about the organization of capital and how it can influence the distribution of wealth and poverty within and between communities and regions.

Human capital theory, of course, represents the most distinctive counterpart to the structuralist perspective thus far in the discussion. Because they work at different levels of analysis with distinctive causal sequences, their unique theoretical properties explaining poverty compliment rather than contradict one another in many respects. Thus, the focus on individual utility maximization and rational underinvestment in human capital presents a concrete, individually-based perspective on why people may choose to live in poverty. The structuralist perspective, on the other hand, provides an important macro-level perspective on intra- as well as interregional variation in poverty based upon concepts such as labor market segmentation and the relative position of industries and extraction firms in profit cycles.

Considerable attention needs to be given to structural analyses of different forms of resource-dependence. This literature provides an overarching context in which to study poverty and social inequality. Direct analysis of wage laborers such as migrant workers, the role of company towns in generating poverty, and the linkages among capital concentration, mechanization, and the impoverization of farm workers are topics needing additional attention. Resource-dependent places are undergoing considerable social change because of the forces we have mentioned. Without increased scholarly attention to these places, many of the traditional resource-based economies literally could disappear without either scientific understanding of how forces of social change have undermined them or appropriate welfare policies.

Moral Exclusion and Rural Poverty

Ascertaining the process of how nature is socially defined is an exercise which goes beyond power-based theory discussed above. Power-based theory raises the question, how is power and domination exercised with natural resource bureaucracies? Theory on the social construction of nature focuses instead on the moral exclusion process or why groups win or lose legitimacy in having rights of access to natural resources controlled by a public authority.

At the heart of this approach, as suggested in Table 5.1, is a dynamic set of shared cultural values about right and proper behavior. These norms both prescribe the rules governing socially appropriate forms of behavior and designate to whom and what we owe restraint and obligation. In the social construction of nature, groups compete for the right to define nature and its socially (morally) appropriate uses with myths or stories about natural objects and their appropriate role in society. Groups who benefit from these myths gain both legitimacy and rights of access and use of the resource.

The potential impoverishment of at least 48,160 forest products workers in the Pacific Northwest because of growing concern for old-growth forests and their ecological structure illustrates the dynamics of moral extension and exclusion, state decision-making and its potential consequences for poverty. In this case one sees how the growing power of a national elite dedicated to environmentalism is challenging the moral legitimacy of both local elites and the national industrial elites who traditionally benefitted from access to and use of natural resources on public lands.[14]

The Greening of America. The greening of America refers to "...the processes by which environmental concerns are nurtured within social groups and modern environmentally-related symbols become increasingly prominent in social discourse" (Buttel 1991:1). Thus, more and more Americans come to share images of the Baby Harp Seal, the toxic waste drum, the Whale, and complex processes such as acid rain, the Greenhouse effect, and nuclear power. Promoted by growing environmental groups and the media, these symbols have powerful emotional and cognitive meaning, and they serve as an important source of motivation for the environmental movement (Mazur and Lee 1991; Szasz 1992).

The process of greening has potential significance for poverty in natural resource-dependent communities. The growth of ecocentric values, as one scholar puts it, can lead to "...the substitution of environmental for social justice discourse" (Buttel 1991:13). That is, environmental groups work to protect natural ecosystems everywhere, even if such protection means that traditional economic development in commercial fisheries, logging, and mining have to cease. The standards of judging successful local development switch from human benefits and costs to biodiverse benefits and costs, opening the door to the argument that human impoverishment may be a necessary consequence of a more appropriate form of community development.

Cultural Themes and Moral Exclusion. Every society is said to contain individuals who share general values and beliefs which either prescribe or proscribe thoughts and actions about appropriate behavior, although everyone may not share the same sets of values and beliefs (Olsen, Lodwick, and Dunlap 1992). Beliefs about the desirability of industrial capitalism and its operation in markets, about our appropriate role in the natural world, and about how we should be governed using democratic principles all represent cultural themes which we share through a common, life-long socialization process. Cultural themes are not reducible to the beliefs and attitudes of individuals. They are shared, taken-for-granted assumptions about how to think or act with respect to a set of situations, and they influence how individuals form their more specific beliefs and attitudes concerning their social and natural environment.

Moral exclusion of those who "harm or abuse the environment" has been one cultural theme associated with the greening of America. Moral objections rather than rational discourse is the common root of conflicts over issues as diverse as timber harvesting, cattle grazing, and animal rights disputes (Jasper and Nelkin 1992).

The idea of a moral community was developed to explain various forms of moral exclusion, including violation of human rights, political repression, religious inquisitions, slavery, and genocide (Staub 1989; Nash 1989; Opotow 1990). The morally excluded are "...perceived as nonentities, expendable, or undeserving; consequently, harming them appears acceptable, appropriate, or just" (Opotow 1990:1). Several issues that are linked by the concept of moral exclusion include abortion, racism, sexism, species conservation, and immigration policies.

Lee (1992) argues that although the Northwest timber supply crisis first appeared to be a conflict between parties struggling for control of economic assets, it now seems to be best explained as a struggle over legitimation of competing moral communities.[15] One moral community is articulated by a wood production coalition of leaders in public-land-dependent wood products corporations, small industry, independent entrepreneurs, community elites, and organized labor. The other moral community is an environmental coalition composed of leaders in local, regional, and national environmental organizations, aided by regional and national mass media and the educational establishment. The clearest expression of the underlying cultural theme is found in attempts by environmental advocates to extend the boundaries of moral community to include animals, plants, and other natural objects (Nash 1989; Devall and Sessions 1985; Devall 1988).

Although an emerging environmental coalition seeks to displace the historically dominant position of the wood production elite, the contest is not simply a prolonged conflict between social classes or economic interests. It is instead primarily a struggle to control public sentiment and natural resource bureaucracy officials by manipulating cultural symbols displayed in the media. The struggle is illustrated by the fact that the wood production coalition and the environmental coalition are the primary contestants in this struggle, while corporations owning timberland are posturing to defend their turf from environmental regulations while preserving a fall-back position from which they could capture windfall profits.[16]

Myths as Instruments for Legitimation. Myths are basic ingredients and first-order consequences of cultural processes that result in political legitimization (Berger and Luckmann 1966). The process of legitimization involves justification for inequality in the attribution of value to a resource (Cohen 1975). The acid test for legitimacy is the differential behavior of contestants whose relationship is structured by unequal distribution of access to a particular resource. Greater latitude of behavior is enjoyed by those who have acquired greater control over a valued resource. As noted earlier in this discussion, the opportunities for making choices reduce the vulnerability, isolation, and powerlessness that are associated with poverty (Chambers 1983; Sen 1985, 1987; Kusel 1991a).

Myths are managed in two different ways: (1) cultural extension; and (2) cultural substitution. Cultural extension involves legitimation of present actions by sacralizing or portraying them as an outgrowth of a society's most respected history and cherished vital traditions. Cultural substitution involves emphasis on a utopian future rather than a sacralized past. The past is portrayed as irrelevant, or even malevolent. The substitution of new and often alien, cultural values for indigenous values are advocated as the only way for the society to survive. Myths become especially important as a means for replacing ordinary notions of historical time with the sense of timelessness portrayed by an hypothetical future and discredited past.

Lee (1992) has examined the strategies employed by both the environmental and the wood production coalition in the Northern Spotted Owl controversy. His objective has been to document how moral communities have been defined and legitimated. Particular attention is given to how the assignment of boundaries to moral communities may have resulted in moral exclusion, as well as how such moral exclusion has been legitimated. He has placed particular emphasis on the terms on which social and economic justice is to be extended to wood products workers, since these terms are essential for understanding the processes by which they may be pushed or recruited into poverty.

Myths of the Environmental Coalition. Environmentalists have articulated an elaborate set of myths or cultural interpretations to justify old-growth preservation and exclude wood products workers from their moral community.

Two classes of interpretations are most evident: (1) myths about natural objects, including forests, ecosystems, and animals; (2) myths about wood products workers, emphasizing their immorality, potential for moral transformation, and justification for suffering if they are unable or unwilling to reconcile themselves with the emerging moral community articulated by the environmental coalition.

Myths emphasizing cultural extension are manifested in sacralized values assigned to forests "so old that they stand outside ordinary time" (the ancient forest) and irreplaceable biological legacies, including endangered species and entire ecosystems. The ancient forest is openly acknowledged as a symbol of immortality, or biological continuity.

Similar unquestionable value is assigned to species thought to depend on old-growth forests. Using biological research published by the U.S. Forest Service, the environmental coalition selected the Northern Spotted Owl as an "indicator species" with old-growth habitat requirements shared by innumerable other species (Carroll 1991). "The owl" has become a true icon, representing the ancient forest and all the species that inhabit it.[17] The character of the owl as an icon capable of resolving contradictions is revealed by the fact that its mythical/legal status remains unquestioned, especially when a rational assessment would suggest that there may be a wide range of alternatives for preventing the owl's extinction.

A separate set of myths has been constructed about people who depend on the harvesting and manufacturing of wood taken from old-growth forests. Members of the environmental coalition have described old-growth loggers by using images such as "buffalo hunters," "tree murderers," and "rapers of the land." Such vilification of loggers is pervasive, appearing in political cartoons, magazine articles, and environmental newsletters (Lee 1990).

Cultural substitution is evident in the ways by which environmentalists adopt two myths of reconciliation to define the terms on which loggers may re-gain membership in the moral community. The first is the traditional belief in the mobility of labor. Here faith is placed in the capacity of rural labor markets to automatically redistribute dislocated workers to jobs in industries that are "kinder and gentler" to the environment (Anderson and Olson 1991). Members of the environmental coalition conventionally assume such employment transformations will occur because people respond rationally to adversity by seeking a new job, retraining if necessary, or moving. Contradictions between the idealized vision of a perfectly efficient labor market and the realities of highly inefficient rural labor markets are masked by the popular ideology of *laissez faire* market solutions (Lee 1990; Carroll 1991).

A second myth of moral transformation is expressed in current legislative proposals to compensate dislocated loggers by employing them on publicly funded projects to restore ecological integrity to streams and watersheds damaged by logging. Although there are sound social, economic, and ecological justifications for such projects, restoration work would also have symbolic significance in immediately qualifying dislocated loggers for membership in the environmental coalition's moral community. Environmental restoration work would signify their commitment to repairing the damage they have done to the environment in their previous work as loggers.

Myth Management by the Wood Products Coalition. The wood products coalition formed in response to the surprising influence of the environmental coalition on public sentiments. Jobs, family, and community were selected as key symbols (Lee 1990). A strategy of cultural extension sought to justify continuity, or at least a reasonable compromise, in old-growth harvesting.[18] Values such as family and community and the dignity of holding a job have long been celebrated as unquestioned traditions in American culture. The home also became an important symbol in the management of myths, both in the sense that wood products have been essential for building affordable homes and in the sense that wood products workers' homes are threatened by sudden timber harvest reductions. An attempt was made to appeal to the common humanity of all people, and to exclude those who would deny people work, harm families, deny people homes, and destroy communities.

Comments. Scholarly work on the use of myths in the social construction of nature and moral exclusion compliments research on power theories of natural resource bureaucracies. It explains how people may be impoverished through social processes where a traditional rural lifestyle, once revered as a fundamental part of American culture, is becoming an anathema which must be curbed. The moral exclusion process is a result of the gradual greening of America since World War II. Thus, the recent Northern Spotted Owl controversy is not a unique regional phenomenon. Rather, it is part of a larger impoverishment process in which resource extraction is no longer condoned. This problem undoubtedly will extend beyond the confines of public lands, since environmental groups are equally concerned with the protection of ecosystems, irrespective of their legal status.

The cultural substitution of environmental preservation policies for more utilitarian resource policies presents a particularly thorny social problem for at least three reasons. First, those who bear the burden of moral exclusion are deeply committed to their work and its all encompassing lifestyle (Carroll 1991). Second, many of the people who will be excluded from working in the forest products area lack resources such as landownership, so their ability to survive this social change without experiencing some unknown period of poverty or economic hardship is reduced. Third, even remotely parallel forms of employment such as construction work or heavy equipment operation may be less available in the future since so many of the newly created employment opportunities are in the service sector.

Research on moral exclusion and the social construction of nature is the newest in this discussion, and it can be expected to play an important part in the field. In reviewing work on power-based theories of resource bureaucracy and poverty, we noted that there is evidence of fluidity in the nature of bureaucratic domination in time, but this fluidity is not well documented in different settings. Theory on the social construction of nature provides an avenue for explaining the dynamic qualities of bureaucratic domination and control. In doing so, it directs attention to actors beyond those groups with the capacity to gain a direct foothold on the agencies, including the mass media. It also suggests that status groups as well as classes can play a significant role in social change, even when they compete with larger resource extraction firms for rights to public land. Thus, theory of the social construction of nature provides an important counterpoint to the more economically deterministic structural theory. In addition, it suggest ways that people form expectations, accurately or otherwise, about the future consequences of particular sets of actions involving the commitment of time, money, and other resources. One suspects that human capital theorists and social constructionists have mutual interest that could help build even better theories. Even their interests in attributing value to some sequence of events with respect to a material object or social agency or investing in human capital seem parallel, although the language of the two theories may keep them apart.

Discussion

We have examined four theories having explanatory value for understanding relative and absolute poverty in rural resource-dependent communities and regions within the United States. Human capital theory explains rural poverty under these conditions in terms of rational underinvestment. Those living in poverty do not have the educational background or aspirations necessary to take advantage of new employment opportunities as more traditional forms of earning a living in agricultural or extractive regions decline because of resource exhaustion, mechanization, capital disinvestment, or environmental preservation. Rather than "blaming the victim," however, human capital theorists make causal connections between people who have underinvested in their own educational development and financially limited taxpayers, accountable local officials, labor unions, and absentee-owned resource extraction firms. As yet, the parallel effects of the resource extraction firms and environmental organizations have not been recognized, but we see no reason why environmental organizations could not readily be integrated into the theory. As the theory stands, mining, ranching, farming, fishing, and timber harvesting firms are especially important because they set wages, control vast land holdings, and are locally influential enough to be able to pass tax burdens onto other local residents, thereby making a major contribution to the fiscal and social conservatism in these communities.

Human capital theory is an important and fundamental part of this literature because it offers testable hypotheses directly related to the questions as to why people in resource extraction regions experience high rates of poverty. Consider, for example the argument that people in resource-dependent communities are more likely to undervalue investment in their own human capital than people living in other kinds of communities. This hypothesis is based upon an assumption that people strive to maximize their expenditures of time and energy in the acquisition of marketable skills and commodities. These forms of human capital could be considered as forms of property rights, broadly defined as rights to opportunities for acquiring income and wealth. How one develops aspirations and expectations with regard to levels of human capital investment and resulting property rights, however, is not strictly a matter of individual rational choice. The community institutional context in which one acquires information leading to expectations about returns on human capital investment is critical in the process, even though the theory ultimately is one about individual decision-making and its consequences for poverty and personal well-being.

Human capital theory explains well-being as a function of property rights earned through investments combined with the terms of trade which one encounters in labor and other markets. Thus, poverty is the product of diminished property rights and adverse terms of trade. Since both the sum of individual property rights and the terms of trade which present themselves to residents in sites of resource extraction are the result of forces which are included within the domains of other theories in this discussion, it is a logical starting point. Further advances in the field will need to examine the precise ways in which human capital theory can be integrated with these other theories.

Large resource extraction firms historically also have played an important role in the decision-making of natural resource bureaucracies. However, at times power-oriented theorists find cooperative domination and domination through constellation of interest, which implicates state officials as well as private capital in setting the conditions in which poverty and wealth develops. Cattlemen, working with the cooperation of the Forest Service, displaced small Spanish-American ranchers from range lands in the West and contributed to the creation of absolute poverty and malnutrition. Large firms have also prevented Native-Americans from exploiting coal and oil on their reservations, and they unsuccessfully challenged Native-American fishing rights on the Great Lakes. In the latter case we actually have both class and status groups working for bureaucratic largess. The sportfishing industry, a class, worked in concert with a state sportfishing association whose members share a common lifestyle or status. That example and several others found in our work exemplifies the mobilization of people living in relative poverty and is an important occurrence worthy of considerable attention. As mentioned earlier, it also presents an opportunity to integrate power-based theory with resource mobilization theory in the literature on social movements.

Structural theory, including recent work on profit cycles and the development and behavior or firms, provides the most abstract, comprehensive view of urban and rural economies and the numerous ways in which they can be linked with poverty and well-being. As the literature stands, phenomena such as profit cycles, labor market segmentation, economic restructuring, and core-periphery relationships are treated separately. However, they can be integrated and developed as a relatively powerful explanation for poverty in resource-dependent areas. Historically, extractive regions have been under the influence of large, often monopolistic firms administered and controlled from metropolitan centers. The development of empirical measures to ascertain the degree of asymmetry in the exchange of capital and natural resources between rural and metropolitan areas in the United States would seem to be a theoretically meaningful and important avenue for research. To the extent that asymmetrical economic relationships exist between peripheral extraction regions and core production sites, one could also examine how such relationships influence rates of poverty. The extent to which resource extraction communities and regions have experienced capital disinvestment in recent years, the utility of profit cycle theory in explaining such disinvestment, and the ability of these places to pursue effective economic development efforts are equally important topics which, as yet, have not received the kind of scholarly attention they deserve.

A puzzling observation that one can make in looking at the literature on the structure of agriculture and other resource extraction activities is that employment in monopoly sector firms is associated with relatively high paying, stable jobs. Yet, wage labor employment in agribusinesses is shown to associated with very low wages and poor working conditions. In the case of the forest products industry, employment in large, state-of-the-art wood or paper production facilities is found to be economically rewarding with high wages and steady work. However, the ratio of capital to labor, in comparison with the past several decades, is high, so many prior employment opportunities have been lost to automation. Moreover, profit cycle theory tells us that even the most stable employment structure will shrink in time. Thus, work on poverty under conditions of resource dependence requires very careful distinctions about the precise sector with which one is working, whether the dominant local economic activities involve extraction or processing of a natural resource, and the stage of local extraction or processing firms in the profit cycle.

Large, absentee-owned resource extraction firms, however, are not the only agents influencing the wage and employment opportunities in resource extraction regions. For those regions where natural resources (especially untapped or undeveloped resources such as old-growth forests) are controlled by public agencies, environmental groups are now competing with traditional corporate actors for moral claims concerning their appropriate use. Since scholars see an unlimited future for the environmental movement in the United States, conflicts among environmentalists, organized labor, and natural resource extraction firms and the consequences of these conflicts for poverty and well-being are as important as any phenomena meriting attention in the field. It provides an opportunity to examine the veracity of traditional assumptions about the mobility of labor within the oldest, most traditional sectors of the U.S. economy. More generally, both qualitative and quantitative research on this topic will document what amounts to the historically significant conflict between capitalism and environmentalism and the social forces which shape how state officials resolve it.

These theories and the underlying social processes creating the phenomena which they are designed to explain suggest that rural Americans in resource-dependent communities face unprecedented obstacles in their ongoing development, and curbing growing rates of poverty will be no small challenge. The emergence of a global economy literally puts them in competition with communities in the Southern Hemisphere where wages are but a fraction of those in the United States. In addition, some communities with abundant range land or forests may not be able to develop extractive economies because of the greening of America. Of course, the United States has some of the most productive agricultural and forested land in the world, so conflicts between environmental groups and resource extraction firms are more likely than complete capital disinvestment from sectors such as mining, forestry, fishing, and agriculture.

It should also be noted that not all poverty in resource-dependent communities is directly linked to extractive activities or to rational underinvestment in human capital. Fortmann and Peluso (1992) and Nord (1991) recognize a diversity of processes at work which create different types of poverty. Life-cycle poverty occurs through age-related poor health or changes in family structure such as the death of a breadwinner or divorce. Poverty importation occurs where inexpensive housing and opportunities for subsistence living serve as incentives for rational investment in human capital through in-migration by poor households (Fitchen 1981; Berardi 1991; Muth 1990).[19] Non-resource-dependent working poor have been impoverished by firms moving into a resource-dependent community in search of low-wage labor. Ethnic minorities with some of the highest rates of poverty are impoverished through long histories of discrimination in the provision of basic public services, including public education (Greenstein 1989). The landless poor are impoverished by having lost ownership of land that could have been used for sale or development as a fallback in periods of unemployment, poor health, or other personal difficulties (Geisler 1991). While some of these forms of poverty can be explained with the theories selected for this discussion, the variety identified here also suggests, as we stated in the introduction, that our analysis has not been an exhaustive one.

While the four theories examined in this discussion compliment each other in certain ways, or at least have the capacity to do so, they also differ in many respects. We already identified how they represent different levels of theoretical abstraction. However, they also point toward contradictory implications. Some work suggests that the structure of resource extraction is conducive to poverty because the firms operate in areas without alternative sources of employment, and the firms are increasingly encountering competition from parts of the world with very low wage rates. Work on the Northern Spotted Owl controversy, on the other hand, suggests that if work in the old growth forests of the Pacific Northwest is terminated to avoid species extinction, poverty will increase.

This contradiction in the discussion appears to point toward a dilemma encountered by local community leaders and other residents of remote or inaccessible communities with an abundance of any given natural resource. The likelihood of such areas receiving capital investment and economic development is predicated on the willingness of community residents to become part of a resource extraction economy. Yet, if they do, they may become even more impoverished. In the short run, this could be caused by the nature of the wage rates in these firms. In the long run, poverty levels may increase because of profit squeezes, environmentalism, foreign competition, or other factors. Thus, communities in geographically remote locations are caught between a future of economic stagnation and one which is riddled with uncertainty, domination by absentee-owned firms, and the possibility of moral exclusion by increasingly influential environmental groups.

Faced with this kind of choice, most communities will probably risk the uncertainties of seeking public or private investments in their local economies. Otherwise, they are likely to face out-migration, rising unemployment, and relatively high rates of poverty. Economic development efforts are an important part of community life throughout rural America. With the ratio of capital to labor increasing in resource extraction and processing, however, traditional economic development efforts along these lines are unlikely to absorb all the surplus labor. In addition, deindustrialization in urban as well as rural areas in recent years reduces the alternatives which displaced workers have during their working years. Research by members of this Working Group also indicates the positive commitments and cultural affinities which loggers and undoubtedly other workers in the extractive sector have toward their occupations and lifestyles. Even if this were not the case, lower levels of investment in human capital in these communities limit employment alternatives.

Thus, we come to the question of what kinds of economic development are resource-dependent areas likely to experience over and above whatever may occur because of natural resource extraction? Without changing the normative climate in these localities with respect to educational aspirations, a future based on a service economy requiring relatively unskilled workers is one possibility. However, the services most likely in relatively remote locations are of two kinds: (1) activities involving land uses judged to be undesirable in other rural or urban areas such as the management of toxic waste, waste incineration facilities, and the development of public institutions such as prisons and mental hospitals; and (2) seasonal work in recreation and tourist businesses. Both alternatives are important in that they must occur somewhere. Whether either of these possibilities has the capacity to overcome the employment problems and poverty rates in resource extraction regions, however, remains uncertain.

Alternatives to this scenario are recognized in the literature, but they will not occur without imaginative efforts by highly motivated, powerful coalitions of community leaders, the unemployed, state officials and others. Human capital theory indicates that the financial and educational resources of these communities are limited and often controlled by firms with restricted interests in the social well-being of these communities. However, work by Vail indicates that international competition is driving either large or small resource extraction operations in commercial logging to upgrade the technology and skills of workers. We also find a growing literature on the potential for flexible manufacturing systems with computerized information processing capabilities, so manufacturers can produce a diversity of products, thereby reducing the risks associated with more specialized industry (Kenney et al. 1989:144). Thus, we find computerized systems weaving a wide variety of textiles in parts of rural Italy and aircraft and computer assembly operations in parts of rural France (Piore and Sabel 1984). When the demand for a particular good declines, the flexible systems can be reprogrammed for alternative products. Whether such alternative production systems have developed in rural areas of the United States, the social dynamics by which they occur, and the impact of such development on poverty and wealth is, as yet, unknown.

For such development to occur in resource extraction regions of rural America, at least three major changes probably would have to occur. First, rural public education would have to be uncoupled, to some extent, from its dependence on local property taxes. Second, higher educational expectations would have to be promoted, perhaps through state standards and tests. Third, the telecommunication infrastructure in rural areas would have to be brought into line with that in urban areas. Even service enterprises such as motels and resorts now require telecommunication equipment to handle advanced bookings and communication with travel agencies throughout the country. These changes are unlikely to occur without the development of new alliances between local groups and state officials mentioned above, since some resource extraction firms and officials in natural resource bureaucracies gain opportunities for capital accumulation and political power under the status quo. Whether these alliances emerge at all or emerge from either the creative leadership of those concerned about rural poverty or the more desperate and perhaps radical tactics of a growing strata of unemployed and disenfranchised rural people is a question that can only be answered in time.

An alternative to the above scenario involves the formation of coalitions among small farmers, forest landowners, social movement organizations concerned with public health and/or the environment, and the rural poor. Increasing the labor intensity of farming or forest harvesting and soil and forest regeneration could serve a number of interests. First, it would help reduce environmental problems associated with the aerial spraying of herbicides in reforestation projects or biocides in agriculture by using human labor and organic forms of pest management and soil enrichment. Second, it would reduce input costs to farm operators and forest landowners. Third, it could stimulate the kinds of cooperative arrangements such as we find among Swedish forest landowners, since viable, labor intensive agriculture would require changes in the organization of production as well as a shift to more organic forms of production technology.

We have not developed this scenario extensively in the discussion, however, It could only become a significant one if it were promoted by alliances among workers, private landowners, environmentalists, and others. It would require commitments from scientists in research universities and state officials in natural resource bureaucracies to the pursuit of alternatives for agriculture, forestry, and other forms of resource extraction. While this second condition may be developing in state agencies and land grant universities, the first condition at times can be problematic. We know that labor unions, civil rights groups and national environmental groups are forming coalitions, especially in opposition to the siting of toxic waste management facilities in rural and urban communities. However, the divide between labor and environmentalists in the Spotted Owl controversy suggests that the formation of a broad-based coalition of different groups working for improvements in social and environmental welfare can be very challenging. Efforts to stem the incidence of poverty and the struggle for a safer, healthier environment will require that residents in resource-dependent communities and regions, as elsewhere, begin to search for common ground and beginnings toward common action.

Notes

This chapter was prepared by Craig R. Humphrey, The Pennsylvania State University; Gigi Berardi, Gettysburg College; Matthew S. Carroll, Washington State University; Sally Fairfax, University of California-Berkeley; Louise Fortmann, University of California-Berkeley; Charles Geisler, Cornell University; Thomas G. Johnson, Virginia Polytechnic Institute and State University; Jonathan Kusel, University of California-Berkeley, Robert G. Lee, University of Washington; Seth Macinko, University of California-Berkeley; Michael D. Schulman, North Carolina State University; Patrick C. West, University of Michigan.

1. The Orshansky Index assumes that one third of a lower income family's budget is allocated for food. Thus, the Index is based on three times the cost of the U.S. Department of Agriculture's low cost food budget after regional and rural-urban adjustments in the cost of living (Katz, 1989:115).

2. For an important exception to this trend, see Brunelle's (1990) discussion of the changing structure of the forest products industry in the Pacific Northwest. Tracing lumber and plywood production by different sizes of firms between 1978 and 1985, Brunelle (1990:112) finds "...a shift in lumber production from National firms towards Regional and Local firms between 1978 and 1985." Whether comparable trends are evident in other sectors of the extraction industries remains uncertain.

3. For a detailed account of how managers or owners of resource extraction firms, notably coal companies, are able to influence local government in their assessment of corporate land holdings for purposes of taxation, See Caudill (1962).

4. Both the authority and the implementation capacity of a natural resource bureaucracy have to be considered in deciding exactly what kind of policy the agency has or represents. Shover et al.(1986), for example, show that the authority of the U.S. Office of Surface Mining was undercut in the early 1980s by budgetary restraints and opposition from both the Reagan administration and state-level natural resource bureaucracies, making it very difficult for officials to enforce strip mining regulations established during the Carter administration.

5. Much of this work is derived from classical social theory in the writing of Weber, particularly his *Economy and Society*, written between 1910 and 1920. The work was not fully translated into English until 1968. Thus, the reference to Weber (1968). For more on Weber, see West (1982a).

6. Weber (1968:943) has observed that domination through constellation of interests can develop into domination proper or power domination. It can also interact with other forms of domination that can enhance the power base for other forms of domination (West 1982a: 121). According to West (1992), "These are important caveats to watch out for, for they are far from trivial in their consequences for the rural poor."

7. For a parallel example, see the case involving a coalition between the National Park Service and the Sierra Club opposing efforts by the Havasupai Indians to regain control of their ancestral land on the rim of the Grand Canyon. While the interests of the Havasupai prevailed, their use of the rim is restricted to grazing, a limited advantage because of poor soil quality (Hirst 1985; West 1992).

8. For important exceptions see Culhane (1981) and Shover, Clelland and Lynxwiler (1986).

9. State-specific *Land Loss Prevention Manuals* are published by the Federation through their Land Assistance Fund.

10. That some originally resource-dependent communities such as Pittsburgh and San Francisco did eventually diversify and change their status from periphery to core areas only lends more credibility to Bunker's (1989) argument that generalizations about these places and their futures are extremely difficult. But when the resource is depleted, or when substitutes are found elsewhere, the potential for increased levels of either short- or long-term poverty certainly exists.

11. Similar trends are evident in the forest products industry. With the ratio of capital to labor in core, state-of-the-art integrated lumber and paper mills as high as it is, producers avoid plant shutdowns and layoffs to ensure the proper operation and maintenance of equipment and inventories (Marchak 1983: 172-190). Workers in the peripheral sector, including family-based firms in logging and timber hauling, offer inexpensive contracting services to producers on a piece-rate basis. Not unlike the survival of small farmers in an era of agribusiness (Buttel 1982:25-26), small private

contractors in the forest products industry work long hours for low wages to remain in forested rural regions and participate in the industry of their parents.

12. Goldschmidt examined wages, employment turnover, security in labor, social isolation of workers, labor participation in important community decisions, and the strength and diversity of community institutions and infrastructure.

13. The influence of state policies on employment opportunities in resource-dependent communities is important enough to warrant a separate chapter in this volume. In addition, Hooks (1990) discusses how the U.S. Department of Agriculture shifted its support to large scale industrial farming between 1948 and 1952. Macinko (1991) discusses the importance of state policy-making for commercial fisheries in the United States. Work on the role of state policy-making in influencing communities near public forests is discussed by Drielsma et al. (1990), Schallau (1990) and Lee (1990).

14. The term "elite" refers to the "...highest stratum within a field of competence. The elite is composed of those persons who are recognized as outstanding and are considered leaders in a given field...members of an elite have an important influence in shaping the values and attitudes held by their segment of society (Theodorson and Theodorson 1969)."

One could focus on how elites are influencing policies with implications for poverty and well-being in other natural resource contexts as well. Economic activity dependent on agricultural irrigation, hydroelectric power generation, and agricultural and silvicultural practices is likely to be heavily affected by efforts to save threatened or endangered salmon species on the Snake and Columbia rivers. Reduction or complete elimination of cattle grazing on public lands throughout the West could threaten the economic viability of much of the traditional ranching industry. Further restrictions on the subsistence uses of game and fish in Alaska could threaten traditional lifestyles for isolated native and non-native communities (Berardi 1991; Muth 1990).

15. The researchers employed ethnographic methods to study people in timber-dependent communities, including 194 in-depth interviews with a cross-section of those parties involved in the controversy, content analysis of media coverage, and scientific advisory service. For details see (Carroll 1991a; Warren et al. 1991; and Lee 1991).

16. Large timber companies will enjoy substantial windfall profits from price increases accompanying restrictions on supply if public timber is withdrawn from the market. Total asset transfers to foreign and non-restricted domestic suppliers could total as much as $4.7 billion (Lippke et al. 1990).

17. Szasz (1992) defines icons as cultural signs or symbols which have "...highly-condensed and unarticulated meanings and highly-charged value and emotional components conveyed through vivid visual images (and their aural equivalent, 'the sound bite')."

18. Two bills introduced into Congress in 1991 reflect these values: (1) the Forest and Families Protection Act; and (2) the Forest and Community Survival Act.

19. Practices such as hunting and fishing, living in substandard housing, sharing quarters with relatives, gardening, and pooling the costs of utilities (Nord 1991).

6

Persistent Rural Poverty
and Racial and Ethnic Minorities

Introduction

Persistent rural poverty is a problem that afflicts some groups more than others. Historically, Hispanic, African-American, and American Indian communities have endured the most intense forms of economic deprivation and its consequences: malnutrition, ill-health, malaise, and violence. These communities also have in common the experience of brutally repressive measures directed at them for the purpose of maintaining their disadvantaged position. Any meaningful discussion of persistent rural poverty simply cannot overlook the experiences of these groups because their communities are too often at the core of this problem.

Despite the frequently presumed homogeneity of rural America, the social landscape is dotted by a variety of ethnic minority communities. These communities have a distinctive cultural mileau and may be German, Scandinavian, Amish, Mormons, or any number of other ethnic populations who settled the rural countryside in this and the preceding century. They are ethnic minorities but they are not the subject of this discussion.

These groups settled across the countryside in places of their own choosing, often in highly desirable locations, pursued their chosen livelihood, lived as they wished, and often prospered. Few, and possibly none of these things are true for African-Americans, American Indians, and Hispanics living in rural areas. These groups have in common that they are still living in places near the locations where they were first enslaved, placed on a reservation, or exploited for cheap labor and above all, kept under the heel of the dominant society.

Oppressive institutions such as slavery were fundamental in guaranteeing the privileges of white American society. They established the caste system of southern society, made accessible the natural resources of North America, and made available cheap labor for twentieth century agribusiness. The wealth taken out of rural America, and the prosperity of white society in particular, was possible because of institutions that subjugated minority populations. And the circumstance of rural minorities today--blacks, Hispanics, Indians--is that they still live in close proximity to the remnants of these institutions. For instance, Jim Crow as a system of racial oppression is no longer intact but elements persist, as does its legacy. Persistent rural poverty among these minority groups is one legacy of these institutions.

A Working Definition

This discussion focuses on persistent rural poverty as an economic phenomenon, a condition measurable in dollar units, but this premise is certainly open to question. Hypothetically, income is an accurate index of consumption levels, assuming a homogenous urban environment in which currency is the only medium of exchange and where prices for goods and services are invariant. These hypothetical conditions, of course, do not describe rural economics. The worth of subsistence activities such as hunting or fishing cannot be easily assigned a cash value. Because bartering and other subsistence activities are typically overlooked by income measures of poverty, such measures may overstate levels of economic hardship. On the other hand, telephone service and other utilities are often costly or unavailable in rural ares, transportation costs are high, and access to basic services such as health care often is limited or nonexistent. These conditions make rural life costly in ways seldom captured by poverty indices based on income.

Furthermore, there are many kinds of poverty afflicting rural communities besides economic poverty. Another way of looking at it is from the standpoint of deprivation. Poverty represents the deprivation of those elements of daily life considered normatively and physically necessary for leading a life free of sustained physical and psychological hardship. From this perspective, income is only one dimension of poverty. Poverty may also manifest itself in discrimination, physical violence, the denial of opportunities, cultural oppression, and in the countless other ways that deprivation causes personal harm. Income is certainly an important element in this perspective but needless to say, there are many other ways in which groups such as American Indians or African-Americans may experience deprivation.

Nonetheless, income is a substance that is more easily obscured and measured than other types of deprivation. Perhaps for this reason, the social sciences have been fixated on income-based measures of poverty, exclusive of other perspectives. Because of this deeply ingrained tradition, this chapter necessarily is organized around a view of poverty primarily as an economic phenomenon. And despite this narrow focus, readers should be aware that this is but one dimension of a multifaceted problem.

Demographic Background

Considering the amount of attention devoted to the problem of urban poverty, it is perplexing that rural[1] poverty seldom attracts much notice. Official poverty rates are consistently higher in rural areas, regardless of race. Yet a breakdown of poverty rates by race shows that without exception racial and ethnic minorities bear the brunt of economic hardship in rural areas. Rural African- and Mexican-Americans[2] and American Indians consistently rank among the poorest of this nation (see Table 6.1). In 1989, rural poverty rates were 40 percent for African-Americans, 35 percent for Mexican-Americans, and 30 percent for American Indians. Poverty rates for rural whites stood at nearly 13 percent in the same year. In metropolitan areas, poverty rates were 7 percent for whites but higher were urban African-Americans (29 percent), Mexican-Americans (28 percent), and American Indians (16 percent).

It is important to understand that some of these residential differences are compositional. That is, rural areas typically have sizable concentrations of persons who have a high risk of being in poverty regardless of where they reside. Persons with a high risk of being in poverty are economically marginal persons by virtue of their age, education, physical condition, or other work limiting characteristics. Rural areas often have a disproportionate number of such persons, causing rural areas to have even higher rates of poverty than might be otherwise expected.

Rural families also tend to be larger than urban ones and this is certainly a risk factor for poverty, insofar as large numbers of children limit women's labor force participation and strain scarce family resources. However, child-care duties notwithstanding, one of the most proximate causes of poverty for able-bodied working age persons is the inability to find employment, or employment with above-poverty level wages. Existing data clearly show that rural minorities are disproportionately represented among the ranks of low income persons living at the margins of poverty.

The statistics in Table 6.2 reveal that American Indians and African-Americans living in nonmetropolitan areas are twice as likely as their urban counterparts to have near poverty-level incomes despite the fact that these individuals were employed in full-time, full-year jobs. Among full-time, full-year workers, 26 percent of rural American Indians and 25 percent of rural African-Americans did not earn enough to raise themselves about the margins of poverty. Rural Mexican-Americans, with 28 percent near poverty, fared worse than rural blacks or Indians but the gap between them and their urban counterparts was not as great.

TABLE 6.1 Poverty Rates for Individuals by Race/Ethnicity and Residence, 1989

| Race/
Ethnicity | Total | Nonmetro | Total
Metro | Metro | | Weighted N[a] |
				Inside Central Cities	Outside Central Cities	
Total	12.9%	15.9%	12.1%	18.7%	7.6%	158,079
White	8.4	12.6	7.0	9.3	5.4	120,122
African American	30.8	40.0	29.1	33.2	20.0	19,270
Hispanic	26.3	34.5	25.7	29.4	18.5	13,342
Mexican	28.6	37.9	27.7	29.3	21.8	8,543
Other Hispanic	22.2	21.8	22.2*	29.5	11.8	4,799
Native American	22.9	30.3	15.7	15.7	14.3	887
Other	14.5	16.7	14.3*	19.8*	9.7	4,459

* Difference with respect to the nonmetropolitan rate is not significant at .05 using a two-sample test for the significance of differences in proportions.

[a]Weight is divided by mean weight to yield N's approximately equal to CPS sample size. The total metro column includes some cases that, to protect confidentiality of respondents, we suppressed on the central city/non-central city identifier.

Source: March, 1990 Current Population Survey.

Considering that fully one-fourth of full-time, full-year rural minority workers have incomes near or below official poverty thresholds, their tenuous economic position is even starker in the area of underemployment. Underemployment includes the unemployed, "discouraged" workers, part-time workers desiring additional hours, and full-time workers with earnings 125 percent below the official poverty level. By this definition, it is obvious that every segment of rural America is chronically underemployed.

However, compared with white workers, the connection that rural minorities have with the labor market is fragile at best (Table 6.3). Nearly one-half (46 percent) of American Indians are underemployed. African and Mexican-Americans are only slightly better off, as these groups have underemployment rates of 44 and 42 percent respectively. As before, the rural-urban gap is smaller for Mexican-Americans than for blacks or Indians but for all these groups, it is consequential in size.

An important insight into why rural minorities have lower incomes and more underemployment than rural whites or urban minorities can be found in

TABLE 6.2 Near-Poverty Rates Among Those Employed Full-time, Full-year, 1990

Race/ Ethnicity	Total	Nonmetro	Total Metro	Metro Inside Central Cities	Outside Central Cities	Weighted N[a]
Total	6.9%	11.3%	5.8%	8.1%	4.2%	53,890
White	5.1	9.8	3.7	4.1	2.9	42,839
African American	13.2	24.6	11.4	13.4	8.4	5,454
Hispanic	18.3	25.8	17.8	19.6	15.4	3,884
Mexican	22.3	28.3	21.8	22.2*	20.7	2,331
Other Hispanic	12.3	17.6	12.1*	16.4*	7.0	2,553
Native American[b]	18.4	26.2	13.6	27.1*	7.0	216
Other	5.3	7.0	5.2*	4.9*	4.9*	1,497

* Difference with respect to the nonmetropolitan rate is not significant at .05 using a two-sample test for the significance of differences in proportions.

[a]Weight is divided by mean weight to yield N's approximately equal to CPS sample size. The total metro column includes some cases that, to protect confidentiality of respondents, we suppressed on the central city/non-central city identifier.
[b]Estimates for Native Americans should be regarded with caution given low N's. The sample contains 190, 237, 80 and 92 Native Americans aged 25-64 in nonmetro, metro, central city and suburban areas respectively.

Source: March, 1990 Current Population Survey.

Table 6.4. It is obvious that rural minorities have a serious human capital deficit compared to rural whites or urban minorities. About 81 percent of nonmetropolitan whites have at least the equivalent years of a high school diploma. Yet only 65 percent of American Indians, and 42 and 58 percent of Mexican- and African-Americans had an equal amount of education. The rural-urban education gap for African-Americans is an especially striking 18 percentage points.

The rural-urban difference in education for these minority populations may be partially explained by migration: better educated persons leave rural areas to pursue opportunities in urban labor markets. Certainly, lower levels of schooling are consistent with some explanations about the causes of poverty. In fact, there is a rich array of models available to explain poverty among rural

TABLE 6.3 Percent Underemployed by Race/Ethnicity and Residence, 1990[a]

Race/ Ethnicity	Total	Nonmetro	Total Metro	Metro		Weighted N[b]
				Inside Central Cities	Outside Central Cities	
Total	28.2%	33.4%	26.8%	28.6%	25.0%	76,449
White	26.9	32.1	25.3	25.2	24.6	59,634
African American	33.6	43.7	31.8	34.7	25.5	8,393
Hispanic	33.4	41.7	32.7	33.8	29.4	5,982
Mexican	35.9	41.5	35.4	35.4	32.2	3,718
Other Hispanic	29.2	42.2	28.6	31.7	24.6	2,263
Native American[c]	38.4	46.3	32.0	44.7*	23.8	370
Other	26.1	32.9	25.7*	27.8*	23.6	2,070

* Difference with respect to the nonmetropolitan rate is <u>not</u> significant at .05 using a two-sample test for the significance of differences in proportions.

   [a]Following Clogg and Sullivan (1983) the underemployed include the unemployed, discouraged workers, part-time workers who would like to work more but cannot, and full-time workers whose earnings are below 125% of official poverty thresholds.
   [b]Weight is divided by mean weight to yield N's approximately equal to CPS sample size. The total metro column includes some cases that, to protect confidentiality of respondents, we suppressed on the central city/non-central city identifier.
   [c]Estimates for Native Americans should be regarded with caution given low N's. The sample contains 190,237, 80 and 92 Native Americans aged 25-64 in nonmetro, metro, central city and suburban areas respectively.

Source: March, 1990 Current Population Survey.

minorities. These models can be represented by two types of perspectives: human resource deficits and structural discontinuities.

Explanations for Persistent Rural Poverty

Human Resource Deficits

   Human capital theory is a neoclassical economic model that posits that workers are compensated in proportion to their productivity in the workplace. In this context, productivity is a function of skills acquired through education,

TABLE 6.4 Percent of Those Aged 25-64 Who Have Completed Twelve or More Years of Schooling, 1990

Race/ Ethnicity	Total	Nonmetro	Total Metro	Metro Inside Central Cities	Metro Outside Central Cities	Weighted N[a]
Total	82.8%	78.1%	84.0%	79.5%	86.9%	81,528
White	87.1	80.9	89.0	89.0	89.9	63,453
African American	73.1	57.7	76.0	73.8	82.4	9,042
Hispanic	53.3	48.9	53.6	48.8	57.7	6,298
Mexican	46.5	42.2	46.8*	43.9*	47.9*	3,786
Other Hispanic	63.7	68.9	63.4*	54.8	73.5*	2,512
Native American[b]	71.1	65.4	75.8	77.7	74.5*	428
Other	84.4	82.8	85.0*	80.9*	88.5*	2,308

* Difference with respect to the nonmetropolitan rate is <u>not</u> significant at .05 using a two-sample test for the significance of differences in proportions.

[a]Weight is divided by mean weight to yield N's approximately equal to CPS sample size. The total metro column includes some cases that, to protect confidentiality of respondents, we suppressed on the central city/non-central city identifier.
[b]Estimates for Native Americans should be regarded with caution given low N's. The sample contains 190,237, 80 and 92 Native Americans aged 25-64 in nonmetro, metro, central city and suburban areas respectively.

Source: March, 1990 Current Population Survey.

training, and work experience (Becker 1964; Ehrenberg and Smith 1982). A large number of studies have corroborated this view with findings showing a positive relationship between earnings and measures of human capital such as schooling and work experience (McLaughlin and Perman 1991).

This framework explains income (or more precisely--earnings) differences among groups such as men and women, rural and urban residents, or blacks and whites as reflections of differential human capital resources. Rural African-Americans earn less than rural whites, for example, because rural blacks have fewer human capital resources than white workers. Empirically, the human capital deficits of rural minorities relative to white workers are certainly consistent with this perspective (Bean and Tienda 1987; Farley and Allen 1987;

Snipp 1989). Of course, the explanation scarcely addresses the subject of *why* rural minorities have less education.

Status attainment research is a body of literature closely paralleling human capital theory. Both regard variability in the distribution of education as crucial for understanding inequality in the distribution of other valued resources. Status attainment research is distinct from human capital theory partially because it focuses on earnings as well as on indicators of social status, occupational status in particular. Education plays a key role because it is crucial for attaining high status, well-paid occupations. Status attainment research extends the basic human capital model by attempting to explain variability in the distribution of educational resources as well as variability in status and income (Blau and Duncan 1967; Sewell, Haller and Ohlendorf 1970).

Status attainment models specify that variability in educational resources is a function of family background, ability, and social psychological factors such as ambition and the encouragement of others. These background factors are responsible for educational attainments which in turn, lead to achievements in occupational status and income. A wealth of empirical data has been martialed in support of these models, and there is little question that these background factors play a major role in educational achievement and ultimately success in adult life (Haller 1982).

The implications of these models for persistent poverty among rural minorities are fairly clear. The disadvantaged position of rural minorities is directly connected to low levels of educational achievements among these groups. The absence of schooling among these groups is, of course, due to their limited background resources, especially the low social status of their families, limited ambitious, encouragement from others, and poor academic skills (McLeod 1987; Mizruchi 1967; Bandura 1986; Wilson 1991).

Viewing income and social status as the cumulative end-product of lifetime achievements does allow for the possibility of racial discrimination beyond the workplace--as it is so confined in human capital theory. In other words, racial discrimination can affect adult achievement in the workplace, at school, or in the encouragement that a student might receive from teachers and peers. Studies have shown that African-Americans receive less schooling than whites with similar social backgrounds (Featherman and Hauser 1978).

In recent years, interest in status attainment models has declined. However, extensions of this work have incorporated the Labor Utilization Framework and found that blacks are substantially more likely than whites to be underemployed (Clogg, Ogenda, and Shin 1991). Lichter (1989) used this framework to examine the position of blacks in the rural South and found that they were more likely to be underemployed than urban blacks in the South, northern blacks, and whites.

"Cultural capital" (Bourdieu and Passeron 1977; Collins 1979) is another, more difficult to quantify human resource that enhances, or impedes access to labor markets. "Cultural capital" includes certain kinds of behavior, tastes, and attitudes that are markers of social class. Upper class parents, for example, imbue their children with attitudes and behaviors valued by other members of the same social class, and in doing so, provide their children with a resource that will help them gain entry and acceptance in upper class circles. Access to these social networks also means access to school and job opportunities as well as other kinds of economic advantages. From this perspective, minority populations are disadvantaged because they have cultural practices that differ from those valued by economic elites, and lack the cultural resources that might help them obtain access to elite networks.

While the notion of cultural capital has been used to explain the reproduction of privileged classes in society, "culture of poverty" perspectives (Lewis 1969; Duncan and Tickamyer 1988; Tickamyer and Duncan 1990) deal directly with the persistence of poverty among ethnic minorities. Cultural capital is a positive resource that can be used to gain access to economic resources but the so-called culture of poverty is a collection of behaviors, attitudes, and tastes that are at best unhelpful in the job market, and more commonly are detrimental. Culture of poverty perspectives allege that the lifestyles of ethnic minorities are organized in a manner that limit economic success. For example, this view would argue that American Indians who are fully committed to the ceremonial life of their tribe cannot expect to become economically successful because their ceremonial obligations might prevent them holding steady employment.

The idea of cultural capital has not been used to explain persistent poverty among rural ethnic minorities. However, the culture of poverty has been widely invoked in the past to explain this problem, and its failings as an explanation have been well critiqued. Culture of poverty explanations suffer from several shortcomings. One problem is that they are virtually impossible to verify with empirical research. Pinpointing the elements of minority culture that can be consistently and directly linked to economic failure is a futile exercise. Not surprisingly, another problem with this perspective is that it lacks empirical support. A third problem is that culture of poverty explanations fail entirely to recognize practices such as racial discrimination; and that ostensibly maladaptive cultural practices may in fact be rational responses for dealing with oppression imposed by the dominant society.

Structural Discontinuities

Dissatisfaction with human capital and status attainment models in the 1970s spurred the development of models explicitly concerned with the impact of social structure and labor market organization. While human capital and status attainment models were concerned with conditions in the labor supply, critics argued that these models paid insufficient attention to factors affecting labor demand. These critics also charged human capital and status attainment models with being overly individualistic and unmindful that circumstances beyond the control of workers also can play a key role in their well-being.

Dual labor market theory is concerned with the effect of labor market organization on worker outcomes. As its name suggests, this model posits that the U.S. labor market is divided into two discrete segments: primary and secondary employment sectors. These sectors differ by the occupations found within them. Jobs in the primary sector are secure, well-compensated, and offer opportunities for career advancement. Conversely, jobs in the secondary sector have few fringe benefits, are poorly paid, unstable, and offer few opportunities for promotion (Doeringer and Piore 1971; Kalleberg and Sorenson 1979; Snipp and Bloomquist 1989).

Dual economy theory closely parallels dual labor market theory. This perspective is concerned with the structure of industrial production and how it affects worker well-being. Again, this theory posits two sectors of industrial production designated as core and periphery (Beck, Horan and Tolbert 1978; Tolbert, Horan and Beck 1980). Industries in the core sector are large-scale, capital intensive operations with a highly unionized workforce. Workers in these industries enjoy higher wage rates, more stable employment, and better working conditions than workers in the periphery sector. Periphery sector industries tend to be smaller firms with labor intensive production technologies. They are often economically marginal operations and this makes their workers vulnerable to lay-offs, low wages, and poor working conditions.

Relatively little work has been done using dual economy or labor market theory to explain persistent poverty among rural minorities. Yet the implications of these models for this subject are fairly obvious. Presumably, minorities in rural areas find themselves concentrated in the secondary/periphery sectors of the economy, hence their low wages and other economic disadvantages. However, the empirical data bearing on this idea presents a more complex picture. There is little systematic evidence that economic structure adversely affects the earnings of black workers more than whites (Parcel and Mueller 1983; Hodson 1983), meaning that racial segregation is not endemic to economic segmentation. At least one study indicates that racial discrimination is greater in core than in periphery industries (Beck, Horan and Tolbert 1981). There is general agreement, however, that within sectors, black workers typically have lower-paying, less desirable jobs than whites (Snipp and Bloomquist 1989).

Beyond these limited findings, the economic segmentation literature offers few insights into rural poverty. And it is important to remember that there are other structural discontinuities besides economic segmentation. Uneven development is a particularly important matter because there is considerable evidence that economic growth does not equally benefit all groups in rural areas. Rural minorities seldom receive significant benefits from economic development (Summers et al. 1976; Colclough 1988; Falk and Lyson 1988).

Some analysts have argued that the structure of economic inequality has an important spatial dimension (Snipp and Bloomquist 1989). Models of "uneven development" posit that certain areas or places are subject to economic exploitation by other places or areas. These models typically specify that a "core" metropolitan region economically exploits less urban "periphery" places by using their size, influence, and power to obtain inexpensive raw materials, cheap labor, and otherwise prevent economic resources from reaching these places (Baran 1957; Frank 1967; Hechter 1975). This perspective has been used to describe the distribution of inequality in the U.S. south, especially in the so-called black belt (Falk and Lyson 1988), and the exploitation of natural resources on American Indian reservations (see Snipp 1988 for a review).

The formation of ethnic enclaves is another type of development about which little is known. In urban areas, there is some research suggesting that enclave economies provide a protected environment for ethnic entrepreneurs (Waldinger et al. 1990). Some analysts also argue that enclave economies are beneficial because they provide opportunities for escaping dead-end secondary labor market jobs in the mainstream economy (Portes and Bach 1985). Yet the evidence supporting this idea is limited and controversial (Sanders and Nee 1987, 1992; Portes and Jensen 1992).

In relation to rural minorities, the dynamics of enclave economies are poorly understood. However, rural minorities often live in deliberately created enclaves--segregated neighborhoods, reservations, and colonias. Yet these places are ordinarily bereft of the kinds of activity associated with enclave economies. Why there is so little economic activity in these communities is puzzling, especially given the experience of urban minorities such as Cubans. Nevertheless, the absence of capital (physical and human), infrastructure, and the absence of other conditions necessary to stimulate economic growth are problematic. And last, but certainly not least, the proximity of rural minority communities to the historic institutions of social oppression should not be underestimated.

The Inadequacy of Existing Perspectives

Social scientists have been actively involved in poverty-related research for well over 25 years, and longer considering that the study of inequality has been a preoccupation since the earliest days of the discipline. Despite this long-standing concern, the fact remains that the U.S. continues to have significant numbers of its citizens living in severe economic hardship. This alone should underscore the inability of contemporary social science to provide meaningful alternatives that might significantly reduce the prevalence of poverty, if not eliminate it altogether.

Models such as human capital and status attainment have been faulted for a variety of shortcomings (for a review see Snipp and Bloomquist 1989). Human capital theory, for example, rests on a number of assumptions from neo-classical economic theory which may or may not be empirically true about market conditions and behavior; for example that all workers are competing for the same pool of jobs, or that all workers have the same knowledge about market conditions. Status attainment and human capital theories focus exclusively on supply-side variables to explain the genesis and reproduction of inequality and poverty. This emphasis, of course, leads to policy implications suggesting that individuals are in some way responsible for their lack of economic success, and a premium is placed on strategies for modifying individual behavior and characteristics.

The shortcomings of perspectives such as human capital and status attainment, especially the absence of concern with demand-side conditions, prompted much of the work dealing with structural discontinuities. However, from the standpoint of rural minorities, this work also leaves much to be desired. First, this literature is bereft of studies dealing directly with poverty among racial and ethnic minorities in rural areas. Certainly there are conclusions that can be drawn but what can be learned from this literature is at best indirect and inferential. A related problem is that this work neglects almost entirely the problem of market discrimination, and if anything, treats this subject in a manner identical to the way it is handled in status attainment and human capital theory--as a residual net of all other known antecedents to poverty and income. Finally, while this approach deals with "structure" in a narrowly defined economic sense, it does not deal with other types of social organization known to affect the economic well-being of minority populations; that is, the institutional structures mobilized to maintain the subordinate position of minority communities in rural areas.

One of the principal weaknesses of the existing literature concerning rural poverty is that it fails to address the position of minority communities within the larger social and economic matrix of the dominant society. Rural racial and ethnic minorities live in physically distinct communities, isolated to a greater or lesser degree from Anglo society. Explanations of poverty and inequality that fail to appreciate this isolation also fail to deal with its impact on rural minorities. Such models assume a market in which, at most, individual workers are discriminated against by individual employers. Such perspectives overlook entirely a much more complex reality in which multiple barriers surrounding minority communities exist for the purpose of denying them access to resources enjoyed by the dominant society. These barriers are much more formidable because they transcend market relations and defy narrowly constructed economic solutions to rural poverty.

Put another way, these perspectives neglect the fact that rural minority populations live in communities, that these communities are more or less separate from those of whites, and that the well-being of institutions within these communities is vital for the people living within them. It is simply impossible to address the needs of individuals without also addressing the needs of the communities in which they live. In desperately poor minority communities, it may be possible to help a few by giving them the skills to succeed elsewhere, but many others will be left behind and ultimately those left behind will become the poorest of the poor. From this perspective, communities are the incubators of persistent rural poverty.

Reservations, Colonias, and the Other Side of the Tracks

Taking a community perspective on the matter of persistent rural poverty among rural racial and ethnic minorities means going beyond the usual focus on market processes and worker outcomes characteristic of most poverty-related research. A community perspective necessarily has to be much more broad-gauged in scope, dealing with the internal dynamics of minority communities as well as the political economic context in which these communities exist. Understanding these issues for rural American Indian, African-American, and Hispanic communities sets the parameters for the next generation of research.

Reservations

There can be little mistake that American Indians in rural areas, most of whom reside on federal reservations, live in the shadow of the institutions created for their subordination. The original motive for creating reservations in the 19th century was for isolating and containing American Indians in places distant from the mainstream of American society. In the early years of the reservation system, these places functioned as internment camps where Indian communities were supervised by military and other federal authorities. It was expected that eventually, with education, Christian conversion, and other measures designed to "civilize" Indians, reservations would no longer be needed.

In the early years of their existence, reservations functioned fully as concentration camps where Indians were quarantined, isolated, and kept out of the mainstream of American society. Until the *Standing Bear* Supreme Court decision in 1879, American Indians were not considered persons entitled to *habeas corpus* rights. Reservations were also places where American Indians were deprived of their self-sufficiency; they were not allowed to pursue game off the reservation, nor were they allowed to possess firearms. Under such circumstances, reservation Indians depended entirely on rations provided by their military overlords. On many reservations, modern welfare dependency differs from the past only in substituting cash payments for military rations.

By the early 20th century, most observers expected American Indians to vanish entirely but defying these expectations, the American Indian population has grown rapidly throughout this century, including the numbers of Indians living on reservations. However, reservations have shed their old function as internment camps. As the last remaining land base, reservations have taken on new importance as places central to tribal culture and social life. By virtue of a complex legal history of treaties, court decisions, and other agreements, American Indians living on reservations continue to exercise a certain amount of jurisdiction over the affairs of their communities. This is made possible by the doctrine of tribal sovereignty, a legal theory that allows tribes a high degree of autonomy from state and local authorities yet keeps them subordinate to the federal government. Reservation lands are not only a place for the practice of tribal culture, they also represent political boundaries in which American Indians still enjoy a measure of self-rule.

Tribal sovereignty is enormously important for a number of reasons, especially for tribal survival and improving living standards. Recognition of tribal sovereignty allow tribes to collectively purchase lands that are immune from taxation and alienation. It also allows tribes control over land use, especially for taxation, zoning, and development purposes.

The unique political and legal status of reservations is not without liabilities however. Because of the special relationship that tribes have with the federal government, the Bureau of Indian Affairs (BIA) exists solely for the purpose of managing reservation matters. Historically, the BIA has been a coercive institution charged with implementing policies designed to maintain the subordinate position of American Indians. In recent decades, the problems associated with the BIA stem less from deliberate malice and more from persistent problems of incompetence, fraud, and mismanagement. For example, the BIA has been frequently censured for mismanaging tribal resources, especially the vast energy resources found on some reservations (Ambler 1990). Similarly, one assessment of BIA administration found that fully one-third of the BIA budget is devoted to administration, and for every federal dollar spent on Indian affairs, only 12 cents ever reaches an American Indian (White 1990:274).

Reservations also are heavily dependent on the federal government for the resources needed for local administration. This, along with the dearth of economic activity on most reservations means that the federal and tribal governments typically are the single largest employers in many of these communities. This also means that a large share of the reservation workforce is highly vulnerable to shifting political agendas. Reservation workers are impacted by political developments in Washington, D.C. as new programs are funded, or as old ones are discontinued. Similarly, changes in tribal administration may create new jobs or eliminate old ones. Unemployment on many reservations skyrocketed following the large cuts in federal funding in the early 1980s.

The vulnerability of reservation economies to external politics, especially in Washington, D.C., has caused tribal leadership to look for other sources of revenue. "Economic development" has become a shorthand expression for a variety of tribal ventures in private enterprise. Some of these developments have involved leasing tribal resources but the standard of living for tribes with energy resources is not very different from those without resources (Snipp 1988). Other ventures have ranged from tourist developments to light manufacturing. The results of these efforts have been mixed successes.

Many reservations have exploited their sovereign status to obtain a competitive advantage. Activities such as the sale of tax-free tobacco products and tax exemptions for outside businesses are examples. Perhaps most lucrative has been the development of gambling related tourism. Although state governments frequently object to reservation gambling, the principle of tribal sovereignty puts this activity beyond their control, at least for awhile.

Cornell and Kalt (1990) argue that tribal political organization and the rights and jurisdiction associated with tribal sovereignty also represent resources for economic development. They argue that tribal control and a direct stake in tribal interests are central to the creation of successful economic development projects (Cornell and Kalt 1990). Case studies of successful tribal ventures indicate that effective leadership with a free hand to direct tribal efforts result in profitable tribal ventures (White 1990).

Cornell and Kalt (1990) also contend that tribal culture has an important, if elusive, impact on reservation development. By stating this, they are not resorting to old ideas about the "culture of poverty." However, in the course of observing successful and unsuccessful development projects, they conclude that successful developments were often projects that did not conflict with tribal values or lifestyles. From this perspective, the key to planning a successful project is to be able to identify ones that are "culturally appropriate" to the community.

At this time, American Indian communities are among the most impoverished in the nation. Dependency on the federal government has done little to alleviate this problem, and some would argue that this has exacerbated the problem. Yet many tribes have taken steps to bring jobs and income to their communities and to obtain revenues to provide for those who cannot work. The eventual success of these efforts will be crucial for community well-being but at this time, success is by no means assured.

Colonias

Since the early years of this century, migrant labor has been a mainstay in American agriculture. Nowhere has this been more true than in the agricultural regions of the west, especially in California, Texas, and other regions of the southwest. The overwhelming majority of this labor has been supplied by immigrant Mexican workers and Mexican-Americans from south Texas, especially since the early years of this century. Although mechanization has had a tremendous impact on the amount of labor required by western agribusiness, farmworkers are still an essential part of this industry, especially in vegetable crop production.

One consequence of the exploitation of Mexican labor by western agribusiness has been the formation of *colonias*. Colonias are small settlements of Mexican workers scattered throughout rural western areas, especially in California and south Texas. These communities formed to meet the needs of migrant workers for inexpensive housing, but are plagued by a lack of public services, and a variety of health problems. Colonia residents include a sizable number of immigrant workers but often, the majority are native-born. In south Texas, about two-thirds of colonia residents were born in the U.S. (Texas Department of Human Services 1988).

Colonias formed in the early part of this century when a variety of "push" and "pull" factors stimulated Mexican immigration into the United States. The Mexican revolution of 1910 was a major impetus for early immigration as migrants fled the unrest and instability of this conflict. Around the same time, the introduction of modern irrigation technology and the growth of western agribusiness fueled the demand for cheap labor to work the fields and harvest the crops. The influx of destitute immigrants was a boon for western agribusiness in search of cheap labor but did little beyond yielding a subsistence living for the workers.

The onset of the Great Depression was a major set-back for Mexican workers because many were deported or forced to repatriate. Mexican workers also became the objects of racially motivated attacks by jobless white workers seeking agricultural employment (Galarza 1977). Although colonias dwindled in numbers during this time, they were especially important as refuges from the hostility of surrounding Anglo communities.

The slack demand for farm labor changed abruptly with the outbreak of World War II. In response, the Bracero Program was legislated in 1942 to encourage Mexican immigration and insure an inexpensive source of farm labor. This program granted easy entry into the U.S. for Mexican workers seeking temporary employment in agriculture. Although the Bracero Program was originally passed as an emergency war time measure, it remained intact until it was abolished in 1964; while in effect, it provided between 40 and 70 percent of the work force for specialty vegetable and fruit crops (Mehra 1989 quoted in Castillo 1991).

The Bracero Program had two major impacts on western colonias. One is that the influx of new immigrant workers swelled the numbers living in colonias. This, of course, stretched already scarce resources such as housing and sanitary facilities. The other impact of the Bracero program is that it changed the demographic composition of the colonias. In particular, colonias became filled with single young men in search of work. This altered employment patterns as younger male workers were used to displace older, more established workers-- braceros could be used as strikebreakers (Mines and Anzaldua, quoted in

Castillo 1991). This undermined the position of older, more established Mexican immigrants, many with families, and helped to depress the wages paid to farm workers.

The emergence of colonias has been instrumental for agricultural production. On one hand, they have served as "ports-of-entry" for Mexican immigrants, providing access to necessities such as cheap housing, social and family contacts, and information about employment. At the same time, their proximity to large-scale agricultural production has made these places into labor "reservoirs" that can be tapped at will by agribusiness interests. The labor supply is further leveled by the ebb and flow of migrant workers in colonias.

The subordinate position of colonia residents has been sustained in a number of ways. The overwhelming dominance of agribusiness in the market for low-skill labor means that immigrant Mexicans with little education have few other alternatives for employment. Furthermore, U.S. immigration policies can be used to take advantage of the massive population growth in Mexico by ensuring an abundant supply of workers. Under these circumstances, agribusiness interests are well-positioned to dictate the price they pay for labor.

In response to the disproportionate power exercised by agribusiness interests, farm workers have attempted several times in this century to organize for their mutual protection--the United Farm Workers are the best known and most successful effort (Thomas and Friedland 1982). However, these efforts met with brutal attempts to repress them, usually with physical violence and strikebreakers. Mechanization also has been a potent weapon aimed at under-cutting the bargaining power of farm workers, as it has given growers an alternative, albeit an expensive one, to paying higher farm labor wages.

Mechanization and other technologies also had an impact on growers themselves. Mechanization changed the structure of western agribusiness by increasing the capital intensity of agricultural production, and this eliminated many smaller producers and concentrated ownership among a few large producers. The changing structure of western agriculture had a rebounding effect on farm labor and the colonias. Palerm (1988) argues that the changing technology in modern agriculture has been accompanied by increasing differentiation in the agricultural labor force. Some farm workers are skilled, relatively better-paid, and are mostly sedentary. Others are less skilled, more migrant, but able to find year-round employment. A third group are unskilled, highly mobile workers who experience sustained spells of unemployment, are poorly paid, and easily exploited.

The differentiation of the colonia workforce has implications for the internal stratification of these communities. Certainly the presence of sedentary workers will give longevity to these localities. However, it is not clear whether this will alter the position of these places in the local or national economies, especially because colonia workers have increasingly become employed in non-agricultural industries such as garment production in Los Angeles. However, this has not fundamentally altered their subordinate position in the workforce, as colonia residents are increasingly employed in sweatshops and low-paid assembly work.

Compared with American Indian reservations, nearly all of which have some type of land base and political organization, colonia development faces major obstacles. Unlike Hispanic communities such as Cubans in Miami, colonias do not have integrated industries characteristic of enclave economies. In fact, they have few retail or other kinds of establishments; they are dependent on nearby Anglo communities for consumer goods as well as for employment. This dependence has prompted some observers to invoke an analogy with colonialism to describe the position of colonias: cheap labor is the raw material extracted from these settlements, while their dependence on external sources of consumer goods is imposed by a variety of institutions ranging from racial discrimination to immigration policies.

The Other Side of the Tracks: Rural African-Americans

Before 1865, rural African-American communities were atypical. The existence of African-American communities today are linked directly to the abolition of slavery and not surprisingly, most are dispersed throughout the South. There are rural black communities in other regions of the United States, especially in the West, but certainly they are fewer in number than in the South. Reconstruction and the adoption of Jim Crow legislation helped ensure that these communities were isolated from the white mainstream, and economic practices such as sharecropping and employment discrimination have made these places among the poorest in America.

Poverty in the African-American population has been a longstanding research issue since the publication of *The Philadelphia Negro* by W.E.B. Dubois in 1899. Yet, with only a few exceptions, the plethora of studies dealing with African-American poverty have focused almost exclusively on urban areas. The lack of attention given to rural black poverty is puzzling but for no other reason than the simple fact that conditions are worse in rural areas than in urban ones.

The legacy of American apartheid is perhaps no more evident anywhere else in the United States than in the old South where rural black communities are still concentrated, especially in the region known as the "Black belt" (Falk and Lyson 1988). Segregation as a legal institution played a central role in maintaining the isolation of these communities and denying them access to resources available to nearby white communities. For example, during the 1930s, cooperatives formed by the Rural Electrification Act were kept racially separated (Suitts 1991). Other rural development activities in the 1930s such as the Farm Security Administration (FSA) were kept racially segregated and ultimately these efforts fell under the control of wealthy white farmers (Suitts 1991).

The repressive social climate of the Jim Crow South and the collapse of its agriculture economy, especially cotton, sustained the northward migration that had started around the turn of the century (Fligstein 1981). Fligstein (1981) also points out that boll weevil infestation and mechanization had a devastating impact on black tenant farmers, effectively displacing them and black farm laborers from agriculture altogether. The displacement of blacks from agriculture was another impetus for migration.

The northward migration of rural southern blacks had two important consequences. One is that it contributed to the urbanization of the black population and their concentration in northern cities. The other outcome is that it caused many rural African-American communities to dwindle. Between 1920 and 1950 the southern rural black population declined from 6,733,00 to 5,426,000. In the same period, the number of blacks living in urban areas of the north and west grew from 1,424,000 to 4,790,000 (U.S. Bureau of the Census 1976). As of 1980, 85 percent of the black population lives in urban areas with 46 percent concentrated in the north and west; barely 14 percent of the black population lives in the rural South[3]. There is little doubt that the depopulation of rural black communities in the South robbed these places of vital human resources as the ablest left in search of opportunities elsewhere.

The mechanization of cotton production in the South and the burgeoning post-War economy of the North fueled the streams of out-migrants from rural black communities in the 1950s and 1960s (Fligstein 1981). However, the Civil Rights movement swept across the South during this period and was responsible for abating some of the most repressive practices of the Jim Crow South. Although politically liberating, the Civil Rights movement provided little relief from the economic hardship plaguing these areas. In fact, the Civil Rights movement, to the extent that it opened opportunities elsewhere, may have spurred talented African-Americans in rural areas to leave these places behind at an even more rapid rate. As Wilson (1980) argues, the Civil Rights movement was a predominantly middle-class movement. African-Americans who benefitted most from the movement were those who already were well-positioned to take advantage of the opportunities it produced, namely the black middle-class. For this reason, the Civil Rights movement produced limited economic gains for poverty-stricken rural blacks, despite the fact that rural black communities were engulfed by some of the most intense conflicts.

In every sense of the term, rural black communities have become "places left behind." In recent years, much has been written, especially in the popular press, about the return of African-Americans to the South. Arguably, these return migrants have been attracted by growing black political power and especially by the southern economic boom of the 1970s and 1980s. However, black return migration coupled with economic growth in the South have not meant that rural black communities are being rejuvenated. As Falk and Lyson (1988) point out, economic development in the South is highly uneven, and concentrated in urban areas; once again, leaving behind rural black communities.

As places left behind, the poverty-stricken character of these places contrast starkly with the affluence of white society, and with the growing urban black middle-class. In many respects, this disparity mirrors the stratification of blacks in urban areas--especially the division between middle-class blacks and the so-called urban underclass (Wilson 1987). However, the plight of rural African-American communities have been virtually unnoticed compared with the attention devoted to the urban "underclass."

No doubt gang warfare, drugs, and violence attract more attention than the quiet poverty of rural black communities. Nonetheless, there are ways that the experiences of poor rural blacks parallel those of the urban underclass. For example, families headed by single women have increased dramatically since 1960 in rural areas, more than doubling within two decades. In 1960, 27 percent of poor black families in rural areas were headed by women and by 1980, this number had risen to 59 percent (Dill and Williams 1992). The result is a large concentration of African-American women and children living in poverty conditions.

Predictably, there are enormous barriers facing any attempt to rejuvenate rural black communities. However, Horton (1992) proposes a five-point plan designed to rebuild and fortify the institutions of rural African-American communities. Echoing Alinsky, his plan begins with the premise that strategies for coping with rural black poverty must be focused on the community as a whole, and it must be a solution that arises from the community and not imposed by external agents. The five elements of the Black Organizational Autonomy (BOA) model include (1) Economically autonomous black social institutions; (2) internally developed and controlled data sources; (3) an emphasis on black history and culture; (4) the development and incorporation of black women in leadership roles; and (5) socially inclusive leadership.

Economically autonomous black social institutions are central to the BOA model. Financial independence provides the foundation for the other elements in the model by allowing for the development and implementation of programs free from external interference. A weakness of existing programs for disadvantaged communities is that their unpopularity with the white middle-class makes them vulnerable to political scapegoating.

The need for community-based data sources may appear less crucial but such information is vital for planning and managing community development efforts. An emphasis on history and culture is especially important for unifying the black community, especially in the face of growing class divisions between rural and urban populations, by reminding community members of their common origins and cultural heritage. Community development efforts also must be socially inclusive. Horton (1992) maintains that too often in the past, most of these efforts have tilted toward the urban black middle-class, and have included too few women.

The BOA model has not been widely adopted as a strategy for community development. However, it represents criteria that might be considered as a general framework for rural black community development. The utility of this model remains to be seen but without doubt, it underscores the basic elements needed to revitalize rural black communities.

Common Problems and Unique Situations

The single, most obvious characteristic that reservations, colonias, and rural black communities have in common is that all of them are desperately poor places--among the poorest places in American society. Another trait they have in common is that they are isolated from the rest of American society. By definition, their rural location makes them physically isolated from the urban mainstream. These communities also have been devastated by racial discrimination and repressive measures that have kept them socially isolated from an otherwise prosperous society.

Reservations, colonias, and rural black communities, unlike other communities, share the experience of living nearby the historical remnants of institutions designed to conquer and oppress them. A list of these institutions is depressingly long: the Bureau of Indian Affairs, tribal police, labor contractors, immigration authorities, slavery, Jim Crow, sharecropping and plantation agriculture--to name only the most obvious ones. These institutions, along with unremitting discrimination and the constant threat of physical harm, have been extremely effective in subordinating minority communities throughout the history of this nation. Despite these common experiences, it is important to remember that these communities also have unique qualities that defy generalization.

American Indian reservations, for example, have a unique political and legal status. The doctrine of tribal sovereignty guarantees tribes a measure of political autonomy seldom found in colonias or rural African-American communities. Furthermore, most tribes have some kind of reservation land base. Reservation lands may or may not be well-endowed with natural resources but at the very least, they are property that tribal communities may claim in common. Political sovereignty combined with land, and possibly natural resources, offer tribes development opportunities that have been limited by institutional barriers erected in the past.

Colonias have the doubtful benefit of being more recent in origin, and escaped the most brutally repressive periods in U.S. race relations history. They have not experienced violence on the same scale as that used to maintain slavery or establish the reservation system. Besides their relatively recent origins, these communities are perhaps most unique for their dynamic populations. From their inception, colonias have been primarily immigrant communities, and as such, they have had abundant populations, and especially abundant numbers of able-bodied workers. They are communities with a rich reserve of undeveloped human capital. Colonias also are unique because they have the distinction of being concentrated in the most economically dynamic region of the nation--the so-called "sunbelt". The combination of human capital reserves and proximity to southwestern "sunbelt" economic growth presents these communities with development opportunities not available to either reservations or rural black communities. However, colonia residents must find ways to overcome the institutional barriers that in the past have prevented them from developing the human capital of their workers and that have denied them access to the mainstream economy of the southwest--overcoming the institutional measures that have enforced their isolation.

Rural African-American communities are unique for many reasons. One is their legacy from slavery, the most oppressive of all known social institutions. Another is their place in the Civil Rights movement, one of the most important events in American history that ultimately empowered all minority communities. Although rural black communities gained few economic benefits from the civil rights movement, the struggles for these rights took place in venues like Philadelphia, MS. They are rich in the culture and heritage of all African-Americans, and revitalizing rural black communities may depend heavily on support from this urban constituency. And in many respects, urban middle-class blacks who have reaped the benefits of the civil rights movement owe a debt to these places.

Sustained out-migration and the absence of a land base means that rural black communities have few of the human or physical resources that could potentially be developed in colonias or reservations. However, given the niche that these communities occupy in the heritage of African-Americans across the country, it does not seem unreasonable to consider mobilizing support across the nation for measures to re-develop these communities. Providing jobs, affordable housing, and other amenities in these communities not only would help slow out-migration, but also might attract return migrants and newcomers from urban areas.

Ultimately, dealing with the problems in rural black communities may depend heavily on the support of the urban African-American population, and especially the support of the black middle-class. The basis for this support may not be self-evident but without question, there is at least one very important historical precedent in the Civil Rights movement. As noted above, middle-class blacks benefitted most from the Civil Rights movement but their gains also resulted in political empowerment for blacks and other minorities across the nation, including those in rural communities. Given this precedent, combined with the electoral power of a unified black vote, an appeal to African-American unity to mobilize African-American political organization on behalf of these communities might serve as a powerful impetus for action.

The expansion of the black middle-class and growing class divisions in some respects might make an appeal for unity with impoverished blacks more difficult. Nonetheless, successfully mobilizing this constituency, as a matter of preserving African-American culture and heritage, would certainly be a potent force in bringing resources for development in these communities.

New Opportunities for Coping with Poverty

Right Answers to the Wrong Questions

For nearly three decades, social scientists have been struggling to understand the problem of poverty: the causes of poverty and ways to reduce it. This has been an enormous undertaking involving uncountable hours of scientific labor whose efforts have been documented in millions of printed pages. The amount of money this has required probably will never be known but it has been a sum reaching the tens and perhaps hundreds of millions of dollars.

Most of this work has been organized around an implicit framework concerning the supply and demand for labor. This approach is driven, of course, by moral assumptions about the inherent goodness of work, that the able-bodied should work, that hard work should be justly rewarded, and that some individuals such as the disabled or elderly should be exempt from work. In a prosperous society, poverty is neither a just reward for hard work nor an acceptable condition to be inflicted upon children or the infirm. From this perspective, poverty is a problem to be solved by adequately providing for those unable to provide for themselves, and by making sure that everyone else has gainful employment.

Given this perspective, providing cash and in-kind benefits to the deserving poor is hardly problematic. However, managing the dynamic conditions of labor markets in a way that all able-bodied persons can be assured of gainful employment with an adequate standard of living is a considerably more complicated problem in a free market economy. This has challenged social scientists to focus on ways of helping the unemployed find work, and ways to ensure better wages for the working poor.

The volumes written about poverty deal with this problem almost exclusively in terms of this narrow focus on labor force participation, unemployment, and wage rates. Given the level of effort devoted to these subjects, it might be reasonable to question the success of this work: the models are not perfect and there is still room for much improvement. Nonetheless, social scientists do know a great deal more about these subjects than they did 30 years ago. There is a considerable body of evidence to suggest that social scientists understand the most important antecedents of poverty, especially if the problem is limited to stimulating local economies and obtaining employment.

Stating that social scientists know how to reduce, if not eliminate poverty clearly runs afoul of the empirical reality that poverty exists and may even be increasing. If we know how to solve this problem, why does it persist, and if it persists, then do we really not know enough about it? Assuming that social scientists know enough about poverty to suggest steps to reduce it, the persistence of poverty is a paradox. However, there is another way of looking at this situation. Namely that social scientists have been very good at finding the answers to their questions but they have done very poorly in asking the right questions in the first place.

The Growing Irrelevance of Rural Sociology

Social science has an elaborate system of scientific principles for evaluating the acceptability of an answer to any given question. Eventually, these answers become accepted as scientific knowledge. Unfortunately, the social sciences have never developed a parallel set of principles to decide whether the correct questions have been asked. This means that it is possible to have large bodies of knowledge that are fairly ineffective in dealing with the problems they were meant to confront. Despite the large and growing body of knowledge about poverty, the persistence of poverty seems to suggest that social scientists have been asking the wrong questions.

This matter is especially relevant to the problem of persistent poverty among rural minorities. Understanding the factors affecting the supply and demand for labor hardly begins to address the root sources of economic disadvantage among these populations. Certainly labor market factors are important but clearly they are not the only considerations. For example, this literature deals with discrimination as an unaccountable residual quantity, and typically, it receives much less attention than other known factors.

The existing literature on poverty among rural racial and ethnic minorities fails to deal with a wide variety of issues that might be germane to this problem. There is little recognition, for instance, of the impact of living in the aftermath of slavery and colonialism. There is little awareness about how institutions such as slavery and Jim Crow might reverberate across generations and manifest themselves in contemporary society. And there is little knowledge about the historical persistence of these institutions across generations.

Furthermore, traditional views of poverty as a problematic market outcome often have a highly individualistic orientation. That is, poverty is presented as a problem afflicting individuals, families, or households. However, individuals, families, and households also live together as communities, and communities are seldom considered to be valid units of analysis. For rural minority populations, communities are a powerful and important unit of social organization bound by ethnicity and kinship.

Overlooking communities in poverty research has meant that this literature also has failed to comprehend the meaning and significance of ethnicity, kinship, traditions, culture, and other factors that bind these communities together. For example, labor mobility models typically ignore the importance of communities by assuming that labor will freely move to take advantage of economic opportunities wherever they exist. From this perspective, rural ethnic minorities such as American Indians who refuse to abandon their homes in pursuit of opportunities elsewhere appear irrational, foolish, or both. However, the "immobility" of labor makes a great deal more sense in the context that community life, shared traditions, and a sense of place also have a great value. For ethnic minority workers, this value may well exceed potential though unrealized economic benefits outside the community.

The myopia that burdens traditional views of poverty also means that recommendations for remedying poverty will be equally handicapped. By failing to deal with poverty as a problem for communities as well as for families and individuals, a critical gap exists in dealing with the aftermath of poverty. Many of the problems associated with poverty (crime for example), reflect the breakdown of social relations that bind community members together and in this respect, poverty is as much a problem for communities as it is for individuals.

There is yet another way traditional views of poverty are misdirected. Given the large body of knowledge about the market forces affecting poverty, there are many options for addressing this problem. In particular, there is a great deal known about how to redistribute income and its effect on poverty. Poverty among the elderly, for example, was substantially reduced in the late 1970s and early 1980s simply by retooling the Social Security system. It would not be an inexpensive matter but it is entirely possible to use existing measures such as the tax system to redirect income to targeted groups such as children or rural communities with large minority populations. If this is true and it is possible to reduce poverty, then why has this not been done?

The likely answer to this question is fairly simple. The political wherewithal to implement income redistribution or other measures that would sharply reduce poverty does not exist. For at least the past decade and perhaps longer, the white middle-class that makes up the majority of voters has shown little or no interest in abating poverty, and especially for minority populations (Bobo 1991; Heclo 1992). It is not a theme enunciated by elected officials, the media, or other opinion-makers. There is however, considerable popular enthusiasm for initiatives dubbed the "New Paternalism" and designed to insure that the poor adhere to the values of the white middle-class (Heclo 1992); making marriage a condition for welfare benefits, for example. Measures that actually reduce poverty are an important issue only among a small circle of activists, academics, and fringe candidates for office.[4]

For social scientists truly concerned with poverty, a critical question should be why there is so little popular concern about reducing poverty. Instead of yet another regression model of earnings and education, social scientists would do well to turn their attention to the politics of anti-poverty measures and the problem of incipient racism among the electorate. Racism in particular is a volatile issue that needs to be more clearly understood but in the current political climate, most social scientists are reluctant to even utter the word, much less take it up as a subject for serious study.

In fact, focusing on labor market behavior diverts attention from what is undoubtedly the most important reason for why there is as much poverty as there is today. There is too little public concern about poverty to accept the serious measures that it requires; especially in a political climate more disposed to "reforming" the poor than to dealing with income inequality. This question alone is important above all because without the political support to implement measures to reduce poverty, billions of dollars and millions of hours could be spent on studying poverty and not a single person living in poverty would benefit from it. By failing to address the white middle-class' apathy of urban America toward the rural poor, and their antagonism toward minority populations (rural or urban), social scientists are knowingly or unknowingly collaborating with those who would do nothing about poverty. Much has been written about the biases of race and class, and about poverty, but little has done to understand how these issues affect rural poverty, and what might be done to abate these problems. Feigning ignorance and continuing to study poverty as it has been studied, in ever finer detail, is an all too convenient excuse for inaction. It diverts attention from the realities of material deprivation and economic hardship and redefines the problem of poverty as one of insufficient research; for this social scientists are as much to blame as anyone in the public debate over poverty.

Rural sociologists are as guilty as any other discipline in their preoccupation with poverty as a problem defined by labor market behavior. As a result, the contributions that rural sociology might make toward alleviating poverty seem irrelevant at best and counter-productive at worst. This is especially true for rural minorities because rural sociologists have never shown much interest in these communities, have never been too interested in studies of racism and its consequences, nor in thinking about poverty as more than a matter of income.

Unless rural sociologists are willing to refocus their attention, it is virtually certain that their work on rural poverty, especially in relation to ethnic minorities will remain an essentially scholastic exercise. However, this situation can be avoided if they are willing to expand the scope of poverty research for understanding issues such as the expansion of neo-colonialism, the historical persistence of institutions that perpetuate discrimination, segregation, and other racist practices, as well as viewing minority communities as organic places steeped in ethnic traditions and culture. Furthermore, rural sociologists should address the hard question of why white middle-class Americans are content to live with the knowledge that millions live in desperate conditions in places not far from their homes. If rural sociologists are not willing to extend their interests beyond the labor market, toward the social environment in which they exist, then poverty research is likely to remain the scholastic and often pointless exercise that is too common in the literature today.

Notes

This chapter was prepared by Matthew Snipp, University of Wisconsin-Madison; Hayward D. Horton, Iowa State University; Leif Jensen, Pennsylvania State University; Joane Nagel, University of Kansas; and Refugio Rochin, University of California-Davis.

1. The statistical data presented in this paper are for metropolitan and nonmetropolitan areas, as defined by the U.S. Bureau of the Census. Strictly speaking, "rural" areas are not the same as "nonmetropolitan" areas but for the sake of convenience, the terms "rural" and "nonmetropolitan" are used interchangeably in this discussion. None of these data are for rural areas as defined by the Census Bureau.

2. Readers should be aware that most rural Hispanics are Mexican-Americans or Mexican immigrants.

3. It is important to remember that the overwhelming majority of the nonmetropolitan African-American population continues to live in the south.

4. The 1992 riots in Los Angeles and elsewhere following the Rodney King court verdict have made the problem of poverty more visible in the media. Whether this marks a renewed interest in this issue remains to be seen.

7

Women and Persistent Rural Poverty

Introduction

Research increasingly demonstrates that women comprise the majority of the poverty population. They are especially vulnerable in rural areas, where limited economic opportunity provides few means of escape. Yet the study of women's poverty at the empirical level is seldom matched by theoretical work which explicitly treats gender as a social process.

In this chapter we review past efforts to explain rural poverty, paying particular attention to women as a group and gender as an analytic category. Measured against a set of theoretical criteria, we find that most past work is incomplete, failing critical tests for good theory or research. This review provides the foundation for an integrative account of gender, place, and poverty. In addition, we examine the implications of this approach for future research, data requirements, and policy concerned with poverty in rural America.

Our perspective attempts to bridge a sustained division between theories of poverty conceptualized in terms of either people who are poor or places that are poor. Although clearly not independent concepts, only rarely are the two explicitly linked. Research from the *people-based* conceptualization shows that women have always been more likely than men to be poor, and that the numbers and proportions of poor women have increased dramatically over the last two decades (Pearce 1990). We also know that women are more likely to become and remain poor, experience spells of poverty, and transmit poverty to their children (Pearce and McAdoo 1981). Importantly, initial accounts of the feminization of poverty focussed on gender-based sources of poverty, thereby muting race, ethnic, and regional variations in causes and vulnerability. More recent work recognizes that minority status is intimately intertwined with the relationship between gender and poverty and attempts to disentangle the conflation of these factors (Amott 1990; Dill and Williams 1992; Mink 1990; Tickamyer and Latimer 1992).

Place-based accounts of poverty emphasize regional variability in resource endowments, infrastructural investments, and economic growth. Such studies demonstrate the extent to which poverty differs not only regionally, but also within and between urban and rural areas (e.g., Morrill and Wohlenberg 1971). Some macrolevel accounts of gender and poverty's spatial attributes demonstrate spatial variation in opportunity structures for women in formal and informal global, national and local economies (Jones and Kodras 1990; Gringeri 1990b; Portes, Castells and Benton 1989; Tickamyer and Tickamyer 1988). One can also see this in regional and local demographic structures and processes (O'Hare 1988), and in programs and policies at state and local levels (Jones 1987; Jones and Kodras 1986; Rank and Hirschl 1988; Sanders 1991). Yet the growing number of studies that analyze aggregate characteristics of impoverished places rarely focus on the intersection of gender, race, and ethnicity.

These constellations are particularly important. While women are fairly evenly distributed across the landscape, their social attributes and available types of household arrangements and economic opportunities are not. Women of color are concentrated in particular regions or places, confounding attempts to present a general account of poverty processes. Women's chances of being poor increase for some types of women and in some places more than others. Therefore, a comprehensive understanding of gender and rural poverty must examine both the social and spatial components of women's poverty.

The theoretical account constructed in this chapter attempts to bridge these divisions by drawing on two developing bodies of theory. First, we consider the new feminist scholarship. It seeks to understand the intersection between gender and other spheres of social life, including the economy, the reproduction of households and communities, and the state. Second, we ground our understanding of rural poverty in recent efforts to re-theorize the role of space in social life. These two perspectives enable us to construct the broad outlines of a theory of *women's rural poverty* which moves beyond the descriptive accounts these terms have previously implied. We begin by reviewing the available data on rural women's poverty and discuss its limits. We next elaborate the characteristics we expect adequate theory to have, and then evaluate contemporary theory in light of these criteria.

Poverty Data: What Do We Know?

The most comprehensive sources of demographic and economic information are the decennial census and current population surveys. These sources provide an overview of the poverty population's characteristics and its economic correlates, yet they remain inadequate on two levels. First, basic demographic information disaggregated by gender, race and ethnicity, region, household type, age, and residence are frequently not collected or published. While we can often analyze one or a select combination of these dimensions, we lack information on their more complex intersections. Second, neither source provides adequate information on the relationship between poverty and participation in the economy. Such data typically provide even less resolution than poverty data alone, or the data reflect a male bias in which formal economic activities are privileged over other forms of work. The consequence of these data inadequacies can be felt at the theoretical level, where processes may be conceptualized in monolithic terms and at the empirical level, where detailed answers to questions regarding poverty, work, and their intersection remain unknown. In the following, we illustrate these issues with a brief examination of existing data.

Table 7.1 shows the prevalence of poverty across race/ethnicity, region, residence, sex, and age in 1990. Depending upon their region, nonmetro women of all colors tend to experience poverty at rates between one-in-ten and one-in-five. Rates are highest in the south and lowest in the northeast census regions, while women living in nonmetro areas tend to experience higher poverty rates than their metro counterparts. Rates vary considerably once we control for race and ethnicity. African-American and Hispanic women tend to experience much greater levels of poverty than white women, with rates worse than one-in-three common in many areas. Moreover, with few exceptions across the spectrum of region and place of residence, women were more likely than men to live below the poverty level. The differences by sex are largest in the nonmetro south, and are higher for African-Americans than for other groups.

Table 7.1 also shows the 1990 distribution of poverty across the life course. Poverty rates for children are much higher than for the general population. Especially alarming is the fact that over half of African- American children in nonmetro areas live in poverty. Although male and female children under 18 experience, as expected, nearly equivalent poverty rates, the labor market years, 18-64, demonstrate a pronounced gender gap. This differential closes in the early post-retirement ages, 65-74, but increases again after age 75, where poverty rates equal to or exceeding those for children are common.

Table 7.2 provides a spatial/temporal perspective on poverty among female-headed households. The proportion of such families living in poverty is higher in metro areas than nonmetro areas. But whereas female-headed family poverty growth stalled in the 1980s in metro areas, growth has continued in nonmetro areas, leaving one-in-four of white families and one-in-two of African-American families in poverty.

A temporal portrait of poverty rates for "unrelated" males and females is shown in Figure 7.1. While conditions for women in nonmetro areas do not appear to have become worse since the 1970s, they have not become much

TABLE 7.1 Percent of Metropolitan and Non-Metropolitan Populations Living in Poverty by Race, Ethnicity, Region, Sex and Age: 1990

	All Races		White		Black		Hispanic	
	Male	Female	Male	Female	Male	Female	Male	Female
Metro								
Total	11.0	14.3	8.6	11.1	26.0	33.7	25.7	29.8
< 18 years	19.8	20.2	15.1	14.9	42.0	44.3	39.3	37.1
18-64 years	7.8	12.1	6.6	9.5	16.6	28.2	18.5	26.1
65-74 years	5.6	11.1	3.7	8.9	20.2	31.6	15.7	22.0
> = 75 years	7.7	17.7	6.1	15.5	26.8	40.7	18.6	29.5
Non-Metro								
Total	14.5	18.1	11.8	15.0	37.2	44.0	31.8	32.3
> 18 years	23.1	22.7	18.4	18.4	53.4	51.7	42.6	38.6
18-64 years	11.1	15.6	9.6	12.9	24.8	39.0	23.5	28.1
65 74 years	8.9	15.9	6.5	13.9	41.2	41.7	39.4	29.7
> = 75 years	15.2	24.8	11.8	22.3	50.3	54.2	40.0	38.5
Northeast								
Metro	9.5	13.4	7.4	10.6	26.1	31.7	31.3	41.4
Non-Metro	9.2	11.3	9.0	11.4	11.8	3.0	14.3	16.7
Midwest								
Metro	10.2	14.0	6.8	9.3	31.0	40.7	19.6	26.3
Non-Metro	12.0	14.3	11.3	13.8	27.5	30.0	17.9	20.5
South								
Metro	12.0	15.7	8.9	11.5	24.9	32.5	24.8	26.7
Non-Metro	18.0	22.7	13.0	16.8	37.8	44.9	37.8	37.2
West								
Metro	11.6	13.8	11.0	12.8	19.0	27.1	25.2	27.6
Non-Metro	13.0	16.6	12.1	15.8	41.7	38.2	28.1	30.0

Source: U.S. Bureau of the Census, Current Population Reports, Series P-60, No. 175, Poverty in the United States: 1990, Washington, D.C.

TABLE 7.2 Household Composition of Persons Living in Poverty by Race and Residence

	All Races			Whites			Blacks		
	1990	1980	1970	1990	1980	1970	1990	1980	1970
Metro									
Total	24,510	18,021	13,378	15,711	11,201	9,107	7,696	6,172	4,129
Female Headed	40.1	40.3	35.5	29.6	29.6	25.5	63.7	62.3	58.9
All Other	37.0	37.5	40.6	43.8	44.6	53.2	20.1	21.8	27.6
Unrelated									
Females	13.9	14.2	17.2	16.6	17.4	21.3	9.0	9.2	8.7
Males	9.0	7.9	6.8	10.0	8.4	7.4	7.2	6.7	4.8
Non-Metro									
Total	9,075	11,251	12,142	6,615	8,494	8,464	2,141	2,406	3,520
Female Headed	30.3	25.3	23.7	23.5	19.1	17.5	51.4	47.4	37.6
All Other	49.3	54.9	61.4	53.1	59.0	66.1	37.1	38.8	54.7
Unrelated									
Females	13.1	13.8	10.6	15.5	15.9	13.1	6.0	7.9	7.5
Males	7.3	6.0	4.3	7.9	6.0	3.3	5.5	5.9	0.2

Source: U.S. Bureau of the Census, Current Population Reports, Series P-60, No. 175, Poverty in the United States: 1990, Washington, D.C.

Figure 7.1 Percent of Nonmetropolitan Males and Females Not
Living in Families Living in Poverty: 1970–1990

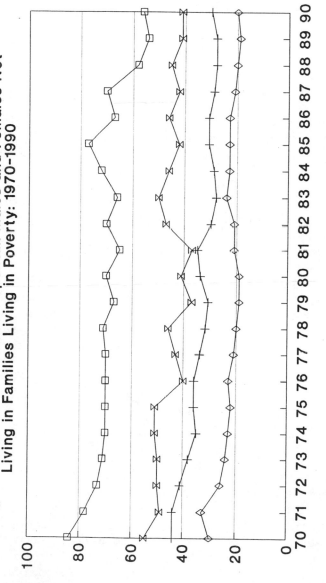

Race/Sex

Source: US Bureau of the Census, Annual Current Population Reports, 1970-90, Washington, D.C.

better either.   Poverty rates declined slightly for white and black nonmetrowomen in the early 1970s, but these patterns were not matched by equivalent decreases in subsequent years.   Poverty rates rose for nearly all race/sex groups in the latter half of the recession-prone 1980s. African-American women did close part of the poverty gap relative to other groups by the end of the decade.

It's difficult to understand the relationship between these demographic patterns and the rural economy.   Women simply do not figure prominently in regional comparisons of sector employment growth or labor market areas.   It is even more difficult to obtain detailed information by multiple demographic categories.   We do know that poverty has persisted in nonmetro areas even though women's participation in the labor force has increased.   Labor force participation rates for women in nonmetro areas rose from about half that of males in 1970, to over three-quarters that of males in 1989.   This increase may partly account for the decline in the gap in poverty rates between "unrelated" males and females in nonmetro poverty between 1970 and 1989 (Figure 7.1). Nevertheless, labor force participation does not guarantee an income above poverty level, as the large number of rural working poor illustrates (Deavers and Hoppe 1992; Tickamyer 1992).

We also can determine that the ongoing economic restructuring taking place in the U.S. provides no relief to women.   Census data show that the largest shifts in the employment composition of the female nonmetro labor force between 1970 and 1989 are from finance and insurance, service industries and from the manufacturing sector to retail trade.   Yet women earn significantly less than males in each of these industrial groups.   While the 1989 ratio of women's to men's earnings for full-time, year-round employment in manufacturing was 0.61, the gender wage gap is equally bad in retail trade (0.59), finance and insurance (0.49), and services (0.63).   Thus, women do not stand to gain from the economic shifts currently taking place.   Please remember that these data only suggest more specific trends, and are difficult to obtain by race, residence, and region.

The data problem is further compounded by a bias in the categories used to create official accounts of economic activity and employment.   Men's historic domination in the paid labor market, combined with traditional gender role ideologies, disguises the significance of women's work.   Not only are employment opportunities for nonmetro women limited by discrimination, traditional attitudes, and a lack of flexibility in home-work schedules, but women contribute a substantial amount of unacknowledged unpaid labor.   This effectively limits women's paid labor force participation.   Public record data underestimate the labor women provide to meet a broad range of reproductive needs through their labor contributions to household, farm, and family enterprises.   Reducing economic activity to formal employment categories ignores the diverse sets of tasks women perform (Levitan and Feldman 1991). These activities may include subcontracting arrangements with firms operating within the formal wage-based economy, and piece-work arrangements sold to independent middle-persons. They may also include forms of self-employment not fully acknowledged on tax returns, or payment for services rendered "off the books" or outside of tax laws characteristic of wage employment (AB 1978; Mattera 1985). These myriad work and labor relations represent what Mingione (1991:20) has called "the spectrum of human activities contributing to reproduction," and make up an increasing share of the rural economy. Yet they are virtually ignored in official statistics.

Finally, even studies attempting to remedy past omissions by differentiating economic contributions of all types by sex may continue to ignore the significance of patriarchal social relations which actually construct gender differences. These omissions reveal a narrow interpretation of the rural economy and an underestimation of the myriad activities shaping production, exchange, and consumption relations in rural communities. In part, these observations provide the impulse for the following section, in which we examine the criteria we shall use in attempting to construct new theoretical frameworks to explain women's poverty in rural America.

Criteria for Theory Construction

Rural women's poverty has most often been conceptualized as an empirical phenomenon and has seldom been the object of theoretical work *per se*. This is doubtless due to the fact that gender and space have not been key themes of the social disciplines. In contrast, our criteria attempt to locate gender and space as central analytical categories in assessing poverty. A number of related criteria emerge from this critical, feminist, and reflexive position. Together these form the basis for a grounded critique and guide our recommendations for strengthening theoretical work on women's rural poverty.

Our criteria for theory development in women's rural poverty ask whether the theory recognizes that:

1. *Social reproduction and production are inseparable, necessary, and co-equal processes*. Production refers to social relations that sustain the material conditions for social life. Reproduction refers to relations central for the reproduction of households and communities. Significant for our purposes is the central role that gender plays in enabling, sustaining, and integrating both relations of production and reproduction. One can demonstrate the linkages between patriarchy and capitalist production by the facts that (1) without women's domestic labor in social reproduction, waged labor geared toward production could never take place, and (2) women engaged in waged labor are

exploited not only as members of a particular class, but also as women (as the literature on occupational segregation and women's wages demonstrates only so well). As a result, women's subordination must be seen as woven into the very fabric of exploitation in capitalist societies and not simply as the result of sex role socialization.

2. *Gender, race, and ethnicity are integrated into the theory rather than "tacked on."* Early efforts to rectify the neglect of women in social science took an "add women" approach, in which researchers sought to expose the hidden work, contributions, and victimization of women (Harding 1987:4). Similar observations can be made about race and ethnicity. These researchers have not explained how such differences are constructed or how the systems of which women are a part inform social understanding. Rather, they often merely supplement the formerly all-male studies with studies of women or blacks or even black women. We maintain that gender, race, and ethnicity are socially constructed processes of equivalent significance and complexity to that of class. As such, they should be integrated into abstract, theoretical accounts rather than added as an elaboration merely complicating the resolution of concrete, empirical studies.

3. *Individuals and social structures are mutually defined.* The poverty literature is replete with instances of conceptualizations which are either overly volunteerist or reductionist. Volunteerism undergirds many conservative and neoclassical accounts of poverty, while reductionist impulses are associated with certain forms of structural Marxism as well as with culture of poverty theories. We favor a middle ground reconceptualization of the relationship between individuals and social structures. Social structures, such as culture and the economy, are seen as both medium and outcome of individual action and agency (Giddens 1984). In recognizing this duality, we conceive individuals to be conscious agents who operate within a matrix of social relations, but who also have a reservoir of power for transforming these relations through their own action.

4. *Social processes are embedded in time and space.* Core concepts of functionalist theory, such as modernization, industrialization, and urbanization, fail to incorporate adequate notions of temporal or spatial processes. These "unfolding models of change" (Giddens 1979) are ahistorical, despite purporting to explain change, and aspatial, despite describing changes which extend across natural and constructed landscapes. Other theories incorporate one dimension but rarely both simultaneously. For example, political economy theories of social change have a reasonable claim to historical authenticity but still struggle with spatiality. Theories which explicitly incorporate space often do so in a reductionist and deterministic way. We align ourselves with contemporary theory in sociology and geography which seeks to understand social processes

as contingent on space and time. Moreover, space, when conceptualized in terms of a socio-spatial dialectic, is seen to be both outcome and mediator of social processes (Soja 1989). Thus the spatial unfolding of social processes is conceptualized in terms co-equal to their temporality. By linking time and space in this way we focus attention on the processes which continually reconstitute "rurality" in both social and spatial terms.

5. *Local events and processes are linked to global ones.* Instead of conceptualizing rural areas as somehow analytically separate from urban ones, theory should grasp the complex inter-linkages between all locales (cf., Duncan and Goodwin 1982; Murgatroyd et al. 1985; Urry 1981). Not only do locally contingent social and economic processes mediate large-scale global ones, global processes must also be viewed as comprised of many local level restructurings. Conceptualizing locales in this way has important implications for the research distinctions between "rural" and "urban." Both labels suggest a spatial "framing," placing primary or sole emphasis on locally contingent conditions while ignoring the dual intersections between local and global processes. We seek to understand rural poverty as inescapably interconnected to large-scale processes beyond the redress of rural locales; these, in turn, are not only the result of events taking place in other rural areas but also in urban ones.

6. *The state is neither wholly subordinate to society nor independent of it.* Two separate perspectives dominate the literature known as state theory. In society-centered theories, state activity is understood as the direct outcome of processes in society at large. In state-centered theories, the state is conceptualized as a relatively autonomous entity capable of defining its own agendas for action. We seek to integrate both of these perspectives while maintaining the force of each (Jessop 1990). The state is a social relation whose activities are always embedded in the wider social sphere. At the same time, the state is comprised of actors with specific enabling powers, and thus one must recognize the implications of state activity in the wider society. Applied to women's rural poverty, this perspective assists us in understanding social policies such as public assistance in gendered terms, while nevertheless recognizing the potentially positive role that such policies may have in alleviating deprivation. Indeed, it is precisely because of these possibilities that the state must be viewed as a site of social contest and struggle.

Theoretical Review and Critique

Just as empirical work differentiates poverty of people from poverty of place, one also can organize theoretical accounts in terms of their emphasis on social or spatial organization and process. These categories largely transcend ideological stance and level of analysis. In this section, the broad outlines of influential models are discussed for their relevance to women and rural poverty.

Social Organization: Poverty of People

Poverty of people theories direct attention to the social conditions in which deprivation is clearly apparent. Such accounts include micro-level models which focus on various aspects of an individual's endowments or decision-making, and macro-level theories concerned with a group's culture, class, or demographic situation. In all cases, differentiations in economic well-being occur along social, rather than spatial, lines. One does not measure the distinctiveness of rural poverty by the processes which endow some places with growth and others with stagnation. Rather, one examines the extent to which the relevant social conditions are located in some places rather than others.

1. *Human Capital Theory* (HCT) explains employment and wages in terms of an individual's efforts, capabilities, and human capital investments, on the one hand, and labor supply and demand on the other. HCT assumes a smoothly functioning and harmonious labor market. Rational, knowledgeable, and mobile workers select among opportunities for employment offered to individual workers based upon their contribution to the marginal product. Poverty arises from deficits in human capital acquisitions and enhancements, and in its extreme version may be thought of as the result of nothing more than an individual's failure to invest or to put forth an adequate work effort. Human capital acquisition and retention may be particularly problematic in rural areas.

In a particularly controversial corollary, women's observed depressed labor market opportunities and outcomes result from reduced human capital from a variety of gender related sources. These include sex role socialization, lower skills investment, self-selection into sex-segregated occupations, and high turnover rates. These also include interrupted work histories resulting from women's primary roles in reproductive labor that detract from their value to employers.

In spite of several decades of research, HCT has not explained persistent wage differentials between women and men or the occupational sex segregation which reinforces the gender gap. Despite strong empirical evidence for structural barriers and discrimination in the operation of labor markets, this approach either does not recognize the impact of these factors or conceives of them as transitory aberrations (cf., Blau and Jusenius 1976, England 1982).

2. *Culture of Poverty* theorists originally hypothesized that exclusion from the cash economy creates individual apathy, alienation, and deviance, as well as community disorganization that ultimately becomes part of the poor's lifestyle (Lewis 1966). Subsequent appropriations of the model ignore the links to economic opportunity posited by Lewis, emphasizing instead the self-defeating, vicious circle in which the poor are blamed for adopting and perpetuating deviant values, behaviors, and lifestyles that devalue work (Banfield 1970; Valentine 1968). A key component of this formulation is the breakdown of normative patterns of family formation and sexual control, resulting in the

widespread increase in early and extramarital pregnancies. This is cause and consequence of a "vicious cycle of poverty" in which women with few other options transmit the deviant poverty culture to their children. This perspective underlies the policy prescriptions of more recent conservative thinkers such as Gilder (1981) and Murray (1984), who argue for the elimination of income support programs on the grounds that they are incubators of welfare dependency and thus, sources for the culture of poverty.

Significant for our purposes, none of the culture of poverty theorists adequately address gender issues. Such models attribute poverty to family dissolution, extramarital childbearing and rearing, and other violations of midcentury idealized gender roles, family forms, and bourgeois lifestyles. They emphasize women's domestic roles as appendages of traditional family structures and have little interest in gender as an analytic category or as a key ingredient in poverty analysis.

3. *Demographic Explanations* of poverty address the ways in which demographic factors interact with social and economic processes. Three such explanations are relevant to gender and rural poverty: cohort size, family structure, and migration.

Easterlin's (1980) explanation of changes in economic well-being focused on long-term swings in the size of generational cohorts. The relatively small depression era birth cohort enjoyed prosperity as they entered a high demand labor market with relatively low entrance requirements. When the much larger baby boom cohort entered the labor market the picture changed dramatically, with declining real wages because of increased job competition. Industrial restructuring increased educational requirements for entry-level jobs at the same time large numbers of women entered the labor force, thereby exacerbating the competition for employment.

There are several difficulties with this analysis for understanding rural poverty. In particular, economic processes are assumed rather than explained, either in terms of restructuring or of government policies. Moreover, the substantial differences between men and women's employment characteristics tend not to be addressed. Levy and Michel (1991), for example, fail to consider either the impacts of Reagan administration policies upon the supply of low-wage jobs or the power differentials which relegate women to particular types of employment or to household reproductive activities.

Family structure explanations of women's poverty point to the post-1960s increases in the number of female-headed families. Such families are formed through marital disruption (e.g., divorce, separation, or widowhood) or out-of-wedlock fertility. Family disruption has severe consequences for family income (Duncan and Hoffman 1985), and divorce is a strong predictor of poverty status (Coe, Duncan, and Hill 1982). The problem is exacerbated by most fathers' failure to provide adequate child support (Bane and Ellwood 1989).

In spite of the strong correspondence between the spatial-temporal dynamics of family disruption and growth of women's poverty (see Jones and Kodras 1990), the implications of such an explanation are problematic. First, the thesis directs attention away from the more significant question of why women find it difficult to support their families as the sole breadwinner. To see familial disruption as the primary *cause* of poverty is to ignore the many barriers to employment that remain for women, and especially for women from disadvantaged class, race, or ethnic backgrounds. Second, by focusing attention on the "breakdown of the family," researchers may implicitly endorse the maintenance of incompatible and even violent relationships. Underlying this perspective is an ideological bias which suggests that female-headed families are in some way not "whole" without a male partner.

Migration is a third demographic process applied to poverty research. From the standpoint of many economists and demographers, migration functions as a relief valve which siphons off excess labor from regions with high levels of underemployment and low wages towards more prosperous regions (Lowry 1966). The *in situ* effects of such movements are a decrease in labor supply in the origin and a corresponding increase in its wage levels. These changes are counterbalanced by an increase in labor supply in the destination. As a consequence, regional wage differences and unemployment narrow between the two regions until either regional economic changes alter production patterns or until pecuniary or institutional impediments to migration are reached.

Researchers have long recognized that the labor force adjustment model, while plausible in theory, is in practice deficient on several grounds. First, it tends to treat migrants as an undifferentiated group with similar education, age, and class backgrounds. Migrants are not, however, a random sample of the origin population. Those persons who expect higher lifetime earnings, i.e., the young and relatively better educated, are more likely to migrate (Morrison 1972). This can offset gains to the origin region as its stock of human capital is depleted through migration. Second, labor tends to be less mobile than financial capital or even some forms of fixed capital. Therefore, the equilibrating tendencies stemming from the labor migration may not compensate for the capital investment movements. Third, migration decisions are often made at the household and family levels rather than at the individual level. This may decrease labor mobility or negatively impact the incomes and careers of trailing partners (most typically women). Finally, the labor force adjustment model diverts attention away from structural dimensions of the economy (that make certain regions especially vulnerable to economic downturns), toward the victims who are left to "vote with their feet."

4. *Marxist Theories* traditionally focus on waged labor to explain poverty, but do not view the market mechanism as an impartial "invisible hand" smoothly regulating the exchange of labor for wages. Rather, Marxist models scrutinize the conflictual and contradictory relationship between capital and labor. One's

relationship to the means of production determines wealth and income and hence poverty. Moreover, the determinants of different levels of human capital are structurally and institutionally shaped in such a way that these individual characteristics are actually a consequence of structural inequality patterns. Within this framework, the likelihood of being poor varies directly with dependence on wage labor (Wachtel 1973).

Among rural and agriculturally based households, traditional Marxist interpretations miscalculate the determinants of rural poverty since various forms of self-employment are common for many of the poor. Moreover, with the restructuring of the economy and the increasing proportion of individual and family income secured from wages, self-employment and informal labor exchanges, efforts to explain poverty based on wage income alone fail to fully explain why people are poor. For example, contemporary changes in wage employment (e.g., the decentralization of production, increases in out-work, subcontracting, and home-based work paid on a piece-rate system, as well as the growth of self-employment), would be inadequately understood by a traditional Marxist interpretation of poverty based solely on a formal definition of wage labor. Similarly, women's work, both within the formal labor market and in various forms of unpaid labor, is not adequately explained within a traditional Marxist framework in which relations of production are given primacy (Hartmann 1976). Traditional Marxist analyses give inadequate attention to the gendered nature of both production and reproduction.

5. *Welfare State Theories* examine the intersection of poverty with welfare programs and work effort. In an early account, Brehm and Saving (1964) analyzed income and the receipt of public assistance in terms of the more general model of the demand for leisure. Their microeconomic analysis postulated that the choice between income and leisure depended upon the indifference curve, the wage rate, and the support level provided by the state. An increase in wages would have a positive effect on work effort, but this effect could be undercut by rising levels of state support which could increase the demand for leisure. The equilibrium position determining the degree of work vs. leisure would be determined by the level of income support and the wage rate.

Such neoclassical formulations, continued in the work of Gallaway and Vedder (1986), hold individuals responsible for exhibiting work effort while at the same time condemning the state for what is seen as overly generous public assistance levels. In contrast, other authors have rejected the work disincentive model in favor of labor market driven factors (e.g., Kodras 1986; and Jones 1987).

By focusing attention on the interaction between work and welfare, and not the gendered nature of each of these systems, researchers within this tradition have adopted largely acritical stances towards women's poverty. In rural areas a woman's vulnerability to poverty is compounded by the double jeopardy of more restricted labor market opportunities with jobs that pay subpoverty wages (see Bloomquist 1988; Gorham 1992). In addition, she is also likely to receive subpoverty level welfare benefits (Vinson and Jesberg 1981, Watkins and Watkins 1984). Furthermore, feminist theorists have developed a critical perspective on welfare programs, arguing that they perpetuate both systems of class and gender repression (Gordon 1990; Pearce 1979). And since women predominate as both welfare recipients and employees of the welfare state, "the fiscal crisis of the state coincides everywhere with...the feminization of poverty" (Fraser 1989:144).

Spatial Theories: Poverty of Place

Place-based theories of poverty focus more explicitly on the spatial side of the rural poverty equation. They include spatial models developed by regional economists and Marxists, human ecology approaches, and rural development theory. All share a concern with the unevenness of economic development and the consequent poverty in rural communities and regions. Importantly, spatial theories assume that the economic well-being of a place will be transmitted to social institutions and individuals alike. A sound economic base in a given locale allows those who live and work there access to incomes and resources to meet their family needs. In this way, the individual's poverty is remedied by addressing the poverty of place.

1. *Spatial Theories* underpin many of the place-based growth and development models. In the neoclassical economic growth version, inequality among a country's various regions first increases and then declines. The factors hypothesized to account for growth polarization in core areas are manifold. Williamson (1965) suggests that the pattern is related to production flows between regions, the extent of interregional linkages, and government policy. Others have offered a 'leading sector' hypothesis, noting that a core region's formation is often associated with specific resource or locational endowments in particular places and historical junctures which facilitate the establishment of a crucial industry or economic sector (Perloff and Wingo 1961; Pred 1973). Once established, the core region tends to grow at the expense of the periphery, from which are channeled resources, labor, and capital. Divergence ensues as a pattern of circular, and cumulative causation is set in motion (Mera 1973; Myrdal 1957; Parr 1973).

Core-periphery frameworks also inform Marxist and neo-Marxist models of uneven development, which were originally used to explain colonial exploitation patterns and the "development of underdevelopment" in developing nations (Frank 1967). Regional inequality is seen as the outcome of capitalist development logic, with its exploitive capital-labor relations and ruthless drive for capital accumulation. That drive leaves rural areas vulnerable to exploitation for their natural resources and cheap labor (Markusen 1987; Weaver 1984).

The dependency framework places core-periphery relations within a theory of unequal exchange, the politics of comparative advantage, and an historical understanding of colonial and post-colonial regimes.   However, when the analogy of core-periphery is used to explain regional inequality in the U.S., these components of the theory are frequently ignored. Therefore, many core-periphery studies of U.S. rural poverty are primarily descriptive. Core and periphery serve as synonyms for urban and rural, advanced and backward, rich and poor.   In other cases, these approaches are overly reductionist and deterministic. They rely on the dominance of particular industries in defining the social relations of production to explain regional inequality (cf. Billings and Tickamyer 1990 for detailed discussion and examples).   Finally, all spatial models tend to neglect the role of reproduction, culture, ideology, and gender.

2. *Ecological Models* have re-emerged in studies of inner-city urban ecology that investigate the community characteristics creating and reinforcing poverty (Wilson 1987; Lemann 1991; and Jencks and Peterson 1991).   In these models, economic crisis, restructuring, and industrial relocation have eliminated jobs for core urban areas, leading to vastly reduced opportunities for lower and working class African-American men.   Simultaneously, the Civil Rights movement's limited success in reducing racial barriers in jobs and housing for educated, middle-class blacks has resulted in an outmigration which has emptied these communities of their stable, productive members. Left behind are the "urban underclass"--persons who exhibit the characteristics ascribed to the culture of poverty.   The result is communities with high levels of under- and unemployment, underground and criminal activity, adolescent pregnancies, female-headed households, and welfare dependency.   The disorganization of such communities, with their lack of visible or viable economic opportunity and middle class family stability, perpetuates and augments the underclass behaviors that lock people into poverty.

This theory has provoked much controversy because of its similarity to culture of poverty models, its focus on urban centers, and its undue emphasis on male opportunity and female dependency, thus reinforcing the failure to recognize how gender structures opportunity.   The centrality of specifically urban social forms and populations makes it of dubious value to understanding rural poverty, although there has been some speculation about similar community effects models to areas of rural persistent poverty.   Such accounts focus on lack of social support and infrastructure rather than lack of human and cultural capital.   They also point to the relative absence of "underclass" behaviors in rural areas (Duncan and Tickamyer 1988; Tickamyer and Latimer 1992).   There has been little discussion of whether it is even appropriate to reformulate the model for rural America.

3. *Rural Development Theory* emerged in the late nineteenth century as a dominant mode of organizing thinking and action.   It came in response to the uneven impact of capitalist accumulation on regions throughout the U.S. From

their earliest manifestations, rural America problems were conceptualized as the failure to keep pace with urban development rather than more fundamental systemic failures. In the terminology of the modernization and dependency frameworks, rural America was viewed as an underdeveloped region requiring programs "...to raise rural America to twentieth century standards of urban social and economic organization and efficiency" (Summers 1986:349). We pay special attention to the discourse surrounding rural development because it is the centerpiece of much rural sociological theory and practice, is closely connected to other influential paradigms, and is the mainstay of public policy dealing with rural economic development.

The rural development discourse is summarized by a few key statements. First, rural people and rural places are "unfinished" vis-a-vis urban people and urban places. Second, the assessment of "development" is based on measurements calibrated solely on an economic basis. Since rural problems are defined in terms of capital and technology deficits, solutions are also couched in such terms. Third, the unquestioned desirability of economic growth within a market economy precludes from valuing all but production oriented economic activities. Fourth, movement toward the goal of "being developed" implies a transition from one end of a growth or development continuum to another. It confers upon the rural development process a progressive, orderly and stable character, thus betraying the perspective's functionalist underpinnings.

By conceptualizing the problems of rural America in this way, attention is focused exclusively on the modern production economy and the role of the modern *producing* subject within it. Obscured or undervalued are "informal activities, self-provisioning, the economic role of family and ethnic relationships and [a] variety of household strategies" (Mingione 1991:1).

This limited conceptualization of "work" especially undervalues the worth of women historically responsible for reproductive activities within the household and the many activities within the shadowed or informal economy. This has had a number of consequences for development planning. One is the tendency to think in terms of dichotomies: modern vs. traditional sectors, economic vs. volunteer activities, productive vs. reproductive activities. Activities which are not modern or not performed for money are not productive and hence, aren't work. Such thinking emphasizes reliance on statistics reporting economic activity in the business sector, with little attention to informal activities, many of which are dominated by women. Modern, progressive rural development is not supposed to include an informal economy.

While much of the work on women and rural development policy focuses on conditions within the Third World, conditions within the U.S. can be used to illustrate this point. For instance, Tinker (1981) suggests that the rise of two-income families has made visible the once informal activities of women, such as meal preparation, nursing the sick, and volunteering. Women no longer have time for such activities; their roles have been replaced by those in the service industry, which is considered to be productive yet retains a peripheral and marginal status. The informal economy, meanwhile, is thought to be related to inequities in allocating resources and opportunities in the formal sector. Thus development theory focuses on economic activities and neglects questions concerning who benefits and how.

Another factor largely ignored by development policy is the importance of women's activities for family survival (Tinker 1981). Women retain responsibility to feed, clothe, shelter and educate their families. In modern society this often is through their own economic activity because they are single parents or their husband's income is inadequate or unavailable. Furthermore, with shifts in cultural and family practices (e.g., acceptance of divorce and illegitimacy, rejection of alimony), women are more vulnerable in times of economic crises (Voydanoff 1990).

Little attention has been given to how rural development programs affect rural families and women. This neglect reinforces sex stereotypes and creates an environment in which women are dependent on men. Policies and programs are consequently formulated for male dominated economic activities, constructing or deepening women's dependency. For example, feminists argue that the introduction of advanced technologies are more likely to benefit men. First, technology development has been more rapid in areas of men's work, e.g., cash crops vs. food crops and small animal breeding. Women are thus less likely to benefit from advances in commercial farming. Second, women have limited access to land, credit, and training. This creates additional barriers to exploiting new technologies. As a result, in rural areas, and particularly farming areas, women either increase their dependence on men, work off-farm to meet household needs, or migrate to urban areas.

Women, moreover, are seldom acknowledged or involved in policy formation. Little if anything is known about the differential impact of U.S. development policies and programs for women. The state has played an important role in this regard. For example, state generated "rural revitalization" strategies have shaped the responses of rural communities to the impacts of the global restructuring that has gone on since the early eighties. The strategies have called for attracting vigorous industries to rural communities to hire the underemployed and unemployed. Attempts to diversify the economy continue to frame problems without regard to gender, class and race. As such, they fail to account for changes conditioned by the reality that "the growth in the number of informal-sector and women workers is the centerpiece of global restructuring" (Ward 1990:2).

Carr (1981) calls for planners who recognize women as workers and plan for them to work more productively through access to credit, training and other facilities. She explores the popular notion of appropriate technology and notes the tendency to ask, "appropriate for whom?" Technology developed for "women's" work often is not acceptable to women. Furthermore, as Papanek

(1981:225) points out, rural development planners and scholars must pay attention "to the work of women not only because that is good for women....(They) must also realize that it is good for development".

Summary. The shortcomings of each of these theories for a theory of women and persistent rural poverty is that they almost universally fail to incorporate gender. They generally ignore women and the activities women most often perform, or they incorporate and promote a myriad of hidden assumptions about women's subordinate roles in the economy, the community, the labor market, the family, and the household. None comes close to doing anything more than "tacking gender on" when forced to confront gender's relevance for rural poverty and development. Theories applied to poverty as a characteristic of people do little to consider spatial variation, assuming an undifferentiated economy in which economic status is situated. On the other hand, theories of place typically are highly simplistic in their understanding of space. They fail to meet criteria for mutual dependency between the local and global. And they do not recognize historical and temporal dimensions or come to grips with the intersections between the social and the spatial. Approaches vary in the degree to which they recognize state level activity and mediation, but these too have been shown to be inconsistent or ideologically formulated.

The Feminist Critique

The most unified and consistent criticism of past theory and research on poverty comes from the burgeoning feminist literature on production, reproduction, and the welfare state. In contrast to virtually every other approach to understanding poverty, feminist perspectives emphasize the extent to which women's economic opportunities are conditioned and shaped by their disadvantage in the wage labor market; by their high participation level in informal and unpaid labor, both productive and reproductive; and by state policies toward women, work, and welfare. In this section we discuss research in these areas and show how these factors can be integrated to produce a feminist perspective on rural women and poverty.

It's All Work: The Formal, Informal, and Household Sectors

Although relatively few studies examine distinctly *rural* women's experiences, we do know that women's opportunities are more limited in rural areas, and that these limits are related to local economy structure and the impacts of global restructuring on the formal, informal, and household sectors (Bokemeier, Sachs, and Keith 1983; Bokemeier and Tickamyer 1985, Gorham

1992, Lichter 1989, Lichter and Landry 1991, McLaughlin and Sachs 1988, Tickamyer and Bokemeier 1988, 1989; Tienda 1986).

Formal Work. Given the male bias in data collection procedures, it is not surprising that we know more about women's engagement in formal economic arrangements than in their informal ones. Socio-demographic characteristics interact with economic ones to directly and indirectly affect female-headed household poverty rates in rural areas (Tickamyer and Tickamyer 1988; Tickamyer 1992). Women have much more limited employment opportunities and flatter earnings curves in areas dominated by agriculture and mining (Tickamyer and Bokemeier 1988). They are less likely than men to benefit from human capital investments that increase earnings within a particular labor market, and they are more likely to experience under- and unemployment in rural areas (Lichter 1989). In spite of these disadvantages, research has revealed that women's wages and incomes are the resources that sustain both family and farm in times of severe economic need. During the farm crisis of the 1980s and the continued squeeze on farm income, the persistence of small farms has been attributed to the willingness of farm women to self-exploit--to expand their workloads to include off-farm wages and to compromise their standard of living (Flora 1992; Haney and Knowles 1988). As both farm and rural nonfarm women increase their participation in the non-agricultural labor market, occupational sex segregation has increased in rural communities (Rogers and Goudy 1981; Seminoyov 1983).

Global economic restructuring in the form of the spatial reorganization of the international division of labor has had profound effects on rural economies, communities, and regions. The changes defining rural life include declining living standards, growing under- and unemployment, a feminizing of the labor market, increasing numbers of households dependent on more than one income to meet their needs, and increasing numbers of families with incomes below the poverty line.

Standard accounts of the globalization of the economy tend to identify the determinacy of multinational corporations and the supra-state in shaping regional economic conditions (e.g., Frobel, Heinrichs, and Kreye 1980). This is useful in connecting local outcomes to global scale processes. However, this work can be criticized for fostering an undifferentiated image of women workers that fails to recognize that "...female labour is not available in a pre-packaged form...both the State and capital need to intervene to release this labour power in the particular form required by concrete production conditions" (Pearson 1988:450-56). Pearson's reflexive and constructionist approach to labor market relations refines the interpretation of economic restructuring, the concomitant processes of industrial relocation and the feminization of the labor force. Low-wage manufacturing occupations, in particular, are the product of the new demands of international capital and people's living conditions and experiences in communities, which mediate how economic restructuring and the reorganization of daily life actually unfold.

These contingencies provide a necessary frame for analyzing rural poverty since they draw attention to the interaction among macro-economic processes, institutional decision-making, and social action. Increasing numbers of women have been drawn into wage and other forms of remunerated as well as unpaid labor. In addition to understanding the importance of the absolute and relative increases in female labor force participation rates, it is also important to understand how labor deployment patterns have altered the structure and pattern of daily life. The pressures for women to earn wages has required a renegotiation of the normative definitions of women and work and a redefinition of the relationship between family structure and gender ideology. This redefinition of the "cult of domesticity" has the potential to challenge not only how we now understand contemporary work patterns and household relations, but also how we have traditionally understood the organization of rural production and the relationship between work and family, family and household, and household and community. The feminization of the labor force, the increasing demand for women workers, and women's increased demand for employment also challenge how we think about the "family wage," low-wage and low-skill employment, and the segmentation of the labor market. Finally, these changing circumstances highlight the complexity and embeddedness of work-family relations that can no longer be ignored nor adequately captured by conventional information collected on employment.

Informal and Unpaid Work. Another major concern of feminist research is the reconceptualization of informal and unpaid labor as central objects of study. Indeed, the failure to adequately conceptualize, measure, and study nonformal labor market activity may be the biggest deficiency of past research. Many women in the informal sector supply goods and services to those working in both the formal and informal sectors. These activities include petty commodity production, support for small-scale entrepreneurial initiatives, various forms of home-based production, and an increasing array of subcontracting and out-sourcing arrangements. In times of crisis women take on tasks to reduce their dependence on paid services by increasing their contribution to service provisioning (Beneria and Feldman 1992). During the Great Depression, for example, women's egg and butter money sustained farm families throughout the Midwest (Fink 1986).

In contemporary times these activities have become more complex as the need for survival strategies increases, and as the informal sector has likewise been transformed by the social and economic changes attending global economic restructuring. The "exploitive use of informalization," a process by which corporate firms restructure in order to reduce labor costs and increase profits has had a profound impact on women's lives throughout the world. Within many rural areas in the U.S., exploitive informalization has resulted in the development of unregulated enterprises and home-based industries targeted specifically at attracting women. They offer piece-work, provide neither security nor benefits and are often high-risk occupations.

Women's unpaid activities may contribute to either production or social reproduction. The activities embrace a range of exchanges not measured or paid for with money, but rather in currencies where value is measured by gratitude, bonding, a sense of mutual obligation, reciprocity, or efforts at redistribution (Mingione 1991; Levitan and Feldman 1991). This labor includes household work geared toward reproductive activities such as child care, education, and meal preparation, and a variety of self-provisioning and reciprocal goods and services exchanges. For women in rural economies, particularly those engaged in agriculture, the lines between paid and unpaid labor, productive and reproductive work, and labor market and household activities may be extremely permeable and demonstrate the interdependence among categories.

Household Work. Much unpaid work occurs within households, the locus of social relationships necessary for production and reproduction of social and economic life (Collins and Gimenez 1990). Households are dynamic units in which life course stage relates to members' productive and reproductive capacities and to the need for particular social services such as child and health care, whose provision may be problematic in rural areas (Bokemeier and Garkovich 1991; Wenk 1989).

Although households are a central conceptual tool for gender analysis, feminist scholars take issue with how they are typically conceptualized and studied. Especially in family studies, the household and family often are conflated and depicted as a consensual, integrated, affective, and homogeneous social unit, acting in the collective interests of all members. Feminist scholars instead regard the household as itself contested terrain. A growing body of research on Third World households confirms that households are shaped by contradictory and contested interests, especially regarding expenditure decisions and resource allocation (Sen 1990; Fapahounda 1988; Stichter 1990). There are few equivalent studies of U.S. households, where the assumption of household unity prevails despite many indications to the contrary.

In periods of economic distress, households tend to be fluid in composition, residence, and resource distribution and consumption (Fitchen 1991; Stack 1974). Among the poor, for example, the least expensive goods and services are used by those able and willing to contribute unpaid efforts to their final consumable form (Smith 1984). The ability to reduce the cost of purchased commodities by adding labor time to their use value is especially important in financially stressed households where women take responsibility for preserving the value of commodities outside the wage economy. Thus, poor women are likely to purchase and prepare less costly food, requiring a greater contribution of their labor than would be the case if they purchased ready-to-eat, prepared food items. This means that women in poor households will often trade an increase in the time they invest in meeting household responsibilities with reductions in out-of-pocket expenses.

Migration studies illustrate both the complexities of household linkages to labor markets and the consequences of failing to recognize divergent interests within households. Migration decisions impact both individual workers and the market but they are articulated at the household level, and their impact is felt by all household members regardless of their economic activity or individual capital investments. The decision to move differs by gender in the relative impact on labor or economic activity of family members. In the traditional family, moves benefit husbands' careers at the expense of their wives' employment opportunities.

These examples suggest that both production and reproduction depend upon the availability of unpaid, nonwage, often female, labor. As such, when women are required or find it necessary to share their labor time between household and workplace, they must either expand the number of hours they work or increase the support they receive for meeting household obligations. Studies reveal, however, that the most obvious sources of support--male partners--are not always willing to assume responsibility for housework, regardless of employment status (Saraceno 1992).

State Policies

Comparative studies show that the U.S. is virtually the only industrialized nation with family and welfare policies that do not explicitly provide for women's dual role or that has any but punitive assistance to poor mothers and their children (Kamerman 1984). The failure to value reproductive labor results in a segmented welfare system comparable to the segmented character of the labor market in which women work (Nelson 1990; Pearce and McAdoo 1981; Pearce 1990). The secondary welfare system applies primarily to women and their children. In this system welfare is a privilege rather than a right; coverage is uncertain, stigmatized, and variable by locale. This contrasts with universal entitlements such as unemployment compensation and social security that are both more available and more rewarding for men. Second-class treatment is reinforced by the disempowering effect of negotiating the welfare bureaucracy, which increases disadvantage and quiescence and makes resistance unlikely, if not impossible (Nelson 1984).

In addition to the gender subtext of the welfare state, there is also an unmistakable spatial/regional subtext. For instance, inequalities among states in entitlement levels translate into significantly lower levels of assistance payments for states with large rural populations (Watkins and Watkins 1984). No state pays benefits substantial enough to raise families receiving AFDC above the poverty line. The less affluent rural states, poor by virtue of historical patterns of uneven regional development and characterized by weak economic bases and smaller tax revenues, pay the lowest benefits and are least likely to lessen vulnerability to poverty (Vinson and Jesberg 1981; Watkins and Watkins 1984). Not coincidentally, these states also have large minority populations.

We don't know what this implies for rural women vulnerable to reliance on the state welfare system since the data that would help make a more meaningful assessment are not available. However, the available information suggests that nonmetro women have poorer employment options, experience more occupational segregation and have lower earnings than women in metro areas. Therefore they face the double jeopardy of more restricted labor market opportunities and welfare entitlements which more likely than not provide subpoverty benefits (Watkins and Watkins 1984).

These trends converge with the growth of households headed by women, who are more likely to rely on welfare benefits and with the movement of poor people who seek relief by migrating from urban areas into rural counties (Cervantes 1988; Gwynn et al. 1989). All told, these trends place additional demands on a welfare system in crisis and in the process of being down-scaled. There have been recent reforms such as the Family Support Act of 1988, which is designed to move people from welfare to work and to reduce the state's role in mediating the worst impacts of the current economic crisis. These reforms seem particularly insensitive to the poor labor market conditions faced by rural people in general and rural women, in particular.

Integrating Production, Reproduction, and the State

The above discussion demonstrates that the feminist perspectives provide a more expansive and embracing view of the rural economy and recognize the crucial role women play in agricultural, non-farm, informal, and home-based enterprises. It forces us to rethink what constitutes work and how work contributes to rural production and to the needs and interests of rural communities. Further, it results in more complex notions of types of work and types of workers constitutive of labor deployment. In addition, it gives a broadened view of household production, and provides an important opening for exploring the recursive relations shaping work-household/family interactions. We need to recognize the importance of the rural household for maintaining agricultural production (as in family farming), and for sustaining petty commodity production, self-employment, and home-based enterprises. This helps to promote a broadened view of the domestic economy overall and its significance for analyses of rural poverty and rural economic change.

Work concepts which ignore or obscure the complex activities and relations both inside and outside the marketplace and the household reify the dichotomy between productive and reproductive activity. In other words, within a market-based view of the economy the household is seen as an arena which subsidizes wage employment and offers "a haven in a heartless world," at least for men.

However, it ignores the labor invested by women to enable the separation in the first place. Limiting the definition of work to paid employment and forms of self employment fails to recognize that unpaid family labor (which is not calculated in employment statistics) may be used to subsidize paid employment and that the well-being of the family enterprise often depends upon the unpaid labor of household members to realize its productive capacity. In fact, using unpaid labor directly in production may be a necessary, if not sufficient, contribution to both the reproduction of the enterprise as well as to the reproduction of the household. Since unpaid labor contributions are not generally defined by hours worked, wages, and *a priori* notions of hierarchy and control, they are likely to be ignored or underestimated in studies identifying employment demand should the household enterprise fail or be reconstituted.

Significant for our purposes, rural women's contribution to production, whether through household, home-based, resource-based, informal or formal sector work, or through reciprocal or redistributive exchanges, is likely to be more complex than in urban areas. This is particularly true given the range of structural, institutional, organizational, and ideological factors characterizing rural-urban differences. In addition to free family labor used inside or outside agricultural production, nonremunerated labor also may include the conscious deployment of women's labor to replace the need for hired labor. It is well established that women take on tasks to replace the need to hire labor or to reduce the dependence on paid workers, the family enterprise or the self-employed (often male), worker can no longer afford. Under these circumstances it is usually only the self-employed worker who is captured by employment statistics or studies. However, women may support the family enterprise by contributing to petty entrepreneurial sales and service activities as well as by engaging in other income producing activities.

Rural areas also differ by the available technical and social infrastructure such as a transportation network or public transportation arrangements. For example, using informal networks to generate child care services may depend on the availability of nearby residential space, the disregard of rental contracts, or tactics which subvert legal barriers to informal child-minding arrangements. Even access to large and heated spaces may be more difficult than for those with more abundant child care resources.

The above examples suggest that if one limits employment data to paid, formal sector work, and studies premised solely on the availability of these data, one underestimates the contribution of unpaid family labor in analyses of work and employment. Additionally, self-provisioning and housework activities, even when necessary to realize the productive capacity of a family enterprise, also are assumed to be inconsequential in analyses of employment. While such labor deployment patterns may be heuristically distinct from paid employment, interactions between paid and unpaid may in fact affect employment demand and supply, the outcome of various types of employment generation schemes (especially programs designed to enhance entrepreneurship), and research findings purported to examine but one side of the work equation.

For the poor, underestimating the effects of paid and unpaid work interactions ignores the increasing labor time women are likely to invest in self-provisioning and cost-reducing work for themselves and their families. Ignoring or underestimating the unpaid household labor time that women and other family members contribute to meeting the costs of social reproduction inhibits the successful implementation of local and federal policies, which assume the availability of women's labor and women's time.

Finally, feminist perspectives enable us to connect work issues with an understanding of the gendered nature of state welfare policies. Under such perspectives, welfare is seen as a system of oppression which not only reproduces historically-embedded ideologies about the roles of women in society, but which also serves to discipline labor in a variety of forms. For example, Gordon (1990) has argued that traditional ideas about gender roles were constituted on the basis of cultural and class norms that proffered white middle-class notions about the male-supported nuclear family. She posited that a woman's primary source of income would be from the wages earned by a man and that whatever a woman earned from her own labor would be simply supplementary. Once these norms were encoded within the American social-welfare system, they insured women's structural vulnerability to poverty. Benefits are kept so low and the process of recipiency is so demeaning that women are often forced to alternate between the subpoverty wages of the female labor market and the subpoverty benefits of the female welfare system.

Abramovitz (1988) argues, moreover, that longstanding gender ideologies provide the basis for the mutual reinforcement of patriarchy and capitalism by insuring that the productive sector has access to the benefits of reproductive activities at minimal costs. By denying the value of reproductive work carried out primarily by women, capital is valorized and sustained. Patriarchy is in turn strengthened by the differential values accorded productive ("male") and reproductive ("female") labor, respectively. Moreover, when denied a living wage except through their ties with men participating in the labor force, women are faced with exchanging dependence on men for dependence on the state. Longstanding gender ideologies ultimately provide for the institutionalization of patriarchy and the continued subordination and oppression of women.

When combined with the emerging theoretical work on spatiality, feminist theory provides a number of incisive conceptualizations for better understanding the dynamics of rural women's poverty. For instance, in addition to having a profound affect on the rural economy, economic restructuring also results in destabilizing and restructuring those welfare programs disproportionately affecting women. Thus, a picture begins to emerge of rural women under siege, caught between the interplay of a variety of forces. Historically rooted gender ideologies have conditioned rural women's structural vulnerability to poverty due to the gendered inequities of welfare programs. In addition, the successful intermeshing of patriarchy and capitalism has intensified women's structural vulnerability to the dislocations of capital and the attendant fiscal crises of the welfare state. Consequently, rural women whose employment opportunities have been eroded by the processes of economic restructuring also face the further erosion of already inadequate welfare entitlements as a result of the same economic processes.

Discouraging as this interpretation may seem, Fraser (1989) suggests that by theorizing the gendered nature of the welfare state, we confront de-gendered interpretations that serve to normalize, naturalize, and depoliticize the welfare problematic. In so doing we provide the potential for praxis by acknowledging welfare as a fundamentally political discourse, a contested domain of interpretation. In this domain the potential for agency and struggle could transform consciousness and pave the way for transforming the material circumstances of many women's lives.

Conclusion: Toward New Explanations of Rural Women's Poverty

Scholarship on the rural economy has typically emphasized analyses of the farm structure, the capitalization of agriculture, and the changing production and labor relations shaping the use of landed property. This emphasis has especially characterized scholarship in the U.S., thus explaining the relative neglect by rural sociologists, development economists, and rural policy analysts of women's contribution to the rural economy. In the face of rural income and resource diversification and a resurgence of Marxist and other critical interpretations of rural labor relations, there has been increased recognition of the salience of the non-farm sector as an important production arena. It interfaces with and helps to structure agricultural capacities. The concept rural, in other words, has been recast from an identification solely with agricultural activities to one including a range of non-farm, wage-based activities and self-employment ventures.

This reconceptualization also reflects the contribution of feminist scholars to analyses of rural work and rural poverty. These scholars have identified the contribution of women's home-based productive activities (such as subcontracting arrangements and out-sourcing relations), as well as women's unpaid and previously unrecognized labor contribution to the household and to economic capacity. Additionally, feminist research on domestic labor and the importance of unpaid domestic work, whether viewed as a subsidy to capital or as patriarchal relations of subordination and labor control, draws attention to the necessary contribution of women's paid and unpaid labor in constructing daily life.

The feminist critique points to new directions for theory and research on women's poverty. Feminist theory provides the basic tools for constructing a theoretical model to apply to the problem of rural women's poverty. It properly focuses attention on gender, space, and the economy, relations of production and reproduction, and the ways these are embedded in social institutions. Yet it is our contention that for the most part, previous theoretical accounts have erred by providing a too limited understanding of the intersection of each.

At the outset, we claim that it is an error to conceptualize women's rural poverty solely in terms of gender and the family. To do so only 'tacks gender on' as an empirical apparatus, long after the theoretical issues concerning rural poverty have been decided. Such approaches may capture significant elements of women's role in the social reproduction of the family, but they often fail to recognize the significance of women in the process of production.

In addition, we maintain that conceptual claims made on behalf of the distinctiveness of the 'rural' confound our ability to understand the web of social relations which connect all spaces, from the global metropolis to the rural farmstead. What is at issue is the tendency to conceptualize poverty in such contexts outside of the larger space-economy within which these regions are embedded. Rural poverty, in short, must not be seen as a particularly rural question, but one that cuts across all spaces, from urban to rural and from local to global.

Finally, we also question those frameworks which seek to understand poverty solely in economic terms, i.e., outside of either its gender or spatial contexts. Such analyses tend to so over-emphasize the role of waged labor that questions regarding uncompensated work in the household are never asked; or they suffer from a spatial myopia which treats poverty as a monolithic phenomenon instead of one outcome of a geographically differentiated production system.

In contrast, the conceptualization we offer positions theories of women's rural poverty within a larger theoretical framework, and in the process seeks to provide the grounds for a more complete understanding of the range of social processes involved. This framework synthesizes theory and research from diverse sources and perspectives to focus on the intersections between social reproduction, production, and the state, as these are embedded in time and space.

In summary, in this chapter we have attempted to show that the gendered nature of rural women's poverty operates at four levels of abstraction:

1. *In lived experience of poverty.* We have argued that poverty itself is "gendered," i.e., the causes, consequences and experiences of poverty differ in significant ways for women and men. This is not to ignore or deny the many commonalities in men's and women's poverty or that they share many of the same root causes in the operation of the economy. At the same time there are fundamental differences stemming from women's and men's different locations in social relations of production and reproduction and in the way the state mediates these relations.

2. *In theories that explain poverty.* Our review of poverty theory found that most standard explanations of poverty, either of people or place, do not take account of gender differences or do so only to a very limited extent. Most typically this involves recognizing an empirical difference in poverty rates or dichotomizing gender to demonstrate that women and men differ in their access to resources, without explaining how or why this occurs (or in some cases, as in human capital theory, providing inadequate or discredited explanations). We argue that poverty theories that do not recognize the gendered nature of poverty and fail to understand it in these terms can never fully explain poverty, let alone understand women's poverty.

3. *In data about work and poverty.* A major conclusion of this review is that data collection on social and economic conditions for people and places is highly biased by the failure to recognize the gendered nature of all social relations. Official statistics often ignore gender or gender related activities. Concepts such as employment, unemployment, labor market, and labor force are the focus of official data collection efforts, and are formulated and used as if they were gender neutral. Thus, they obscure differences in the activities of women and men. The failure to regularly or consistently conceptualize and collect information on other forms of work conceals much of what occurs in women's daily life and diminishes much of the real work performed by women. This in turn makes it difficult to honestly assess causes, consequences, and experiences of poverty or to formulate realistic policies and programs to counter it.

4. *In public policy aimed at poverty.* Feminist analyses of the welfare state and welfare programs show how deeply patriarchal ideology and assumptions pervade these domains. The existence of a dual or segmented welfare system parallels and reinforces disadvantage in a segmented economy, thus exacerbating the gendered aspects of poverty. The devaluation of women's work, the failure to acknowledge women's work as such, and the lack of information on this work contribute to misinformation and confusion about the nature of the welfare system and debate over the forms that fair and effective social support policies should take.

We have shown that feminist scholarship is responsible for exposing the gendered nature of poverty, providing important advances over previous work which has ignored this aspect of the problem. However, feminist theory as it currently stands is also subject to criticism, particularly in its treatment of social and spatial diversity of the poor. There is little in current feminist scholarship on poverty that examines the problems of rural women, or of different groups of rural women, or that would suggest that poverty is anything but an undifferentiated national (or urban) U.S. problem or an issue for third-world development.

Our goal has been to demonstrate how a feminist analysis can advance understanding of women's poverty in rural America, but it should be obvious that the task has barely begun. Understanding gender and poverty is predicated on reformulating conceptions of gender and space and thus women's position within the rural economy. Much of this effort must be directed at new theory, new research, and new data to permit this reformulation. We must incorporate both relations of production and reproduction to understand how capitalism and patriarchy shape people's lives--women's and men's--in specific locales embedded in an expanding global political economy but in a contracting world.

Notes

This chapter was prepared by Ann Tickamyer, University of Kentucky; Janet Bokemeier, Michigan State University; Shelly Feldman, Cornell University; Rosalind Harris, University of Kentucky; John Paul Jones, University of Kentucky; and DeeAnn Wenk, University of Oklahoma.

8

Rural Families and
Children in Poverty

(T)he situation in the open-country pockets of poverty in the 1970's seems less depressing than some of the present rural poverty situations. Where there were stable jobs, family-based support networks, enduring marriages, and home ownership then, now in many rural places there appear to be inadequate jobs, fragile man-woman relationships, smaller and weaker social networks, and a mobility and insecurity of housing tenure that keep many people on the edge of poverty--and some of them on the edge of homelessness.

—Fitchen (1991).

Introduction

The processes that create and perpetuate poverty among rural families and children are poorly understood and seldom studied. The paucity of rural research stands in dramatic contrast to active scholarship on urban, notably ghetto, poverty. The urban underclass literature provides coherent, albeit competitive (Prosser 1991), explanations that link the characteristics of the local/regional labor market, residency patterns, and community institutions to family dynamics, child rearing practices, and child outcomes. Analyses of the urban underclass and children at risk of developmental delay are controversial. Nevertheless, the literature postulates specific, observable relationships across levels of analysis.

No comparable analytic framework exists for rural families and children in persistent poverty. Macro-level analyses of poverty emphasize the structure of economic opportunity, local labor market characteristics, job quality, and returns to investment in human capital. The consequences of such structural realities for people are relatively ignored. Micro-level analyses typically emphasize coping behavior and how people respond to adverse circumstances. The context of such reactions is usually assumed rather than explained. Sociologists and economists lean towards macro-level explanations, while psychologists favor micro-level ones. Structural/attitudinal explanations also provide bases for alternative policy recommendations (Kane 1987).

Even the most cursory literature review reveals the need for a comprehensive conceptual orientation that integrates macro- and micro-analyses and provides a sensible framework within which to explore multiple levels of determination. Rural poverty is not a singular phenomenon. Families confront socioeconomic realities that are both historically and regionally specific (Jensen 1990). Individuals have characteristics that reflect their own accomplishments, but they also confront structural realities such as social class membership, gender, and ethnicity. Parents must make hard decisions as they balance personal preferences and responsibilities for their children. These decisions likely reflect parents' realistic alternatives and personal maturity as well as their capacity to meet children's needs. All this means that a family's race or ethnicity, social class, life course, and children's developmental status are the smallest set of factors that poverty analyses must situate properly in time and space.

The macro/micro interface is an issue in sociology because overly deterministic analyses at both the macro- and the micro-levels have not successfully accounted for the diversity of human responses. The important anthology by Knorr-Cetina and Cicourel (1981) reflects the leadership of micro-level theorists, while the works of Giddens (1981, 1984) and Mingione (1991) depart from macro-level concerns.

Although a satisfactory theoretical synthesis has not emerged, some viable methodological procedures have been articulated. Innovative studies in a variety of substantive areas analyze individual survey data in their ecological contexts (Gottfredson and Taylor 1986; Entwistle, Casterline, and Sayed 1989; Sampson 1991; Garbarino and Kosteling in press). Nevertheless, the potential to incorporate aerial data concerning the institutional and socioeconomic of survey respondents remains "both large and untapped" (Elder 1985:39).

All these methodological observations focus attention on mediation processes, i.e., how structural factors limit alternatives and how individuals modify their own environments. Given this problem definition, census or survey data analysis can provide incomplete insights into poverty. Ethnographic research is a necessary complement. Qualitative studies can make a substantial contribution to our understanding of social processes, how individuals appraise their situation and select a course of action. A synthesis between quantitative and qualitative methodologies is virtually required by the problem posed. Moreover, both quantitative and qualitative researchers strengthen their work by bringing a longitudinal perspective to their studies.

To date, neither the theoretical nor the methodological potentials have been realized in research on poverty among rural families and children. In fact, little research specifically address rural families and children in poverty and nothing focuses on family dynamics and processes that foster or impede the transmission of poverty from one generation to the next. Consequently, it is necessary to extrapolate from disparate but relevant studies.

The purpose of this chapter is to demonstrate how sensitivity to issues at the macro/micro interface can refocus existing research traditions and provide a temporal dimension to social process analysis. We reviewed the major theoretical perspectives that figure prominently in the literature on families and children in poverty, focusing on their contributions to our understanding of rural poverty. We were compelled by the paucity of scholarship to develop integrating themes and found that the macro/micro interface was a useful organizing principle. We were particularly concerned to explore mechanisms by which poverty was or was not transmitted from parent to child, and these mechanisms drew our attention to parenting in its longitudinal and social context.

Social institutions intrude on all intimate relationships, but poor families and children are particularly vulnerable to social policy. Analytically, the design and delivery of social services stands at the nexus of the macro/micro interface. Accordingly, we incorporate service delivery as a theme and advocate integrating service providers and clients into the process of problem identification, policy analysis, and program evaluation.

Rural Context for Families

It is difficult to be poor in any community, but certain paradoxes are specific to rural areas. Traditionally, a rural life style has been associated with self-reliance, neighborliness, conservative values, and respect for tradition. Phrased less positively, rural residents are regarded as nosey, behind the times, and resistant to change. Independent of value judgments, people's lives are grounded in both family and community (Waltman 1986). Those who live on land settled by their ancestors experience an attachment that is increasingly rare in geographically mobile societies. Attuned to their heritage, families can live modestly, yet not perceive themselves to be deprived (Kermit Nash, personal communication). Furthermore, the decision to "live poor" may reflect a deliberate choice, an alternative life style elected for religious or secular reasons (Ward 1988).

Families and children who are poor do not necessarily think they have problems or need help, especially if they compare favorably with their daily associates (Jencks and Mayer 1990). Nevertheless, an urban-oriented mass media certainly makes the rural poor realize that they are different. What it means to grow up poor and rural in the age of Nintendo and MTV is a paradox worthy of study.

Rural communities both attract and repel residents, and this is an enduring paradox of rural living. Poor families have limited choices and those living in rural areas have even fewer choices. For example, there is typically one public school but no private ones with specialized programs. In addition, one public health clinic may exist, but no hospital or private physician. And, there are very few family daycare providers and virtually no centers with sliding fee scales. Still, some people prefer the rural environment and never leave. Others sample city life and return to the social supports and familiar lifestyle of their rural community. Some may have "failed" in the city, but other return migrants consider themselves to be rich, if not in money, in security, autonomy, and personal relationships.

Another important paradox concerns economic maintenance. Rural wages are lower than urban wages, but the possibilities for self-provisioning are greater. Nevertheless, families who participate actively in the non-market economy can enjoy a higher living standard than monetary income alone would suggest. In order to do so, however, they must work. Families with access to land may be able to use well water, collect firewood, grow vegetables and fruit, and raise barnyard animals. Barter is common in rural communities, so labor and/or goods can be exchanged outside the cash nexus. Production may also be designed to bring in cash, which may invite state regulation. Local ordinances can prevent rural residents from exercising initiative. In a Gullah community in South Carolina, one woman noted:

> Seem like when you try to do something for yourself, they try to stop you. We always doing something fo' hunt money. You got something you raise, you can make, you can make some money selling. And doing them a favor bringing fresh, nice things to sell. And white people buy it, too. Now they say the fish and things stink up the city (Adra Gaillard, in Young, in preparation).

Despite opportunities for self-provisioning, contemporary rural families have a substantial need for cash income. Processed food, transportation, utilities and health care are proportionately more expensive in rural areas (Ghelfi 1988). Consequently, an important paradox of rural poverty is the need to earn cash income and the high cost of doing so. Travel is problematic. Distances are great, public transportation is limited, and back roads are in poor repair. A reliable automobile is virtually a necessity, almost a precondition for obtaining the job that would pay for the car. Transportation is a serious limiting factor for all aspects of rural life, especially employment, training, child care, and service utilization. It is also a major item in rural school budgets, which limits the programs that can be offered.

Rural communities with small tax bases experience problems in providing public services. Nevertheless, benign neglect generates another paradox for poor rural families. Low taxes, few ordinances, and liberal zoning restrictions allow rural families to meet their housing needs more economically than their urban counterparts. The quality may be marginal, but flexible housing arrangements provide some measure of relief to poor families. The family who owns several acres can move a mobile home onto the property and establish a multi-generational homestead. This could permit a daughter going through divorce to retain custody of her children, save money, and engage in activities like training or work (Fitchen 1981).

The accessibility of relatives introduces another paradox of rural poverty. Rural residents are likely to know which families have serious problems, so children in need of protection or mentoring are likely to be identified. On the other hand, being born into a family of ne'er-do-wells can stigmatize children and make it less likely that the community will rally to their support. When relationships are positive, the coincidence of kith and kin can provide powerful support networks for poor families.

Children with access to their extended family have many opportunities to experience potentially enriching relationships. This is frequently cited as a positive characteristic in the black community, because extended families are nearly twice as prevalent among blacks than whites (Tolson and Wilson 1990). Extended families relieve parents of some of the child rearing burdens, which might improve the parent/child relationship. Nevertheless, successful children raised in extended families are obligated to those who sacrificed on their behalf. Kin support is double edged (Emily Arcia, personal communication).

Even if an entire family in a traditional rural community has a negative influence on a child, adults in the school, church, or other institutions may exercise a countervailing influence. When communities lose population through outmigration, there are fewer institutional supports for families. Churches close, schools consolidate, women who previously volunteered seek paid employment. Families left to their own devices may be the very ones who would benefit from a dense network of community support. To the extent that community institutions are undermined by demographic change, the possibilities of social disorganization increase. Families and children with few resources suffer.

When community supports are disintegrating, the negative consequences of being born "on the wrong side of the tracks" are probably greatest. Fitchen (1981) illustrates how class prejudice operates even within ethnically homogenous communities. She argues that the hidden injuries of class begin early and become intensified during adolescence. Supporting the notion of stereotyping, Bleckman (1982) reports that teachers attributed classroom performance problems to children known to be from single parent or poor homes, whether or not there was corroborating evidence. All available research suggests that stigma has serious, negative influences on children.

Families and children who are poor find it both easier and harder to live in rural rather than urban environments. The paradoxes of rural poverty are apparent. Tradition is both comforting and stifling; self-provisioning is both viable and exhausting; kin networks are both protective and smothering; ties to place are both comforting and constraining. When greater economic opportunity lies only beyond family and community, people raised with traditional rural values experience conflict. There is a specificity about rural poverty, but it is subtle.

Demographic Perspectives

Little research has focused specifically on poor rural families and children, but most of what exists is written from a demographic perspective. The general question posed is how rural poverty is similar to and different from urban poverty. The child rather than the family is the preferential unit of analysis for the study of childhood poverty (Preston, 1984).

Trends in childhood poverty are fundamentally similar in urban and rural areas. Eggebeen and Lichter (1991) demonstrated that the proportion of all children in poverty decreased between 1960 and 1980 and increased thereafter. Deep poverty, defined as 50 percent or less of the official poverty level, represented a substantial proportion of all child poverty. Poverty was more prevalent among black than white children. Indeed, "Apart from disability of the household head, rural location is the most powerful factor associated with black childhood poverty" (Duncan and Rodgers 1988:1013).

Ethnic and racial minorities are particularly vulnerable to poverty if they live in rural areas. Kraly and Hirschman (1990) provided an essential historical perspective on childhood poverty among Mexicans, Native Americans, and blacks. This research documents the fact that minority parents were generally unable to provide children with economic advantages, especially if they resided in rural communities. Jensen and Tienda (1989) analyzed more recent data on families and reported that both minority and residential status were associated with family income levels. Nevertheless, no adequate multivariate analysis of childhood poverty captures the diversity of ethnicity in the contemporary United States. Data analysis is limited by the small size of certain ethnic groups, who may nevertheless be very visible in particular communities. Arcia, Keyes, Gallagher, and Herrick (1992) estimate that fully 32 percent of children under five are members of ethnic minorities. They map the proportion of young minority children by state, thereby illustrating concentrations of black, Hispanic and/or Native American children, especially in the southeast and southwest. Minority children are already the majority in places like California and the District of Columbia. Major sections of the United States will be predominantly black or Hispanic within another generation. Multiculturalism is a reality, not just a slogan, in rural as well as urban communities.

Poverty rates are higher among children resident in non-metropolitan counties. Child poverty declined dramatically between 1960 and 1970, only to increase between 1980 and 1990. Childhood poverty and deep poverty both remain prevalent (Lichter and Eggebeen 1992). This is important because taking the child rather than the family as the unit of analysis can overestimate the incidence of poverty and underestimate its depth (Smith 1989).

Non-metro children have higher poverty rates, regardless of family type. Poor non-metro children are more likely than their metro counterparts to live in two-parent families. Children in female-headed households are more likely to experience poverty, regardless of residence. Indeed, Lichter and Eggebeen (1992) report that increased rates of child poverty attributable to higher prevalence of female headed households more than offset the economic improvements attributable to increases in female employment, rising levels of parental education, and decreasing family size. Duncan and Rodgers (1991) reported similar results, although they provided no metro/non-metro comparison.

The effect of family composition varies by ethnic group. Black children continuously living in two-parent families were as likely to experience poverty as white children who always lived in single-headed families. The poverty experience may also vary by family type. Ross and Morrissey (1989) found that children in non-metro, male-headed families tended to be temporarily poor, while those in female-headed families disproportionately experienced persistent poverty.

These findings do not mean that marriage cures poverty. Female heads of house are a heterogeneous group because ever married and never married mothers have different demographic characteristics. Fitchen (1992) argues that marriage alone cannot change the poverty status of most rural, never married mothers because the low wages that potential mates could earn in depressed labor markets would keep the family among the working poor.

What is specific about childhood poverty in rural areas is how recent macroeconomic changes have had differential, negative consequences for young families (O'Hare 1988). Between 1979 and 1986, real median family income declined by 10 percent while the poverty rate increased 55 percent among young adults in rural areas. Fully one-fourth of all non-metro children lived in poor households by 1986. Considering only households headed by persons 18-29, the poverty rate increased 13 points to 32 percent between 1979 and 1986. Young Hispanic families experienced a 16 point increase to 46 percent, while blacks saw a 22 percent increase to 68 percent.

Many of these poor families have wage earners. Nearly one-third of young rural families with one wage earner were poor in 1986, and nearly 10 percent of those with two or more workers still did not earn enough to bring family income above the poverty line. Unemployment, underemployment, and low wages are all implicated in high levels of poverty among children in young, non-metro families (O'Hare 1988).

Children born into poverty can realistically expect to spend much of their pre-adult lives poor. Morrissey (1991a) found that approximately 12 percent of young adults had been persistently poor as both children and adults. Intergenerational poverty was higher among non-whites, Southerners, non-metro residents and those raised in female-headed households. Other evidence comes from statistical analyses. Bane and Ellwood (1986) found that children born into poverty experienced very long periods of disadvantage, especially if they were black. Adams and Duncan (1990:14) focused on the long-term poor. They note: "(C)hildren account for the majority of people living in households with able bodied heads but in long-term poverty. This holds for both blacks and whites, within and outside metropolitan areas and in both the recent (1979-1986) and early (1967-1979) period." Rogers (1991) provided a complementary analysis. She reported that the strongest predictors of the adequacy of income to family needs were parental education, number of siblings and marital status. Metro/non-metro residence had a statistically significant effect. Nevertheless, in separate metro and non-metro models, the variables behaved similarly, suggesting that the same fundamental processes were at work (Carolyn Rogers, personal communication).

The demographic literature provides important perspectives on childhood poverty in rural communities, but it does not capture the complexity of children's experiences with poverty. Duncan and Rodgers (1988) emphasized the frequency that children made transitions into and out of poverty, but recent work (Devine, Plunkett, and Wright 1992) suggests that chronic as opposed to episodic poverty has stabilized at higher levels during the 1980's than during earlier periods. Persistent poverty may become a reality for increasing numbers of urban and rural children.

These findings raise important questions. Does it matter how old children are when they experience their first spell of poverty? How important is the depth of poverty and its persistence? Do children experience poverty differently if it is relatively common or uncommon among their peers? How does household composition mediate the way poverty impacts children? How do secular economic trends influence children's perceptions of economic opportunity? What are the likely consequences for the intergenerational transmission of poverty? How can social policy address these issues?

These questions indicate that demographic perspectives on childhood poverty need to be integrated with other substantive conceptual orientations. In all cases, a longitudinal perspective is essential, whether it derives from economic history, developmental psychology, life course studies, and/or the family stress and coping literatures. The demographic literature will thereby be able to transcend description and embrace interpretation.

Family Process Perspectives

Most poverty researchers proceed from macro-level concerns and ignore how people react to economic hardship. Most family dynamics researchers proceed from micro-level concerns and fail to focus on the families experiencing economic hardship. If one were to represent contemporary scholarship in a Venn diagram, there would be little overlap between the circles at the macro/micro interface. Moreover, virtually none of the overlap would concern poor, rural families. This reflects major conceptual and empirical weakness.

It is overly ambitious to develop in this chapter a comprehensive conceptual framework that successfully integrates macro- and micro-level processes. Nevertheless, existing scholarship provides an important beginning. New analyses of household survival strategies are being conducted in an explicitly historical and structural context. These approaches invite one to consider combinations of market and non-market activities, the former meditated and the latter not mediated by a cash nexus. This distinction casts literatures concerning family stress and social support networks in a new light because scholarship can be interpreted as exploring how market and non-market activities interact at the household level and how families exchange goods and services outside a cash nexus. The life course literature can also be subsumed under a general survival strategies framework. Because life course analysis works at the interface of history and biography, it provides important insights into the macro/micro interface. A more comprehensive conceptual framework could be developed if future conceptual and empirical efforts focused on these issues.

Survival Strategy Perspectives

The concept of strategy figures prominently in social scientific research. Strategy usually implies that individuals or collectivities make conscious and rational decisions, taking into account their immediate needs and long-term goals. Structural constraints limit viable alternatives. Indeed, Crow (1989) suggests that the most potentially interesting strategies to sociologists are those developed under conditions of severe constraint.

Analyses of the survival strategies of poor families have encompassed urban and rural families in countries with very different economic development levels. Consequently, the survival strategy literature is the least parochial of all perspectives on poor rural families and children.

Most analyses of survival strategies focus on particular households (e.g., Stack 1974) or prototypical agricultural social strata (e.g., Garrett 1986). Researchers seek to emphasize the logic people use when they allocate scarce resources such as land or time to different activities like self-provisioning or wage labor. They use actor-centered language, which can highlight differences in the perceptions of actors and observers. Nevertheless, analyses generally reflect the theoretical predilections of researchers. Rarely are survival strategies defined as the deliberate, self-conscious formulations of householders. Whatever researchers observe can be interpreted to reflect actors' survival strategies, as devined or perceived by these researchers. This is the classical functionalist dilemma.

Analyses of survival strategies can escape the limitations of functionalism only if researchers identify structural factors that limit choice and favor certain patterns. One viable analytic framework is that of Mingione (1991), who works within a Marxist paradigm. He assigns considerable importance to processes of social reproduction, which are undertheorized in classical Marxist analyses. Marxist analysis has been bedeviled by the question: How do households reproduce the social relations of production specific to a given mode of production? When inquiry focuses on capitalism, the query is more insistent: Once there is an alienation of production from the household, how do household dynamics and economic dynamics interrelate? This focuses on the diverse conditions and organizational relations which allow human beings to survive in various social contexts.

Households embody social relations ordered by mutual obligations that collectively allow participants to survive. They are differentiated collectivities. Households exhibit an internal division of labor with regard to decision-making and allocating tasks and rewards. They are characterized by resource pooling and reciprocity and embedded in their social context of friendship and community networks.

Fundamentally, households are interdependent with the cycle of capital, so survival strategies must be analyzed in their macroeconomic context. This is the major principle distinguishing Mingione's approach from other analyses of survival strategies. One previous cycle of capital was associated with the incorporation of children into wage labor, another with the corresponding incorporation of married women. The current cycle reflects the increase of surplus population in industrialized countries and the diffusion of informal activities.

Global economic restructuring has eliminated or redefined many jobs in the formal economy, so workers must support themselves and their families in other ways. The macroeconomic situation encourages workers to engage in self-provisioning and informal activities, work that produces goods or services for domestic use outside the cash nexus. Self-provisioning and informalization are both examples of non-commodified relationships in which labor power is not exchanged for a cash payment. An irony of advanced capitalism is that non-commodified relations become increasingly common while early capitalism destroyed them.

Households have different capacities to engage in self-provisioning and informal labor, and these differences reflect both household composition and economic resources. Rural households with access to productive resources are advantaged over urban households in the same social class. Nevertheless, small, poor families are most disadvantaged in the informal economy because they have few human or material resources to deploy.

Family Stress and Social Support Perspectives

The family stress and social support literatures use the language of social systems. This is both a strength and a weakness. The idea that all system elements are interrelated discourages parochial attention to a limited range of variables, but it also encourages interpretations suggesting that the patterns observed reflect system imperatives. Underdetermination and overdetermination are the two sides of the functionalist coin.

If one abandons functionalism, it is possible to integrate the family stress and social support literature into the more general conceptual framework developed by Mingione (1991). One can impose the fundamental distinction between commodified and non-commodified relations and argue that these literatures basically explore non-commodified relations. The subset of research about economic hardship probes the consequences of major changes in commodified relations (e.g., job loss or persistent poverty) for non-commodified relations (e.g., parenting style or network support). This problem definition situates family processes research at the macro/micro interface, where it is more likely that students of the family will recognize the implications of their research for economic development and public policy.

The family stress literature includes a subset of work on economic distress. Substantial research has focused on stress associated with major life transitions (e.g., marriage/divorce, childbirth and parenting, moving, loss of a loved one). In economic hardship studies, the precipitating factor may be divorce or separation. This literature focuses on the economic deterioration experienced by women and their children (Sidel 1986). Poverty may also be precipitated by job loss or irregular employment. There is a substantial literature, mostly focusing on men. Little of this work is written from the family stress perspective (See Voydanoff 1984; Voydanoff and Donnelly 1988).

Studies of economic distress provide several important insights into family dynamics. Economic distress is associated with marital dissolution and increased mental and emotional disturbance. Persistently inadequate economic resources and the perception of economic hardship are associated with depression, loss of self-esteem and feelings of mastery. The length of joblessness is important because the long-term unemployed are likely to experience chronic distress and depression that may encourage unconstructive behaviors. Some individuals blame themselves for their job loss, while others blame factors beyond their control. Those who can count on the support of family and friends weather stressful experiences better than those whose support networks are weak. "(T)he combination most productive of psychological distress is to be simultaneously single, isolated, exposed to burdensome parental obligations and--most serious of all--poor" (Pearlin and Johnson 1977:714 cited in McLoyd 1990:320).

Parental behavior mediates the effects of economic hardship on children. The critical mediating factor is how fathers react to job loss. Paternal punitiveness and low nurturance cause the father-child relationship to deteriorate. Children's responses may include socioemotional problems, somatic symptoms and reduced aspirations and expectations (McLoyd 1989). Parents who are poor are reported to value obedience, rely on corporal punishment, express little affection, and fail to respond to the child's socioemotional needs. One can attribute these behaviors to emotional distress caused by substantial environmental stress (McLoyd 1990). Parents experiencing economic hardship and social isolation can neglect and/or abuse children. Indeed, McLoyd (1990) believes that the literature supports a causal relationship between poverty and child abuse.

The social stress literature is not well integrated with the social support literature. Nevertheless, it appears that social networks moderate tendencies toward punitive parenting and arbitrary discipline. Networks can provide emotional support, informational support and role modeling, parenting support, and intervention in the case of abuse or neglect (McLoyd and Wilson 1990).

Social networks can be overwhelmed by demands made on them. During the recent farm crisis, many families lost their farms and in some areas, farm loss was of epidemic proportions. Formal and informal support networks disintegrated (Heffernan and Heffernan 1986). This highlights a key feature of social support networks--they are reciprocal. They break down when participants do not have the time, energy, and/or resources to dedicate to mutual support. It is easier for the non-poor than the poor to maintain effective and extensive social support networks (Mingione 1991).

In summary, the family stress/family support literatures provide powerful evidence regarding the deleterious consequences of economic distress and poverty for family relations in general and child development in particular. Available scholarship has several important weaknesses. It does not disentangle the effects of culture, ethnicity, household composition, and social class membership. It does not focus on persistent poverty and the likely cumulative, negative effects on children. And, it fails to explore economic hardship in the context of rural environments, except in the special case of farm loss.

More generally, the family stress/social support literatures are not integrated into a structural analysis of the conditions that families confront. The basic distinction between commodified and non-commodified relations recasts research in a neo-Marxist rather than a neo-functionalist framework. This reformulation permits an explicit analysis of the macro-micro interface. This may serve to humanize analyses of global economic restructuring and to ground family dynamics analyses in their specific socioeconomic contexts.

Life Course Perspectives

Life course perspectives figure prominently in family studies, especially in sociology and social history. They explicitly ground individuals in time and space, and place individuals in the context of significant others. Consequently, life course orientations provide a generalized ecological perspective on human development that one can readily integrate with a comparable approach in developmental psychology (e.g., Garbarino 1985).

Several concepts figure prominently in the life course literature. The concept of cohort, explicitly adapted from demography (Ryder 1965), situates age-mates in historical time; the concept of social age situates age-graded social statuses and normative role sequences in the life course (Elder and Caspi 1988). One's personal biography reflects a specific combination of trajectories and transitions, qualitative changes in at least some aspect of daily living (Harris 1987).

Elder's research on children of the Great Depression is a seamless web that documents the consequences of economic hardship. He found that adult men and women experienced decrease or loss of earnings differently, because the breadwinner role was traditionally salient for men. The long-term consequences of economic hardship for mental health were more negative for men than women (Elder and Liker 1982). Paternal behavior, notably punitive parenting, mediated the impact of economic hardship on children (Elder 1974). Both the age and gender of children and the match of temperament between child and parent influenced the consequences of parental behavior (Elder 1979; Elder, Caspi, and Van Nguyen 1986; Elder, Liker, and Cross 1984). These studies suggest that child characteristics and parental behavior are both important determinants of the consequences of economic hardship for children. Finally, the consequences of economic hardship for adult women varied by social class membership (Elder and Liker 1982:267): "Neither a privileged life nor one of unrelenting deprivation assures the inner resources for successful aging."

The life course perspective has several important strengths. It provides a vocabulary for conceptualizing linkages across levels of analysis, space, and time, so it invites multidisciplinary collaboration. A life course perspective is sensitive to the interface between personal and historical time and explicitly considers the relationship between individual and family time. Research appropriately focuses on family dynamics, and in the case of the literature under review, on interpersonal behaviors that are reactions to economic stress. Finally, it identifies potentially critical "transitions" that represent opportunities to redirect the life course.

The logic of life course analysis would argue that observed relationships are strongly conditioned by history and location as well as by personal and family characteristics. The conceptual orientation would, therefore, require that reactions to economic hardship be evaluated in a variety of circumstances. If behavior, and therefore its interpretation, is historically conditioned, it would be sensible to develop linkages between the life course and structural forces that influence it. Harris (1987:28) advocates a classical dialectical approach to study how people "both constitute and are constituted by the socio-historical process." Mayer and Schoepflin (1989) direct particular attention to the state's role in shaping individual lives. With regard to life course transitions like employment and marriage, they argue:

> The state turns these transitions into public life events and interlocks organizationally and functionally differentiated domains of society as people flow through them…(T)he state (also) accentuates transition events, age brackets, and life segments, and provides external rather than individually created order throughout life. In this way the state clearly contributes to a differentiated structure of the life course (Mayer and Schoepflin 1989:203).

This provocative argument has not been developed by researchers working within the life course perspective, although, given the common vocabulary of "transitions," no conceptual translations are required. This approach has particular salience for those interested in poverty. Public policy as implemented by local bureaucracies impinges on people in regular ways at specific points along the life course. Consequently, it may be useful to consider the relationships among personal biographies and public policy, thereby facilitating the systematic analysis of relevant micro/macro linkages. Just as state policy changes, the nature of these linkages should change. The resulting analysis should, therefore, be dynamic rather than static, specific to time and place rather than disembodied in the historical present.

Social Service Perspectives

Human service professionals perhaps come closest to integrating the divergent perspectives on family and child poverty addressed in this chapter. To them it is clear that definitions of "rural" and "poverty" are comparative constructs having importance but not immediacy. Simple numerical definitions, whether for rurality or poverty, ignore heterogeneity and complexities of the person/environment relationship. It has been suggested that social service workers accept "rural" as a philosophical entity, taking into account the character, values, and cultural expectations of the rural resident (Tippin 1980). Accepting self-definition by the poor is another alternative (Collier 1984).

An ecological-systems, person-in-the-environment perspective is at the core of social work practice (Meyer 1987). It requires the melding of macro and micro perspectives. Understanding derived from social network, organizational, and stress theory also may be used. Generally, however, practitioners have found the predominant theoretical approaches more helpful for explanation than for change (Briar 1987).

In rural areas, social service resources are very limited. Most existing services are mandated by federal law--e.g., income maintenance, child welfare, supplemental nutrition programs, vulnerable adult protection, and foster care. Private programs generally supplement the public services with timely and individualized responses, particularly for short-term needs--e.g., food shelves, shelters for the homeless and for battered women and their children. While both sectors recognize the need for prevention and integration, neither seems willing or able to mobilize forces to synchronize political, economic, education, familial institutions.   Nor are they able to implement nationally the intensive, comprehensive and flexible family- and community-centered services which have proven effective at state and local levels (Schorr and Schorr 1988).

Social welfare programs, particularly income transfers, have substantially alleviated poverty among the elderly over the past fifty years, doing so at the expense of families and children (Preston 1984).   They have also had some impact on conditions of the urban poor, but have been significantly less successful in ameliorating poverty in rural areas (Jensen 1989).

Research has verified that rural residents are less likely to receive benefits from welfare programs and transfer payments than are urban residents. These programs are, therefore, less successful at ameliorating rural poverty (Jensen 1989; McLanahan 1985; Rank and Hirschl 1988; Rogers 1991). Explanations for the lack of success divide along individual and structural lines. Poor rural families may be ineligible for welfare programs because they are married, employed or homeowners. Even those assets used in work (e.g., cars, trucks, equipment) may disqualify families from food stamps or other programs (Jensen 1989), but new policies that would encourage and enable accumulation of assets by those with low income are proposed (Sherradan 1991).   New federal legislation mandates the AFDC/Unemployed Parent program that should benefit the rural poor who were disproportionately excluded from benefits.   The Children's Defense Fund recommends supplementing adequate funding for child care, Head Start, and health care with progress to meet the "special needs of children in vulnerable families who face the effects of drug use, emotional problems, abuse, and neglect" (Sherman 1992:10).

Socioeconomic, linguistic, and cultural barriers contribute to underutilization of services (Garcia Coll 1990). Arcia, Keyes, Gallagher and Herrick (1992) developed a generic model of service utilization.   They emphasized the interaction among three sets of variables: predisposing family factors, the family's perception of its problems, and enabling elements for services that can address the problem. Family characteristics associated with underutilization of health and social services include minority ethnic status, young parental age, low parental education, female-headed householder, and large family size. Among the important disenabling factors are the costs--time, inconvenience, and money--associated with procuring services. These disenabling factors are clearly implicated in the underutilization of services in rural communities. In rural areas it is often difficult to obtain information about, and access to, existing social services. Important limiting factors include illiteracy, lack of information and outreach, lack of public transportation and expense of private transportation. Programs designed and administered at the county level are particularly vulnerable to local prejudices against poor and minority populations, especially in the southeast, with its highly stratified communities (Duncan and Tickamyer 1988). Local officials may also "keep quiet" about programs and benefits or fail to offer programs that they find incompatible with prevailing power relations (Gene Summers, personal communication).

Rural people subscribe to values of independence and self-sufficiency and, determined to do it themselves, may purposefully not avail themselves of services offered (Waltman 1986). Some of the reluctance to use existing services also may be due to a hesitation to expose private family matters, fear of stigma (Rank and Hirschl 1988), previous disappointments when seeking services (Cynthia Johnson, personal communication) or fear of retaliation from officials (Wellstone 1978). These attitudes are consistent with a generalized reluctance in the United States to permit public policy to intervene in the private sphere of the family (Korbin 1992).

Because there is no one cause of poverty, there is no simple cure. Those who would help get rural families with children out of poverty must first be aware of differences in needs (Ross and Morrissey 1987), the variety of existing programs, their histories, and the ideologies on which they are based (Ropers 1991). It is important to have the best possible data that social scientists can generate, but perhaps it is most important to listen and work closely with those whose lives are directly affected (Fitchen 1991).

Intergenerational Reproduction of Poverty

A powerful predictor of children's developmental status and their subsequent economic position is the socioeconomic status of the families in which they are raised. This not only reflects the inexorable dynamics of social stratification but also the consequences of social policies. Most industrialized countries implement policies that actively support families and children (Kamerman 1984; Lubeck and Garrett 1988). Conceptually, such policies socialize some of the costs of raising children and redistribute resources to families with children. Subsidized services may include child allowances, health care, and early childhood education. The United States has no comprehensive family policy to mitigate the effects of economic disadvantage. Consequently, socioeconomic status is a more powerful predictor of child development in the United States than in Europe (Korbin 1992).

Poor children are at risk for negative outcomes. There is controversy in the literature about the relative importance of specific risk factors, but there is broad consensus that multiple risks produce what Sameroff and Chandler (1975) call a "continuum of caretaker casualty." Developmentalists are particularly concerned about environmental and biomedical insults that have long-term, negative consequences. Poor children are more likely than others to experience preterm birth, handicapping conditions, hunger and malnutrition, parental substance abuse, and homelessness. These experiences create problems that are permanent or highly resist remediation. Their effects are cumulative and jointly constitute lifelong barriers to achievement. They are critical factors in the intergenerational transmission of poverty.

Maternal and Child Health

The limited availability, affordability, and accessibility of health care in rural areas is a major contributor to the physical conditions that reduce people's capacity to work and earn a living wage. Maternal poverty can place children at risk for developmental delay. Women suffering the effects of stress, poor nutrition, and inadequate prenatal care are at risk to deliver preterm or low birth weight babies (McBarnette 1987). Indeed, the low birth weight in poor rural counties was 30 percent above the national average in 1985 (DeLeon, Wakefield, Schultz, Williams and VandenBos 1989:1299). Fragile children may also intensify demands on an already stressed caretaking environment (Sameroff 1986).

The vast majority of areas with health personnel shortages are rural. This is partially a consequence of public policy. Medicare and Medicaid reimbursements to physicians and hospitals are half those in urban areas (DeLeon, Wakefield, Schultz, Williams and VandenBos 1989:1299). Without adequate finances rural communities cannot attract or retain physicians or maintain small hospitals and primary care units (Doelker and Bedics 1989). Medical care, both preventive and curative, becomes less available. The time and expense of traveling to facilities also limits their utilization, especially for preventive care (Geiger 1984).

Health insurance is less available to minorities and rural residents (U.S. Senate Special Committee on Aging 1988). Minority children are especially likely to lack insurance and a regular source of medical care (Butler, Winter, Singer, and Wenger 1985). The kinds of firms that predominate in rural areas--like small retail operations, locally owned mills and manufacturers, and self-employed farmers--generally offer no health insurance (Perales and Young 1987). Vast numbers of poor families are covered by neither private nor public insurance. In 1990, nearly one-third of married-couple families with incomes below the poverty line had no health insurance; the comparable figure for female-headed families was 13 percent (U.S. Department of Commerce 1991:Table 24).

Comparative research, summarized in Sameroff (1986), demonstrates that rates of mild mental retardation are substantially higher in the United States than in European countries with comprehensive public health and social service systems. Within the U.S., areas with poor prenatal care, limited health care, and lower socioeconomic levels have a greater incidence of mental retardation and learning disabilities (Schrag, Farago and Walker 1983). In fact, persistently poor communities, such as those described by Geiger (1984), are home to a disproportionate number of children with handicapping conditions. Early and appropriate intervention can often prevent disabilities from becoming handicaps. In rural communities, however, the lack of professionals makes early diagnosis and treatment problematic. Moreover, low population densities make it difficult to serve persons with conditions that have low prevalence (Shelly Heekin, personal communication). Current policies for screening and diagnostic assessment focus on the child and fail to address the interactions of the child and its environment (Harbin 1990). This approach is particularly problematic in rural communities. It is only by assessing the child in the explicit context of family and community that one can identify resources that can be mobilized to foster development.

Hunger and Malnutrition

It is a common belief that hunger is not a reality in modern America. Food stamps, WIC, and emergency food programs are available to rural, as well as urban residents. Nevertheless, the Community Childhood Hunger Identification Project (CCHIP) recently documented cases of families so poor that they must choose whether children or adults eat what little food is available (Wehler, Scott, Anderson and Parker 1991). While rural families are more likely to participate in the Food Stamp Program than any other "welfare" program (Rogers 1991), many eligible families simply do not apply. Even those who do participate in the programs may find they must use relatives, friends, and emergency food programs to supplement the program benefits. Free breakfast and lunch programs are effective during the school year, but transportation problems and regulations insensitive to rural populations make it difficult to provide supplementary feeding programs during the summer months (Linda Stone, personal communication).

The effects of hunger and malnutrition are well known. Hungry children are more likely than non-hungry children to experience debilitating physical symptoms including fatigue, irritability, headaches, ear infections, and colds. These problems make them more likely to miss school or be unable to concentrate on learning if they attend. Educational underachievement is the result.

Undernutrition, failure to thrive, and trace-metal deficiencies are all more common among poor children (Lozoff 1989). Undernourished infants act as if they are conserving energy. They explore and interact with caregivers less, so parents may not take the initiative to stimulate the child (Carolyn Campbell, personal communication). Families stressed by poverty are the least likely to be able to offer experiences that might compensate for physical deficits and lags caused by undernutrition, even if they accurately assess the reason for the child's apathy and withdrawal.

Parental Substance Abuse

Developmentalists emphasize interactions between biomedical and interpersonal factors. Nowhere is this interaction clearer than in the case of physical conditions that are caused by maternal substance abuse. Intrauterine exposure to crack cocaine and HIV is more prevalent in urban, especially inner city neighborhoods, but drug abuse also affects rural communities. Historically, the drug of choice was alcohol. A high incidence of fetal alcohol syndrome (FAS) and fetal alcohol effect (FAE) is documented in Native American populations (Dorris 1989). These syndromes can easily be confused with mild retardation or antisocial neuroses and character disorders, and they likely exist, unidentified, in other persistently poor communities.

Maternal alcohol abuse during pregnancy is clearly implicated in the intergenerational perpetuation of poverty. Dorris describes his son's lack of "imagination," by which he means the inability to foresee consequences and develop an appropriate strategy to set and achieve goals. To the extent that maternal alcohol abuse results in a learning disability--the inability to generalize cause and consequence thinking--it may underlie the lack of motivation that was once assumed to a legacy of the "culture of poverty" (Texidor del Portillo 1987).

Family Disruption

It is well established that marital disruption is an important factor in precipitating spells of poverty for women and their children. The problem of family disruption, however, is more basic than conventional analyses suggest. Children whose parents are absent because of abandonment, incarceration, substance abuse, and/or death now represent six percent of all children (Annie C. Casey Foundation 1992). The New York Times (March 29, 1992) labeled them the "new orphans."

Excluded from these tallies are children not resident with biological parents because they are in foster care. Researchers routinely identify poverty as an attribute of families whose children are placed in foster care. What they consistently overlook, however, is the long term, cumulative stress generated by persistent poverty. Some children are in foster care "because the parents literally had no money to buy food, pay the rent, or keep the house heated in winter" (Bush, 1988:249). Families who experience prolonged loss of income risk being labeled "neglectful." Parents may see their children removed to foster homes and their parental rights terminated (Boehm 1970).

One study found that families of children placed in foster care had been known to Social Services for an average of eight years after an initial application for financial assistance (Governor's Advocacy Council on Children and Youth 1978). Another study (Thieman, Fuqua and Linnan 1991) reported the highest out-of-home placement rate from children in the lowest family income bracket. Despite the obvious importance of poverty, social programs generally do not seek to provide sufficient income but to improve family functioning and parenting skills. If those efforts fail, professionals begin proceedings to terminate parental rights and place the child for adoption in a family with suitable resources.

Children from minority and single parent households are more frequently placed in foster care than other children. Ethnic and class differences are both important: "(W)hite workers confront barriers of language and custom, rely on conscious or unconscious cultural stereotypes, and misinterpret conditions of poverty as conditions of neglect" (Norman 1985:36). A realistic fear that officials might put their children in foster care discourages homeless parents from using services. Once the children have been removed "the parents are caught in a Catch-22. Without their children they are not eligible for welfare or housing assistance as families; without income and housing, it's very difficult to get the children back" (Pearce 1992:214).

The numbers of children being removed from families to foster care is increasing, but there are also nationwide efforts to preserve and reunite families. These are having positive effects in rural as well as urban areas (Norman 1985). However, children are unlikely to reunite with families where the parents lack education and income and where there is parental hospitalization, incarceration, or substance abuse (U.S. Department of Health and Human Services 1978). These children are likely to remain poor.

Homelessness

Homelessness and near-homelessness pose special risks for children. In both rural and urban areas, significant mobility often precedes homelessness (Fitchen 1991; Rossi and Wright 1987). Poor families may move repeatedly in response to eviction or in search of affordable housing, temporary jobs, or extended family support (Bassuk, Rubin and Lauriat 1986). The family may "double up" with relatives or friends for a time. Overcrowding may exacerbate tensions, especially if there are pre-existing problems such as domestic violence or substance abuse. Parents may separate temporarily, or everyone may live together in the car.   Repeated moves disrupt children's ties to schools, playmates, pets, and familiar places.

Shelters exist for families both in urban and rural areas.   Homeless rural families frequently seek employment in urban areas and temporarily live in urban shelters. A pattern of urban-rural-urban migration is common (Pat Smith, personal communication). The best shelters provide predictability, privacy, and opportunity for children's play (Cryer and Harms 1990).   The worst expose children to violence and disease. Layzer, Goodson, and Delange (1986) found that fully half the infants in shelters had health problems, but few shelters have the capacity to screen for, let alone treat, disease.

All available research, reviewed by Johnson (1989), Redmond and Brackman (1990), Whitman, Accardo, Boyert and Kendagor (1990), and Rescoria, Parker and Stolley (1991), suggests that the cognitive and socioemotional development of homeless children is substantially worse than for similar children who have residences. School-age children experience no educational continuity and little academic success. Preschoolers seem to suffer even more because their days lack consistent structure. Children of all ages must deal with parents, many of whom are overwhelmed by the calamity that has befallen the family (Debby Cryer, personal communication).

Most professionals expect that children who experience homelessness, especially long periods of transiency, will suffer developmental and educational delays. These foster the intergenerational transmission of poverty.

The Silent Dialogue with the Culture of Poverty

We have structured our discussion of the intergenerational transmission of poverty in a silent dialogue with the culture of poverty. We are concerned that the persistently poor will become increasingly different from others, not because they share different values but because they are exposed to different risks. We have documented the fact that poor rural children are at considerable risk of developing conditions that will limit their ability to work as adults, either directly as in the case of handicapping conditions or indirectly as in the case of undereducation. We know that the single most powerful determinant of poverty is work disability status. Only a comprehensive, multi-sectoral policy supportive of families and children can reduce the negative consequences of poverty and impede its intergenerational transmission.

Transcending Persistent Poverty

We know very little about how children transcend the limitations imposed by a childhood lived in persistent poverty. We know that all children born to disadvantaged parents do not necessarily grow up to be poor and that the intergenerational transmission of disadvantage is not automatic. What we do not understand is how children mobilize their resources to beat the odds against them.

One way to visualize the issue is a decision tree. A decision made early in life leaves some alternatives open, even as it closes off others. Using this model, one can imagine specific sequences of contingent events that occur in children's lifetimes and influence whether they do or do not escape poverty as adults. Children's lives are deeply affected by their individual physical and psychological resources, by the sequence and timing of events in their family's history, by networks of community and institutional resources, and by national and international events.

With so many opportunities for variation, we would expect that more than one sequence of events could result in positive outcomes for children (Schaefer 1987). Unfortunately, we are not able to describe alternative trajectories that allow children to transcend persistent poverty. With some notable exceptions (Werner and Smith 1982; Shonkoff and Meisels 1990), existing scholarship rarely adopts a longitudinal perspective. Rather, research has focused on children at particular points in time and explored the relative importance of specific variables to child outcomes. Available scholarship freezes biography, so the temporal dimension of children's lives as lived is lost. Nevertheless, the literature is valuable because it identifies critical nodes on the decision tree.

Social scientific research has identified several sets of factors relating to child outcomes--individual, family, community, and macroeconomic characteristics. We begin with the child because we seek to emphasize the highly contingent nature of child development and exits from persistent poverty. We explore what Edwards (1976) labels "successful deviance."

Children are individuals who both influence and are influenced by their social environments (Jewett 1978; McLoyd 1990). Although this assertion seems self-evident, scholarship distributes itself along a continuum of child agency to social determinism. The extreme of the child agency position is the intellectual equivalent of Teflon children. Resilient children are vulnerable but invincible. Such language is more appropriate to sloganeering than to scholarship because it renders an important phenomenon inaccessible to analysis. It also trivializes economic hardship and diverts attention from the real price children pay who manage to escape persistent poverty.

Relatively little scholarship has seriously considered how children enhance their own socialization experiences. Children who are wanted, born without complications, and responsive to their surroundings are advantaged from the start. Bright, resourceful, easy-going, alert, attractive children are more likely than others to elicit positive responses from adults and other children. Even in poor surroundings, they have better chances of getting their needs met (Parker, Greer, and Zuckerman 1988).

The dominant assumption in the literature is that children are influenced by others. The roles of parents and other powerful figures are presumed to be central, especially for young children. Such family-centered analyses must be moderated, however, given recent trends that have relevance to childrearing. The majority of mothers now return to work when their children are very young (Wenk and Garrett 1992). Consequently, youngsters have extensive and intensive extra-familial exposure at early ages. Although much child care for infants and toddlers is family-based (Garrett and Lubeck 1988), older preschoolers are likely to be in group-based care. These child care experiences are important to children's socialization, as are the school experiences of older children (Baydar and Brooks-Gunn 1991).

Longitudinal research has followed several panels of youngsters who received enriched early childhood education experiences. Small numbers of children were served over several years, generally in university-based or research-oriented programs. Programs provided high quality childcare, access to medical care and other services, and parent education. Although these programs are expensive, they are cost effective (CLS 1983). Head Start is also a comprehensive program, serving both children and their parents. This program is also cost effective (Haskins 1989). Nevertheless, Head Start serves less than one-fifth of eligible children. High quality early childhood education programs and Head Start are less available in rural than urban areas (Sherman 1992).

Parents raise children in a social context. Consequently, the quality of services provided in public and private institutions influences child development. The quality of childcare services reflects state regulations establishing minimum standards and parent's ability to pay for services exceeding the mandated minimum (Phillips 1987). The more time that children spend in extra-familial care, the more child outcomes reflect social policy and family dynamics. For this reason, the family/policy interface is critical to any evaluation of how poor children transcend poverty.

The literature about children at risk for developmental delay is predicated on the assumption that "children from poorer families have poorer intellectual and social outcomes" (Sameroff 1986:193). Accordingly, research and early intervention programs focus on potentially negative influences and "protective factors" that enable children to evade harm. Among the protective factors are the personality characteristics of the child, a supportive and stable family, and an external support system that enhances coping and projects positive values (Garmezy 1992). Additional protective factors include sociability, high activity level, the presence of multiple caregivers, and attentive parenting during infancy (Werner and Smith 1982). Dubow and Luster (1990) highlight the quality of parent/child relationships. They conclude that children's developmental status is enhanced by a cognitively and emotionally supportive home environment; that self-esteem is fostered by authoritative parenting styles by which parents set clear and consistent limits within which children are empowered to make decisions. A positive self-concept is fostered by secure and harmonious personal relationships and successful task accomplishment appropriate to the developmental stage.

Ogbu (1981) conceptualizes childrearing as a culturally organized system of transmitting competencies to successive generations. Even in the face of poverty, family and community members can encourage children to feel competent. The literature emphasizes feelings of self-worth, efficacy, mastery, and self-esteem as products of an intense relationship with a parent or another significant adult (e.g., grandmother, teacher). Such children can experience a "cycle of success" (Parker, Greer, and Zuckerman 1988:1235).

Certain maternal characteristics, notably older age, higher education, and greater intelligence, are associated with positive child outcomes. Adolescent mothers are observed to be less verbal, more physical, less responsive, and more punitive in interactions with infants than older mothers (Garcia Coll 1990). Maturity, and the attendant readiness to parent, is a general asset (Hofferth 1987). A specific issue that figures prominently in the literature is linguistic stimulation. Older, educated mothers tend to provide a linguistically rich environment that enhances cognitive development (Bock and Moore 1984). Linguistically impoverished children are at a severe disadvantage in school, but children who are fluent in another language rapidly acquire fluency in English (Emily Arcia, personal communication). Above and beyond language, if children learn cultural patterns of interaction at home that are inconsistent with school culture, they will experience disadvantage (Ogbu 1981).

There is substantial evidence that children raised in single parent households are disadvantaged in comparison to children raised in families with two adults (Hetherington, Camara, and Featherman 1983). Poverty, largely attributable to the low average earning power of women, is clearly an important factor. Time is also crucial. Many single mothers are overburdened and simply lack the time and endurance to devote to activities which would enhance their children's development and support their achievements (McLanahan and Booth 1989; Astone and McLanahan 1991).

Children benefit from stable homes with multiple caregivers (Werner and Smith 1982). Nevertheless, the role of fathers in child development is generally ignored (Lamb and Sagi 1983). Scholars have not pursued how the characteristics of unwed fathers influence relationships with mother and/or child. Rather, what has been documented is that men in intact families spend little time in childrearing (Berk and Berk 1979). Observational studies suggest that men interact differently with children, e.g., roughhousing (Radin and Russell 1983). As anyone who has ever tried to put an overstimulated child to bed knows, this has advantages and disadvantages.

Family and children are generally regarded as a female domain, and scholarly attention reflects that bias and focuses preferentially on women. The presence of a grandmother is associated with positive outcomes for both child and mother (Furstenberg, Brooks-Gunn, and Chase-Landale 1989; Pearson, Hunter, Ensminger, and Kellam 1990). Several interrelated processes seem to be at work. Grandmothers who are themselves knowledgeable about childrearing can encourage good parenting skills in their daughters by modeling appropriate behavior. Grandmother's care also supplements maternal care, so children receive more and better attention than if the mother-child pair lived independently. Childcare by grandmothers can relieve mothers of substantial burdens, thereby permitting young mothers to complete their educations, train for jobs, or seek employment. These accomplishments enhance their employability. If mothers also learn to practice birth control effectively, they enhance their marriageability.

Poverty is generally not romantic, but neither is it inevitably disruptive of human relationships. People in poor communities necessarily learn that both they and their work are undervalued. However, poverty and pride can coexist. Poor adults in rural areas are not necessarily stigmatized, since social status is not determined solely by money. Contribution to community welfare is valued.

Domestic service is among the least desirable, poorest paid jobs. It recruits women whose racial, ethnic, and/or immigrant status limit their occupational alternatives. Nevertheless, domestics enjoyed prestige within the black community. Moreover, in the hope that opportunities would eventually open up, domestics learned how to guide their own children to goals that were beyond their personal experience (Dill 1980).

An important theme in the literature on rural, black, southern communities is their integrity. Lee (1985) found that successful, rural, black adolescents came from close families, well integrated into community support networks and institutions. They had positive role models, and they wanted to succeed in school and at work. Finally, they held strong religious convictions, conservative moral attitudes, and limited black consciousness. This is a specific illustration of Hill's (1972) more general appraisal of the strengths of black families, which include strong kin bonds, adaptable family roles, strong work commitment, high achievement orientation, and deep religious orientation. Interestingly, similar themes appear in explanations of academic success among Asian Americans in comparison to the academic failure commonly experienced by black children living in inner city ghettos (Slaughter-Defoe, Nakagawa, Takanishi, and Johnson 1990). Clearly, cultural values are more relevant than ethnicity.

Academic success, defined minimally as completing high school, is regarded as a requisite for subsequent occupational success. Academic achievement has been related to a sense of personal efficacy (Bowman 1977) and proactive orientations towards racial barriers (Ogbu 1981). However, scholarship reports an inconsistent relationship between income and sense of efficacy (Kane 1987). Families can socialize proactive orientations towards existing racial inequity. This results in an internal sense of efficacy plus an external orientation toward racial barriers as reflected in ethnic pride, egalitarian beliefs, and a commitment to self-development (Bowman and Howard 1985). Such a future orientation need not be blind to contemporary discrimination, but it is most efficacious when educational and employment opportunities are actually available (Ogbu 1981).

The literature on successful children emphasizes the congruence between familial and societal values. It does not emphasize the price that children pay for success. Must children renounce their ethnic heritage in order to succeed? Must they renounce their class background? Must they become genderless? These are serious questions, for which current scholarship provides no ready answers. It is likely, however, that the price of success is high.

People who are poor need not embrace majority emblems of success. Criminality is stereotypically associated with urban rather than rural residence. Urban areas may provide more lucrative venues for certain illegal activities, but the countryside provides special opportunities. Growing marijuana, smuggling illegal migrants, and escorting drug traffic are among the illegal activities commonplace in depressed rural areas. Certain specialized illegal services, e.g., providing bear parts traded in international markets (National Audubon Society 1989), require a rural environment.

Macroeconomic factors govern both illegal and legal activities and exert an overwhelming influence on the ability of poor children to escape poverty as adults. Although a rising tide does not raise all boats, economic stagnation or decline makes it difficult for people to maintain, let alone improve, their economic position over a working life. International and national level processes have specific manifestations at the local level, so some regions provide more opportunities than others. The secular trend, however, is that the availability and quality of jobs are deteriorating and the pace of deterioration is accelerating (Mingione 1991). To the extent that macroeconomic improvements were historically important in the reduction of poverty, such beneficial trends are less likely to occur in the future. Consequently, the macroeconomic picture for today's children is bleak, especially if they are poor, female, and/or minority.

Strengthening the cultural fabric of a community may help some children transcend poverty. All members can benefit from community assets like educational and religious institutions, history, architecture, ceremony and ritual. Nevertheless, community ties and local attachments are customarily perceived as obstacles rather than assets (Martinez-Brawley 1990). Opportunities for participation in local planning and political process, popular in the 1960's, can empower parents and encourage advocacy for children. An interdisciplinary community project combining research and action in Nova Scotia focused on improving the "level of socio-cultural integration." The project staff believed that increased economic and educational opportunities would not be sufficient to transform a "disintegrated community." Consequently, they worked to reduce the interpersonal hostility, anxiety, depression, and suspicion. Indigenous leadership developed to build community cooperation and pride, which in turn elevated individual adult self-esteem that was expressed in home improvement and job seeking (Leighton 1965). May we assume that children of the community benefitted?

Parents must make concerted, even heroic, efforts to protect their children from the negative effects of poverty. Their task is difficult when economic deprivation is brief, and virtually impossible when poverty is a persistent reality. Transcending poverty is especially difficult if positive factors do not exist at individual, familial, and community levels. The literature suggests that the children of Ozzie and Harriet could survive on Walton's Mountain, but the resulting script hardly addresses the reality that poor, rural families confront. Household composition in the contemporary United States looks little like that of the 1930-40's, and economic growth does not approximate that of the 1950-70's.

Parental and household characteristics figure prominently in the literature on children at risk for developmental delay because families virtually do it all. Few social policies in the United States actively support families and children and supplement the inadequate resources that some parents bring to childrearing. Children experience the disadvantage that results from low socioeconomic status, and they are not afforded an equal opportunity to succeed. Many able but disadvantaged children fail to achieve their potential. Those who succeed in overcoming the limitations they incurred by being raised in persistent poverty are special, as are those who raised them. Such heroics must be interpreted in the context of social policy. Schorr (1992:335) draws an analogy:

> It is as if poor families are out in the ocean, swimming against the policy tide. Only the heroes or the very fortunate make it to shore. A society that wishes to reduce the number who swim only to drown has to do something about the tide.

Conclusion

In this chapter, we explored alternative approaches to learning how macro- and micro-level factors influence the lives of rural families and children in poverty. We were compelled by the paucity of scholarship to look beyond studies with this precise focus and to search for insights in divergent research traditions. We believe that future research needs to build on current knowledge, and we recommend some guidelines for future research.

We have argued that analyses of poverty should be grounded in time as well as space. At the macro level, secular changes are captured by history. At the micro level, structural realities are experienced in personal biographies.

Together, history and biography provide potentially complementary insights into complex social processes.

With the exception of Fitchen's (1981) pioneering work, we have not identified any studies that truly integrate history and biography in the exploration of rural poverty. Ethnographic research, grounded in both time and space, is particularly suitable to achieve this synthesis. Nevertheless, quantitative analysis can be designed to be more comprehensive and address issues at the macro/micro interface. We recommend that researchers consider ways to operationalize concepts at different levels of analysis and to integrate different types of longitudinal data into their studies.

Historical, macroeconomic data exist. Mingione (1991) provides a powerful framework for conceptualizing secular trends at the international, national, and regional levels. Public agencies routinely gather and publish statistics, which are subsequently analyzed by social scientists. Data collection can always be improved, but it is possible to rely on existing scholarship and develop meaningful periodizations for the analysis of poverty. Recent work by Duncan and Rodgers (1988) and Devine, Plunkett, and Wright (1992) illustrate how historically specific economic conditions can be taken into account in the analysis of survey data. These studies make a substantial contribution to the literature concerning families' experiences with poverty because they deliberately model historical periods.

Longitudinal, microeconomic data now exist on several panels of American families. Consequently, it is possible to study biographies of poverty and identify common coping strategies. The Panel Study of Income Dynamics (PSID) provides a twenty-year perspective on household economies, even following children as they establish independent households. The National Longitudinal Study of Labor Market Experience/Youth Cohort (NLS/Y) is a thirteen year panel, and it includes assessments of the development status of children born to women in the original sample. Scholars working with these data sets have shown little interest in children and rural poverty. New research on the PSID (Adams and Duncan 1990) is provocative but descriptive, and current work by Garrett, Ng'andu, and Ferron (in preparation) on the poverty experiences of young children as captured in NLS is not yet complete. Appropriate multivariate analyses of the PSID and NLS data sets would substantially enhance our understanding of rural poverty.

We believe that analyses should be grounded in space as well as time. There are many studies of poor places, but few analyses of survey data locate people in space. This reflects conceptual limitations. The nature of the macro/micro interface is not theorized. The socioeconomic structure of a community has no hypothesized, systematic relationship with family and/or individual characteristics. Consequently, even spatial variables like region and residence are treated as characteristics of individuals in the demographic literature, although they are clearly ecological or contextual variables.

Ecological data provide the spatial context within which individual outcomes can be analyzed. Geocode files come with the NLS and the latest releases of the PSID. Alternatively, individual level data from the Current Population Survey (CPS) can be aggregated to a regional level (e.g., Lichter and Costanzo 1987). Not all national data sets permit the integration of individual and regional analysis. When integration is feasible, the influence of important regional characteristics like labor market areas can be assessed. Research designs that explore individual and ecological variables would substantially enhance our understanding of rural poverty.

Qualitative research on poverty is also important. Anthropologists and other field workers encourage informants to articulate their visions of the world and to explain why they act and react as they do. Such insights can inform the design and analysis of survey research. Social workers and other direct service providers also bring important perspectives to the understanding of rural poverty. Scholars can expand the research cannon by collaborating with service providers and the recipients of services (e.g., Martinez-Brawley and Blundall 1989).

A few simple principles could reorient research in interesting directions:

- Ground interpretations in time and space. Context has consequences that do not disappear simply because they are ignored.
- Adopt a longitudinal perspective. Personal biography, regional development, and historical balances of international power all matter.
- Integrate individual and contextual variables. People are influenced by and themselves mold their environment.
- Think praxis. Theory, analysis, and program are inexorably interrelated.

Notes

This chapter was prepared by Patricia Garrett, University of North Carolina, and Naurine Lennox, St. Olaf College, with assistance from Janet Fitchen, Ithaca College; Constance Hardesty, University of Oklahoma; Cynthia Johnson, North Carolina State University; and Maxine Thompson, North Carolina State University.

9

The Rural Elderly and Poverty

Introduction

The declining significance of old age as a determinant of economic well-being has been a prominent theme in the literature since the early 1980's (e.g., Preston 1984). Poverty rates among all elderly have declined over the past twenty years from 24.6 percent in 1970 to 12.2 percent in 1987 (U.S. Bureau of the Census 1991c). Despite these gains for elderly individuals, overall, certain groups of elderly persons continue to face much poorer economic prospects than others. Among these are nonmetropolitan elders.[1]

The purpose of this chapter is to examine existing poverty theories and apply those theories to the situation of the rural elderly poor. We recommend a number of extensions of existing theoretical perspectives and we discuss several methodological issues that, if resolved, would clarify factors associated with the dynamics and persistence of rural elderly poverty. Two themes guide our discussions. First, we recognize the spatial variation in poverty and that rural areas are diverse in the extent to which poverty is characteristic among the rural elderly population. Second, we recognize that poverty varies over time according to historical context for individuals, communities and regions. We stress the importance of individual variation over time and across the life course.

Our discussions include both individual and structural factors that constrain the economic well-being of the rural elderly population. First, we examine the prevalence of poverty among the rural elderly and search for causal factors as revealed by such analyses. Next, we review theories of economic advantage and disadvantage for their applicability and adequacy in explaining poverty among the rural elderly population. Two subgroups of the rural elderly population receive special focus--women and minorities. Gender, race and ethnicity have a prominent influence on economic well-being throughout the life course, including old age, and some explanation of the interface with poverty among the rural elderly is important to our discussion. We evaluate absolute, relative and subjective poverty measures, and how well they capture the dynamics and persistence of rural elderly poverty. Finally, we recommend theoretical and research developments that would extend our knowledge of poverty among older rural residents.

Prevalence of Poverty Among the Rural Elderly

Elderly individuals, those ages 65 and over, comprise a larger share of the nonmetropolitan than metropolitan population, making the issue of poverty among the elderly particularly salient in nonmetropolitan areas. This was true in 1980, when 13 percent of the nonmetropolitan population consisted of individuals over age 65 compared to the 10.7 percent of the metropolitan population that was over age 65 (Glasgow 1988). Over the next decade the elderly population grew as a percentage of the population in both metropolitan and nonmetropolitan areas; in 1990, 14.5 percent of the nonmetropolitan population was over age 65, compared with 11.3 percent of the metropolitan population (unpublished data calculated from the 1990 Current Population Survey). This pattern of population concentration of the elderly in nonmetropolitan areas results from the historical net inmigration to nonmetropolitan areas of individuals ages 60 and over (Glasgow 1988; Lichter, McLaughlin and Cornwell 1992) and the net outmigration of younger individuals from nonmetropolitan areas, especially during the late 1980's. Declines in fertility, improvements in health care and declining mortality also contribute to the increase in the elderly population.

In 1979, 20.5 percent of persons ages 65 and over living in nonmetropolitan areas were poor, compared with 12.0 percent of metropolitan elderly persons (Table 9.1). Lower poverty rates were recorded in that year for the total population of nonmetropolitan than central cities of metropolitan areas. However, elders in nonmetropolitan areas recorded higher poverty rates than did central city elderly residents. By 1990, the overall situation had improved such that 16.1 percent of nonmetropolitan elders were poor and 10.8 percent of metropolitan older individuals were poor. Despite this improvement, nonmetropolitan elderly persons were 50 percent more likely to be poor than their metropolitan counterparts. Their poverty rates had moved closer, but were still higher than those experienced by their central city peers. Nonmetropolitan elders also were more likely than metropolitan elders to have incomes close to the poverty threshold, making them more susceptible to moving into poverty as they grow older (McLaughlin and Jensen 1991).

These differences in poverty rates for nonmetropolitan and metropolitan elders may be due in part to differences in the composition of the elderly population in the two types of locations, rather than to a higher risk of poverty among

TABLE 9.1 Poverty Rates Among Elderly Individuals by Race and Residence, 1979-1990

	All	Whites	Blacks
1990			
Metropolitan	10.8	8.8	30.1
Central city	14.6	11.0	31.6
Nonmetropolitan	16.1	13.6	35.6
1987			
Metropolitan	11.1	9.3	29.6
Central city	14.3	11.3	29.2
Nonmetropolitan	15.6	12.6	46.5
1983			
Metropolitan	12.1	10.2	30.5
Central city	14.3	11.5	29.6
Nonmetropolitan	17.8	15.2	49.5
1979			
Metropolitan	12.0	10.2	30.4
Central city	15.7	10.7	31.1
Nonmetropolitan	20.5	18.4	46.3

Sources: Current Population Survey, U.S. Bureau of the Census, U.S. Department of Commerce, 1980, 1984, 1988, 1991c.

the rural elderly. For example, a higher proportion of the nonmetropolitan than metropolitan elderly population is 75 years or older. Since among the 65+ population, older age is associated with a higher likelihood of being poor, this difference in age composition would alone raise poverty rates in nonmetropolitan areas, even if no single age group was more likely to be poor in nonmetropolitan than metropolitan areas. Other compositional factors may also play a role. For example, the lower education levels of nonmetropolitan elders would raise poverty rates (Glasgow 1988). On the other hand, the lower proportion of blacks and higher proportion of married people among the nonmetropolitan population would serve to lower poverty rates.

A cursory look at poverty rates in metropolitan and nonmetropolitan areas by race (Table 9.1) and by age and sex (Table 9.2) suggests that compositional factors alone are unlikely to explain the difference in poverty rates between metropolitan and nonmetropolitan elderly residents. For both whites and blacks and for women and men ages 65-74, poverty rates in nonmetropolitan areas

TABLE 9.2 Poverty Rates by Age, Sex, and Residence, 1990

	Males			Females		
	All	White	Black	All	White	Black
Age 65 - 74						
Metropolitan	5.6	3.7	26.2	11.1	8.9	31.6
Central City	8.5	4.5	22.5	15.1	11.4	30.6
Nonmetropolitan	8.9	6.5	41.2	15.9	13.9	41.7
Age 75+						
Metropolitan	7.7	6.1	26.8	17.7	15.5	40.7
Central City	9.9	6.8	30.1	22.0	18.1	44.6
Nonmetropolitan	15.2	11.8	50.3	24.8	22.3	54.2

Source: Current Population Survey, U.S. Bureau of the Census, U.S. Department of Commerce, 1991c.

remain higher than in metropolitan areas, and, surprisingly, the discrepancy is even greater among nonmetropolitan than center city elderly black residents.

Investigators have attempted to measure more precisely the extent to which differences in poverty rates between metropolitan and nonmetropolitan areas can be attributed to population composition differences (Glasgow 1988). One recent test was carried out by McLaughlin and Jensen (1991). Using 1990 Current Population Survey (CPS) data, they estimated logistic regression models of poverty status for metropolitan residents (distinguishing those living in the central city and in noncentral city metropolitan areas) and nonmetropolitan individuals ages 65 and over. Variables that controlled for differences in sociodemographic composition of the population were gender, age, race, education, disability status, marital status, and living arrangements. Even after controlling for these composition characteristics, a residence effect remained. The higher poverty rates in nonmetropolitan areas cannot be explained by compositional factors alone. Indeed, the study by McLaughlin and Jensen (1991) found that the size and significance of the nonmetropolitan effect on poverty increases when controlling for other factors. This is evidence that adjusting for population compositional differences would in fact increase the differential between metropolitan and nonmetropolitan poverty rates for the elderly.   Thus the explanation for differences in metropolitan and nonmetropolitan poverty rates among the elderly must rest on explanations for why poverty rates would be higher for each population subgroup in nonmetropolitan areas.

In the United States, the income of the elderly derives from two major sources: an earnings-based income support system (i.e., Social Security and employer-provided pensions) and a means-tested income transfer system (i.e., Supplemental Security Income) for those whose income and assets fall below set thresholds. The nature of this mixed public-private income system for elderly individuals means that explanations of poverty among elders should be consistent with explanations of earnings disparities among nonelderly persons. We discuss the major theoretical perspectives below. We argue, however, that in order to adequately address the income differences among elders across space and time, one must incorporate the importance of the experiences of individuals over the life course, and examine how those experiences are likely to vary for different cohorts of elders across geographic space.

Theoretical Perspectives on Poverty Among the Rural Elderly

Clues to sources of differences between nonmetropolitan and metropolitan elders can be derived from cross-sectional analyses of poverty among the elderly. These studies generally describe the poverty experience by concentrating almost entirely on current characteristics and living arrangements of elderly individuals. They show that individuals more likely to be poor are older, less educated, black (or nonwhite), women, widowed, divorced or separated, and living alone. In the discussion of prevalence, we have described why these correlates of poverty among the elderly do not explain the difference in observed poverty rates across geographic areas. Thus, it must be that either metropolitan and nonmetropolitan residences have a different contemporaneous impact on the risk of being poor during the later years of life or that the process of becoming poor is different in those two areas. That is, while cross-sectional studies describe the poverty status across individuals at a given time, the poor in metropolitan and nonmetropolitan areas may have very different poverty histories. Theories about why some individuals end up poor and others do not must encompass the experience of all poor individuals, both those who were poor throughout their adult lives and those who entered poverty late in life and are unable to escape that status.

Before describing how one can apply theoretical perspectives to explain the difference between the economic prospects of metropolitan and nonmetropolitan elders, it is necessary to distinguish between changes in the risk of being poor as experienced by individuals and as reported by place. This distinction is important in evaluating changes in poverty rates, which must necessarily be measured across groups of individuals. For example, poverty rates may rise or fall over time, even though no change in the incomes of those who were poor in the initial period occur. It is broadly agreed that a large part of the improvement in economic well-being of elders over the past twenty years results from the movement of larger, younger, more economically well-off cohorts into old age (Riley 1987). The economic position of elders as a group thus improves even though no particular elderly person's income has in fact improved. Similarly, improvements in the economic position of elders in metropolitan and nonmetropolitan areas are the result not only of who becomes old, but who moves to or from metropolitan and nonmetropolitan areas. Thus, in examining factors related to poverty, we must be careful to distinguish those determining the well-being of a particular individual and whether that individual's well-being will change, from those affecting poverty reported by place.

Changes in the economic circumstances of elders as a group and as individuals over time highlight the necessity of using a life course perspective to understand poverty. Such a perspective allows us to understand current economic well-being and poverty among elders, as well as the process by which individuals become poor, and the situations that place individuals at greater risk of becoming poor. Because individuals of different ages have different life experiences set in different historical and geographic contexts, their economic well-being is likely to vary even when other aspects of their lives appear similar. The economic opportunities available in the 1930's and 1940's in rural Appalachia were much different from those available to blacks in the Mississippi Delta, or to whites in Pittsburgh or Detroit. Thus, when examining economic well-being and poverty among elders, existing theories must be extended to reflect the historical and geographic variation in individual life experiences and how they affect economic status in old age.

Work history influences the current poverty status of older individuals through its effect on levels of lifetime earnings and wealth accumulation. Higher earnings facilitate saving for retirement, and lifetime earnings and quarters of labor force participation are used as part of the formula that determines Social Security benefit levels (Svahn and Ross 1983; Ycas and Grad 1987).

Employment also may provide pension income [in 1984, 38% of aged family units had private or government pension income (Ycas and Grad 1987)], and continuation of medical or health care coverage into retirement. Not all employers provide the same benefits nor do all jobs offer the same wages (Beller 1981). Accordingly, the following review of theories outlines how lifetime work experiences relate to the demographic attributes of individuals and how these affect the poverty status of elderly individuals. We also incorporate how or why these theories may operate to differentially influence well-being for certain groups and for those in nonmetropolitan areas.

We review three theoretical perspectives that have been used to explain poverty among working age persons. We outline why human capital, status attainment, and labor market structure theories are relevant for explaining the economic well-being of elders, whether they live in metropolitan or nonmetropolitan areas. We then propose some preliminary ideas for extending these theories to the case of nonmetropolitan elders and to a life course perspective.

As initially developed, these theories explained differences in earnings and occupational attainment of individuals at a given time. We suggest that they can be equally applicable to understanding life-long economic well-being and the ability of individuals to accumulate resources for use in old age. We also suggest that incorporating local geographic context further improves understanding of the causes and consequences of poverty among elders and why some groups are more at risk of being poor than others. Our attempt to extend these theories of working age poverty to explain elderly poverty can be combined with existing empirical approaches, which tend to stress current conditions of elders--marital status, living arrangements, health and other demographic attributes of elderly to explain poverty (Bound, Duncan, Lauren and Oleinick 1991; Coe 1988; Worobey and Angel 1991).

Poverty theories generally provide either individualistic or structuralist explanations. Individualist explanations suggest that individuals control their fates, and that they make decisions that either enhance economic well-being or place them at an economic disadvantage. Structural explanations suggest that conditions beyond the control of individuals also play a critical role in influencing individual well-being.

Human Capital Theory

Human capital theory concentrates on workers' characteristics that increase their value to employers (e.g., education, work experience, job skills) (Becker 1964; Mincer and Polachek 1975). Individuals make decisions about investing in human capital. The level of investment, in turn, determines an individual's success in the labor market. Workers with higher levels of human capital command higher wages and benefits, enabling them to accumulate more resources for use in old age than those with lower investments. In this theoretical perspective, it often is assumed that human capital investment affects earnings unhampered by discrimination based on age, race, or gender, or by the individual's geographic location.

A significant volume of research testing human capital theory has shown that returns to human capital, especially education, are lower for minorities, women (Bibb and Form 1977), and those working in nonmetropolitan areas, with women and minorities in nonmetropolitan areas facing a double-jeopardy situation (McLaughlin and Perman 1991a). Thus, individuals with the same apparent levels of human capital have much different success in turning their human capital investments into resources for use in old age.

Human capital theory also fails to incorporate explicitly the idea of career paths or ladders that result in differential rates of movement from entry level to higher level positions (Spilerman 1977). Over a person's work life, the value of human capital depends on the levels of human capital of competing workers when they enter the labor force and on the opportunities (or lack thereof) for upward mobility throughout their careers. Generally, those with higher levels of education and training are more competitive initially in the job market, and are more likely to obtain jobs with advancement potential. Once again, however, research has shown that certain individuals (women and minorities) are not given access to the same career paths as white men. Career paths have also been found to be more limited in nonmetropolitan areas (Doeringer 1984). Individuals are unable to convert their human capital investments into opportunities for advancement throughout their careers, thus reducing their ability to accumulate assets for later use. In addition to the role that education plays in giving workers access to certain employment opportunities, it also is argued that those with higher levels of education are better-equipped to plan for retirement.

Using either explanation, human capital theory as commonly used is a static theory. Its value to explaining economic well-being among the elderly could be enhanced if the role of education in affecting job transitions and, especially opportunities for upward job mobility, were given careful attention. In addition, one must carefully consider the concept that educational attainment is relative. A much higher proportion of those currently elderly never finished high school, increasing the value of a high school diploma for those who did finish. In the same way, upward mobility paths were much different while currently older individuals were in the labor force, possibly providing a much greater return to lower levels of education than can be expected by those in today's labor force. One must also consider the differential success of women and minorities in converting human capital investment to earnings and pensions and the fact that geographic variation in opportunities further confound the supposed direct link between human capital and earnings attainment and wealth accumulation.

Status Attainment Theory

A few studies have concentrated on using individual's characteristics prior to retirement to explain postretirement economic well-being (Campbell and Henretta 1980; Henretta and Campbell 1976). They found consistency (for men) in the characteristics from status attainment models that explain economic attainment both before and after retirement. These studies provide a starting point for developing theories based on life experiences that will ultimately aid in explaining economic well-being among the elderly. Once again, however, these models use individual and background characteristics to explain current status (occupational or earnings) or to explain a change in status (usually occupational status) over time. To date, the few studies of this type that have been completed only examine the relationship between characteristics prior to retirement and economic well-being after retirement for white men. These studies have not addressed the role of gender and race, or of local conditions in moderating this relationship. In particular, such studies do not address why or how individuals maintain their economic attainment, nor do they incorporate life course events, such as widowhood, divorce, or illness, that might alter the economic well-being of particular individuals. In short, these studies do not look at the processes by which individuals maintain particular occupations or levels of income.

Labor Market Segmentation Theory

The labor market structure perspective stresses the types of employment available and whether access to good jobs is restricted to certain groups. This structural perspective combines several related theories, such as dual labor market, dual economy, and labor market segmentation, to build a model that links earnings and the quality of employment offered by particular employers. Dual labor market theory ties higher skill requirements of occupations and higher costs of replacing workers to employers offering jobs with higher wages, benefits, upward mobility and stability (Doeringer and Piore 1971; Dickens and Lang 1985; Piore 1975). Dual economy, and other economic segmentation theories, argue that the position of an industry or firm in the product market determines its ability to reward workers (Baron and Bielby 1980; Hodson 1983; Tolbert, Horan and Beck 1980).

Core industries are those with large profit margins in monopolistic industries, often are unionized and tend to offer higher wages and benefits to all workers. These industries also are more likely to offer upward mobility opportunities to their workers. Peripheral industries face competitive product markets which result in lower profit margins. They are more likely to have smaller firm size, and generally are associated with lower wages, lower likelihood of being unionized, and fewer opportunities for advancement within a firm.

Labor market segmentation theory suggests that certain groups of workers--women and racial and ethnic minority men--operate in separate labor markets; they do not compete for the same jobs as white men and that opportunities differ (Gordon, Edwards and Reich 1982). This is primarily evidenced by occupational and industrial segregation of these groups from white men (Beller 1982; Jacobs 1989; Perman and Stevens 1989). Within the structural explanations of employment quality, women and racial and ethnic minority men are much more likely to have poor jobs in the peripheral industry sector of the economy and in secondary occupations. Low upward mobility, low earnings and interrupted employment translate into lower Social Security benefits and often no pension benefits for these groups once they reach older ages. Lack of employer-sponsored retirement benefits and the inability to accumulate wealth prior to retirement almost guarantee individuals with these types of jobs poverty or near poverty income after withdrawal from the labor force.

From a life course perspective, the labor market segment in which workers find themselves, determines their ability to improve their status through upward job mobility. Those workers in the secondary occupational sector--that is, characterized as lacking opportunities for upward mobility--are likely to experience little improvement in their situation unless they change both employers and occupations.

These theories have also been used to extend human capital theory under the hypothesis that returns to education vary with occupational and/or industrial sector, as well as by gender and race within sector. Thus, to fully understand the ability of individuals to accumulate wealth and access to pensions and higher Social Security levels in old age, we must be able to identify not only their human capital, but the industrial and occupational sectors of their employment, and the types of job mobility they have experienced throughout their lives. The gender and race of individuals further influences their access to particular types of jobs and the returns they receive for their education and other human capital attributes. An additional consideration is that both occupational and industrial structure vary by geographic area, changing the opportunities for advancement and the access of certain groups to particular types of jobs.

Given the reliance of the elderly on incomes generated through their prior and (infrequently) current labor force participation, individuals in nonmetropolitan areas are particularly disadvantaged. The over-representation of poor jobs in peripheral industries and small firms in nonmetropolitan areas results in fewer choices and poorer employment opportunities than are found in metropolitan areas (Doeringer 1984; McGranahan 1988). Combined with relatively low employee power, workers with relatively low levels of human capital and low unionization rates in nonmetropolitan areas, nonmetropolitan workers are now and have been economically disadvantaged when compared with metropolitan workers (McLaughlin and Perman 1991a). The characteristics of employment available in nonmetropolitan areas are much more similar to those found in peripheral industries and secondary sector occupations. They are much less likely to lead to opportunities for advancement within a firm, and the opportunities for mobility across employers may be limited by the small number of alternative employers in any given geographically-defined labor market. Migration in search of better opportunities is one of few options available to nonmetropolitan residents with the human capital and willingness to move. In recent years the nonmetropolitan economic structure has become more similar to that of metropolitan areas (Tienda 1986). The economic structure in nonmetropolitan areas in earlier decades, however, was much more reliant on resource extractive industries such as agriculture, logging, quarrying and mining. Reliance on such industries may place those currently elderly in nonmetropolitan areas (who have been long-time nonmetropolitan residents) at a special disadvantage because of the cyclical nature of the success of these industries.

The Special Case of Women and Minorities

Minorities and women in nonmetropolitan areas are especially disadvantaged (Jensen and Tienda 1989; Lichter 1989; McLaughlin and Perman 1991b). The high poverty rates among minority populations are a major social concern; among the nonmetropolitan elderly being black is associated with a risk of poverty that is almost three times that for the white population. Being female raises the poverty risk among whites; among blacks, however, women and men have surprisingly comparable poverty rates (Table 9.2). Thus, any theory that purports to describe the outcomes for elderly individuals in nonmetropolitan areas must describe why white women fare worse than white men, but black women and men have very similar rates of poverty.

In considering the economic situation of today's elderly women and minorities, we must remember that their life experiences varied considerably from those of minorities and women currently of working age. The permeability of the educational system and of the labor market by gender and race differed greatly in the 1940's as compared to the 1960's and now. Social role expectations and socialization further limited the employment opportunities and advancement options for women and minorities who currently are over 65 years old.

Women. Fifty-seven percent of all poor individuals living in nonmetropolitan areas in 1990 were women, but among nonmetropolitan elders they account for fully 70 percent of all those in poverty. In this country, in general, the vast majority of elderly poor people are women. Examination of women's poverty in old-age is made complex by the fact that individual characteristics useful in explaining men's poverty are less useful for explaining women's poverty. This results from most currently elderly women's near total reliance on the benefits that accrue to their spouse in determining their own economic well-being. Given the gender division of labor into household and market work prevalent in the United States while women currently aged 65 or over were of working age, the current economic status of the majority of women will be determined by their spouses' earnings and pension income (Sorenson and McLanahan 1987). In addition, for women, marital disruptions and becoming widowed are more important predictors of women's economic well-being than are the women's own education and employment history (O'Rand and Landerman 1984; Smith and Moen 1988; Sorenson and McLanahan 1987; Warlick 1985). Thus for this group, poverty in old age will be the result, for some, of changes in family status and economic opportunities as they age, and for others of life-long poverty that continues into their retirement years.

Theories about the causes of poverty among currently elderly women must incorporate the importance of changes in their family status as they age and of both their own life employment experiences as well as those of their spouse(s). Given the low lifetime labor force participation of women who currently are elderly, human capital, status attainment, and structural theories that describe a woman's current employment experiences and characteristics do not provide comprehensive explanations of an elderly woman's economic well-being. Even among never-married women, labor force conditions and opportunities open to women who currently are elderly were likely to limit the benefits associated with a college education or continuous labor force participation. Examining the joint influence of the husbands' and wives' characteristics and how these are played out over their remaining lifetimes would increase the relevance of human capital, status attainment and structural explanations in understanding women's poverty.

Older Women, Widowhood, and Poverty. Any explanation of poverty among the elderly must take account of the poverty observed among elderly women, a group for whom both numbers and rates are high. Among currently elderly women, statistics underscore the tremendous influence of marital status and living arrangements on poverty status. In 1990, eight percent of elderly couples in nonmetropolitan areas were poor, while over 33 percent of elderly women living alone were poor (Table 9.3). This rate was higher than that for the comparable group in metropolitan areas, including the central city (Table 9.4). Over two-thirds of nonmetropolitan elderly black women living alone were in poverty in that year. Theoretical explanations of poverty among the elderly must encompass the causes and paths into poverty among women, and, for older women, that pathway is often via widowhood. Thus, this section focuses on widowhood and why it has profound implications for the income and poverty status of older women.

The data in Table 9.3 compare poverty rates for three groups of elderly women: married couples in which the householder is age 65 or older, women who head a family that does not include a spouse, and women living alone. Women are buffered by the presence of other family members--especially when one of those members is their husband. Even among black elderly women, for whom poverty in marriage is a major cause of being poor when widowed, unmarried status is associated with a sharply higher risk of poverty.

When women do little or no paid work outside the home during marriage, they will share in the returns their husbands receive from labor market efforts. His below-poverty earnings will result in her poverty as well. When wives also participate in paid work, the family's economic status results in part from the rewards to her labor market efforts. For poor families and women, the earnings-related retirement systems in the United States--Social Security and

TABLE 9.3 Poverty Rates of Elderly Individuals in Nonmetropolitan Areas by Marital Status and Race, 1990

	All	Whites	Blacks
Married Couple Families	8.1	6.0	41.2
Female householder, no spouse	15.9	8.8	(a)
Unrelated Females	33.4	31.2	67.9

(a) rates not provided because of small number of observations.

Source: Current Population Survey, U.S. Bureau of the Census, U.S. Department of Commerce, 1991c.

employer-provided pensions--directly link poverty during younger years to poverty in retirement and widowhood.[2]

As data in Table 9.3 suggest, however, the high poverty rates observed for unmarried elderly women are not solely a function of poverty when married. Explanations of high poverty among unmarried elderly women also rest in reasons for the abrupt diminution of income upon the death of husbands. In an earnings-based Social Security system, survivors of workers are explicitly provided with the means of sharing in the worker's retirement income even after the worker's death. Social Security payments continue through survivor benefits paid to wives and husbands of deceased workers. Spouses, at age 60, are eligible for a benefit approximately equal to the deceased worker's full benefits. In employer-provided pension plans survivor benefits are paid if workers choose a joint and survivor benefit option.[3] Workers may make alternative choices, however, choosing a single-life benefit--one that ceases when the worker dies, a lump-sum payment, or benefits paid to survivors only during a specified fixed period. Asset income may also diminish upon widowhood. Except in marital property states where half of all income and assets acquired during marriage belongs to each spouse, assets held in the name of only one of the spouses may be willed to persons other than the surviving spouse.

The transition from wife to widow has proven to be crucial to the economic status of many elderly women. We thus review available research on the transition from married to unmarried status among elderly women and what that research implies about the source of higher poverty for them. Because this

TABLE 9.4 Poverty Rates of Elderly Unrelated Females, 1979-1990

	All	Whites	Blacks
1990			
Metropolitan	24.7	21.5	58.2
Central city	29.2	24.0	57.8
Nonmetropolitan	33.2	31.0	68.7
1987			
Metropolitan	23.4	20.2	57.1
Central city	27.2	22.5	55.0
Nonmetropolitan	31.5	26.8	79.9
1983			
Metropolitan	24.9	21.9	56.4
Central city	28.2	24.2	55.4
Nonmetropolitan	32.8	29.2	80.6
1979			
Metropolitan	26.3	23.4	57.9
Central city	28.8	24.8	58.0
Nonmetropolitan	38.2	35.2	82.4

Sources: Current Population Survey, U.S. Bureau of the Census, U.S. Department of Commerce, 1980, 1984, 1988, 1991c.

section is concerned with poverty among nonmetropolitan elderly women--specifically, the reasons for their higher incidence of poverty--the discussion is oriented around describing potential metropolitan and nonmetropolitan differences in the process, the causes and the consequences of poverty among elderly women in metropolitan and nonmetropolitan areas. Understanding the economic changes that occur when women become widowed and during the years they remain unmarried requires longitudinal data.

Using longitudinal data, one can observe the precise timing and magnitude of changes in income, assets, family structure, and poverty status. Only since the advent of nationally representative, longitudinal panel studies with large samples of elderly families--for example, the longitudinal Retirement History Study (RHS), the National Longitudinal Panel of Mature Women, and the Panel Study of Income Dynamics (PSID)--have we begun to understand the causal pattern of poverty among elderly women.

There are three major conclusions drawn from longitudinal studies on widowhood that we discuss in turn and link to the issue of poverty for nonmetropolitan elderly women:

1. Widowhood is likely to occur earlier or at younger ages among low income couples, implying that some of the higher poverty rate for widows compared to married women is due to the selective attrition into widowhood of women who were poor when married.
2. The event of widowhood is associated with a sharp rise in poverty. In fact, at all income levels widowhood brings a major change in economic well-being with income changes absolutely greater among women initially at higher income levels. It appears that husbands--even those in high income groups--fail to adequately insure their wives against the economic consequences of widowhood.
3. While some widows are able to escape poverty, the majority will remain in poverty. This permanence is associated with the forces that place women at a disadvantage in the labor market, especially when gender inequality is compounded by older age.

Some of the poverty observed among widows is a continuation of poverty when married. Differences in poverty between metropolitan and nonmetropolitan elderly women will reflect in part the lower earnings and higher poverty among younger married families in nonmetropolitan areas. Because Social Security benefits are earnings-related, geographic differences in earnings histories of men and women will be reflected in the Social Security benefit amounts they receive when retired and widowed. Pensions are also earnings-related, and, likewise, will reflect those differences.

Numerous studies have found that morbidity and death are inversely correlated with indicators of socioeconomic status such as educational attainment, income, and husband's employment stability (Becker, Landes, and Michael 1977; Hoffman and Holmes 1976; Hurd and Wise 1989; Martin and Bumpass 1989). Data from longitudinal studies of widowhood corroborate such findings: the income of couples who are soon to be widowed are lower when married than is the income of those who remain intact during the specified observation period (Holden, Burkhauser, and Myers 1986; Mott and Moore 1978).

Because earlier widowhood is selective of those relatively less well-off to begin with and more likely to become poor with a small decline in income, differences in poverty rates between married and unmarried women tend to exaggerate the poverty associated with the transition to widowhood. The reason for the relationship between poverty and spouse's death is not entirely understood, but it likely has two sources: the long-term health problems of some husbands that cause both their lower life-time earnings and early death, and the causal effect of long-term poverty on health status.[4]

Longitudinal studies of elderly women suggest that prewidowhood poverty is a modest contributor to the higher poverty rates of unmarried than married women observed in the cross-section. Hurd and Wise (1989) report an increase in poverty rates for women widowed during the RHS from 9 to 42 percent. Holden, Burkhauser, and Myers (1986) report a rise in poverty rates from 9-16 percent in the last year of marriage to 38-50 percent in the first year of widowhood. While Burkhauser, Holden, and Myers (1986) show that poverty during the first year of widowhood may have been overestimated in both studies, even after appropriate income adjustments, poverty among this group is estimated to almost double, from 14 percent to 26 percent (Holden 1989a). Among more recently widowed women, Holden (1989a) finds that poverty rose from just 6 percent when married to 15 percent immediately after the husbands' deaths. If all income previously paid to the couple continued to the surviving spouse, or declined only in proportion to the decline in consumption needs of the smaller household unit, economic well-being of wives would not change upon widowhood. Longitudinal data, however, show that on average widows are left with far less income than is necessary to maintain the same living standard enjoyed when married.

Table 9.5, which reports total incomes and pensions, suggests important sources of income change when women in metropolitan and nonmetropolitan areas are widowed. These are cross-sectional data from the 1987 panel (wave 4) of the Survey of Income and Program Participation, disaggregated by age to partially control for differences in the age distribution of metropolitan and nonmetropolitan elderly women. A major difference between married and unmarried women is the percentage reporting pension income. We focus on company pension receipt, which excludes government and veteran pensions, since it will more likely reflect differences in pension coverage of metropolitan and nonmetropolitan firms. The smaller percentage of nonmetropolitan married couples receiving company pensions is a reflection of lower coverage. In both areas, unmarried women are even less likely to receive a pension, a reflection both of the lower pension coverage of working women and the chances that husbands will choose a pension that does not continue to the survivor. Holden and Burkhauser (1986) report that for the RHS cohort, fewer than half of all married men covered by a pension chose a survivor option. The incomes reported by married women as their own are shown in parentheses in Table 9.5. If these data represent accurately the effect of a marital status change, a surprisingly small share of the income of unmarried women comes from sources linked to their husbands.

Pensions are not the sole source of the change in income when wives become widows. The data on pensions are useful in indicating that the same puzzles remain to be answered for nonmetropolitan women as have been raised for

TABLE 9.5 Income Received by Elderly Unmarried Women, Married Couples and (Married Women), Metropolitan and Nonmetropolitan Areas, 1987

Age	Metropolitan		Nonmetropolitan	
	Unmarried Women	Married Couples	Unmarried Women	Married Couples
Mean Monthly Total Income				
65-74	$1,010	$2,494 (750)	$856	$2,148 (702)
75+	918	1,844 (633)	718	1,496 (487)
Percent Receiving Company Pension Income				
65-74	21.7%	53.0% (18.0)	14.8%	35.3% (7.8)
75+	20.8	41.3 (11.2)	10.3	24.4 (2.7)
Mean Monthly Company Pension Income[a]				
65-75	$204	$528 (172)	$263	$494 (251)
75+	221	332 (194)	177	659 (224)

Note: Company pension excludes government and military pension income.

[a]by those receiving company pension.

Source: Unpublished data from the 1987 Panel, Survey of Income and Program Participation, U.S. Bureau of the Census, U.S. Department of Commerce.

elderly widows in general: why is it that women are so much worse off in widowhood than in marriage?

Research supports the hypothesis that it is the insurance that husbands hold against their deaths that makes a difference in the degree of financial change suffered by newly widowed women. The few studies of husbands' insurance decisions imply that husbands greatly underestimate the needs of their widows in their financial planning (Auerbach and Kotlikoff 1987; Holden and Burkhauser 1986). Nonmetropolitan status is likely to matter if prewidowhood differences in insurance coverage exist between metropolitan and nonmetropolitan residents or if the insurance choices of husbands are different in some systematic way. We know virtually nothing about the financial decisions nonmetropolitan couples make about their retirement. The data in Table 9.5 suggest that disadvantage is greater for nonmetropolitan couples because of lower pension coverage. Even for couples with pensions, the widow may not be fully protected.

If husbands leave large estates to widows, income-based measures would underestimate the actual level of economic well-being of women following widowhood. Indeed, the claim is often made that income discrepancies between metropolitan and nonmetropolitan elderly may be partially offset by accumulation of assets. While a full accounting of assets is necessary to understand the relative economic status of the nonmetropolitan elderly, for women, the issue is whether the share of the married household's assets given to the wife following the husband's death compensates for the loss of his income.

Available evidence on the wealth of the elderly in general does not support the likelihood that the higher poverty among nonmetropolitan women will be offset by their higher assets. Already poor or near poor couples generally have little to bequeath in terms of tangible assets and property, such as homes, other real estate, businesses, savings, and marketable securities (Holden and Smeeding 1990). In part because of age, the most valuable assets held by couples in which one subsequently dies are their house, pension, and Social Security. A full measure of well-being would include some value for these. "Bequeathable" wealth is surprisingly small--$11,005 (1979 dollars) among those who were not poor prior to widowhood (Hurd and Wise 1989). This amount is significantly lower than among other "intact" couples, and is in part a reflection of the selectivity of death. More striking is the fact that annuity wealth (pensions and private annuities) is almost dissipated upon the husband's death; the relative economic status of women as widows is changed only slightly when full measures of wealth are compared in marriage and widowhood (Holden 1989b; Hurd and Wise 1989).

The level of poverty observed at any time among elderly unmarried women is the net result of the consequence for poverty risks when husbands die, and the probability of escaping poverty. Widows could exit poverty, for example, through greater work effort, the initiation of survivor benefits from Social Security or private pensions, or remarriage. Short-term poverty from which there is full recovery demands a different policy response compared to poverty that persists.

It is generally assumed that the possibility of economic recovery for older women diminishes as remarriage probabilities and the chances of successfully entering the work force diminish with age. To the extent that nonmetropolitan areas present relatively limited job opportunities for older women, the chances of recovery from widowhood-related income falls may be even smaller. Moreover, older nonmetropolitan women are less likely to have participated in the labor force than metropolitan women (Bokemeier, Sachs and Keith 1983). Thus it would seem--although we do not know--that for nonmetropolitan women the gender and geographic inequalities in economic opportunities, compounded by their age and widowhood, will be reflected in the greater permanence of their poverty.

The relative importance of the woman's own characteristics and experiences as compared to those of her spouse(s) is likely to vary across cohorts. As younger cohorts enter old age, women are more likely to have extensive labor force participation and to be covered by Social Security and pension plans in their own right. In addition, these women will have access to Social Security and pension plan benefits earned by their spouse, and vice versa. Younger cohorts of women with greater commitment to the labor force and access to occupations with high wages and benefits are more likely to qualify for adequate levels of Social Security benefits and pension income based on their own employment, reducing the importance of spousal benefits in determining a woman's economic well-being (Hess 1986). In general, we have an incomplete understanding of the determinants of the economic status of elderly women and the changes associated with the move from being married to widowed. This is even more so for nonmetropolitan elderly women, for whom the absence of data restricts what we know about them. The economic status of these widows remains closely linked to that of their husbands, since husbands' earnings, savings and retirement decisions prior to death determine to a large extent what income and assets remain for widows.

Taking all evidence together, we must conclude that much of the association between widowhood and women's economic insecurity lies in the failure to guard through insurance against the potentially catastrophic consequences of the husbands' death, and in the inability of widows to counteract these consequences through their own labor market work or retirement income. To the extent that women in nonmetropolitan areas face different probabilities of widowhood early in their lives, have husbands who are less likely to be covered by pensions or have life insurance through employers, and themselves face a poorer job market through which to build their own retirement resources, nonmetropolitan elderly women will be less secure as they age. Restricted work opportunities for men and women, larger percentages of self-employed workers, and fewer jobs with pension coverage reduce the planning options available for nonmetropolitan families against the financial consequences of widowhood. We know little about how families think about and plan for the eventuality of one spouse's death. And we do not know how families in metropolitan and nonmetropolitan areas differ in the decisions they make.

Minorities. Among all groups of elders, minorities--both men and women--have the highest rates of poverty in nonmetropolitan areas (Table 9.2). Given the very high rates of poverty among working age minorities in nonmetropolitan areas, poor minority elders are likely to have spent their entire lives in poverty, rather than becoming poor as they aged. The special disadvantage of African Americans, American Indians, and Hispanics in nonmetropolitan America can be traced to their distinct histories of forced entry or forced movement within the United States. These patterns of forced migration have led to rural elderly blacks being concentrated in the Southeast, American Indians in the Southwest and Northern Plains, and Hispanics in the Southwest. Rural minority elders at highest risk of being poor, thus are concentrated in various parts of the Southern region. These groups' social and economic histories in those spatial locations are intertwined in ways that make the economic disadvantage of minority elders of grave proportions.

Several factors we touched on in the earlier theoretical discussion combine to place minorities in nonmetropolitan areas at a special disadvantage. First, minorities, and especially minorities over age 65, have very low levels of educational attainment when compared with whites. This gap is especially large in the South where nonmetropolitan minorities are concentrated. These low education levels result from social expectations about the economic roles of blacks during the time those currently elderly were of school age, and the segregation of educational systems by race. Without question, primarily black schools received lower levels of investment, a pattern that is argued to continue today in areas with predominantly black populations. Thus, even when blacks were able to attend school, the quality of the education received was much different from that of their white counterparts. This educational disadvantage, combined with expectations about appropriate economic roles for blacks were the beginnings of the economic hardship faced by black elders today.

Local labor market conditions and structures also have a profound influence on employment and earnings histories and consequently on the accumulation of advantage and disadvantage over the life cycles of older individuals. Rural minorities are concentrated in regions with widespread, persistent underdevelopment (Brown and Warner 1991; Colclough 1988). These regions are characterized by economic structures and labor relations that exploit cheap labor and in which there has been and continues to be little incentive to improve wage rates, skills, employee benefits, or working conditions.

Whether employment has been in plantation agriculture and tenant farming, farming and ranching on tribal lands, or as migrant farmworkers and subsequently in manufacturing or service sector jobs, minorities typically have been employed in low-wage, low-skill jobs, with no benefits and often without public, much less private, pension coverage.

Because of their lower levels of educational attainment and the types of jobs historically considered "appropriate" for minorities, these individuals have had few opportunities to improve their economic conditions over their work lives. Rural minority elders suffer from lifetimes of accumulated disadvantage that are even more severe than those experienced by their metropolitan counterparts. This is evidenced by the higher poverty rates among nonmetropolitan than metropolitan minority elders, including those in central cities.

One theoretical perspective proposed for understanding well-being, both economic and psychological among minority elders is that of double jeopardy. Those supporting this theoretical proposition suggest that minority elders face even more severe deprivation than minorities of other ages--they are even worse off than might be expected because of the operation of the "double jeopardy." While limited support for this theory has been found when comparing U.S. black and white elders (Markides 1983), it may be more useful in explaining the severe economic deprivation of minority elders in nonmetropolitan areas. In these areas, minorities suffer a triple jeopardy--that of being older, being minority and living in nonmetropolitan areas. We know of no empirical test of this hypothesis as it relates to elderly minorities in nonmetropolitan areas.

Elderly minority women in nonmetropolitan areas may be somewhat unusual in that they are more likely than white women to have spent their lives working as household servants or as farm laborers. These women may have had some experience in the labor market, even if in the informal labor market, during the working ages. The jobs they held, however, are unlikely to have provided earnings sufficient to raise them above poverty during their working lives, and certainly did not offer access to pensions--or even to Social Security benefits. The experiences of minority women also are likely to vary with the racial and ethnic group to which a woman belongs. Again, the specific experiences of currently elderly minority women in nonmetropolitan areas require further study. Generally, however, we can hypothesize that these women most likely were poor throughout their lives, regardless of the presence or absence of a male partner, and that their poverty continued into old age. Thus, these women are less likely to experience changes in their poverty status once they have reached old age, since they already are suffering life-long poverty.

Context of Poverty

A limitation of this review is that we have concentrated on factors that explain poverty among elderly individuals. We have not discussed the relevance of poverty of place. There is no question that some areas are poverty stricken and have much higher poverty rates at all age groups than other areas. These areas of very high poverty are geographically concentrated in the Mississippi Delta, in Appalachia, in certain areas of the Southwest and the Great Plains. Cruise (1991) also has identified areas of extremely high poverty rates among elderly individuals. These counties, like those with high poverty rates overall, are overwhelmingly found among nonmetropolitan counties. Individuals who spend their lives in these counties face   much different opportunities than those residing elsewhere. The risk of being or becoming poor in these areas is likely to be much higher whether one is of working age or elderly, and being poor in such an area may be a much different experience from poverty elsewhere. Local conditions can influence not only the risk of becoming poor, but the options available for dealing with poverty. This is true not only of elders, but of individuals of all ages. While we have concentrated on theories that explain an objective measure of poverty--that of income available during a given year--elderly individuals in poverty are likely to face much different conditions and options for dealing with their poverty depending on where they live.

Economic Well-Being: Measurement and Meaning Among the Elderly

Studies often use income poverty as the sole measure of economic well-being among metropolitan and nonmetropolitan residents. Poverty status is a widely used indicator of vulnerability to a variety of economic, social, and health hazards. Its widespread use is attributable to consistency in measurements of cash income values across geographic areas and over time. Cash income--even when received from a wide variety of sources--is a concept that can be consistently defined across families and cultures, has a value that can be recalled relatively easily when the income has been received in the recent past, and is uniformly measured at its face value. Income is, however, an incomplete measure of economic well-being. When using poverty rates to compare the economic vulnerability of elders in metropolitan and nonmetropolitan areas, it is important to recognize its limitations.

In this section we describe important aspects of economic well-being that are not included in an income-based poverty measure.   Others have provided thorough critiques of the official definition of poverty (Ruggles 1990; Sawhill 1989).   The focus of this discussion is to hypothesize how unmeasured components of well-being may vary in metropolitan and nonmetropolitan areas and affect economic vulnerability of the elderly. We discuss four aspects the income-based measure of poverty fails to capture in assessing comparative well-being: the exclusion of resources that enable individuals to enhance their command over goods and services, the higher cost and physical difficulty that some individuals face in obtaining those goods and services, variations in how individuals view their particular economic circumstances, and the ability to capture the dynamics of economic well-being over time and space.

Measuring poverty is important for the implications of poverty's consequences--as a reflection of objective hardships due to the lack of income necessary to achieve even a minimally adequate level of consumption (Binstock 1986). What that level of "adequacy" is can be determined by a relatively fixed social norm (absolute measures), by comparison to income or consumption levels achieved by other individuals or by the person at an earlier period in life (relative measures), and by comparison to some self-reported threshold below which the individual feels resources would be insufficient (subjective measures).

The official U.S. poverty threshold is an indicator of the first type. It measures well-being against an income threshold, defined in 1964 on the basis of the food expenditure patterns of low-income families, taking account of family size. Since then, it has been adjusted only for annual price increases (Orshansky 1965). The poverty measure counts only income, ignoring other resources that may enhance individual well-being.

Studies that expand poverty measures to include the value to recipients of in-kind programs (U.S. Bureau of the Census 1990e) generally show diminished poverty among the elderly compared to younger age groups. Expanded poverty measures that include nonincome resources have rarely been used to compare different groups of elders, among whom coverage and eligibility for programs--even those targeted to this age group--may vary (Holden and Smeeding 1990). Comparing income-based poverty rates for metropolitan and nonmetropolitan elderly populations will fail to reflect true differences in economic hardship to the extent that there is inequality between metropolitan and nonmetropolitan areas. This inequality could exist, for example, in the ownership and value of property, in health insurance coverage, and in access to federal and state in-kind transfer programs. Consequently, it is important to complement income based analyses with data on the broader network of resources--including the in-kind services of friends and family--that may differentially buffer the consequences of low income.

Housing is one key resource that influences the standard of living but which is not included in income measures. The nonmetropolitan elderly reside in what constitutes much of the sub-standard housing in the United States (Glasgow and Beale 1985; Talbot 1985). Significant percentages of rural elders live in poorly insulated dwellings that are structurally unsound and lack running water, adequate wiring and heating (Fitchen 1990). Talbot (1985) noted that in 1975 more than 30 percent of the rural elderly lived in homes without plumbing and 50 percent had no central heating. Higher poverty among the nonmetropolitan elderly suggests that because they are more likely to lack the resources to improve, maintain and repair their homes, the value of housing services may decline in nonmetropolitan areas as individuals age. Whether this deterioration proceeds at a faster pace for nonmetropolitan than metropolitan homeowners is an empirical question.

Another important component of economic well-being is coverage by public or private insurance for health care costs. Elderly without insurance coverage will face higher out-of-pocket expenditures or, should they choose not to seek uncovered health care, more rapid deterioration in their health. Only a small proportion of all elderly individuals have no health insurance coverage. There are reasons to suspect, however, that this proportion and the proportion with Medicare only, are higher in nonmetropolitan than metropolitan areas. Nonmetropolitan workers are more likely to work in jobs--e.g., farming, other self-employed work--that may have no Social Security coverage. They are also more likely to have worked in jobs without employer-provided health insurance coverage (Jensen 1982; Jensen and Salant 1985), thus eliminating the possibility of continuing to obtain employer-subsidized and/or group health insurance into retirement. Lower group coverage for health insurance suggests that the nonmetropolitan elderly may be more often subject to the higher premium charges of nongroup insurance (Jensen 1983).

A second limitation of income-based measures in assessing economic well-being is that income enables but does not guarantee access to goods and services. Limited access to services in nonmetropolitan areas may place the elderly poor at a disadvantage (Glasgow 1991). Rural areas typically are deficient in physicians and medical personnel because they lack threshold populations with incomes sufficient to sustain such services. Mental health services are often not available (Fitchen 1991). The higher costs to rural local governments of providing and delivering services in rural areas reduces the availability of services to the elderly poor (Cordes 1989; Ecosometrics 1981). Indeed, some evidence suggests that poor rural areas may be especially underserved. A study of home care services in a rural Maryland county found that the fewest services were being received in districts with the lowest incomes (Hayslip et al. 1980).

Transportation is a serious problem for the rural elderly that is exacerbated by the geographical separation and low population densities characterizing rural America. Many do not own automobiles and many of those who do are no longer able to drive due to disabilities or failing health (Talbot 1985; Glasgow 1991). The problem is further exacerbated by the lack of public transportation in rural areas. Talbot (1985) notes that only 12 percent of communities with populations of less than 2,500 have access to public transportation. Taxi service is not often an available option.

Subjective measures of well-being typically obtain information from individuals on their own perceptions of economic hardship. These measures are potentially meaningful indicators of well-being--especially in comparing the consequences of poverty across space--for two reasons. First, such measures can reflect how individuals may differentially adjust to a given income level and, consequently, provide a personal perspective on economic hardship. Second, these measures may help resolve the issue of how to identify the existence of difficult-to-identify and difficult-to-value non-income resources that differentially buffer individuals against the consequences of income poverty. For example, an elderly couple just below the poverty threshold may report feeling their income is adequate if they are protected by a good employer-provided retiree health insurance plan, own their own home, have other assets that can be drawn on in an emergency, and are in a closely knit community where they can call on friends and children for transportation, home maintenance and repair, and home health care if needed. Another couple with the same income would not only feel but would, in fact, be far more economically vulnerable if they have only Medicare to cover medical expenditures, live in nonsubsidized rental housing, have no savings, and live in an area with few neighbors and no children on whom they could call for help. A subjective measure would correctly identify the greater security of the first couple, while income-based measures would not. Difficulties in obtaining full resource measures in a population for whom in-kind transfers and services are important but differentially distributed may indicate promise for using subjective measures of well-being to capture these differentials.

Unfortunately, subjective measures of well-being have not been used widely enough for us to understand how responses vary across individuals and families and over time (Hagenaars and de Vos 1988; Dinkins 1991). On average the elderly express greater security at lower income levels than do the nonelderly. However, no study has yet sorted out whether that is a cohort effect that will disappear over time, a lowered expectation about consumption demands as individuals age, or because elderly on average have acquired additional resources that reduce their dependence on income for consumption needs and that provide insurance against income changes.

The value of pursuing research on subjective measures of well-being is supported by the limited available evidence. Much of the research on the nonmetropolitan elderly suggests that in spite of inferior objective living circumstances, levels of subjective well-being, as measured by diverse indices of morale and life satisfaction, are surprisingly high and higher than among the elderly in metropolitan areas (Donnenwerth, Guy and Norvell 1978; Grams and Fengler 1981; Hynson 1976; Lee and Lassey 1980). Coward and Kerckhoff (1978) suggest that 90 percent of the rural elderly considered their incomes to be "adequate" (see Grams and Fengler 1981). Scott and Roberto (1985) found a pattern of heavy reliance on family for both practical assistance and social support among a sample of 245 nonmetropolitan west Texas older adults whose income fell below the poverty level. In rural Appalachia a tradition of close-knit families and strong family interdependence has traditionally provided an important buffer against the hardships of poverty (Beaver 1986; Bryant 1981; Schwarzweller, Brown and Mangalam 1971; Weller 1965). These studies, however, provide no evidence on whether these support mechanisms are stronger or weaker among the elderly poor in urban communities. Reasons for this relative satisfaction may be because impoverished nonmetropolitan elderly people may not perceive themselves as poor when they compare themselves with their parents or with the circumstances of their younger neighbors. In addition, the promise of Social Security benefits may introduce a valued stability and predictability to their economic well-being that they did not have earlier.

We emphasize, however, that the issue is whether subjective well-being measures are able to capture differentials in the objective hardships faced by the elderly poor. It is this usefulness in understanding differentials between metropolitan and nonmetropolitan areas that we argue is worthy of being explored, but the outcome is by no means certain. For example, one could argue that rural environments provide particularly supportive contexts for aging that ameliorate the effects of poverty. In addition, changes over time may reduce accessibility to the supports that buffered the nonmetropolitan elderly in the past against the consequences of poverty. Coward (1987:44), however, argues that "...there is no convincing evidence that the rural poor who are elderly have a more active or pervasive informal support network than their urban elderly counterparts in poverty."

Thus, rather than assuming inherent differences among social support networks in metropolitan and nonmetropolitan areas, one might hypothesize that community support arises from a "social contract" enforceable within a fairly stable and homogeneous community (Lozier and Althouse 1974; Pihlbald 1975; Rowles 1980). Over the years individuals accumulate "social credit" from being a good worker, a conscientious parent, or from making other contributions to the community. They draw on this credit in old age. This generates an expectation within the community that those who can provide assistance to the older person will furnish needed support as an accepted part of their own accumulation of social credit. Thus even among those for whom poverty has been a persistent state over generations, the family can act to insure individuals against even greater hardship in their old age (Kotlikoff and Spivak 1981). The issue then becomes the extent to which these social contracts have differentially existed in metropolitan and nonmetropolitan communities, and the extent to which changes over time in community stability undermines them. This issue is amenable to empirical research on social support network differences in metropolitan and nonmetropolitan areas.

There are two major problems in using available research on subjective well-being and social buffers against income poverty to infer the relative levels of hardship faced by the rural and urban elderly poor. First, none of the cited research speaks specifically to relative satisfaction levels of the rural and urban elderly in comparable economic circumstances. Research compares satisfaction levels of the elderly of all ages or speaks only about the rural elderly poor without an urban comparison. Further, our earlier discussion indicated that the composition of the rural elderly was different from that of urban elderly. Controlling for the racial, age, and marital status differences between these two groups is likely to diminish any difference between the (higher) satisfaction of rural residents and that of their urban peers.

Second, the concept of poverty, whether measured in absolute, relative, or subjective terms, is a static measure that fails to capture the dynamics of poverty over people's lives and generations. By this we mean the movements of individuals into and out of poverty and the movements of individuals who are at risk of being poor from one geographic area to another (e.g., a married woman who undertakes a retirement move with her husband and then becomes poor when he dies). Exits from poverty demonstrate people's ability to mobilize resources that improve their income status--and presumably reduce the associated hardships. Long-term poverty is likely to represent greater hardship for those who have no additional resources to mobilize. While it is presumed that the elderly are less likely than other age groups to exit from poverty, research shows that during the first few years after entering poverty, exit rates are high for this group (Bound et al. 1991; Burkhauser, Holden and Myers 1986; Coe 1988; Smith and Zick 1986). Although marriage, a prominent source of exit among young adults, does not contribute much to the exit chances for the elderly, retirement income and their own increased work are important. We have no information on whether the poor in metropolitan and nonmetropolitan areas face different exit chances. The fact that single month and annual poverty rates for the elderly are more alike in nonmetropolitan than metropolitan areas suggests that long-term poverty among the elderly may be a greater problem in the former (unpublished tabulations from the Survey of Income and Program Participation).

Geographic population movements complicate the ability to assess geographic influences on the chances of becoming and remaining poor. Economic activity takes place within a definable geographic area and the returns from that activity are distributed to individuals with well-defined residential locations. When residence changes, individuals take with them the legacy of economic activity (for example, their education, their savings). Thus, once removed from its place of economic origin, the fruits of economic activity that accrued to the recipient can be misidentified as to its geographic origin. This is a particular problem in identifying the sources of rural versus urban poverty since poverty "in place" might have had its origin in some quite different geographic setting. In part this reflects the fact that individuals make decisions over their lifetimes about the use of income for consumption in the year received, and its use to increase consumption in later years to a level above that which would otherwise be attainable. Current income used to purchase income-producing financial assets will increase the individual's income in future years. On the other hand, income used to purchase housing or other nonincome producing assets will raise economic well-being in later years without a measured increase in income. Thus, while income measures may be a reasonable indicator of the comparative well-being of individuals when received, they become an increasingly flawed measure of well-being over the life course of individuals. Concurrent correlations between the chances of elderly groups entering poverty and the geographic circumstances of their life, may not reveal the influence of earlier environments on those decisions that brought them to their current financial position.

Conclusions and New Directions for Theory and Research

We have covered two main themes in our discussions of poverty among rural older people. First, we stressed variation in conditions across rural areas and the need to incorporate aspects of that diversity in theoretical models and empirical research on poverty among rural elders. At the same time, we have argued that rural residence has a negative effect on the economic well-being of its residents, whether young or old. Second, we stressed that a life course perspective is necessary to a full understanding of poverty among older rural residents. Poverty for some is predictable long before those individuals become elderly. For others, life course transitions that occur primarily during old age (such as widowhood) greatly increase the risk of poverty.

A major correction needed in theories of poverty among rural elders is the inclusion of a life course perspective. Only then can poverty among the rural elderly be understood in terms of a life-time of labor market experience. Many rural elders were poor before they became old or the outcome was predictable because of the nature of labor market structures and dynamics and their participation in the marketplace before they retired.

A life course perspective speaks dramatically to the consequences of what is happening to large numbers of people presently in the working ages. Unless today's workers are able to accumulate "delayed income" for their elder years, they will be impoverished. The future is bleak for the sizable proportion of nonelderly women who head single-parent families. Their high poverty rates, combined with family obligations that limit opportunities for human capital development and labor force participation portend poverty in old age. The point is that cohort differences understood from a life course perspective give us a powerful tool for understanding the dynamics and persistence of poverty among rural elders.

Another extension of theory and research needed in studies of rural older people and poverty is the rural context. What we define as rural is a proxy for the characteristics and attributes of places that shape the life experiences of those who live in rural or "nonmetropolitan" areas. The true task is to identify and define the specific characteristics or aspects of "rural" life that result in those in certain areas having poorer economic outcomes than those in urban areas.

Rural communities are the context within which individuals experience life and that affects individuals' economic success or failure. Inclusion in our models of geographic differences in economic structure, access to resources and services, and other conditions that determine the experiences of rural individuals (including the elderly) takes us beyond traditional sociological and economic theories for explaining poverty to incorporate the idea that these broader theories play themselves out over space. Characteristics that we define as relevant for economic attainment (higher levels of education, employment in certain occupations) may be less influential in some areas than others, depending on the conditions in those areas.

We need meaningful extension of existing theories to incorporate the many potential combinations of structural and individual characteristics across space that determine each package called "local conditions." Testing this theoretical extension is difficult because rather than focus on understanding what it is about space, structure, and conditions in certain areas that lead to poorer economic well-being, we have been limited to rural and urban, or metropolitan and nonmetropolitan because of data availability. Only recently have data become available that allow the study of a broad range of diverse areas.

Investigators of social disparity face the problem of high levels of variation of structure and conditions across areas traditionally defined as nonmetropolitan. Summaries based on rural/urban or nonmetropolitan/metropolitan distinctions are certainly useful. Any attempts to understand and successfully explain a nonmetropolitan effect, however, are likely to meet with only moderate success in defining with any precision the specific place characteristics that condition economic success. The diversity of local conditions must be acknowledged and brought to bear on the problem of rural poverty. Even if we are able to develop theoretical models that include an understanding of the effects of context or local conditions, a second problem arises. Lack of data prevent the adequate testing of theories that incorporate local conditions as a factor in understanding economic well-being in later life. A few data sets exist that allow existing theories of spatial development and effects of local structure to be tested (an ideal example is the PUMS-D labor market areas file from the 1980 Census of Population). It is unclear, however, that such a data set will be built from the 1990 Census, or that the units will retain the same boundaries to allow comparisons across time. This type of data is extremely useful, but it must be linked with individual level (particularly panel) data to allow researchers to model and test theories that incorporate a life course perspective on economic well-being with aspects of the place(s) in which people spend their lives.

The addition of geographic identifiers beyond metropolitan/nonmetropolitan classifications, which makes the estimation of contextual models possible, is essential if researchers are to develop theories that incorporate local conditions and specify models that adequately test those theories. To explain geographic differentials in well-being of the elderly, we must consider the diversity of areas commonly considered rural or nonmetropolitan, and the fact that different aspects of local conditions may operate to influence labor market or employment quality than explain the adequacy of health service provision. We need to think about defining local conditions that are relevant for the problems and issues being studied. Rural and urban areas, for example, differ in economic structure, demographic size and composition, and the effectiveness and capacity of local institutions to provide access to essential services and facilities (Brown and Glasgow 1991). By acknowledging that social structures vary across space and by trying to understand how that variation affects the experiences of individuals and the sociological outcomes of interest, we add to our ability to understand and explain what we observe.

In turning our attention to those subgroups of the elderly population that are particularly disadvantaged, other research and policy issues become prominent. For example, the decades over which panel studies collected data on income, assets, family structure and poverty status included important changes in pension and Social Security policy that were enacted specifically to improve the economic security of widows.[5] Thus, they are rich sources of information on how women are protected (or not) by legislation, employer policies, and intra-family decisions against sudden, sharp, and permanent changes in economic well-being when husbands die.

The richness of these panel studies is, however, offset by their smaller sample size compared to large national cross-sectional data sets, a difference necessitated by the expense of gathering data at frequent intervals over a long period. The number of any single type of event observed over the period of the panel may limit the ability to draw conclusions with confidence. Widowhood, although a status in which a large number of elderly women are observed at any point in time, is an event that is experienced in any year by a small percentage of married women. The number of "widowing" events observed in a panel study is reduced further by the attrition precipitated by reluctance to be interviewed soon after a spouse's death.

When the numbers of events are relatively small, it is especially difficult to compare differences in the incidence and consequences of events between metropolitan and nonmetropolitan populations.[6] It is only with panel data that investigators can accurately assess the relative contributions of life course events, rural and urban community characteristics, and individual attributes on the chances of elderly individuals becoming and remaining in poverty. However, a large share of comparative research on the well-being of metropolitan and nonmetropolitan elderly must continue to be based on cross-sectional data. It is important to understand, however, the limits of using cross-sectional data. For example, longitudinal research on elderly women in general must continue to inform the investigations of conditions in nonmetropolitan areas. The value of longitudinal data suggests attention to obtaining larger nonmetropolitan samples in panel studies.

We have discussed shortcomings of income-based poverty measures and how that limits our knowledge of the dynamics and persistence of poverty. What we conclude is that income-based poverty measures provide an imperfect indication of the economic hardship faced by individuals and may obscure potentially important differences across time and space. Asset holdings and eligibility for in-kind benefits from government agencies or from employers have been incorporated in some poverty measures, but rarely have they been applied to compare metropolitan and nonmetropolitan areas. Researchers must attempt to expand understanding of the different distribution of non-cash resources among the elderly in metropolitan and nonmetropolitan areas. That there may be a measurable difference is suggested by studies on the coverage of private and public retirement and health insurance programs, and on the availability of transportation, and health services.

We have suggested that subjective well-being measures may be able to capture the influence of unmeasured components of well-being. Investigators, however, must be cautious that reports of subjective well-being may be biased, if, as suggested by Pihlblad (1975:54-55), the principle of "independence and individual responsibility for one's own fate," is more dominant in small town ethos and is there more likely to be translated into a prevailing view that "...some hardship and poverty must be borne without complaining."

Subjective measures may also better capture declines in well-being that occur even as income rises in nonmetropolitan areas. The greater integration of isolated, nonmetropolitan regions of the country into the national society and economy, may undermine indigenous "networks of mutual aid and exchange" (Batteau 1983; Schwarzweller, Brown and Mangalam 1971). Major demographic changes in nonmetropolitan America that are transforming rural society may threaten the local extended kinships and family networks of elderly people, especially for those whose family have long since departed the area. As a result, income-based poverty may not grow worse, but its consequences may deepen.

The widespread use of current income measures as indicators of economic well-being coupled with investigation of concurrent geographic attributes fail to capture the reasons (versus correlates) of why rural elderly individuals occupy particular positions in the income distribution at a point in time. For the elderly, financial status is a result not just of current income flows, but of earlier financial decisions that are not likely to be fully reflected in traditional income measures of well-being. A large body of literature has investigated life cycle savings patterns, the accumulation of assets, and the influence of pensions and Social Security on savings, consumption, and retirement timing (e.g., Kotlikoff 1989). To ignore these important components of wealth in measuring economic status distorts income distribution results. The challenge to investigators of rural elderly "poverty" is to map the historical path individuals and families took, to where they happened to be when data on them were collected. Their relative status when older can only be understood in a life course context reflecting not only the fabric of their lives but also that of the communities in which they lived over significant periods of their lives.

While our discussions have considered the measurement of subjective dimensions of the individual's experience of poverty, there is a need to probe more deeply into the *social meaning* of poverty, the ideology that conditions conceptions of poverty that are implicitly accepted and reinforced by "insiders" within particular rural environments.   Local ideology may be a critical determinant of both individual and community responses to poverty.   For example, in parts of rural Appalachia, historical involvement in a self-sufficient economy focused on family-based subsistence farming, involves immersion in a system in which social and economic relationships are inextricably interrelated (Precourt 1983). Because of this intimate relationship, poverty, as defined by income criteria, has limited meaning because it inappropriately separates economic status from its social context.   What this means is that, from the perspective of traditional rural Appalachian culture, an egalitarian ideology, grounded in kinship structure and community-wide networks of mutual aid and exchange, serves as a buffer to the manifestation of poverty.   Other rural environments may have few buffers to poverty and different ideologies of poverty.   A need exists, therefore, to explore the social meaning of elderly poverty in different rural environments.

In conclusion, we have demonstrated that poverty among the elderly differs from that experienced by younger persons because it depends on the accumulated impacts of labor market experience, marital and family history, access to and involvement in public programs, residence in diverse community environments and macro-structural historical events specific to particular cohorts. We have shown that income security is lower among rural than urban elderly because their life-time experiences in all institutional domains provided less benefit and because their current residences are less capable of providing access to essential goods and services.

Notes

This chapter was written by Nina Glasgow, Cornell University; Karen Holden, University of Wisconsin-Madison; Diane McLaughlin, Pennsylvania State University; and Graham Rowles, University of Kentucky.

1. Data on persons classified by size of place in which they reside typically adopt either a rural/urban classification or a metropolitan/nonmetropolitan distinction. These terms are defined by the Bureau of the Census. Most data and studies cited in this chapter use the metropolitan/nonmetropolitan distinction, and thus we use this term throughout our discussion. The rural/urban distinction is used when the study cited has used this classification in the data analyses. Our general discussion uses "metropolitan" and "nonmetropolitan" and "rural" and "urban" terminology interchangeably.

2. Though some poor couples and widows may be eligible for means-tested benefits from the Supplemental Security Income program (SSI), they are not likely to be raised above the poverty threshold. The maximum federal SSI benefits in 1990 of $386 a month for an individual and $579 for a couple were below the respective relevant monthly poverty thresholds of $522 and $659.

3. Since the passage of the 1974 Employee Retirement Income Security Act, pensions must offer a joint and survivor benefit (that is, a pension some share of which continues to the survivor) as the default form. Because some husbands may choose a single life pension (although since 1984 the wife must concur) or a lump sum payment, women who when married shared in the pension income of their husband may receive none of that pension when widowed.

4. Health expenditure studies show that higher earnings (through better health care, and more "healthy" lifestyles) reduce the risk of illness and morbidity (Anderson and Burkhauser 1985).

5. Legislation includes the 1974 Employee Retirement Income Security Act mandating the provision of survivor benefits, the 1984 Retirement Equity Act mandating spousal consent when those benefits are rejected, the 1965 extension of survivor benefits to divorced survivors, and the 1972 increase in Social Security survivor benefits from 82.5 to 100% of the deceased worker's benefits.

6. Confidentiality issues often compound this problem if geographic identifiers are changed or suppressed for small samples. For example, in SIPP state identifiers are scrambled when numbers of persons interviewed in a specific state are small. In some important longitudinal studies, geographic identifiers below the major region are not included.

10

The State, Rural Policy,
and Rural Poverty

Introduction

The national government has done little that really matters in eliminating the causes of rural poverty. At most, U.S. policymakers create marginal relief, disguised behind a thin veneer of political rhetoric. In part, persistent rural poverty occurs because public policymakers have failed to discover--much less apply--the many remedies needed to alleviate U.S. poverty in general. Our concern here is more narrowly focused than suggesting general poverty remedies, however. Market problems and social failures in rural America are different and in many ways more severe than in metropolitan regions (Rodgers and Weiher 1989; Flora and Christenson 1991). We see a near-total inability on the part of U.S. governing institutions to deal successfully with the wide range of rural needs. This chapter will strive to explain why, from an institutional perspective, this has been the case, and explore the potentials and limits of addressing rural poverty. Only by doing this can we shed light on the persistence and the neglect of America's rural poor.

Rural poverty is a contemporary socioeconomic problem that must be dealt with by changing contemporary institutions. The core thesis of this chapter, however, is that to understand the role of the American nation-state and public policy in combatting and reinforcing rural poverty, and to assess the constraints on public policy in addressing rural poverty issues, one must begin with historical analysis. We will demonstrate that rural policy issues have always been defined in agricultural terms, to be solved through modifications of farm programs or supplements to those programs. Also, since farm programs from the outset were developed to achieve increased productivity and technological advance, these programs failed to address the problems of the "people left behind," and actually increased the numbers of those both left behind and left to leave. As an agricultural establishment (USDA, congressional agriculture committees, land-grant agricultural research and extension institutions, general farm and commodity groups) emerged, farm and rural policies became increasingly incompatible. The U.S. was left with no distinct rural vision to guide its politics of places. Institutions could not handle farm and rural policies as separate entities having different purposes. Rural nonfarm policies that did emerge were thus "minimalist," leaving local communities to set and enforce whatever rules local elites could impose on local labor pools. The modest successes that have been achieved in dealing with poverty problems have generally been achieved *indirectly*, through public policies designed to achieve goals other than reducing rural poverty.

While historical analysis is crucial to understanding the role of American public policy in exacerbating and ameliorating rural poverty problems, the emerging macrostructural forces of the 1990s are no less significant. They are changing many of the rules that relate to public policy toward rural areas and rural poverty. The rise of new approaches to federalism, the deepening fiscal crises of national, state and local governments, and increased global economic competition are combining to challenge the agricultural establishment's hold over policymaking. In this chapter, we will build our analysis on micro-level domestic policy decisions of the federal government and then discuss macro- and meso-level structural constraints in the international political economy. It is not our intent to focus on local power structures that we see made possible by the developmental conditions of national policy. That deserving topic is beyond the scope of this chapter.

The Historical Legacy: Rural Policy as Farm Policy

For several sensible reasons, early U.S. farm policy reflected the nation's status as a rural society of farmers and those who depended on them. Indeed, farm policy was rural policy. Culturally, the origins of farm policy were found in the agrarian vision that guided a westward expansion and settlement, that created the hope of establishing producer-landowners as a stable social base, and that justified the governmental costs of encouraging increasing numbers of producers.

Not surprisingly, overproduction of commodities became chronic, since policy was prompted by societal issues rather than what farmers needed to grow to make a profit. Over the years, farm policy shifted from providing benefits all could share in if they made an effort, to new programs emphasizing selective distribution of benefits to individuals on the basis of special status. The process worked most comfortably when specific benefits could be handed out to identifiable constituents.

The Agrarian Myth: Fundamentalist Vision

Public policy decisions are made by choosing among values, and in a democratic society where all values are articulated and pursued, choices are difficult. They cannot be made without some movement toward consensus. It is in this context that agrarian ideology became defined, and also reified, within protective agricultural institutions. As farmers took on near mystical status because of their widespread social importance, the myths surrounding them became equal parts fact and legend. Farmers were seen as facing the uncertain vagaries of weather and climate that often left many of them destitute; they settled most frontier communities after adventurers and pathfinders blazed through, they nurtured scarce natural resources, and they did so at less return on their investment than that gained by other economic factions within society. Farmers' citizenship and moral judgments were seen as sustaining democracy.

Farm Policy As Collective Benefits

The existence of agrarian fundamentalism meant that public policy solutions were at once idealistic in their conception and perceived to be pragmatic in their purpose. While those who worked on farm policy lacked a coherent plan, political and administrative forces converged to offer solutions consistent with agrarian beliefs (White 1958). The early 1860s were, in the midst of the Civil War, an ideal time for farm policymaking in concordance with agrarian imagery. After 20 years of trying in the face of southern opposition, agricultural development proponents finally gained passage of legislation authorizing a U.S. Department of Agriculture (USDA). This organization had a scientific mission: to discover and foster new seeds and plants. Congress moved almost simultaneously on three other, though independent, farm policy bills (the Homestead Act, the Morrill Land Grant College Act, and the Transcontinental Railroad Act). The USDA's scientific emphasis encouraged social and economic development as a new and driving force in agriculture. Not without irony, this meant that the public policy product of simple agrarianism was directed early on toward *modernization* of traditional agrarian society.

This four-fold policy revolution of 1862 was only a first stage. It required substantial elaboration and added policies as time went on and farm problems continued. The combination of public and private investments began transforming the farm sector into a market-oriented, capital-intensive industry. Coupling an expanding number of farms and ranches with an escalating means of production, the modernization paradox of public policy was brought forward: each producer could feed more consumers, but consumers did not demand that much more in products (Cochrane 1979; Johnson 1980). To lower costs and increase consumers' commodity purchases, government farm policy turned more to enhancing productivity and production efficiency. This (1) allowed for continued expansion in the number of producing units, (2) made producers more dependent on government programs while attributing more importance to agricultural institutions, and (3) renewed commitment to transforming U.S. agriculture further away from its European peasant roots (Goss, Rodefeld, and Buttel 1980; Gjerde 1985).

Several important policy initiatives characterized the intervening years between 1862 and 1933, with the later years being a time when farm policy was altered substantially. But it was the culmination of enabling acts that brought forward the land grants, experiment stations and the extension service that created the broad outlines of a publicly-operated structure that would evolve into what Schultz (1943, 1945) later called the "agricultural establishment." Its collective responsibility was to provide for farmers (True 1928; Hildreth and Armbruster 1981). Another act was needed to complete that structural design, however. In 1889, at the insistence of farm groups from around the country, USDA gained cabinet-level status and shed the remains of its image as a minor agency (Herring 1936). Other legislation, again evolving to meet practical farm problems of the moment, provided this agricultural establishment of public organizations with a set of rules to employ on behalf of development goals. This legislation established a farm credit system, exempted farm cooperatives from anti-trust laws, and established regulation of middlemen between farmers and consumers.

In addition, by establishing cooperative farm bureaus in local Extension Service offices, the federal government gave rise in 1919 to a Washington-linked grassroots interest group. These farm bureaus were later ordered separated from the Extension Service of USDA in 1954. However, by then local people had firmed up strong political support for the rules and organizations of the agricultural establishment within government (Kile 1921, 1948; Block 1960; Hamilton 1991:19). That support, especially through the Washington work of the American Farm Bureau Federation, eventually institutionalized private sector interest groups firmly within the establishment's organizational fold (Hansen 1987a, 1991; Browne 1988b).

What characterized the legislative emergence of a publicly-operated and privately-supported agricultural establishment was its emphasis on general social policy. Yet, if all existing farmers had used farm policy benefits, the resource investment of many would have been wasted. Not everyone could grow more productively and still find a market for their goods, at least without all farmers agreeing to produce just enough commodities that would easily sell. Of course, there was no such agreement or a central mechanism to mandate it. Thus, as modernization and development promoted greater industrialization by the 1870s, farmers found even greater price and income vulnerability. In the short term, both farm product demand and supply were becoming less responsive to price changes. But farm production fluctuations did bring wide price swings. These were more easily taken advantage of by consumers (who paid comparatively little of their income for food) than they were by producers (who had sunk what became their family's immobile investment assets into agriculture). Producers, in consequence, had little incentive to vary how much they planted (Cochrane 1979:378-395; Johnson 1980; Robinson 1989:2-18). There was little else they could do with their investments, and feelings of individual control over asset use were lost.

Modernization/development policy, as a consequence, created an early dilemma for agrarian producers. Not to accept the practices advocated by components of the agricultural establishment meant failure, since nonadapters couldn't keep up in a predominantly commercial sector. Rural poverty was thereby ensured for those who would not compete. Otherwise, one left production agriculture and moved to urban locations or, in some places, to local industrial jobs. Of course, only the earliest innovators of new technology gained a market advantage since they produced more of already oversupplied commodities; late adopters struggled in vain to catch up as overall excess production capacity grew (Johnson 1980). Even in an era where technological innovation in agriculture was just beginning, the effects of this treadmill of forced change in production practices ensured that some producers would always face poverty while others prospered (Hamilton 1991:8-25). Creating the agriculture establishment, with its emphasis on technology, brought an inherent inequality to rural America.

By 1928, after several years of complaints of a farm depression following post-World War I price declines, it was clear that political demands generated by economic failure would change U.S. agricultural policy, creating some kind of buffer from the free market. This change to *selective goods* in agricultural policy transformed institutional rules into ones that would alter distribution processes to better hold clients in their relations with policy providers (see Bates 1981, for a similar yet more particularistic distribution pattern in Africa). The Agricultural Adjustment Act of 1933 (AAA) was unlike the previous social policy tradition of U.S. agriculture, in that it provided entitlements to select types of producers, unique from other segments of society as well as from other farmers and ranchers who raised different commodities (Bonnen and Browne 1989; Bonnen 1990). Commodity-specific programs were also distributed selectively. Direct farm payments were based proportionally on the amount of crops grown by each beneficiary. This provided larger incomes for those who grew more.

Commodity programs, as a side effect, induced ever greater inequality among rural Americans. These programs also reduced the risks of expansion by establishing floors under prices. This kept total income to individual program crop farmers guaranteed through a combination of purchase price and supplemental government payments. Land prices were forced so high that many marginal farmers could not afford--or, faced with a good offer, did not wish--to retain property rights. In fostering greater inequality, agrarianism and modernization/development (as complementary cultural ideals that merged the old with the new) gained the upper hand over whatever values U.S. society attributed to social justice.

The creation of the Federal Farm Board in 1929 was an attempt to develop a set of centralized commodity associations to control production and, therefore, limit price vulnerability. There was little hope of the Farm Board succeeding, however. Underestimated were the forces of modernization/development as well as nonexclusive markets that kept farmers from voluntary collective action in making planting decisions. Producers, quite simply, could not cooperate on their own with average production cuts across the sector. Surpluses soared, especially in wheat and cotton. The resulting decline in farm prices and the changing response of the Farm Board brought a death knell for general social policy as a distributional system of collective goods. "Farmers' backwardness, irrationalism, and excessive individualism" (Hamilton 1991:88)--that is, their problems with fixed assets and competition--meant that policy success was only possible if government either forced farmers to comply with policy goals or gave them extra incentives to do so. The Congress, under Roosevelt, accepted policy goals in the AAA that reversed opposition, choosing to listen to farm interest groups and their producer adherents. If policy failed, farm representatives could always be blamed for poor performance and their own enthusiasm for what proved a bad idea (Hansen 1987a, 1991). The easiest way to satisfy a specific group and its lobbyists was to design a government program of direct benefit *only* to them. The desire for more selective benefits gave rise to proliferating programs. This led to a nearly unavoidable biasing of future policy in favor of those already a party to the agricultural establishment.

Rural Policy Came Alive, Almost

The neglect of rural policy should not have surprised anyone. In effect, farm and rural policies were incompatible, since the ideas behind them were in competition. Institutions could not handle developing agriculture as a means of stabilizing rural America *and* investing in community needs as an alternate means to the same end. General responsibility for rural problems came to be seen as the institutional responsibility of USDA as a subset of farm policy and other federally-supported agricultural establishment organizations, namely, the land-grant colleges of agriculture and experiment stations. Rural nonfarm policies thus became "minimalist" (Swanson 1989:15). Government recognized a broader set of rural problems existed but was cautious in dealing with them, most often quite indirectly.

Some rural programs were implemented initially as additional farm programs. These programs had a service mandate of their own for distributing specific policy benefits to farmers, and never compensated for the human costs for those disadvantaged by farm policy. Though each was later extended to other rural residents, ignored were the problems of rural residents who were left behind and off the farm as U.S. agriculture industrialized and modernized, and as farm numbers declined.

Federal recognition of the rural disadvantaged and the need for a more comprehensive rural policy was first articulated in the 1909 Report of the Country Life Commission. That report, prepared with the urging of President Theodore Roosevelt, acknowledged that agricultural development had *so far* failed a large number of farmers, splintering the sector into the proficient and the poor. The Commission made three other points. First, substantial rural progress in stabilizing the countryside was acknowledged, and was attributed to work done by the public organizations of the agricultural establishment. Second, the prevalence of quality of life problems--communications, transportation, health care, soil degradation--was noted for all rural residents. These deficiencies kept rural America from being its normative best, places of superior living. Third, the particular quality of life problems of those left behind were portrayed as important because of the dire consequences they held, not for individuals, but for rural communities and even urban areas to which the displaced fled.

The synthesis of the Country Life report was that a healthy rural society depended directly on a healthy, technologically-progressive agriculture. The federal government thus restated its commitment to industrialized agriculture. The poor, for the good of rural society, were to be freed from poverty's constraints *before* they exited farming. Equally clear in that report was the lack of concern for those poor who either had left the farm or had never been able to achieve success in a rural setting. In particular, there was no expressed concern for the poverty and exploitive conditions that characterized mining and mill towns where local elites controlled labor. Farmers came first because they would stabilize society at large and, with this logic, the local rural community as well. Farmers' stature as *the* key citizens meant they were first in line for the distribution of costly policy benefits and in the formulation of a normative prescription for the specific ills of rural America (Breimyer 1983).

A "farmers first" philosophy was so malleable as to adjust readily to whatever disparate subjects were addressed in the rare, rural community/poverty debates that went on into the 1960s. Only two rural controversies--over the Resettlement Administration during the 1930s and the Rural Development Program during the Eisenhower years--were noteworthy in advancing alternatives. Yet in those times of policy failure, all came back to their unbridled faith in helping even the worst economically-positioned farmers succeed.

It should be noted that even with this pattern of inequality in economic opportunity generated by farm programs, some government services did develop under this "farmers first" ethos to enrich the lives of most rural residents.

Credit, electrification, conservation, and regional development assistance were provided through a new industrial policy logic. These new programs were assigned either to new agencies of the U.S. Department of Agriculture or to independent ones that would soon be incorporated within USDA. That federal department, like no other, burgeoned in size and responsibilities throughout the 1930s as it promulgated new rules (Rasmussen and Baker 1972:30-44). In keeping with the emphasis on selective benefits, each agency within USDA was asked to think broadly about rural resident needs, as long as those needs fell under the existing expertise of the particular agency in question. Agency resources, in a version of farm trickle-down, were targeted to users.

The result, through federal intervention, was a gradual diversification of local economies that had in most regions relied mainly on farmers, agricultural suppliers and marketers. This piecemeal attention produced neither a general assessment of rural needs nor planned growth. New programs and new beneficiaries, coupled with farming's continued displacement of producers, created changing rural communities and regions. By 1985-1986, only 514 of 2443 rural (non-metropolitan) counties were farm-dependent, places where at least 20 percent of total labor and proprietor income came from farming (Ahearn, Bentley, and Carlin 1988).

The results of these changes were intriguing. In a prolonged era of "farmers first" rural policy, program benefits grew from farm agencies as they sought to serve other rural beneficiaries. Yet this change was misleading in both its procedural and substantive effect. It took place for only a select number of USDA agencies, operating only a small percentage of total farm programs. Almost through serendipity (certainly not by agricultural establishment design), the rural economy shifted. The shift was so consequential that areas continuing to be farm-dependent did the *least* to balance community needs and retain population. Yet, from the 1960s through 1990 federal policy debates never shifted away from the emphasis on farm problems to encourage what appeared as the most positive employment and quality of life trends in rural America. That is, rural policy neglected the extremes of both job creation and labor exploitation in rural America.

Getting Rural Policy Attention, 1960-1990

As was true in the period 1909-1959, the contemporary era can be best understood by looking at the recurring themes of policy discussions among the many public officials and private representatives making the decisions. Four topics, all posed as questions, held center stage after 1960: How was the Department of Agriculture to exercise its jurisdictional responsibilities? What mechanisms were to be used in delivering rural development assistance? What was to be done with the persistent, often multi-generational, problems of rural poverty? Why was poverty to be dealt with as a part of rural policy? These four questions were not asked separately. Rather, they were wrapped together and addressed by public officials as parts of an interrelated, but unfamiliar dilemma facing those whose attentions were dominated by modernization and development and never by what was left behind. As a consequence, the four policy questions were reduced to three questions of politics: Who controlled the turf? On what could they agree? Was there anything left with which to serve the poor? This reductionism and alteration of the most relevant questions were not surprising in a special-constituency policy network where original purposes were threatened by change (Robinson 1991).

Who Was in Charge? Agriculture agencies led the way in providing the services necessary for both farm and rural community development, but their resources were insufficient for the task. Over time, several other federal cabinet-level departments and agencies assumed important rural service responsibilities. To clarify roles and provide nominal coordination, President Eisenhower through executive order created the Interagency Committee for Rural Development. It was ordered chaired by USDA. While this committee has since changed several times and added several new participants, the basic unit remains the same. Farm state legislators in Congress, along with USDA program administrators, have insisted on strong agricultural leadership to avoid any erosion of control in designated rural programs with farm policy ties.

Other Service Delivery Obstacles. Since the final year of the Eisenhower Administration, rural poverty has been noted as a specific problem with off-farm implications. Simply articulating its importance has made for political disruptions and, consequently, little policy relief. There have been no exceptions. Despite differences in partisan emphasis, inaction was not caused by party politics or ideology. Rather, three kinds of disagreements were ubiquitous in disrupting policy initiatives for the rural disadvantaged. All were historically rooted in institutions, and not one has been resolved. Consequently, their effect will remain indefinitely. The first disagreement was over whether old institutions, such as the Farmers Home Administration, would lose influence through a change in ruling status. Long-time supporters did not wish to see that occur. The second disagreement was whether, in the face of scarce budget resources, programs for the disadvantaged would be funded at the expense of dollars previously allocated to the institutionalized clientele of farm programs. Farm state members of Congress and farm program administrators were adamant that they would not. Finally, disagreement long existed over who would deliver any new services that grew out of federal programs or reallocated dollars. In all three kinds of disagreements, one common feature prevailed: roadblocks to decisionmaking came as long-time proponents sought to protect institutionalized rules or organizations that were essentially agricultural. This, of course, produced the related effect of keeping national government out of the other problems of rural America, ensuring in the process that local community decisions in a federated system would not be restrained.

When the Poor Benefited. Despite these procedural obstacles, the rural poor have made some policy gains in the past three decades. However, their gains were not made through rural initiatives, even when the Department of Agriculture was responsible for new programs. Economic gains occurred in rural areas, as in urban ones, because poverty programs of the 1960s distributed new social service benefits (Daft 1982; Deavers, Hoppe, and Ross 1986). Other programs for the disadvantaged, for consumers, and more recently, for environmental quality were later added to farm bills of the 1970s and 1980s for this same purpose. Many of these served rural interests. But adding such programs did not mean that the shrinking number of farm state and farm district legislators suddenly agreed to place greater value on, or attention to, how nonfarm policy problems affected rural America. Policymakers were far too embroiled in protectionist controversies set by the demands of an existing modernization/development paradigm. Moreover, the paradigm was kept in motion by the institutionalized maze of public and private organizations and extensive rules of an influential agricultural establishment that was, itself, farm-directed.

The Concentrated, Yet Fragmented, Politics of Farm and Rural Issues

The agrarian myth that propelled farm policy prevailed because it provided satisfying answers, at least in guiding political choices. Yet agricultural policy scholars, all disenchanted with the narrowness of political demands on behalf of farmers, decried the wrongful use of this myth for nearly six decades. The question arises as to how and why it was used, and why the myth failed to evolve?

The structural problems of representing farmers and other rural residents were two-fold. First, farmers were a shrinking minority, and rural residents had long been outmigrants from their regions as well (Paar 1966). Second, representing the many policy facets of agriculture and rural affairs was complex, so that governing institutions had to change their rules to decentralize and specialize. Governing units, within Congress and the administration, grew increasingly fragmented in their policy approaches as they offered selective benefits. Partisan influence was lost and shifted to policy networks. Without central direction or goals, politics and programs meandered along as each new policy initiative or new problem was handled one at a time.

The Evolution of a Farm Policy Network

Governing America was too complicated merely to give farmers what they wanted or to follow a mythic dream. Politics, nineteenth century style, was an amalgam of conflicts. Under such conditions, strong political parties, imposing discipline on members who bore their banner, were valued as among the very few means of lending continuity of purpose to the governing process (Burnham 1965, 1967; McCormick 1986).

Despite the large numbers of farmers in the country, U.S. agriculture was not easily provided for under a strong party government in a laissez-faire state. There was no unified voice. There was no lasting farmers' party. Farmers were well-organized, but in very locally-oriented groups. The net effect of their disruptive ways was that farmers were not invited willingly into decisionmaking by those who controlled the parties and, therefore, the flow of Washington's political debates.

It was in this context of partisan disadvantage and the political inadequacy of existing institutions that the farm bloc emerged in 1921, nearly simultaneously with the crash of farm prices and land values. Its rise radically transformed farm representation as a first move toward concentrated attention to constituent interests (Capper 1922; Kile 1948; Tweeten 1979; Hansen 1987a 1991). Under the farm bloc, farmers forced their way--and the way of the agricultural establishment in Washington--into prominence. They fostered changes in the rules for maintaining the agricultural establishment, moving it from emphasizing only modernization and development through policy-induced technology to also include an emphasis on sustaining political influence to protect that policy paradigm.

The farm bloc, as a loosely organized but formal body of legislators, began first as a Senate coalition called together in the Washington offices of the Farm Bureau. It then moved to the House of Representatives. Led by an Iowa member in each house, with strongest representation in the Senate, the organization won its only legislative battle by fighting the party leaders of most bloc members. The Republican leadership had planned to adjourn Senate deliberations and later move on to a tariff bill. Doing so, however, would have left untended what farm bloc legislators of both parties saw as several important pieces of agricultural legislation. The farm bloc won by resisting partisan initiatives in favor of common constituent problems, halting Senate adjournment, and getting leadership support for half of the pending bills. The ties that well-organized USDA employees had to farmers helped facilitate involvement.

This tripartite network of lobbyists, legislators, and bureaucrats owed its existence in agriculture, as in other policy areas, to several problems of governance. First among them was the problem of how to pass policy specifically for an economic clientele in a laissez-faire government where the market was expected to provide for basic human needs. Second, farmers lacked the prosperity and high incomes to buy political favors when the market did not meet their needs.

Because of its strong grassroots ties and associative state establishment, agriculture gained a reputation as the epitome of the U.S. policy network.

Farmers, it seemed, got just what they wanted (Lowi 1964a, 1964b). But, of course, there was great illusion in that observation. Institutionalization in rulemaking did not translate to omnipotence. Neither farmers nor anyone else in agriculture got all they wanted from public policy (Hansen 1987b). Many needs were left unmet, many proposals unpassed. Traditional network participants restricted their political demands to the programs they desired most or felt most likely to be obtainable (McConnell 1966; Rose 1967; Barton 1976; Hadwiger 1976; Browne 1988b, 1990, 1991). They did not enter into debates about inequities facing others when their own problems were severe and political opportunities so tenuous.

Network politics had the disastrous aforementioned consequences for rural policy, especially for meeting the needs of the disadvantaged. Only a core of programs, ones of the heartland shared by nearly all institutional parts, could be accorded fully protected status (Downs 1966). If either private or public sector experts seriously championed new rural issues, they would have exhausted the political capital and goodwill needed to support their most valued programs. Of course, they avoided such risk. Southern influence in the farm bloc, which was central to its strength after 1929, kept many issues specifically off agriculture's agenda--especially those of race and product processing plants. The result, because of this structural-institutional flaw, was that the agricultural policy network first gave weak support to, and then backed away from, the problems of rural poverty.

How and Why Contemporary Rural Issues Got Lost

Things have not changed. Farm policy advocates hang on very hard, as they did throughout the 1980s, to what policy benefits they still have. And, since 1977, they preached the agrarian doctrine of farm fundamentalism with the same old fire, or they hid behind the firebrands of farm protest who did (Browne and Lundgren 1987).   Therefore, rural policy proposals that reflect a new development paradigm tend to be placed aside, as always, as costly threats. New budget rules have been added that make matters more difficult by requiring a new program to be paid for by savings from an old one (Sinclair 1991). Nonetheless, because some rural problems have gained policy attention while others have not, there are other, very contemporary structural features of government that are also responsible for the specific neglect of the rural poor and disadvantaged today. Two such features stand out. First, the institutional basis of the agricultural establishment has literally exploded in internal conflict over economic interest, bringing far greater scrutiny and risk-avoiding behavior to the rulemaking process (Bonnen 1973, 1980, 1984, 1988; Browne 1988a). Second, the few extant rural institutions, as rooted in farm programs, are the ones perceived as quite significant; they control their parts of the policymaking agenda and tend to squeeze out alternative rural policy ideas.

Explosion. While the agricultural policy network maintained its farm focus throughout the 1970s and 1980s, many new authoritative participants were nonetheless established within it.   Following reform of procedural rules, agricultural legislation continued to move further, but more quickly, to incorporate diverse clientele into new programs. Issues of the environment, international trade enhancement, and food needs have been most fully incorporated.   This attention shift is also played out, however, as a way for more legislators to see district and state reasons to vote for production agriculture.   And the explosion of attention given to new issues, as well as the active involvement of more members of Congress, serves also to drive rural issues and their weaker advocates further to the legislative background.

Turf Protection.   Change that sets new policy directions, such as reforming policy on behalf of the rural disadvantaged, is inconsistent with existing institutional arrangements, threatening some rural programs and organizations. The problem is most evident in Congress, where the agriculture committees hold rulemaking jurisdiction over rural initiatives, particularly those with a development focus.

The implications of such protectiveness of the few existing rural institutions are important and quite negative.   They also are probably unavoidable.   The structural support for rural problems has developed as being so pervasively weak, both within the Congress and within the other agricultural establishment organizations, that policy reform is nearly precluded under present governance rules.   The policy process and its gatekeepers cannot systematically re-examine farm and rural programs on the rulemaking agenda unless an extraordinary level of support exists for doing so.   This support does not exist either through the forces of public opinion or a strong rural policy advocacy network (Browne 1988b).   Thus, for reasons of public policy evolution and institutionalization, re-examination of rural needs has historically failed to occur.

Rural Policy Regimes

The preceding section has demonstrated some of the important historical specifics of how and why direct rural policy came to be largely subsumed within U.S. agricultural policy and why it was so limited in addressing rural poverty and regional inequalities.   At the same time, we stress that the American pattern of rural-related policies is by no means unique among developed countries.   The approaches to political economy or political management of the economy among nationstates can be clustered in three broad groupings or policy regimes: neoclassical, corporatist, and social democratic (Epsing-Anderson 1990). Putting the U.S. into a macro-governing context illuminates much about why its policy processes were conducted as they were.

It helps to begin by noting why a typology of regimes is useful in looking at the political economics of welfare policies, of which attention to rural poverty is a part. First of all, welfare policies should be recognized as being something more than providing state transfer payments to the disadvantaged or state-dependent. A more comprehensive view of the welfare-state assumes that granting social rights should be seen as its core idea. For all practical purposes, the bulk of the gains achieved by subordinate groups and classes in the industrial world since World War II have been based on extension of social rights entitlements like social security (the first social welfare program in most countries), unemployment insurance, inexpensive public education entitlements and entitlements to farm subsidies. Social rights, if they are given the legal and practical status of property rights and are based on citizenship entitlement rather than merely economic performance, will entail a decommodification of individuals in their relationship to the market. Overall, one can identify state systems or regime types on the basis of how their systems of social rights and entitlements are structured in state welfare systems.

Neoclassical regimes, which are laissez-faire in the way the U.S. was described earlier, emphasize the primacy of social choice through relatively unhindered market mechanisms in the realm of social policy and the economy. A citizen's rights to social and economic well-being in neoclassical regimes are very closely tied to the sale of a person's labor as a commodity. Social program benefits are either tied to past labor market performance (as in U.S. social security payments) or emphasize needs tests for access to program benefits. Benefits for the "neediest" tend toward minimal means-tested payments (the point at which the limits of welfare equal the marginal propensity to opt for welfare instead of work) for restricted periods of time. In addition, significant transfers are aimed at the middle classes and modest social-insurance programs. While benefits are targeted closely to low-income recipients, the bulk of public policy spending is aimed in a nontargeted way at the middle classes. Generalized Social Keynesianism--tinkering with fiscal and monetary policy to encourage greater employment or stimulate consumption--predominates. Agricultural modernization and development fits well into this approach. The stratification consequences of neoclassical welfare-state systems are a blend of a relative equality of poverty among state-dependents, and market-differentiated public policy support among the majorities.

Compared to others, the neoclassical regimes restrain the government's coordinating and innovating role in the general economy. There is an instinct, often bordering on religious faith, that unfettered markets are the appropriate vehicle to optimize collective economic performance and well-being. The neoclassical regimes outside the United States include Canada, Australia, New Zealand, and the United Kingdom.

Corporatist policy regimes emphasize a close integration of economy and society. Citizens' access to a minimum of social and economic well-being is a matter of rights rather than demonstrated severe need. Benefits are more generous, cover a wider range of activities, and are available for longer time intervals. Beyond minimum benefits are gradated benefits linked to an individual's rank in the occupational hierarchy. Benefits also tend to be calculated in terms of the perceived rights of family units rather than to individual rights.

Epsing-Andersen (1990) attributes much of the corporatist approach to a pre-industrial conservative political heritage. Society is viewed as a hierarchy of different groups integrated into society. The converse of hierarchy is a sense of noblesse oblige. Salient examples of corporatist approaches to political economy are Germany, France, and Japan. The Japanese corporatism is an exception to the otherwise strong pattern of moderately generous social programs among the corporatist regimes. In Japan, state expenditures on social welfare programs as a proportion of GNP are relatively low because of its strong tradition of providing social benefits through life-long employment with a single employer. The corporatist approach extends from social welfare rights to a sense of the obligation and rationality of governments to coordinate the national economy and promote national comparative advantage. It usually also involves a more cooperative relationship between labor and management than is the case in laissez-faire systems.

Social democratic regimes predicate social policy on an egalitarian system of rights of high levels to social benefits to citizens, independent of their market performance. In contrast to corporatist systems, benefits tend to be allocated to individuals rather than families; child support systems, for example, will be directed towards high day-care payments that encourage a woman's participation in the labor force, irrespective of her spouse's earnings. The social democratic regimes include Sweden, Norway, Finland, Holland, and Austria. The high level of social program benefits imply a high degree of government intervention intended to maintain high employment rates. State-owned enterprises play an important role in the economy. States governed by labor parties, or by opposition parties which are constrained to retain the broad parameters of social democracy when they come to power, exercise a natural expectation that enterprises will actively collaborate with labor unions and the government in formulating economic strategy.

This typology is important to understanding the incidence of U.S. rural policy neglect. With respect to rural development issues, it appears easier to address rural issues in corporatist and social democratic regimes than it is in neoclassical ones. This seems to be the single biggest factor in explaining the exclusionary dominance of the agricultural modernization/development paradigm, especially with its initial nontargeted, collective-goods focus. Corporatist and social democratic regimes attach as much importance to groups as to individuals in the interface between markets and society. A system that specifies group rights by occupation or by social class is more readily inclined to assign group rights by the broad parameters of place than is a highly market-oriented regime. For rural development and rural policy as they affect poverty, corporatist and social democratic regimes appear more able to actively search for fostering the economic viability of rural places than can those in neoclassical systems. This is seen in the recent behavior of European states, the vast bulk of which are corporalist or social democratic, in their negotiations over European Monetary Union, where they renewed the EC commitment to spending programs directed to alleviating the problems of disadvantaged rural regions.

Direct Versus Indirect Rural Policy: Budgets, Social Programs, and Rural Shares of Benefits

A regime taxonomy is not the only one useful in looking comparatively at the state's role in dealing with rural poverty. One can also consider a very simple taxonomy of ways in which state policies may affect the incidence of poverty among rural residents. *Macroeconomic policies* (either designed to affect things such as growth or employment, or designed in response to macroeconomic trends) will obviously affect all citizens, including rural ones. Moreover, they are likely to do so in regional and place-specific ways. Many *sectoral policies* (e.g., agricultural commodity programs) will also have effects on rural poverty levels. *Place-oriented* policies (e.g., regional development programs, rural development programs) are particularly germane to rural poverty. Finally, as noted in the preceding section, *class/entitlement policies* (e.g., social welfare policies, old age assistance programs) will affect the incidence of poverty among rural households and persons. In the United States, the latter three policy types almost always deliver current programs as selectively received benefits, with voluntary use the most important characteristic.

Two of the types of policy influences on rural poverty presented above-- sectoral and place-oriented policies--have conventionally been thought to encompass rural policy. Recognize, however, that these are by no means the only, or necessarily the most important, types of policies that influence rural poverty levels. Such direct rural policies will, in fact, tend to be overshadowed by macroeconomic and class/entitlement policies, which are among the major components of *indirect* rural policy. As suggested earlier, this is particularly true in the U.S. context where rural policy has been largely confined to farm policy, and where there are such pronounced constraints to place-oriented, poverty-alleviation policies. Historically, class/entitlement policies have played a particularly important, but largely unrecognized, role in affecting rural poverty.

The (Disguised Rural) Welfare-State

The previous typology of rural policy regimes is particularly important in considering the extent to which social policies influence poverty levels within a society and the policy institutions that formulate and implement rural policies. Even "regional policies" have been very closely related to social welfare policies. Regional policies have been designed to narrow rural-urban income disparities, and their base of support has been similar to that of social welfare policies in general. Regional policies have been most extensive in Western Europe countries having social democratic and corporatist regimes.[1]

The U.S. Great Society programs that were launched in the 1960s were by and large continued under the three administrations of the 1970s and were modest by the standards of corportist and social-democratic regimes. Nonetheless, as noted, the rise of these programs was very closely associated with unprecedented progress in improving the socioeconomic condition of rural America. Metropolitan-nonmetropolitan disparities in per capita incomes narrowed substantially from 1965 to 1969, and exhibited particularly dramatic convergence from 1969 to 1973. From 1969 to 1973, nonmetropolitan per capita incomes increased at an astounding rate of 5.9 percent per year, compared to 2.7 percent annually for metropolitan counties. These disparities began to widen very slightly in the period from 1973 to 1979, but the federal domestic policies that led to improvement in the condition of rural America in the preceding years remained intact (albeit with some funding declines in real terms). These improvements in rural economic conditions, which at their high-water mark resulted in nonmetropolitan per capita incomes being 78 percent of metropolitan county incomes, did nonetheless represent significant progress (see Henry et al. 1986, for an overview of these trends and USDA, *Rural Economic Development in the 1980s*, 1987, for a useful compendium of information on the changing socioeconomic character of rural America). This period, farm policy successes aside, will no doubt be remembered for some time as the golden age of rural America.

Despite the clear overall improvements in the well-being of rural-nonmetropolitan regions as a result of Great Society programs, several caveats deserve mention. First, the nonmetropolitan "deep" South, which has long had the highest incidence of persistent rural poverty, had less access to Greaty Society funding than did the less disadvantaged border-South region, apparently due in large part to the greater interest of Presidents' Kennedy and Johnson in Appalachia and the unwillingness of southern congressmen to disrupt local political control in their region. Second, the nonmetropolitan "Blackbelt" South developed little, even during the high water mark of the Great Society; the modest improvements in aggregate living levels were probably more due to mass outmigration of the rural poor through the negative consequences of the cotton economy collapse and agricultural mechanization than to structural upgrading of rural economy and society. Third, the nonmetropolitan economy during this period was buoyed by surging raw materials prices and by a temporary pattern of population "turnaround."

The condition of rural America has changed dramatically since the late 1970s, principally as a result of two factors. First, the two Republican administrations of the 1980s and 1990s have progressively--though selectively and somewhat unsuccessfully, from their perspectives--worked to dismantle major components of American social spending that together constituted the heart of the country's most successful part of its rural policy initiative. In addition, the deepening global recession, which began in 1973-74 but which worsened in the early 1980s and again in the early 1990s, has helped to undercut the fiscal basis of federal rural development efforts. It also has contributed, as will be covered later, to a nascent restructuring of the world economy that has potentially adverse consequences for the well-being of nonmetropolitan America.

Several features of U.S. rural policy in the 1960s and 1970s that were alluded to earlier deserve added mention. Great Society-style, U.S. social programs were much smaller in scope and less redistributive (and poverty-reducing) than, and were structurally different from, the social entitlement programs of corporatist and social democratic regimes. The social base of Great Society programs was far more diverse and less unified than the trade union focal point of European social democratic and corporatist social policies. The U.S. variant of the welfare state combined stringently means-tested social welfare programs with broad, nontargeted domestic public investment, social services, and retirement/old age assistance programs within a framework of Keynesian fiscal and monetary policy. This may have been a blessing in disguise for U.S. rural development in two ways. First, rural America did not have to mobilize politically to receive access to these programs. Much of federal rural policy spending was actually a patchwork of nontargeted programs that benefited both metropolitan and nonmetropolitan regions. Second, many of these programs took the form of grants to local government units for constructing infrastructure and operating service facilities, which arguably led to longer-term benefit than if these programs had been directed to income supplements alone (Buttel and Gillespie 1991).

A further aspect of federal rural policy funding that is just now being appreciated is how the selective dismantling of the American welfare state has affected rural development and rural poverty. This dismantling has been centered on the broad social investment, economic development, and service delivery programs that accrued largely to places and organizations rather than individuals (Hardy 1983). By contrast, these administrations have been far less successful in reducing cash transfers through entitlement programs geared to individuals (e.g., social security, medicare and medicaid, government employee retirement programs, food stamps, supplemental security income, aid to families with dependent children, etc.). Government cash transfers, as we suggested earlier, remain very important to the economic base of rural America, and have clearly mitigated the dislocations caused by dismantling other aspects of the welfare state. Retirement programs, especially social security and medicare, have become especially important to rural America as the rural population continues to age (Hirschl and Summers 1984). Nonmetro "retirement counties" (see Bender et al. 1985, for definition) now have the highest per capita income levels of all seven types of nonmetropolitan counties.

Finally, as the character of federal spending shifted dramatically in the 1980s toward military expenditures, nonmetropolitan counties found themselves disadvantaged because military expenditures went mainly to metropolitan counties. Federal defense and space expenditures currently play a large role in contributing to the pronounced advantage that metropolitan counties enjoy over their rural counterparts in per capita federal outlays. The roughly $700 per capita difference in mean per capita federal expenditures on defense and space between metro ($1,011) and nonmetro counties ($303) in FY 1985 is essentially accounted for by the $714 per capita difference in total outlays that could be traced to county levels ($3,192 vs. $2,478, respectively). By comparison, in FY 1978 nonmetro counties received $1,845 per capita, as against $2,007 per capita for metro counties, and the nonmetro-metro differential in defense and space outlays was less than $300 per capita (Hendler and Reid 1980). Thus, the status of rural funding (in the broad sense of both direct and indirect rural policy) has been adversely affected by more than the selective dismantling of the welfare state. The rise of the warfare state has contributed powerfully to the increasing relative disadvantage of rural America as well.[2]

Rural Policy and the Budgetary Process

The politics of the budgetary process is perhaps the single most important arena for ranking the influence of different interests in attaining goals. Budgetary processes proceed in very different ways in parliamentary systems as opposed to the U.S. system of divided and separate powers. Parliamentary budgetary politics proceed mainly behind closed doors, and submitting the budget to parliament is, in one sense, a mere formality: the ruling party is going to vote on the budget as negotiated among its senior ministers. In another sense, the formalities permit a testing of political powers and can result in decisions to modify the budget before it is voted in.

The U.S. division of powers between the executive and the legislative branches creates a budgetary process with multiple points for interest-group representation over an extended time period. After the president submits the administration's budget proposals, the tough negotiations with both houses of Congress begin. The sectoral subcommittees of the budget committees of both houses, plus sectoral committees such as agriculture, give interest groups numerous occasions to intervene. Senators and representatives operate as autonomous political entrepreneurs in a manner that is not possible for the majority of a parliament's members. Powerful congressional committees form the arena where this entrepreneurship is exercised. In contrast, parliament committees are of relatively little importance.

These different systems of budgetary politics have important consequences for rural development. In a parliamentary system, such as exists in Canada, the process is centralized and favors intervention by well-organized groups at the higher instances of the governing party and the civil service. When this is combined with the relatively weak power of local party organizations and the weak influence exercised by the "backbencher" majority of members of parliament, it becomes difficult in parliamentary systems to promote the development interests of predominantly rural areas. Commodity organizations are well poised to intervene on sectoral issues, but rural localities are not. In contrast, it remains true that a number of U.S. Congress members from rural and small town constituencies will have acquired seniority and power. Their power base is primarily in their district, given the very weak discipline of the U.S. party system. They are subject to direct pressures to address (or not address) economic development and other rural policy issues in their districts.

The net result is that despite its minimalist thrust, the United States has a broader range of direct rural policies and a deeper set of institutions to support rural interests than does Canada. It also has more opportunities for protecting local turf by muting some policy alternatives. The resulting modest range of rural policies of the U.S. nonetheless stands in contrast to the paucity of direct rural policies in Canada. On the other hand, spillovers from larger regional development policies and general social programs occur in Canada because a greater share of real policy benefits flow to rural areas in Canada than in the U.S.

All of this can be seen in a brief comparison of U.S. and Canadian national government budgets. In both countries, social programs were the number-one items in the 1989 budgets, accounting for 44 percent of U.S. and 48 percent of Canadian expenditures. Canada, at 13 percent compared to 11 percent for the U.S., spends a modestly higher percentage of national production on these programs. Economic and regional development ranks fourth in both countries, 10 percent in the U.S. and 8 percent in Canada. The entire decade of the 1980s saw comparable appropriations. In both countries, when one disaggregates the rural share of indirect and direct expenditures, government transfers to rural areas come mostly from indirect programs. This is where dependency of the rural disadvantaged lies, not on a net of commodity or modernization and development policies that serve a far narrower set of interests. Quite clearly, because urban interests drive the agenda for indirect policies in both countries, U.S. rural interests beyond farmers have not been able to take advantage of the representative opportunities they enjoy. The cards remain stacked against them.

International and Market Trends Affecting Rural Policy

Beyond the politics of policy emphasis and regime characteristics exist a number of international trends that are often labeled meso-level restraints. Some relate to the internationalization of the global economy. Others are linked to domestic regulatory policies that are largely reactions to international occurrences. Both sets of trends affect not only rural communities but also the supply and availability of jobs and income that can relieve poverty.

Internationalization

While international forces remain on nearly everyone's list of the most potent influences affecting rural America, internationalization is often poorly understood. It is commonly seen as a secular, linear trend or outcome of greater global economic integration, and of the power shift from national states to multinational firms and to such institutions as the World Bank and International Monetary Fund (IMF). Alternatively, internationalization is seen as cyclical expression of the post-war international order crisis that is destined to be reversed as an inevitable new protectionist mood reduces world trade volume and increases the share of trade that is domestically controlled.

In its consequences, internationalization must be seen as broader than either of the above views. It must be conceived of as cause and consequence of the post-War political-economic order crisis under the hegemony of the U.S. Hastened by deficits associated with the Vietnam War, this was essentially a crisis of the dollar as the international reserve currency, leading to the dismantling of the Bretton Woods system in the early 1970s (Block 1977). Bretton Woods, as institutionalized in the World Bank and IMF, and as underwritten by the U.S. dollar, framed the post-War consolidation of national capitalist economies anchored in Keynesian policy. This institutional nexus of international and national political economy anchored a nation-centered social contract between capital and labor. The organization of the national economy pivoted on a particular class structure (mainly the property-owning and working classes associated with manufacturing industry), combined with a policy orientation that depended on national and international regulatory institutions.

The national model of economy was possible only so long as the dollar/gold standard operated. For each state, the requirement of the gold standard was a stable national trade account as a condition of low interest rates and a favorable environment for capital investment. Stable trade depended on balanced participation in the world market (Phillips 1977). Within this model, social protection of economic sectors was legitimized through Keynesianism's emphasis on national regulation. At the same time, the international institutional framework sanctioned free enterprise and trade. This combination of national and international regulation characterizes what Ruggie (1982:393) has termed "embedded liberalism," where "multilateralism would be predicated upon domestic interventionism."

The seeds of the U.S. demise were internal to American hegemony itself. American hegemony encouraged rivalry through international trade and investment among other industrial countries, as their regimes of nationally-focused accumulation suffered declining profitability. The demise released internationalizing forces insofar as the stable, inter-state hierarchy (within the industrialized world and between North and South) unravelled, and as international capital markets came into their own. Both Euro-dollars in the 1960s and petro-dollars in the 1970s fueled this change. The result was the formation, for the first time in world history, of "a single world market for money and credit supply" (Harvey 1989:161). Thus, in the absence of a stable system for regulating class and geopolitical relations, nations and their regimes were set adrift to negotiate their own competitive positions in the world economy. This process of negotiation, across two phases--one of relatively unlimited international liquidity (the 1970s) and the other of relatively limited international liquidity (typified by the 1980s debt crisis)--has had the paradoxical effect of elevating international forces within and among states.

The demise of Bretton Woods was a threshold in the history of nationally-ordered market economies in the sense that it ended national currency regulation on the one hand, and promoted the centralization of world-scale banking capital on the other. The accompanying stagflation (high levels of inflation coincident with high unemployment) brought sustained recession to the industrial countries, followed by relocation of investment to middle-income Third World countries. This hastened the decline of organized labor's power as a political counterbalance in most countries, deemphasizing support for social programs across the board.

At the close of the 1970s, the U.S. devalued its overvalued dollar. This produced a global recession with two notable effects on the internationalization process in the 1980s. First, monetarist ideology and austerity policies led to a dramatic restructuring of class relations, particularly that of widening the gulf between workers based on their conditions of employment (e.g., unionization, job security, eligibility for and extent of benefits). Second, the recession undermined the global debt structure, leading to a redistribution of wealth on a global scale through net South-to-North capital drain (currently in excess of $40 billion annually). This capital drain was largely made possible by the structural adjustment policies imposed on developing country states by international financial institutions to ensure debt repayment. In short, monetarist-type monetary policies (typically combined with the fiscal stimulus of public sector deficit spending) have reinforced the demise of national regulation and exacerbated trends toward restratification of, and inequality among, world nations. Speculative movements of capital and the pressure to export have deepened the crisis of unstable global production in an era of unregulated exchange. As such, internationalizing forces represent attempts by both governments and firms to resolve the economic problems of the modern world economy through new forms of production and new means of regulation.

Internationalization paradoxically involves both de-regulation and re-regulation. Individual states have lost sovereignty, having become "disempowered by the internationalization of capital and weakened by the concomitant collapse of the... Keynesian 'social contract'" (Peck and Tickell 1991:26). Declining sovereignty has thus translated into declining regulatory capacity (e.g., deregulation of financial markets in the U.S., as discussed below). In the vacuum created by the decline of national regulation, two new and immature forms of regulation have appeared. The first is re-regulation such as that proposed for the European Community (i.e., the European Monetary Union). Second, is global regulation, where, anchored collectively by a 1974 agreement of the advanced country central banks (Cox 1987:301), the transnational banks wield influence in the multilateral lending institutions and among policymakers in most developed countries.

This shift in multilateral financial institutions towards global regulation is exemplified in the Structural Adjustment Loan. Adjustment loans extract and underwrite policy changes such as market liberalization, sectoral restructuring, privatization, and export promotion to service debt. These policy shifts redistribute power within the state from program-oriented ministries and departments (e.g., agriculture, education, social services) to the central bank and to national trade and finance officials. In effect, this expresses a decline in the national coherence of states (McMichael and Myhre 1991).

Of particular relevance to rural economies in the U.S. is the spatial reorganization of production relations that has emerged through internationalization forces. A key change has occurred in the relations between developed and developing countries. Once mainly a geopolitical phenomenon, the relation between advanced and developing countries has increasingly been transformed into a *sectoral relation*. New patterns of technology and productive organization, aided by the greater velocity of financial capital (Green 1987), have enabled "enterprises [to] seek greater flexibility in adjusting production to ...differentiated demand" (Cox 1987:321). The links between producing and consuming regions across deregulated national boundaries have been strengthened, while those within nation states have been weakened. The upshot for rural U.S. producers is that they are being subjected ever more directly to competition by foreign producers of food and fiber commodities and industrial goods who have cheaper labor, land, and raw materials at their disposal. This, of course, has real consequences for rural economies.

The Regulation of Markets and Its Spatial Consequences

As the 1990 U.S. census data become available, new forms of inequality that have been documented only anecdotally are becoming visible and attracting increasing public attention. The spatial pattern is complex but recognizable. As noted earlier, broad regional (metro-nonmetro) inequalities have increased, but intra-regional inequalities have widened even more (Christopherson 1991). The emerging landscape is one in which many large cities and small rural communities are faced with serious erosion in median household income and population and, consequently, in "fiscal capacity." The American landscape of the 1990s is also punctuated by suburban "hot spots," such as Contra Costa and Orange Counties in California and Fairfax County in Virginia--places where population and income growth far outpaced national norms during the 1980s. At the same time, urban analysts have focussed on a parallel process which includes the increased concentration of poverty populations in central cities, the loss of inner city population and the increasing disparity between central city and suburbs in almost every respect--jobs, housing, and the quality of public and private services. The third phenomenon is that of the so-called "post-suburban city," the places where employment and investment became concentrated in the 1980s. The evidence here is also compelling, indicating the presence of new agglomerations of advanced business services in suburban counties, leading to job growth and increases in purchasing power for suburban residents (Kling, Olin, and Poster 1991). Although rarely conjoined, the fiscal and economic deterioration of the central cities and of rural communities and the booming growth of suburban "cities" are inextricably linked. They are manifestations within the nation's space economy of adjustment to the internationalization of markets and the division of labor.

The U.S. path to adjustment and its spatial consequences set it apart from other industrialized countries. The distinctiveness of the U.S. path lies in two areas: first, the degree to which the nature of state regulation, particularly during the 1980s, has sharpened firm sensitivity to rapid changes in financial and product markets; and second, the justification and allocation of public expenditures, including social welfare expenditures, in terms of firm "requirements." Taken together, firm-led adjustment to economic internationalization and firm-led social expenditures have affected the locational patterns of productive activities and the place-to-place character of public services and infrastructural investment. The result is a landscape characterized by increasing inequalities among places and people, something that is but a new version of what has long existed for rural America.

Despite the trends noted above, however, the internationalization of markets is not a sufficient explanation for the landscape of inequality taking shape in the U.S. Discussions of competitiveness and market segmentation tell only part of the story, for economic processes continue to be mediated through political processes at national, state, and local levels. Particularly, this goes on as revised expectations of federalism drive many policy decisions to the lowest government level. As noted earlier, this is not a uniquely new U.S. policy response. For this reason, the new spatial inequality requires political-economic rather than simply economic explanations. What must be considered, in particular, is how product and financial markets to which American firms respond have been shaped by government policy and how firms have responded to these markets in ways that have exacerbated intra-regional inequalities. Second, we need to consider how the ability of U.S. firms to adjust to the internationalization of the economy relates to public social investment. The allocation of these investments in the contemporary U.S. has contributed to, rather than having ameliorated, both place-based and prospective equality. The interaction of these closely aligned processes is constructing the emerging space economy.

The regulation of capitalist economies, as this is tied to economic internationalization, has drawn renewed interest in the 1980s and 1990s. These macroeconomic analyses of the relationship between nationstates and markets have been concerned primarily with the direction and control of industrial investment (Zysman 1983; Cox 1986; Hall 1989). A major contention among analysts of the relationship between states and markets has concerned the political basis for these regimes--that is, how governing relationships are established politically, how they are maintained, and whether and under what conditions they can be altered. While all industrialized economies have tended toward some regulation, the form of regulation differs widely. Of the types of regulatory systems governing financial markets in industrialized economies, there are three recognized "types": the *capital market system*, with resources allocated by competitively established prices; the *credit-based system* with administered prices; and the *credit-based, bank-dominated system*. The U.S., quite expectedly given traditions, is the foremost example of the first type. In practice, adjustment to changes in market conditions is formulated and led by individual firms rather than being negotiated by "social partners" (labor and management) as in Sweden, or being state-led through industrial policy, as in Japan. Within a capital market system, as exemplified by the U.S., government ability to influence investment decisions or employment policy is purposively weak in contrast with the other systems.[3]

By definition, capital market systems respond quickly to short-term changes in market conditions and militate against long-term investment strategies. In the laissez-faire U.S., this sensitivity was heightened in the 1980s. Given the relationship between financial market regulation and decisions of firms concerning product markets and labor deployment, the changes in the regulatory regime governing financial markets in the 1980s emerge as central factors reshaping U.S. political economy. Prior to deregulation, in the 1960s and 1970s, non-depository financial institutions, such as brokerage security services and insurance companies, devised short-term investment products or instruments. These instruments yielded a higher return than the interest savings accounts of thrift institutions, which were hindered from competing by interest rate restrictions. At the same time, Eurodollar markets generated other unregulated investment opportunities. Partially as a consequence of these developments, a series of legislative acts removed many of the previous controls on banks and thrift institutions and paved the way for the contemporary financial service industry. As a result, financial institutions no longer rely on a residentiary deposit base to finance lending operations, but rather draw investment funds and invest across regions, countries, and sectors. As a consequence, the industry has changed from one in which the central activity is providing services to a wide range of customers to one in which the central activity is selling financial products to a narrow range of customers.

In general, the removal of national regulatory provisions has made for much more competitive financial markets which, in turn, have affected labor deployment policies and product markets in the U.S. A second change in the regulatory environment that is deepening tendencies toward firm-led adjustment is non-enforcement of anti-trust law, which has accelerated the process of merger and acquisition that began to reshape the industry in the 1970s.

The profit orientation of contemporary financial institutions means that they are strategically targeting certain populations and communities. Bank services appear to be proliferating in some areas, particularly suburban counties, and are being eliminated in less accessible and poorer areas in rural communities and central cities. The move from service to sales and the reorientation of service provision to the high end of the market has been accompanied by an emphasis on short-term commercial loans. This has reduced the availability of long-term, fixed-rate financing crucial to community and small business development. In addition, pressure to leave less profitable areas has led to a less stable local financial market, one more characterized by rapid turnover. Another implication of the emerging distribution of financial services is a loss of certain types of expertise in some locations.

Decisions not to enforce anti-trust regulations are associated with concentration and, by extension, with more centralization of service provision. In rural America, the restructuring of the retail sector has resulted in the so-called "Wal-Marting" of the countryside, or the replacement of locally-owned stores by discount retail chain stores in more centralized locations. The restructuring of retail, stimulated in part by regulatory changes, has encouraged rapid retail centralization and affected most rural communities and some central cities in four ways: decreased sales tax revenue, increased unemployment, redistribution of employment opportunities to higher-order centers, and decreased local investment. The increased debt load carried by firms is encouraging them to restructure operations to reduce labor inputs. This obviously places a greater burden on the contribution of government's social programs to rural areas, and limits the likely impact of rural economic development efforts.

That does not mean government policy is unimportant. Decisions by firms to seek out more profitable markets and less costly production locations obviously take place in response to an already constructed socio-economic terrain, one which is the product of both market and non-market investments. Thus, while firm-led adjustment may not "recognize" the significance of public social expenditures in constructing that terrain, firm locational choices respond to such expenditures. In the U.S., public social investment decisions affect firm-led market decisions in significant ways. First, decentralizing the responsibility for public social expenditures, including everything from physical infrastructure to incarceration, has exacerbated place-to-place differences in fiscal capacity and service quality. This raises the relative cost of doing business in locations with higher fiscal burdens. Second, solutions to lagging economic growth are perceived to lie in dismantling the public sector to mirror existent market processes. Decisions to privatize an already largely private system affect the location and quality of necessary social services. These social investment decisions create the set of location choices faced by firms, affecting the overall social and economic costs of doing business in various places.

In the U.S., the way in which the firm-market relationship has been regulated has flowed from and contributed to what becomes a weakly organized social welfare state. This is exemplified in a number of ways, one of which is the reliance on private employee benefits as a form of social welfare. As a consequence, firm-market regulation policies and social welfare policy move together in a way which departs from the pattern of other industrialized economies. Since U.S. social welfare is tied to the requirements of firms rather than defended in a separate political arena, changes in firm requirements relative to the market are reflected in shifts in the content and extent of social welfare spending and more in the forms of state intervention. The decisions that firms make to adjust to market conditions and the associated shifts in social welfare expenditures translate into investment and expenditure patterns which have a spatial dimension.

Several shifts occurred in the definition and provision of public goods in the U.S. in the 1980s. The first substantive policy change was a break in an already weakly-defined responsibility of the nation-state for the well-being of places located within its boundaries. There was a conscious effort to sever the bond between national and place-based prosperity (Barnekov, Boyle, and Rich 1989). This position was expressed through dramatic cutbacks in non-entitlement human service programs administered by localities in areas such as housing, community development, and employment and job training. Overall, federal spending in these areas declined 35 percent between 1982 and 1986. The second was increased "commodification" of public services, including social welfare services such as health care (Esping-Andersen 1990). Third, state and local assistance from the federal government declined precipitously. The proportion of the federal budget devoted to local assistance programs declined from 15.5 percent in 1980 to 10.7 percent in 1987. Per capita state and local spending increased 31 percent between 1984 and 1988 (in comparison with an 18 percent inflation rate). Much of this growth was driven by health care costs and federal mandates to expand medicaid. At the federal level, the biggest cuts were absorbed by those programs oriented toward "in-need" populations and places. Throughout the 1980s, grants-in-aid programs for rural areas were dramatically slashed. Even basic infrastructural investment projects were eliminated from the budget. Rural communities, as well as central cities, are relatively disadvantaged by the effects of privatization on the location and character of social services. In addition, they are in a much weaker position in terms of basic fiscal capacity, and therefore, *with respect to what they can offer to firms.*

Although the reorganization and redistribution of services is market-driven, it is *also a response to politically-influenced location costs,* including those not immediately related to production--that is, public goods such as education, health services, and physical infrastructure. With respect to the quality and cost of public goods, suburban locations appear to be "more efficient" because of the state-subsidized investment in suburban infrastructure from the 1950s through the 1980s, and because the wealth of the residential population supports higher property tax levels which support local services. In addition, as mentioned before, the defense expenditures of the 1980s were highly skewed toward suburban locations. In contrast, rural America is "less efficient." Not only is its infrastructural base old, it is also underdeveloped because it was intended to serve the more limited needs of a farm economy. Other concerns were largely neglected, leaving a declining and often disadvantaged population that is hard to organize for "efficient" business use. The agriculture modernization/development paradigm, in short, comes back to haunt rural Americans in very pronounced fashion.

In sum, the U.S. is singular among industrialized economies in the degree of vulnerability to market forces because its adjustment is microeconomic and firm-led, rather than mediated through societal-level institutions. Although some state-market regulatory systems such as those of Britain and Canada are quite similar to that of the U.S., there is a prominent difference that increases the risk and vulnerability factors in the U.S. regime. In these other firm-led adjustment systems, a nationally organized social welfare system serves to mitigate the effects of firm-led adjustment policies (King 1989). The lack of such a system in the United States deepens the vulnerability of individuals and regions to the consequences of firm-led adjustment and continues to produce a different set of political responses.

Budget Constraints

During the 1980s the United States went from being the leading creditor nation in the world to being the largest debtor. Had this debt been incurred to undertake investments to stimulate future economic growth, there would not be as much reason for current concern. However, the 1980s were characterized by significant disinvestment in productive capacity. As a result, the U.S. enters the 1990s dependent on foreign borrowing and paying relatively large shares of federal revenue to service outstanding debt. The results are high real interest rates that limit private investment, and restrictions imposed on government policy because resources must be allocated to debt service and maintaining acceptable interest and exchange rates. Because rural areas depend on transfer payments and need major new investments in order to adapt to changing conditions and better use their available resources, the impact of budget constraints on them is potentially devastating.

Further, the budget problems of all government levels are leading to a re-examination of many programs. A more business-like approach is being advocated where returns on investment are calculated to support each program. Although it is difficult to argue with efforts to improve the efficiency of government action, a narrow focus on outlays and monetary returns may not lead to desirable public policy. Many of the actions government undertakes are not readily converted to monetary equivalents and market prices. If they were convertible, there would be less reason for the government to undertake them in the first place because they would be something the market could provide. In addition, the high interest rates prevailing in the private sector tend to push the government into using a relatively high social discount rate, with the result that only projects with short-term returns are undertaken.

Exacerbating the budget problems of governments has been a round of competitive tax cuts. At a time when outlays are exceeding revenues, all levels of government have found themselves in the position of reducing tax levels. This has worsened their financial position and deepened indebtedness for all government levels. Local governments have felt the brunt of this action. They have lost revenue transfers from national and state levels of government, lost access to their own sources of revenue, and have been given additional responsibilities at the same time.

The Forces and Implications Underlying New Rural Policies

In the 1980s, direct rural policy intervention in the United States gradually evolved to a point where it may well have started a fundamental shift in direction. But it may not be a promising one. Ironically, but not unexpectedly given the dictates of history, federal assistance to farming reached record levels during this evolution, particularly when measured on a per-farm basis. Other than for commodity programs, there was a continuous reduction in the level of support provided to rural areas and the rural populace through the wide range of other rural assistance policies (Freshwater 1989). Cuts in infrastructure assistance and reductions in federal support for social programs took place in rural areas at a time when very significant economic dislocations, as mentioned above, exacerbated their effects.

As a consequence, pressure on rural areas from the combination of old and new trends resulted in slower growth rates through most of the 1980s than was the case in urban areas. As rural areas fell further behind, their plight became more obvious and harder to ignore. Yet policy makers saw little in the existing range of direct and indirect public policies that suggested they were adequate to resolve the problems.

There was, at the end of the 1980s, an adjustment in basic rural policy goals that reflected the evolution of the status of rural areas in North America and the forces acting upon them. Prior to 1980 the basic goals of rural policy were entitlement based, grants-oriented and distributional in nature. The policies that were developed employed mostly income transfers to achieve their goals. Objectives of pre-1980s rural policy could be summarized as to: (1) stem the outflow of the rural poor to urban areas by reducing their incentive to leave, (2) protect the income and wealth of the politically powerful in rural areas, particularly farmers, and (3) achieve some measure of equitable access to income and basic services across each nation.

The goals of rural policy, while still politically restrained and modest, have now shifted to more of an investment orientation where benefits are compared to costs. Rural policy goals now include: (1) reducing the burden of carrying the poor and unemployed, (2) increasing the rural contribution to the creation of national income and wealth, (3) protecting the environment, and (4) providing equitable access to income and basic services, but with an emphasis on restricting unwarranted access. While earlier policy goals were oriented to selectively received distributional concerns, the current set of emerging rural policy goals has efficiency as the major focus. And it appears likely to be based on competition between communities, with not all rural places likely to receive support. The shift reflects the influence of a number of old and new trends that were explained throughout this chapter, particularly the reduced ability of rural areas to generate income, a high dependency on income transfers, diminished global competitiveness of the North American economy including agriculture, and budget limits. It also reflects a political philosophy, embedded in neoclassical regime traditions, that favors a minimal role for government unless faced with inordinate pressure to do otherwise.

Another important benchmark for rural policy in the 1980s and 1990s was a public questioning of the levels of public support given to farming, particularly for large commercial growers. Although agriculture in both the U.S. and

Canada received massive levels of support in the last decade, there was increasing realization that those funds did not meet basic social expectations. These supports did not resolve the fundamental problems of the farm sector. And they drew attention to the fact that most commercial-scale farmers who receive the bulk of payments are relatively wealthy, and assisting them provides little benefit to the rural poor. This left open the question as to why support for the modernization/development paradigm was still necessary. By the end of the last decade, there was a greater appreciation in policy circles of the degree of *separation between rural policy and farm policy*, one being for places and the other for an economic sector.

This allowed programs assisting rural areas to be increasingly justified on an economic efficiency basis, rather than for their presumed stabilizing effects. Developing programs are being presented as having a positive return on the public funds invested, or as cost reducing. Recent efforts at revising U.S. rural policy in the 1990 Farm Bill, while still extraordinarily modest in scope by global standards, suggest a rethinking of the appropriate federal role but not the regime orientation. The rural development title offers support for strategic planning, business development, and improving infrastructure as means of making rural locations attractive to those who make firm-induced or market decisions. There are great consequences in this logic for the rural poor, however. As public policy focus shifts from protecting particular industries to enhancing the likely contribution of people, the rationale for autonomous, or place-specific, rural programs disappears. For example, there is little justification in improving the condition of the rural unemployed if this is at the expense of the urban unemployed. A focus on people rather than place leads inexorably to improving mobility of the labor force. If this is combined with an urban environmental pressure that seeks to preserve, and not develop, rural areas, the logical implication is more rather than less rural economic decline. The rural poor, in consequence, seem likely to gain very little.

Conclusion

What we have emphasized in this chapter is a set of institutional restraints on serving the rural poor--agriculture's modernization/development paradigm, forced rural reliance on indirect social programs, the impact of a neoclassical regime, the internationalization of domestic economics, and the reliance in the U.S. on firm-induced decisions which are compatible with laissez-faire traditions. Clearly, though, important changes have taken place in rural areas in North America in the last decade and these are not out of historical context. Some of these changes have reinforced old trends while others have led to a new emphasis. Our analysis indicates that the decade of the 1990s will show important--and likely negative--changes in rural conditions. The set of new forces creating them includes a new federal emphasis that removes much national level support from local communities, a surge in global competition, de- and re-regulation of financial markets, and increasingly binding budget constraint at all government levels.

No matter how successful activists, legislators, and bureaucrats are in generating more comprehensive and meaningfully direct rural policies, these policies, as with the past, will inevitably have less impact on alleviating rural poverty levels than will indirect rural policies--those put in place for reasons other than a desire to improve rural socioeconomic conditions. Increasingly, the predominant policies affecting rural areas are not those specifically designed for rural purposes, but rather broad macroeconomic and social policies that disproportionately benefit or hurt rural areas, usually unintentionally. In the past, the indirect policies contributing most to rural development and poverty alleviation have been those associated with the social-welfare system, broadly construed to mean the system of citizen-entitlements. This system includes not only transfer payments to the state-dependent, but also broad domestic spending programs in areas such as education, infrastructure development, regional policies, service provision, and the like. This system is in decline across the world, due to the exigencies of unstable accumulation, declining state fiscal capacity and endemic fiscal crises, changes in class structures and political mobilization, global economic competition, and the declining coherence and integrity of national economic systems. Portions of this social welfare system will remain--particularly entitlements to the aged and far less generous payments to the state-dependent--and maintenance of these programs will remain crucial to the rural poor. But there seems to be little likelihood of restoring the important non-entitlement components of the U.S. social welfare system any time soon. Other strategies will be needed. Short of a fundamental but unlikely shift in the North American neoclassical regime, a key issue in creating rural jobs and addressing the causes of rural poverty is assigning a higher degree of legitimacy to places in U.S. politics. We advance the proposition that the most viable route for addressing place issues in North America is on the basis of equal access to opportunities: three out of ten North American citizens reside in rural and small town areas where they have distinctively less access to opportunities because of their limited access to programs and facilities fostering economic development. Redress in the form of direct rural development policy is necessary to ensure that this 30 percent of the population can indeed play on the much-vaunted level playing field. The U.S. has had a more formal set of direct rural policies, especially through agriculture, than other neoclassical and even corportist regimes because the political context has allowed a distinct rural group--farmers--to remain identifiable. But other comparable regimes such as Canada have generally provided *more support* to rural areas because the mix of programs has emphasized universality of access to social services. These ultimately are the hard ones to provide without subsidy in rural areas. Effects of distance, lack of economies of scale, and lack of attractiveness to professionals have an impact.

Congressional dissatisfaction with past policy has resulted in a number of rural policy changes being included in the 1990 Farm Bill, including the creation of a new Rural Development Administration (RDA) within USDA. In addition, the Administration has developed its own strategy, based on voluntary councils of federal and state officials to improve the coordination of programs in rural areas. Yet funding has been negligible, now as always. The focus on policy has shifted from the federal to the state level, then down to local units of government. This reflects the growing belief in the benefits of adopting state-based development strategies that reflect the particular conditions of each state and even locale (Fosler 1988). State governors have played an important role in supporting this approach, primarily out of frustration with the limited success of federal programs (DeWitt, Batie, and Norris 1988) and, as we have shown, the limited vision.

Well before the passage of the new provisions for rural development in the 1990 Farm Bill, the USDA had implemented a pilot program to improve the coordination of federal and state programs within a state by establishing State Rural Development Councils (SRDCs). Each council receives assistance from USDA in the form of a USDA staff person and a training program in rural development methods for the members. The intent of the program is to build a consensus development strategy at the state level. Once the consensus is built, federal and state programs can be coordinated to work in tandem to meet the established goals. Plans now call for expanding the number of SRDCs over time until all states are covered.

The 1990 Farm Bill gave the Rural Development Administration authority to manage existing economic development programs within the Farmers Home Administration. Moving the management of these programs to an organization with a specific economic development mandate can provide an opportunity to refocus the federal rural development effort, and create a logical linkage point to the SRDCs. The incidence of real change has been far more problematic, however. Congress has refused funding, resisting any actions that could be seen as refuting the agricultural establishment institutions.

So, in both cases, there is no infusion of new resources, nor is there a significant retargetting of existing funds. Most importantly, there is no commitment that the policies will even survive the next budget cycle. Opposition means RDA activities have not fully been accorded policy status. As a result there is no strong incentive for either state and federal agencies, or dependent communities, to adopt a coordinated approach to rural development, despite the conceptual benefits of doing so.

We have a more fundamental question that undoubtedly concerns RDA funding decisions as well. Given that direct rural policies in the past have been minimalist and have had meager successes in reducing rural poverty, is there a need for explicit rural policy in the U.S.? We believe so. There is an underlying social contract that gives people the right to equal opportunity, and we believe there exists a growing recognition of this right in rural places. While market forces remain the dominant means of allocating resources and distributing wealth, they have never been the sole means of making decisions, even in a neoclassical regime. In the U.S., only the resources and delivery apparatus of the nation-state seem likely to provide equal opportunity. Neither local communities nor the intervention efforts of members of Congress in their districts have escaped the strong tendencies within many communities to exploit their poor and working classes. Although equality is generally seen as a race/gender issue, it is not restricted to these issues. Recently, state courts in Kentucky and Texas have declared the existing school systems unconstitutional, because they did not ensure equal opportunities. While general-purpose programs may go a long way to providing equal opportunities, they may not meet all individuals' needs. Clearly, people in rural areas do better when there is a stronger commitment to general social and economic development programs or betterment. An employment safety net and the broad set of social services narrow the gap between central and peripheral regions.

But general economic and social programs of the sort that are in place, even if extended beyond their current levels, will not be capable of dealing effectively with the problems of distance, scale, and the loss of critical social mass in rural areas. Only by grafting *place-specific programs* onto the set of core social programs will we allow equality of opportunity irrespective of where one lives. While the traditional emphasis on improving human capital to allow outmigration is important and necessary, it too requires place-specific approaches. By ignoring the attachment of people to their rural places, strict market-oriented policy based solely on individual self-interest weakens the likelihood of success of any federally-supported local development program, just as it undermines the sense of community and common purpose.

Notes

This chapter was written by Frederick H. Buttel, University of Wisconsin-Madison; William P. Browne, Central Michigan University; Susan Christopherson, Cornell University; Donald Davis, University of Tennessee-Knoxville; Philip Ehrensaft, University of Quebec-Montreal; David Freshwater, University of Kentucky; John Gaventa, University of Tennessee-Knoxville; and Philip McMichael, Cornell University.

1. As with social-welfare policies, the U.S. was relatively slow to adopt regional policies designed to redress rural-urban disparities in living standards. Even at their apogee in the late 1960s and early 1970s these programs were very modest by European standards. In part, U.S. reluctance to embrace ambitious regional policies was due to the historical tendency of the American state officials to be hesitant to engage in intervention to accomplish social goals. It was also due to the absence of a social-

democratic, welfare-state tradition that would justify intervention to assist the rural disadvantaged, and to the conservatism of U.S. rural regions which precluded articulation of a strong voice in favor of large subsidies to and investments in rural places and people. Also, outside of the South rural disadvantage was generally not so dramatic as to lead to rural-peripheral political movements or political parties whose platforms were aimed at reducing rural-urban disparities (see Hechter 1975, for the contrasting case of the Celtic fringe of Britain).

2. To the degree the military budget is reduced in the post-Soviet era, there may well be further favorable or unfavorable metro/nonmetro distributional impacts. Hardware/procurement cuts would have disproportionately negative impacts on metro places, while personnel cuts would have comparable effects on nonmetro counties.

3. Note that these categories of state regulation of finance bear a strong relationship to the Esping-Andersen (1990) typology of systems of "welfare capitalism." This correspondence suggests that systems through which rights of social citizenship are institutionalized are crucial in distinguishing among state forms and regime types of the advanced industrial nations, and that differences among states in their systems of welfare capitalism have shaped their financial regulatory policies and their overall responses to internationalization forces.

References

Aberly, D. 1970. "A Plan for Navajo Development," in Joint Economic Committee, *American Indians: Facts and Future: Toward Economic Development for Native American Communities*. Washington, D.C.: U.S. Government Printing Office.

Abramovitz, Mimi. 1988. *Regulating the Lives of Women: Social Welfare Policy, from Colonial Times to the Present*. Boston, MA: South End Press.

Across the Board. 1978. "Who Works 'Off the Books'?" *Across the Board* XV(8): 14-15.

Adams, Terry K., and Greg J. Duncan. 1990. "Long-Term Poverty in Nonmetropolitan Areas." Unpublished manuscript. Survey Research Center, University of Michigan, Ann Arbor, MI. January.

_____. 1991. "Closing the Gap: Metro-Nonmetro Differences in Long-Term Poverty Among Blacks." *Rural Development Perspectives* 7(February/May): 2-11.

_____. 1992. "Long-term Poverty in Rural Areas." In Cynthia M. Duncan (ed.), *Rural Poverty in America*. Pp. 63-93. New York, NY: Auburn House.

Advocacy Council on Children and Youth. 1978. "Why Can't I Have a Home? A Report on Foster Care and Adoption in North Carolina." Raleigh, NC: Governor's Advocacy Council on Children and Youth, December.

Aglietta, Michel. 1979. *A Theory of Capitalist Regulation: The U.S. Experience*. Translated by David Fernbach. New York, NY: Verso.

_____. 1982. "World Capitalism in the Eighties." *New Left Review* 136(Nov/Dec.): 5-41.

Agnew, J. A. 1988. "Beyond Core and Periphery: The Myth of Regional Political Economic Restructuring and Sectionalism in Contemporary American Politics." *Political Geography Quarterly* 7(2): 127-139.

Ahearn, Mary, Susan Bentley, and Thomas Carlin. 1988. *Farming-Dependent Counties and the Financial Well-being of Farm Operator Households*. Washington, D.C.: Economic Research Service, U.S. Department of Agriculture, August.

Albrecht, Don E., and Steve H. Murdock. 1988. "The Structural Characteristics of U.S. Agriculture: Historical Patterns and Precursors of Producers' Adaptations to the Crisis." In Steve H. Murdock and F. Larry Leistritz (eds.), *The Farm Financial Crisis: Socioeconomic Dimensions and Implications for Producers and Rural Areas*. Pp. 29-44. Boulder, CO: Westview Press.

Alexander, Arthur J. 1974. "Income, Experience, and the Structure of Internal Labor Markets." *Quarterly Journal of Economics* 88(1): 63-85.

Allen, David N., and David J. Hayward. 1990. "The Role of New Venture Formation/Entrepreneurship in Regional Economic Development: A Review." *Economic Development Quarterly* 4(1): 55-63.

Allen, Joyce E., and Alton Thompson. 1990. "Rural Poverty Among Racial and Ethnic Minorities." *American Journal of Agricultural Economics* 72(5): 1161-68.

Althauser, Robert P., and Erne L. Kalleberg. 1981. "Firms, Occupations, and the Structure of Labor Markets: A Conceptual Analysis." In Ivar Berg (ed.), *Sociological Perspectives on Labor Markets*. Pp. 119-140. New York, NY: Academic Press.

Ambler, Marjane. 1990. *Breaking the Iron Bonds: Indian Control of Energy Development*. Lawrence, KS: University Press of Kansas.

Amin, A., and K. Robbins. 1990. "The Re-emergence of Regional Economies? The Mythical Geography of Flexible Accumulation." *Environment and Planning D: Society and Space* 8: 7-34.

Amott, Teresa. 1990. "Black Women and AFDC: Making Entitlement Out of Necessity." In Linda Gordon (ed.) *Women, the State and Welfare*. Pp. 280-301. Madison, WI: University of Wisconsin Press.

Anderson, H. Michael, and Jeffrey T. Olson. 1991. *Federal Forests and the Economic Base of the Pacific Northwest: A Study of Regional Transitions*. Washington, D.C.: The Wilderness Society.

Anderson, K. H., and Richard V. Burkhauser. 1985. "The Retirement-Health Nexus: A New Measure of an Old Puzzle." *Journal of Human Resources* 20: 315-30.

Anderson, Martin. 1978. *Welfare: The Political Economy of Welfare Reform in the United States*. Stanford, CA: Hoover Institution Press.

Andre, Joyal. 1989. "Les Entreprises Alternatives Dans Le Development Local." *Canadian Journal of Regional Science* 12(1): 75-84.

Annie E. Casey Foundation. 1992. *Kids Don't Count Data Book: State Profiles of Child Well-Being*. Greenwich, CT: Annie E. Casey Foundation.

Arcia, Emily, Lynette Keyes, James J. Gallagher, and Harry Herrick. 1992. "Potential Underutilization of Part H Services: An Empirical Study of National Demographic Factors." Carolina Policy Studies Program, Frank Porter Graham Child Development Center, University of North Carolina, Chapel Hill, NC. April.

Arthur, W. Brian. 1990. "Positive Feedbacks in the Economy." *Scientific American* 262:92-99.

Astone, Nan Marie, and Sara S. McLanahan. 1991. "Family Structure, Parental Practices and High School Completion." *American Sociological Review* 56(3): 309-320.

Auerbach, A. J., and L. J. Kotlikoff. 1987. "Life Insurance of the Elderly: Its Adequacy and Determinants." In Gary Burtless (Ed.), *Work, Health, and Income Among the Elderly*. Washington, DC: Brookings Institution.

Averitt, Robert T. 1968. *The Dual Economy: The Dynamics of American Industry Structure*. New York, NY: W.W. Norton.

Baca Zinn, Maxine. 1989. "Family, Race, and Poverty in the Eighties." *Signs* 14:856-74.

Bandura, Albert. 1986. *Social Foundations of Thought and Action: A Social Cognitive Theory*. Englewood Cliffs, NJ: Prentice-Hall.

Bane, Mary Jo, and David T. Ellwood. 1986. "Slipping Into and Out of Poverty: The Dynamics of Spells." *Journal of Human Resources* 21(1): 1-23.

_____. 1989. "One Fifth of the Nation's Children: Why are They Poor?" *Science* 245(3-2): 1047-1053.

Banfield, Edward C. 1970. *The Unheavenly City: The Nature and Future of Our Urban Crisis*. Boston, MA: Little, Brown.

Baran, Paul A. 1957. *The Political Economy of Growth*. New York, NY: Monthly Review Press.

Barnekov, Timothy, Robin Boyle, and Daniel Rich. 1989. *Privatism and Urban Policy in Britain and the United States*. Oxford, UK: Oxford University Press.

Baron, James N., and William T. Bielby. 1980. "Bringing the Firms Back In: Stratification, Segmentation, and the Organization of Work." *American Sociological Review* 45(5): 737-765.

Barton, Weldon V. 1976. "Food, Agriculture, and Administrative Adaptation to Political Change." *Public Administration Review* 36(2): 148-154.

Bassuk, Ellen L., Lenore Rubin, and Alison S. Lauriat. 1986. "Characteristics of Sheltered Homeless Families." *American Journal of Public Health* 76(9): 1097-1101.

Bates, Robert H. 1981. *Markets and States in Tropical Africa: The Political Basis of Agricultural Policies*. Berkeley, CA: University of California Press.

Batteau, Allen. 1983. *Appalachia and America: Autonomy and Regional Dependence*. Lexington, KY: University of Kentucky Press.

Baumol, William J. 1986. "Productivity Growth, Convergence, and Welfare: What the Long-Run Data Show." *American Economic Review* 76(5): 1072-1085.

Baydar, Nazli, and Jeanne Brooks-Gunn. 1991. "Effects of Maternal Employment and Child-Care Arrangements on Preschoolers' Cognitive and Behavioral Outcomes: Evidence from the Children of the National Longitudinal Survey of Youth." *Developmental Psychology* 27: 932-945.

Bean, Frank D., and Marta Tienda. 1987. *The Hispanic Population of the United States*. New York, NY: Russell Sage.

Beaulieu, Lionel J. 1988. *The Rural South in Crisis: Challenges for the Future*. Boulder, CO: Westview Press.

_____. 1989. *Building Partnerships for People: Addressing the Rural South's Human Capital Needs*. Mississippi State: Southern Rural Development Center.

Beaulieu, Lionel J., Glenn D. Israel, and Mark H. Smith. 1990. "Community as Social Capital: The Case of Public High School Dropouts." Paper presented at the annual meetings of the Rural Sociological Society, Norfolk, VA, August.

Beaver, P.D. 1986. *Rural Community in the Appalachian South*. Lexington, KY: University of Kentucky Press.

Beck, E.M., Patrick M. Horan, and Charles M. Tolbert II. 1978. "Stratification in a Dual Economy: A Sectoral Model of Earnings Determination." *American Sociological Review* 43(5): 704-720.

_____. 1981. "Industrial Segmentation and Labor Market Discrimination." *Social Problems* 28(2): 113-130.

Becker, Gary S. 1962. "Investment in Human Capital: A Theoretical Analysis." *The Journal of Political Economy* 70(5-2): 9-49.

_____. 1964. *Human Capital: A Theoretical and Empirical Analysis, with Special Reference to Education*. New York, NY: National Bureau of Economic Research.

Becker, Gary S., Elizabeth M. Landes, and Robert T. Michael. 1977. "An Economic Analysis of Marital Instability," *Journal of Political Economy* 85(6): 1141-87.

Bellah, Robert N., Robert Madsen, William M. Sullivan, Ann Swidler, and Steven M. Tipton. 1985. *Habits of the Heart: Individualism and Commitment in American Life.* New York: Harper and Row.

Bellamy, Donald L., and Linda M. Ghelfi. 1988. "Southern Persistently Low-Income counties: Social and Economic Characteristics." Paper Presented at the 46th Professional Agricultural Workers Conference. Tuskegee, Al: Tuskegee University.

Bellante, Don. 1979. "The North-South Differential and the Migration of Heterogeneous Labor." *American Economic Review* 69: 166-75.

Beller, Andrea H. 1982. "Occupational Segregation by Sex: Determinants and Changes," *The Journal of Human Resources* 17: 371-392.

Beller, Daniel J. 1981. "Coverage Patterns of Full-time Employees Under Private Retirement Plans," *Social Security Bulletin* 44(7): 3-11, 47.

Bender, Lloyd D., Bernal L. Green, Thomas F. Hady, John A. Kuehn, Marlys K. Nelson, Leon B. Perkinson, and Peggy J. Ross. 1985. *The Diverse Social and Economic Structure of Nonmetropolitan America.* Research Development Report No. 49. Washington, DC: Economic Research Service, U.S. Department of Agriculture, September.

Benería, Lourdes, and Shelley Feldman. 1992. *Unequal Burden: Economic Crises, Persistent Poverty, and Women's Work.* Boulder, CO: Westview.

Berardi, Gigi. 1991. "Native Alaskan Populations at Risk: Putting the Last First." Presentation at the meeting of the Rural Sociological Society, Columbus, OH, August.

Berger, Peter L., and Thomas Luckmann. 1966. *The Social Construction of Reality: A Treatise in the Sociology of Knowledge.* Garden City, NY: Doubleday & Co.

Berk, Richard A., and Sarah Fenstermaker Berk. 1979. *Labor and Leisure at Home: Content and Organization of the Household Day.* Newbury Park, CA: Sage Publications.

Berry, Brian J. L. 1989. "Comparative Geography of the Global Economy: Cultures, Corporations and the Nation-State." *Economic Geography* 65(1): 1-8.

Berry, Brian J. L., and John D. Kasarda. 1977. *Contemporary Urban Ecology.* New York, NY: Macmillan.

Bibb, Robert, and William H. Form. 1977. "The Effects of Industrial, Occupation, and Sex Stratification on Wages for Blue Collar Markets." *Social Forces* 55(5): 974-996.

Bickel, Robert, and George Papagiannis. 1988. "Post-High School Prospects and District Level Dropout Rates." *Youth and Society* 20(2): 123-47.

Billings, D., and A. Tickamyer. 1990. "Development and Underdevelopment: The Politics of Region." Paper presented at the annual meeting of the Rural Sociological Society, Norfolk, VA. August.

Binstock, Robert H. 1986. "Perspectives on Measuring Hardship: Concepts, Dimensions, and Implications," *The Gerontologist* 26(1): 60-62.

Birch, David L. 1987. *Job Creation in America: How Our Smallest Companies Put the Most People to Work.* New York, NY: Free Press.

Bird, Alan R. 1990. *Status of the Nonmetro Labor Force, 1987.* Agriculture and Rural Economy Division, Economic Research Service. Rural Development Research Report No. 79. Washington, D.C.: U.S. Department of Agriculture. I.S Government Printing Office.

Blackly, Paul R. 1986. "Urban-Rural Variations in the Structure of Manufacturing Production." *Urban Studies.* 23(6): 471-83.

Blau, Francine, and Carol L. Jusenius. 1976. "Economists' Approaches to Sex Segregation in the Labor Market: An Appraisal." *Signs* 1: 181-199.

Blau, Peter Michael, and Otis Dudley Duncan. 1967. *The American Occupational Structure.* New York, NY: John Wiley and Sons.

Blaug, Mark. 1976. "The Empirical Status of Human Capital Theory: A Slightly Jaundiced Survey." *Journal of Economic Literature* 14: 827-55.

Blechman, Elaine A. 1982. "Are Children with One Parent at Psychological Risk? A Methodological Review." *Journal of Marriage and the Family* 44(1): 179-196.

Block, Fred L. 1977. *The Origins of International Economic Disorder: A Study of United States International Monetary Policy from Word War II to the Present.* Berkeley, CA: University of California Press.

Block, William J. 1960. *The Separation of the Farm Bureau and the Extension Service: Political Issues in a Federal System.* Urbana, IL: University of Illinois Press.

Bloomquist, Leonard E. 1988. "Performance in the Rural Manufacturing Sector." In David L. Brown, David L. Brown, J. N Reid, J. Bluestone, D. A. McGranahan, and S. M. Maxie (eds.), *Rural Economic Development in the 1980's: Prospects for the Future: A Summary.* Rural Development Research Report no. 69. Washington, D.C.: Economic Research Service, U.S. Department of Agriculture.

_____. 1990. "Local Labor Market Characteristics and the Occupational Concentration of Different Sociodemographic Groups." *Rural Sociology* 55(2): 199-213.

Bloomquist, Leonard E., and Gene F. Summers. 1982. "Organization of Production and Community Income Distributions." *American Sociological Review* 47(3): 325-338.

Bluestone, Barry. 1990. "The Great U-Turn Revisited: Economic Restructuring, Jobs, and the Redistribution of Earnings." In John D. Kasarda (ed.), *Jobs, Earnings, and Employment Growth in the United States.* Pp. 7-37. Boston, MA: Kluwer Academic Publishers.

Bluestone, Barry, and Bennet Harrison. 1982. *The Deindustrialization of America: Plant Closings, Community Abandonment, and the Dismantling of Basic Industry.* New York, NY: Basic Books.

_____. 1988. *The Great U-Turn: Corporate Restructuring and the Polarizing of America.* New York, NY: MacMillan.

Bluestone, Barry, W. M. Murphy, and Mary Stevenson. 1973. *Low Wages and the Working Poor.* Ann Arbor, MI: University of Michigan-Wayne State University, Institute of Labor and Industrial Relations.

Bobo, Lawrence. 1991. "Social Responsibility, Individualism and Redistributive Policies." *Sociological Forum* 6(1): 71-92.

Bock, R. Darrell, and Elsie G. J. Moore. 1984. *Profile on American Youth: Demographic Influences on ASVAB Test Performance.* Department of Defense, Office of Assistant Secretary of Defense. Manpower, Installations and Logistics. Washington, DC: U.S. Government Printing Office.

Boehm, Bernice. 1970. "The Child in Foster Care." In Helen D. Stone (ed.), *Foster Care in Question: A National Reassessment by Twenty-One Experts.* Pp. 220-227. New York: Child Welfare League of America.

Bokemeier, Janet L., Carolyn Sachs, and Ann R. Tickamyer. 1985. "Labor Force Experiences of Nonmetropolitan Women." *Rural Sociology* 50(1): 51-73.

Bokemeier, Janet L., Carolyn Sachs, and Verna Keith. 1983. "Labor Force Participation of Metropolitan, Nonmetropolitan, and Farm Women: Comparative Study," *Rural Sociology* 48(4): 515-539.

Bokemeier, Janet L., and Lorraine E. Garkovich. 1991. "Meeting Rural Family Needs." In Cornelia B. Flora and James A. Christenson (eds.), *Rural Policies for the 1990s*. Pp. 114-27. Boulder, CO: Westview Press.

Bonnen, James T. 1973. "Implications for Agricultural Policy." *American Journal of Agricultural Economics* 55(3): 391-398.

_____. 1980. "Observations on the Changing Nature of National Agricultural Policy Decisions Processes." In Trudy Huskamp Peterson. (ed.), *Farmers, Bureaucrats, and Middlemen*. Pp. 309-327. Conference on American Agriculture, 1977. Washington, D.C.: Howard University Press.

_____. 1984. "U.S. Agriculture, Instability and National Political Institutions: The Shift from Representative to Participatory Democracy." In Department of Agricultural Economics. (ed.), *United States Agriculture Policies for 1985 and Beyond*. Pp. 53-83. Tucson, AZ: University of Arizona.

_____. 1988. "Institutions, Instruments and Driving Forces Behind U.S. Agricultural Policies." In Kristen Allen and Katie Macmillan (eds.), *U.S.-Canadian Agricultural Trade Challenges: Developing Common Approaches*. Pp. 21-39. National Center for Food and Agricultural Policy. Washington DC: Resources for the Future.

_____. 1990. "The Political Economy of U.S. Rural Policy: An Exploration of the Past with Strategies for the Future." Paper presented at the International Symposium on Economic Change, Policies, Strategies and Research Issues, Aspen, CO, July.

Bonnen, James T., and William P. Browne. 1989. "Why is Agricultural Policy So Difficult to Reform?" in Carol S. Kramer, (ed.), *The Political Economy of U.S. Agriculture: Challenges for the 1990's*. Pp. 7-33. National Center for Food and Agricultural Policy. Washington, D.C.: Resources for the Future.

Borts, George H., and Jerome L. Stein. 1964. *Economic Growth in a Free Market*. New York, NY: Columbia University.

Bound, John, Greg J. Duncan, Deborah S. Laren, and Lewis Oleinick. 1991. "Poverty Dynamics in Widowhood," *Journal of Gerontology* 46(3): S115-S124.

Bourdieu, Pierre, and Jean-Claude Passeron. 1977. *Reproduction in Education, Society and Culture*. Translated by Richard Nice. Beverly Hills, CA: Sage Publications.

Bowles, Samuel, David M. Gordon, and Thomas E. Weisskopf. 1983. *Beyond the Waste Land: A Democratic Alternative to Economic Decline*. Garden City, NY: Anchor Press/Doubleday.

Bowman, Phillip J. 1977. *Motivational Dynamics and Achievement Among Rural Black Students in a Community College*. Ann Arbor, MI: University of Michigan Press.

Bowman, Phillip J., and Cleopatra Howard. 1985. "Race-related Socialization, Motivation, and Academic Achievement: A Study of Black Youths in Three-Generational Families." *Journal of the American Academy of Child Psychiatry* 24(2): 134-141.

Braudel, F. 1982. *The Perspective of the World*. Translated by Sian Reynolds. New York, NY: Harper and Row.

Brehm, C. T., and T. R. Saving. 1964. "The Demand for General Assistance Payments." *American Economic Review* 54(6): 1002-1018.

Breimyer, Harold F. 1983. "Conceptualization and Climate for New Deal Farm Laws of the 1930s." *American Journal of Agricultural Economics* 65(5): 1153-1157.

Brewer, H. C. 1985. "Measures of Diversification: Predictors of Regional Economic Instability." *Journal of Regional Science* 25: 463-71.

Briar, Scott. 1987. "Direct Practice: Trends and Issues." In Anne Minahan, Rosina M. Becerra, Scott Briar, Claudia J. Coulton, Leon H. Ginsberg, June Gary Hopps, John F. Longores, Rino N. Patti, William J. Reid, Tony Tripody and S.D. Khinduka (eds.), *Encyclopedia of Social Work,* 18Th Edition. Vol 1. Pp. 392-398. Silver Spring, MD: National Association of Social Workers.

Broder, David. 1989. "Dramatic Changes in Workforce Challenging." *The Greenville, SC News.* Page 4A, Jan. 18.

Broomhall, David E. 1991. "The Influence of Perceived Employment Opportunities on Educational Performance in Appalachia." Unpublished Ph.D. Dissertation. Department of Agricultural Economics, Virginia Polytechnic Institute and State University, Blacksburg, VI.

Brown, David L., J. Norman Reid, Herman Bluestone, David A. McGranahan, and Sara M. Mazie. 1988. *Rural Economic Development in the 1980s: Prospects for the Future.* Rural Development Research Report No. 69. Washington, D.C.: Agriculture and Rural Economy Division, Economic Research Service, U.S. Department of Agriculture.

Brown, David L., and Kenneth L. Deavers. 1987. "Rural Change and the Rural Economic Policy Agenda for the 1980's." In *Rural Economic Development in the 1980's: Preparing for the Future.* Pp. 1-1 to 1-31. Agriculture and Rural Economy Division, Economic Research Service, U.S. Department of Agriculture. ERS Staff Report No. AGES 870724.

Brown, David L., and Mildred E. Warner. 1989. "Persistent Low-Income Nonmetropolitan Areas in the United States: Some Conceptual Challenges for Development Policy." In *Natural Rural Studies Committee: A Proceedings,* edited by Emery Castle and Barbara Baldwin. Eugene, OR: Western Rural Development Center, Oregon State University.

_____. 1991. "Persistent Low-Income Nonmetropolitan Areas in the United States: Some Conceptual Challenges for Development Policy." *Policy Studies Journal* 19(2): 22-41.

Brown, David L., and Nina L. Glasgow. 1991. "Capacity Building and Rural Government Adaptation to Population Change." In Cornelia B. Flora and James A. Christenson (Eds.), *Rural Policy for the 1990's.* Pp.194-208. Boulder, CO: Westview Press.

Brown, Franklin Lee, and Helen M. Ingram. 1987. *Water and Poverty in the Southwest.* Tucson, AZ: University of Arizona Press.

Browne, William P. 1988a. "The Fragmented and Meandering Politics of Agriculture." In M. Ann Tutwiler (ed.), *U.S. Agriculture in a Global Setting: An Agenda for the Future.* Pp. 136-153. National Center for Food and Agricultural Policy. Washington, DC: Resources for the Future.

_____. 1988b. *Private Interests, Public Policy, and American Agriculture*. Lawrence, KA: University Press of Kansas.

Browne, William P. 1990. "Organized Interests and Their Issue Niches: A Search for Pluralism in a Policy Domain." *Journal of Politics* 52(2): 477-509.

_____. 1991. "Issue Niches and the Limits of Interest Group Influence." In Allan J. Cigler and Burdett Loomis. (eds.), *Interest Group Politics*, 3rd Edition. Pp. 345-370. Washington, DC: Congressional Quarterly Press.

Browne, William P., and Mark Lundgren. 1987. "Farmers Helping Farmers: Constituent Services and the Development of a Grassroots Farm Lobby." *Agriculture and Human Values* 4: 11-28.

Browning, Edgar K. 1975. *Redistribution and the Welfare System*. Washington, D.C.: American Enterprise Institute for Public Policy Research.

Brunelle, Andy. 1990. "The Changing Structure of the Forest Industry in the Pacific Northwest." In Robert G. Lee, Donald R. Field, and William R. Burch, Jr. (eds.), *Community and Forestry: Continuities in the Sociology of Natural Resources*. Pp. 107-124. Boulder, CO: Westview Press.

Bryant, F. Carlene. 1981. *We're All Kin: A Cultural Study of a Mountain Neighborhood*. Knoxville, TN: University of Tennessee Press.

Bulow, J., and L. Summers. 1986. "A Theory of Dual Labor Markets with Application to Industrial Policy, Discrimination, and Keynesian Unemployment." *Journal of Labor Economics* 4(3): 376-414.

Bunker, Stephen G. 1989. "Staples, Links, and Poles in the Construction of Regional Development Theories." *Sociological Forum* 4: 589-610.

Burch, Wiliam R., Jr. n.d. "A Sense of Place--When Main Street Becomes a Thoroughfare." Unpublished manuscript, Yale University.

Burch, William R., Jr. 1971. *Daydreams and Nightmares: A Sociological Essay on the American Environment*. New York, NY: Harper and Row.

Burkhauser, Richard V., Karen C. Holden, and Daniel A. Myers. 1986. "Marital Disruption and Poverty: The Role of Survey Procedures in Artificially Creating Poverty," *Demography* 23(4): 621-631.

Burnham, Walter Dean. 1965. "The Changing Shape of the American Political Universe." *American Political Science Review* 59: 7-28.

_____. 1967. "Party Systems and the Political Process." In William Nisbet Chambers and Walter Dean Burnham. (eds.), *The American Party Systems: Stages of Political Development*. Pp. 277-307. New York, NY: Oxford University Press.

Bush, Malcolm. 1988. *Families in Distress: Public, Private, and Civic Responses*. Berkeley, CA: University of California Press.

Butler, John A., William D. Winter, Judith D. Singer, and Martha Wenger. 1985. "Medical Care use and Expenditure Among Children and Youth in the United States: Analysis of a National Probability Sample." *Pediatrics* 76(4): 495-506.

Buttel, Frederick H. 1980. "Agricultural Structure and Rural Ecology: Toward a Political Economy of Rural Development." *Sociologia Ruralis* 20(1-2): 44-62.

_____. 1982. "The Political Economy of Agriculture in Advanced Industrial Societies: Some Observations on Theory and Method." In Scott G. McNall, ed., *Current Perspectives in Social Theory*. Pp. 27-55. Greenwich, CON: JAI Press.

_____. 1983. "Farm Structure and Rural Development," in David E. Brewster, Wayne D. Rasmussen and Garth Youngbert (eds.), *Farms in Transition: Interdisciplinary Perspectives on Farm Structure.* Pp. 103-124. Ames, IA: The Iowa State University Press.

_____. 1991. "Environmentalization: Origins, Processes, and Implications for Rural Social Change," Presidential address delivered to the annual meeting of the Rural Sociological Society, Columbus, August.

Buttel, Frederick H., and Gilbert W. Gillespie, Jr. 1991. "Rural Policy in Political Historical-Perspective: The Rise, Fall and Uncertain Future of the American Welfare-State." In Kenneth E. Pigg (ed.), *The Future of Rural America: Anticipating Policies for Constructive Change.* Pp. 15-40. Boulder, CO: Westview Press.

Buttel, Frederick H., Olaf F. Larson, and Gilbert W. Gillespie, Jr. 1990. *The Sociology of Agriculture.* New York, NY: Greenwood Press.

Cahn, E. S. 1969. *Our Brother's Keeper: The Indian in White America.* New York: World Publishing Co.

Cahn, Edgar S., Jerry J. Berman, S. Dayton Coles, Jr., Nancy Esposito, and F. Browing Pipestem. 1969. *Our Brother's Keeper: The Indian in White America.* New York, NY: World Publishing Co.

Campbell, R., and J. C. Henretta. 1980. "Status Claims and Status Attainment: The Determinants of Financial Well Being." *American Journal of Sociology* 86:618-629.

Caplan, Nathan, Marcella H. Choy, and John K. Whitmore. 1992. "Indochinese Refugee Families and Academic Achievement." *Scientific American* 266(February): 36-42.

Capper, Arthur. 1922. *The Agricultural Bloc.* New York, NY: Harcourt Brace.

Carr, Marilyn. 1981. "Technologies Appropriate for Women: Theory, Practice and Policy." In Roselyn Dauber and Melinda L. Cain (eds.), *Women and Technological Change in Developing Countries.* Pp. 193-203. Boulder, CO: Westview Press.

Carroll, Matthew S. 1991. "Northwest Loggers: An Occupational Community at Risk in the Forest Management Wars." Paper presented at the annual meeting of the Rural Sociological Society, Columbus, OH, August.

Castells, Manuel, and Alejandro Portes. 1989. "World Underneath: The Origins, Dynamics, and Effects of the Informal Economy." In Alejandro Portes, Manuel Castells and Lauren A. Benton (eds). *The Informal Economy: Studies in Advanced and Less Developed Countries.* Pp. 11-37. Baltimore, MY: The Johns Hopkins University Press.

Castells, Manuel, and Lauren A. Benton (eds.) 1989. *The Informal Economy: Studies in Advanced and Less Developed Countries.* Baltimore, MD: The Johns Hopkins University Press.

Castillo, Monica Dianne. 1991. "California's Rural Colonias: A Study of Disadvantaged Communities with High Concentrations of Latinos." M.S. Thesis dissertation. Davis, CA: University of California.

Caudill, Harry M. 1962. *Night Comes To the Cumberlands: A Biography of a Depressed Area.* Boston, MA: Little, Brown and Company.

Cervantes, N. 1988. "Out of the City: Urban Poor Seek Second Chance in Rural America." *San Diego Union*, August 28 and 29.

Chambers, Robert. 1983. *Rural Development: Putting the Last First.* New York, NY: Logaman.

Chandler, Alfred D., Jr. 1962. *Strategy and Structure: Chapters in the History of the Industrial Enterprise.* Cambridge, MA: M.I.T. Press.

Children's Defense Fund. 1991. *The State of American Children 1991.* Washington, DC: Children's Defense Fund.

Christaller, Walter. 1966. *Central Places in Southern Germany.* Translated by Carlise W. Baskin. Englewood Cliffs, NJ: Prentice Hall.

Christopherson, Susan. 1990. "Rethinking Regional Economic Development: How Deregulation and Sectoral Shifts are Changing the Rules of the Game." In D. Otto and S. Deller (eds.), *Alternative Perspectives on Development Prospects for Rural Areas.* Pp. 83-113. Proceedings of Symposium at AAEA Annual Meetings, Vancouver, B.C.: August 4-8.

_____. 1991. "Re-making the Landscape of Inequality." Paper presented at the annual meeting of the Rural Sociological Society, Columbus, OH, August.

Clark, Gordon. 1981. "The Employment Relationship and the Spatial Division of Labor: A Hypothesis." *Annals of the Association of American Geographers* 17:412-424.

Clemente, Frank, and Richard B. Sturgis. 1972. "The Division of Labor in American: An Ecological Analysis." *Social Forces* 51(2): 176-182.

Clogg, Clifford C., Nimfa Ogenda, and Hee-Shoon Shin. 1991. "Labor Force Behavior in the Process of Socioeconomic Attainment: Testing New Seales from the Labor Force Utilization Framework." *Social Science Research* (forthcoming).

Cochrane, Willard Wesley. 1979. *The Development of American Agriculture: A Historical Analysis.* Minneapolis, MN: University of Minnesota Press.

Coe, R., G. Duncan, and M. Hill. 1982. "Dynamic Aspects of Poverty and Welfare Use in the United States." Paper presented at the Conference on Problems of Poverty, Clark University.

Coe, Richard D. 1988. "A Longitudinal Examination of Poverty in the Elderly Years," *The Gerontologist* 28(4): 540-551.

Coffey, William J. 1990. "Comprehensive Bases for Locally Induced Development." In D. Otto and S. Deller (eds.), *Alternative Perspectives on Development Prospects for Rural Areas.* Pp. 51-79. Proceedings of Symposium at AAEA Annual Meetings, Vancouver, BC: August 4-8.

Cohen, Anthony P. 1975. The Management of Myths: The Politics of Legitimation in a Newfoundland Community. *Newfoundland Social and Economic Studies* No. 14, Institute of Social and Economic Research, Memorial University of Newfoundland, Canada.

Colclough, Glenna. 1988. "Uneven Development and Racial Composition in the Deep South: 1970-1980." *Rural Sociology* 53:73-86.

Coleman, James S. 1988. "Social Capital in the Creation of Human Capital." *American Journal of Sociology* 94(Supplement): 95-120.

Collier, Ken. 1984. *Social Work with Rural Peoples: Theory and Practice.* Vancouver, BC: New Star Books.

Collins, Jane L., and Martha E. Gimenez. 1990. *Work Without Wages.* Albany, NY: SUNY Press.

Collins, Randall. 1979. *The Credential Society: An Historical Sociology of Education and Stratification.* New York, NY: Academic Press.

Commins, Patrick. 1990. "Restructuring Agriculture in Advanced Societies: Transformation, Crisis and Responses." In Terry Marsden, Philip Lowe and Sarah Whatmore (eds.), *Rural Restructuring: Global Processes and Their Responses.* Pp. 45-76. London, UK: David Fulton Publishers.

Consortium for Longitudinal Studies (CLS). 1983. *As the Twig Is Bent: Lasting Effects of Preschool Programs.* Hillsdale, NJ: Lawrence Erlbaum Associates.

Cook, Annabel K. 1991. "Economic Recession and the Growth of Producer Services: Metro/Nonmetro Variations." Paper presented at the Annual Meetings of the Rural Sociological Society, Columbus, OH: August.

Cooley, Richard. [1963]. Foss, Phillip O. 1960. *Politics and Grass: The Administration of Grazing on the Public Domain.* Seattle, WA: University of Washington Press.

Cordes, Sam M. 1989. "The Changing Rural Environment and the Relationship Between Health Services and Rural Development," *Health Services Research* 23(6): 757-784.

Cornell, Stephen, and Joseph P. Kalt, 1990. "Pathways from Poverty: Economic Development and Institution-Building on American Indian Reservations." *American Indian Culture and Research Journal* 14: 89-125.

Cosby, A., and P. Steven. 1979. "Some Inequality and Educational Achievement in Rural America." College Station, TX: Texas A&M University.

Coward, R. T., and R. K. Kerckhoff. 1978. *The Rural Elderly: Program Planning Guidelines.* Ames, IA: North Central Regional Center for Rural Development, Iowa State University.

Coward, Raymond T. 1987. "Poverty and Aging in Rural America," *Human Services in the Rural Environment* 11(1): 41-47.

Cox, Andrew 1986. "State, Finance and Industry in Comparative Perspective," in Andrew Cox (ed.), *State, Finance and Industry: A Comparative Analysis of Post-war Trends in Six Advanced Industrial Economies.* New York, NY: St. Martin's Press.

Cox, Robert W. 1987. *Production, Power, and World Order: Social Forces in the Making of History.* New York, NY: Columbia University Press.

Crow, Graham. 1989. "The Use of the Concept of 'Strategy' in Recent Sociological Literature." *Sociology* 23: 1-24.

Cruise, James. 1991. "Does a Rising Tide Lift All Ships?: Community and Regional Dimensions of Elderly Poverty in the Rural United States." Presented to the Rural Sociological Society Annual Meeting, Columbus, OH, August.

Cryer, Debby, and Thelma Harms. 1990. "Services to Families and Children in North Carolina Shelters." Survey Report. Chapel Hill, NC: DC/TATS Media, Frank Porter Graham Child Development Center, University of North Carolina at Chapel Hill. August.

Culhane, Paul J. 1981. *Public Lands Politics: Interest Group Influence on the Forest Service and the Bureau of Land Management.* Baltimore, NJ: Johns Hopkins University Press.

Daft, Lynn M. 1982. "The Rural Poor." *Policy Studies Review* 2(1): 65-71.

Danzinger, E. J. 1974. *Indians and Bureaucrats: Administering the Reservation Policy During the Civil War.* Urbana, IL: University of Illinois Press.

Danziger, Sheldon, Jacques van der Gaag, Michael K. Taussig, and Eugene Smolensky. 1984. "The Direct Measurement of Welfare Levels: How Much Does It Cost to Make Ends Meet?" *Review of Economics and Statistics* 66 (3): 500-505.

Davis, Don, and John Gaventa. 1991. "Altered States: Grassroots Movements and Rural policy Formation." Paper presented at the Annual Meetings of the Rural Sociological Society, Columbus, OH: August.

Davis, Thomas F. 1979. *Persistent Low-Income Counties in Nonmetro America.* Rural Development Research Report 12. U.S. Department of Agriculture: Economics, Statistics, and Cooperative Service. Washington, D.C.: U.S. Government Printing Office.

De Janvry, Alain, and Phillip LeVeen. 1986. "Historical Forces that Have Shaped World Agriculture: A Structural Perspective." In Kenneth A. Dalberg (ed.), *New Directions for Agriculture and Agricultural Research: Neglected Dimensions and Emerging Alternatives.* Pp. 83-104. Totowa, NJ: Rowman and Allanheld.

De Jong, Gordon F., and James T. Fawcett. 1981. "Motivations for Migration: An Assessment and a Value-Expectancy Research Model." In Gordon F. De Jong and Robert W. Gardner (eds.), *Migration Decision Making: Multidiciplinary Approaches to Microlevel Studies in Developing Countries.* Pp. 13-58. New York, NY: Pergamon Press.

De Jong, Gordon F., and Robert W. Gardner. 1981. *Migration Decision Making: Multidisciplinary Approach to Microlevel Studies in Developed and Developing Countries.* New York, NY: Pergamon Press.

De Vroey, Michel. 1984. "A Regulation Approach Interpretation of the Contemporary Crisis." *Capital and Class* 23: 45-66.

Deavers, Kenneth, and Robert Hoppe, 1992. "Overview of the Rural Poor in the 1980s." In Cynthia M. Duncan (ed.), *Rural Poverty in America.* Pp. 3-20. New York, NY: Auburn House.

Deavers, Kenneth L., Robert A. Hoppe, and Peggy J. Ross. 1986. "Public Policy and Rural Poverty: A View from the 1980s." *Policy Studies Journal* 15(2): 291-309.

_____. 1988. "The Rural Poor: Policy Issues for the 1990s." Unpublished paper. U.S. Department of Agriculture, Economic Research Service.

DeLeon, Patrick, Mary Wakefield, Amy   J. Schultz, Jane Williams and Gary VandenBos. 1989. "Rural America: Unique Opportunities for Health Care Delivery and Health Services Research." *American Psychologist* 44(10): 1298-1306.

Davall, Bill, and George Sessions. 1985. *Deep Ecology: Living as if Nature Mattered.* Salt Lake City, UT: Peregrine Smith.

Devall, William B. 1988. *Simple in Means, Rich in Ends: Practicing Deep Ecology.* Salt Lake City, UT: Gibbs-Smith.

DeVanzo, Julie. 1981. "Micro-Economic Approaches to Studying Migration Decisions." In Gordon F. De Jong and Robert W. Gardner (eds.), *Migration Decision Making: Multidiciplinary Approaches to Microlevel Studies in Developing Countries.* Pp. 90-129. New York. NY: Pergamon Press.

_____. 1983. "Repeat Migration in the United States: Who Moves Back and Who Moves On?" *The Review of Economics and Statistics* 65(4): 552-559.

Devine, Joel A., Mark Plunkett, and James D. Wright. 1992. "The Chronicity of Poverty: Evidence from the PSID, 1968-1987." *Social Forces* 70(3): 787-812.

DeWitt, John, Sandra Batie and Kim Norris. 1988. *A Brighter Future For Rural America*. Washington, D.C.: National Governors Association.

Dickens, William T. and Kevin Lang. 1985. "A Test of Dual Labor Market Theory," *American Economic Review* 75(4): 792-805.

Dill, Bonnie Thornton. 1980. "'The Means to Put My Children Through': Child-Rearing Goals and Strategies Among Black Female Domestic Servants." In La Frances Rodgers-Rose (eds.), *The Black Woman*. Pp. 107-123. Beverly Hills, CA: Sage Publications.

Dill, Bonnie Thornton, and Bruce B. Williams. 1992. "Race, Gender, and Poverty in the Rural South: African American Single Mothers." In Cynthia M. Duncan (ed.), *Rural Poverty in America*. Pp. 97-109. New York, NY: Auburn House.

Dinkens, Julia M. 1991. "Perceptions of Well-being Among Three Age Cohorts of Rural Southern Elders." Annual Agricultural Outlook Conference, U.S. Department of Agriculture.

Doelker, Richard E, Jr., and Bonnie C. Bedics. 1989. "Impact of Rural Hospital Closings on the Community." *Social Work* 34: 541-543.

Doeringer, Peter B. 1984. "Internal Labor Markets and Paternalism in Rural Areas," in Paul Osterman (ed.), *Internal Labor Markets*. Pp. 271-289. Cambridge, MA: The MIT Press.

Doeringer, Peter B., and Michael J. Piore. 1971. *Internal Labor Markets and Manpower Analysis.* Lexington, MA: D.C. Heath.

Donnenwerth, G.V., R. Guy, and M.J. Norvell. 1978. "Life Satisfaction Among Older Persons: Rural-Urban and Racial Comparisons," *Social Service Quarterly* 59:578-583.

Dorris, Michael. 1989. *The Broken Chord*. New York, NY: Harper & Row Publishers.

Downs, Anthony. 1966. *Inside Bureaucracy*. Boston, MA: Little, Brown.

Drielsma, Johannes H. 1984. "The Influence of Forest Based Industries on Rural Communities." Unpublished Ph. D. dissertation, Yale University, School of Environmental Studies and Natural Resources.

Drielsma, Johannes H., Joseph A. Miller, and William R. Burch, Jr. 1990. "Sustained Yield and Community Stability in American Forestry," in Robert G. Lee, Donald R. Field, and William R. Burch; Jr. (eds.), *Community and Forestry: Continuities in the Sociology of Natural Resources*. Boulder, CO: Westview Press.

Drucker, Peter F. 1986. "The Changed World Economy." *Foreign Affairs* 64(4): 768-791.

Dubow, Eric F., and Tom Luster. 1990. "Adjustment of Children Born to Teenage Mothers: The Contribution of Risk and Protective Factors." *Journal of Marriage and the Family* 52:393-404.

Duncan, Beverly, and Stanley Lieberson. 1970. *Metropolis and Region in Transition*. New York, NY: Sage Publications.

Duncan, Cynthia M. 1992. *Rural Poverty in America*. New York, NY: New York Auburn House.

Duncan, Cynthia M., and Ann R. Tickamyer. 1988. "Poverty Research and Policy for Rural America." *American Sociologist* 19: 243-259.

Duncan, Greg J., and Saul D. Hoffman. 1985. "A Reconsideration of the Marital Consequences of Marital Dissolution." *Demography* 22(4): 485-497.

Duncan, Greg J., and Willard Rodgers. 1988. "Longitudinal Aspects of Childhood Poverty." *Journal of Marriage and the Family* 50(4): 1007-1021.

_____. 1991. "Has Children's Poverty Become More Persistent?" *American Sociological Review* 56(4): 538-550.

Duncan, S., and M. Goodwin. 1982. "The Local State and Restructuring Social Relations: Theory and Practice." *International Journal of Urban and Regional Research* 6(2): 157-186.

Easterlin, Richard A. 1980. *Birth and Fortune: The Impact of Numbers on Personal Welfare.* New York, NY: Basic Books.

Ecosometrics, Inc. 1981. *Review of Reported Differences Between the Rural and Urban Elderly: Status, Needs, Services, and Service Costs.* Washington, D.C.: Final Report for Administration on Aging, Contract No. 105-80-065.

Edin, Kathryn, and Christopher Jencks. 1992. "Reforming Welfare." C. Jencks, *Rethinking Social Policy: Race, Poverty, and the Underclass.* Pp. 204-35. Cambridge, MA: Harvard University Press.

Edwards, Clark. 1981. "The Basis for Regional Growth: A Review." In Lee R. Martin (ed.), *A Survey of Agricultural Economics Literature Economics of Welfare, Rural Development and Natural Resources in Agriculture 1940s-1970s.* Vol. 3, Pp. 159-282. Minneapolis, MI: University of Minnesota Press.

Edwards, Ozzie L. 1976. "Components of Academic Success: A Profile of Achieving Black Adolescents." *Journal of Negro Education* 45(4): 408-422.

Edwards, Richard. 1979. *Contested Terrain: The Transformation of the Work Place in the Twentieth Century.* New York, NY: Basic Books.

Eggebeen, David J., and Daniel T. Lichter. 1991. "Race, Family Structure, and Changing Poverty Among American Children." *American Sociological Review* 56: 801-817.

Ehrenberg, Ronald G., and Robert S. Smith. 1982. *Modern Labor Economics: Theory and Policy.* Gleenview, IL: Scott, Foresman and Co.

Elder, Glen H., Jr. 1974. *Children of the Great Depression: Social Changes in Life Experience.* Chicago, IL: University of Chicago Press.

_____. 1979. "Historical Change in Life Patterns and Personality." In Paul B. Baltes and Orvile G. Brim, Jr. (eds.), *Life Span Development and Behavior.* Pp. 117-159. New York, NY: Academic Press.

_____. 1985. "Perspectives on the Life Course." In Glen H. Elder, Jr. (ed.), *Life Course Dynamics: Trajectories and Transitions, 1968-1980.* Pp. 23-49. Ithaca, NY: Cornell University Press.

Elder, Glen H., Jr., and Avshalom Caspi. 1988. "Human Development and Social Change: An Emerging Perspective on the Life Course." In Niall Bolger, Avshalom Caspi, Geraldine Downey and Martha Moorhouse (eds.), *Persons in Context. Developmental Processes.* Pp. 77-113. Cambridge, MA: Cambridge University Press.

Elder, Glen H., Jr., Avshalom Caspi, and T. Van Nguyen. 1986. "Resourceful and Vulnerable Children: Family Influence in Hard Times." In R. K. Silbereisen and K. Eyferthand G. Rudinger (eds.), *Development as Action in Context: Problem Behavior and Normal Youth Development.* Pp. 167-186. Berlin, GR: Springer- Verlag.

Elder, Glen H., Jr., and Jeffrey K. Liker. 1982. "Hard Times in Women's Lives: Historical Influences Across Forty Years." *American Journal of Sociology* 88(2): 241-269.

Elder, Glen H., Jr., Jeffrey K. Liker, and Catherine E. Cross. 1984. "Parent-Child Behavior in the Great Depression: Life Course and Intergenerational Influences." In P. Baltes and O. Brim, Jr. (eds.), *Life-span Development and Behavior*. 6: 109-158. New York, NY: Academic Press.

Ellwood, David T. 1988. *Poor Support: Poverty in the American Family*. New York, NY: Basic Book.

England, Paula. 1982. "The Failure of Human Capital Theory to Explain Sex Segregation." *Journal of Human Resources* 17(3): 358-70.

Entwisle, Barbara, John B. Casterline, and Hussein A. -A. Sayed. 1989. "Villages as Contexts for Contraceptive Behavior in Rural Egypt." *American Sociological Review* 54(6): 1019-1034.

Entwisle, Doris R., and Karl L. Alexander. 1992. "Summer Setback: Race, Poverty, School Composition, and Mathematics Achievement in the First Two Years of School." *American Sociological Review* 57(1): 72-84.

Esping-Andersen, Gosta. 1990. *The Three Worlds of Welfare Capitalism*. Princeton, NJ: Princeton University Press.

Evensky, Jerry. 1991. "The Neoclassical Model Enriched by the Structure of Control: A Labor Market Illustration." *American Journal of Economics and Sociology* 50(2): 207-222.

Falk, William W., and Thomas A. Lyson. 1988. *High Tech, Low Tech, No Tech: Recent Industrial and Occupational Changing in the South*. Albany, NY: State University of New York Press.

Fapahounda, Eleanor. 1988. "The Nonpooling Household: Challenge to Theory," In Daisy Dwyer and Judith Bruce (eds.), *A Home Divided: Women and Income in the Third World*. Stanford (CA): Stanford University Press.

Farber, Stephen C., and Robert J. Newman. 1986. "A Test of the Spatial Convergence of Worker Characteristic Prices." Unpublished manuscript, Department of Economics, Louisiana State University, March.

Farley, Reynolds. 1988. "After the Starting Line: Blacks and Women in an Uphill Race." *Demography* 25: 477-95.

Farley, Reynolds, and Walter R. Allen. 1987. *The Color Line and the Quality of Life in America*. New York, NY: Russell Sage Foundation.

Featherman, David L., and Robert M. Hauser. 1978. *Opportunity and Change*. New York, NY: Academic Press.

Felson, Richard B. 1990. "Blame Analysis: Accounting for the Behavior of Protected Groups." *American Sociologist* 22(1): 5-23.

Findeis, Jill L. 1992. "Gender Differences in Human Capital in Rural America." In Lionel J. Beaulieu, and David Mulkey (eds.), *Investing in People: The Human Capital Needs of Rural America*. Boulder, CO: Westview Press.

Fink, Deborah. [1989] 1986. *Open Country, Iowa: Rural Women, Tradition and Change*. Albany, NY: SUNY Press.

Fitchen, Janet M. 1981. *Poverty in Rural America: A Case Study*. Boulder, CO: Westview Press.

_____. 1990. "Poverty as a Context for Old Age in Rural America," *Journal of Rural Community Psychology* 11(1): 31-50.

_____. 1991. *Endangered Spaces, Enduring Places: Change, Identity and Survival in Rural America*. Boulder, CO: Westview Press.

_____. 1992. "Poverty and the 'Single-Parent Family': Is Marriage a Panacea for Poverty?" Paper presented at the annual meetings of the Society for Applied Anthropology, Memphis, TN.

Fite, Gilbert Courtland. 1981. *American Farmers: The New Minority*. Bloomington, IN: Indiana University Press.

Fligstein, Neil. 1981. *Going North: Migration of Backs and Whites From the South, 1900-1950*. New York, NY: Academic Press.

Flora, Cornelia Butler. 1992. "The New Poor in Midwestern Farming." In Cynthia M. Duncan (ed.), *Rural Poverty in America*. Pp. 201-211. New York, NY: Auburn House.

Flora, Cornelia Butler, and James A. Christenson. 1991. *Rural Policies for the 1990s*. Boulder, CO: Westview Press.

Flora, Cornelia, and Jan L. Flora. 1988. "Characteristics of Entrepreneurial Communities in Time of Crisis." *Rural Development News* 12(2): 1-4.

Flora, Jan L., and Cornelia Butler Flora. 1986. "Emerging Agricultural Technologies, Farm Size, Public Policy, and Rural Communities: The Great Plains and the West." In *Technology, Public Policy and the Changing Structure of American Agriculture*. Vol 2, Pp. 168-212. Background Papers, Part D: Rural Communities, Washington, D.C.: Office of Technology Assessment.

Flora, Jan L., James J. Chriss, Eddie Gale, Gary Green, Frederick Schmidt, and Cornelia Flora. 1991. *From the Grassroots: Profiles of 103 Rural Self-Development Projects*. Agriculture and Rural Economy Division, Economic Research Service, USDA, Staff Report N. 9123. Washington, DC: U.S. Government Printing Office.

Forest Trust. 1991. *Forest-Based, Rural Development Practitioners*. Directory 1991-1992. Santa Fe: Forest Trust-The Tides Foundation.

Fortmann, Louise P., and Nancy L. Peluso. 1992. "Processes and Structures that Cause Rural Poverty in Natural Resource-Dependent Areas of the United States." Unpublished manuscript prepared for the Working Group on Poverty and Natural Resources, Rural Sociology Task Force on Persistent Poverty in Rural America.

Fosler, R. Scott 1988. *The New Economic Role of American States: Strategies in a Competitive World Economy*. New York, NY: Oxford University Press.

Frank, Andre Gunder. 1967. *Capitalism and Underdevelopment in Latin America: Historical Studies of Chile and Brazil*. New York, NY: Monthly Review Press.

Fraser, Nancy. 1989. *Unruly Practices: Power, Discourse and Gender in Contemporary Social Theory*. Minneapolis, MN: University of Minnesota Press.

Freedman, Marcia K. 1976. *Labor Markets: Segments and Shelters*. Montclair, NJ: Allanheld, Osmun.

Freshwater, David. 1989. "Synopsis of the Proceedings of the Rural Development Symposium" in Joint Economic Committee. *Towards Rural Development Policy for the 1990's*. S. Prt. 101-50. Washington, D.C.: U.S. Government Printing Office.

Freudenburg, William R. 1991. "Addictive Economies: Extractive Industries and Vulnerable Localities in a Changing World Economy." Presentation at the meeting of the Rural Sociological Society, Columbus, OH, August.

Friedland, William H., Amy E. Borton, and Robert J. Tomas. 1981. *Manufacturing Green Gold: Capital, Labor, and Technology in the Lettuce Industry*. Cambridge, MA: Cambridge University Press.

Friedmann, Harriet. 1987. "Agro-food Industries and Export Agriculture: The Changing International Division of Labor, 1945-73." Paper presented at the annual meetings of the Rural Sociological Society, Madison, WI, August.

Fröbel, Falker, Jürgen Heinrichs, and Otto Kreye. 1980. *The New International Division of Labour: Structural Unemployment in Industrialized Countries and Industrialization in Developing Countries*. Translated by Peter Burger. Cambridge, MA: Cambridge University Press.

Fuchs, Victor Robert, and Diane M. Reklis. 1992. "America's Children: Economic Perspectives and Policy Options." *Science* 255(January 3): 41-46.

Fuguitt, Glenn V., David L. Brown, and Calvin L. Beale. 1989. *Rural And Small Town America*. New York, NY: Russell Sage Foundation.

Fullerton, Howard N., Jr. 1989. "New Labor Force Projections, Spanning 1988 to 2000." *Monthly Labor Review* 112(11): 3-12.

Furstenberg, Frank F., Jeanne Brooks-Gunn, and Lindsay Chase-Lansdale. 1989. "Teenaged Pregnancy and Childbearing." *American Psychologist* 44(2): 313-320.

Galarza, Ernesto. 1977. *Farm Workers and Agri-Business in California: 1947-1960*. Notre Dame, IN: University of Notre Dame Press.

Galbraith, John Kenneth. 1967. *The New Industrial State*. Boston, MA: Houghton Mifflin.

Gallaway, L., and R. Vedder. 1986. *Paying People to Be Poor*. Dallas, TX: National Center for Policy Analysis.

Galston, William. 1988. "U.S. Rural Economic Development in a Competitive Global Economy." In Gene F. Summers, John Bryden, Kenneth Deavers, Howard Newly and Susan Sechler (eds.), *Agriculture and Beyond: Rural Economic Development*. Pp. 1-9. Madison, WI: University of Wisconsin-Madison, College of Agricultural and Life Sciences.

Garbarino, James. 1985. *Adolescent Development: An Ecological Perspective*. Columbus, OH: Charles E. Merrill.

Garbarino, James, and Kathleen Kostelny. In press. "Child Maltreatment as a Community Problem." *Child Abuse and Neglect* (Forthcoming).

Garcia Coll, Cynthia T. 1990. "Developmental Outcome of Minority Infants: A Process-oriented Look into Our Beginnings." *Child Development* 61(2):270-289.

Garfinkel, Irwin, and Sara S. McLanahan. 1986. *Single Mothers and Their Children: The New American Dilemma*. Washington, D.C.: Urban Institute Press.

Garkovich, Lorraine. 1989. *Population and Community in Rural America*. New York, NY: Praeger.

Garmezy, Norman. 1992. "Resiliency and Vulnerability to Adverse Developmental Outcomes Associated with Poverty." In Travis Thompson and Susan C. Hupp (eds.), *Saving Children at Risk: Poverty and Disabilities*. Pp. 45-60. Newbury Park, CA: Sage Publications.

Garrett, Patricia. 1986. "Social Stratification and Multiple Enterprises: Some Implications for Family Systems Research." *Journal of Rural Studies* 2: 209-220.

Garrett, Patricia, Nicholas Ng'andu, and John Ferron. Forthcoming. "The Poverty Experiences of Young Children and Their Consequences for Child Development." Frank Porter Graham Child Development Center, University of North Carolina, Chapel Hill, NC., Forthcoming.

Garrett, Patricia, and Sally Lubeck. 1988. "Family-Based Child Care: Implications for Social Policy." *Journal of Applied Social Sciences* 12(2): 142-169.

Gaventa, John. 1980. *Power and Powerlessness: Quiescence and Rebellion in an Appalachian Valley*. Urbana, IL: University of Illinois Press.

Geiger, H. Jack. 1984. "Community Health Centers: Health Care as an Instrument of Social Change." In Victor W. Sidel and Ruth Sidel (eds.), *Reforming Medicine: Lessons of the Last Quarter Century*. Pp. 11-32. New York, NY: Pantheon Books.

Geisler, Charles C. 1991. "Insights and Oversights: Land Alienation and Poverty in the United States." Presentation at the meeting of the Rural Sociological Society, Columbus, OH, August.

Gershuny, Jonathan I. 1978. *After Industrial Society: The Emerging Self-Service Economy*. London, UK: Macmillan.

_____. 1988. "Time, Technology, and the Informal Economy." Pp. 579-597 in R.E. Pahl (ed), *On Work: Historical, Comparative and Theoretical Approaches*. Oxford, UK: Basil Blackwell.

Getz, Virginia K., and Robert A. Hoppe. 1983. "The Changing Characteristics of the Nommetro Poor," *Social Development Issues* 7(1):29-44.

Ghelfi, Linda. 1988. "About That Lower Cost of Living in Nonmetro Areas," *Rural Development Perspectives* 5(1):30-34.

Gibbs, Jack P., and Walter T. Martin. 1958 . "Urbanization and Natural Resources: A Study in Organizational Ecology." *American Sociological Review* 23(3): 266-77.

_____. 1959. "Toward a Theoretical System of Human Ecology." *Pacific Sociological Review* 2: 29-36.

Giddens, Anthony. 1979. *Central Problems in Social Theory: Action, Structure and Contradiction in Social Analysis*. London UK: MacMillan.

_____. 1981. *A Contemporary Critique of Historical Materialism*. Berkeley, CA: University of California Press.

_____. 1984. *The Constitution of Society: Outline of the Theory of Structuration*. Berkeley: University of California Press.

Gilder, George. 1981. *Wealth and Poverty*. New York, NY: Basic Books.

Gjerde, Jon. 1985. *From Peasants to Farmers: The Migration from Balestrand, Norway to the Upper Middle West*. New York, NY: Cambridge University Press.

Glasgow, Nina. 1988. *The Nonmetro Elderly: Economic and Demographic Status*. Agriculture and Rural Economy Division, Economic Research Service, U.S. Department of Agriculture, Rural Development Research Report No. 70 (June). Washington, D.C.: U.S Government Printing Office.

_____. 1991. "Conceptualization of Poverty Among the Rural Elderly." Paper Presented to the Annual Meeting of the Rural Sociological Society. Columbus, OH, August.

Glasgow, Nina, and Calvin L. Beale. 1985. "Rural Elderly in Demographic Perspective," *Rural Development Perspectives* 2(1): 22-26.

Glasmeier, Amy. 1990. "Rural Development in a Global Economy." In D. Otto and S. Deller (eds.), *Alternative Perspectives on Development Prospects for Rural Areas: Proceedings of Symposium at AAEA Annual Meetings*. Pp. 5-26. Vancouver, B.C., Aug. 4-8.

Goedhart, Theo, Victor Halberstadt, Arie Kapteyn, and Bernard M. S. Van Praag. 1977. "The Poverty Line: Concept and Measurement." *Journal of Human Resources* 12 (4): 503-20.

Goldschmidt, Walter. 1946. "Small Business and the Community: A Study in the Central Valley of California on the Effects of Scale of Farm Operation." Report of the Special Committee to Study Problems of American Small Business, U.S. Senate, 79th Congress, 2nd Session, Committee Print 13. Washington, DC: U.S. Government Printing Office.

_____. [1947] 1978. *As You Sow: Three Studies in the Social Consequences of Agribusiness*. Montclair, NJ: Allanheld, Osmun.

Goldstein, G. S., and T. J. Gronberg. 1984. "Economies of Scope and Economics of Agglomeration." *Journal of Urban Economics* 16(1):91-104.

Goodman, John L. 1981. "Information, Uncertainty, and the Microeconomic Model of Decision Making." In Gordon F. De Jong and Robert W. Gardner (eds.), *Migration Decision Making: Multidiciplinary Approaches to Microlevel Studies in Developing Countries*. Pp. 130-148. New York, NY: Pergamon Press.

Gordon, David M., Richard Edwards, and Michael Reich. 1982. *Segmented Work, Divided Workers: The Historical Transformation of Labor in the United States*. Cambridge, MA: Cambridge University Press.

Gordon, Linda. 1990. "The New Feminist Scholarship on the Welfare State." In Linda Gordon (ed.), *Women, the State, and Welfare*. Pp. 9-35. Madison, WI: University of Wisconsin Press.

Gorham, Lucy. 1992. "The Growing Problem of Low Earnings in Rural Areas." In Cynthia M. Duncan (ed.) *Rural Poverty in America*. Pp. 21-39. New York, NY: Auburn House.

Goss, Kevin, Richard Rodefeld, and Frederick H. Buttel. 1980. "The Political Economy of Class Structure in U.S. Agriculture." In Frederick H. Buttel and Howard Newby, (eds.), *The Rural Sociology of Advanced Societies: Critical Perspectives*. Pp. 83-132. Montclair, NJ: Allanheld, Osmum.

Gottdiener, Mark. 1985. *The Social Production of Urban Space*. Austin, TX: Univerity of Texas Press.

Gottfredson, Stephen D., and Ralph B. Taylor. 1986. "Person-Environment Interactions in the Prediction of Recidivism." In James M. Bryne and Robert J. Sampson (eds.), *The Social Ecology of Crime*. Pp. 133-155. New York, NY: Springer-Verlog.

Gottschalk, P. and S. Danziger. 1985. "A Framework for Evaluating the Effects of Economic Growth and Transers on Poverty." *American Economic Review* 75(1): 153-161.

Grams, Armin, and Alfred P. Fengler. 1981. "Vermont Elders: No Sense of Deprivation," *Perspective on Aging* 10(1): 12-15.

Granovetter, Mark S. 1974. *Getting a Job: A Study of Contacts and Careers.*
Cambridge, MA: Harvard University Press.
_____. 1985. "Economic Action and Social Structure: The Problem of
Embeddedness." *American Journal of Sociology* 91(3): 481-510.
Green, Gary P. 1984. "Credit and Agriculture: Some Consequences of the Centralization
of the Banking System." *Rural Sociology* 49(4): 568-579.
_____. 1987. *Finance Capital and Uneven Development.* Boulder, CO:
Westview Press.
Green, Gary P., Jan L. Flora, Cornelia Flora, and Frederick E. Schmidt. 1990. "Local
Self-Development Strategies: National Survey Results." *Journal of the Community
Development Society* 21(2): 55-73.
Greenstein, Robert. 1989. "Welfare Reform in Rural Areas," in The Congressional
Research Service (eds.), *Towards Rural Development Policy for the 1990'S:
Enhancing Income and Employment Opportunities: A Symposium.* Pp. 35-40.
Washington, DC: U.S. G.P.O., U.S. Government Printing Office.
Greenstein, Robert, and Isaac Shapiro. 1992. "Policies to Alleviate Rural Poverty."
In Cynthia M. Duncan (ed.), *Rural Poverty in America.* Pp. 249-63. New York,
NY:Auburn House.
Greenwood, Michael J. 1975. "Research on Internal Migration in the United States: A
Survey." *Journal of Economic Literature* 13: 397-433.
Grieco, Margaret. 1987. *Keeping It in the Family: Social Networks and Employment
Chance.* London, UK: Tavistock Publications.
Gringeri, Christina E. 1990a. "Industrial Homework as a Rural Development Strategy,"
dissertation proposal, Department of Social Welfare, University of Wisconsin.
_____. 1990b. "The Nuts and Bolts of Subsidized Development: Industrial
Homework in Two Rural Midwestern Communities." Ph.D. Thesis, University of
Wisconsin-Madison.
Gunn, Christopher Eaton, and Hazel Dayton Gunn. 1991. *Reclaiming Capital:
Democratic Initiatives and Community Development.* Ithaca, NY: Cornell University
Press.
Gwynn, D. B., Y Kawamura, E. Dolber-Smith, and R. I. Rochin. 1989. *California's
Rural Poor: Trends, Correlates and Policies.* Davis, CA: California Institute for
Rural Studies.
Hadwiger, Don F. 1976. "The Old, the New, and the Emerging United States
Department of Agriculture." *Public Administration Review* 36(2): 155-165.
Hagenaars, Aldi J. M. 1986. *The Perception of Poverty.* Amerstandm: North Holland
Publishing Co.
Hagenaars, Aldi J. M., and Klaas de Vos. 1988. "The Definition and Measurement of
Poverty," *Journal of Human Resources* 23(2): 211-221.
Hall, Peter A. 1989. *Governing the Economy: The Politics of State Intervention in
Britain and France.* New York, NY: Oxford University Press.
Haller, Archibald O. 1982. "Reflections on the Social Psychology of Status
Attainment." In Robert M. Hauser, David Mechanic, Archibald O. Haller, and Taissa
S. Hauser (eds). *Social Structure and Behavior.* Pp. 3-28. New York, NY: Academic
Press.

Hamilton, David E. 1991. *From New Day to New Deal: American Farm Policy from Hoover to Roosevelt, 1928-1933*. Chapel Hill, NC: University of North Carolina Press.

Hamilton, Stephen F. 1990. *Apprenticeship for Adulthood: Preparing Youth for the Future*. New York, NY: Free Press.

Handler, Joel F., and Yeheskel Hasenfeld. 1991. *The Moral Construction of Poverty: Welfare Reform in America*. Newbury Park, CA: Sage Publications, Inc.

Haney, Wava G., and Jane B. Knowles. 1988. *Women and Farming: Changing Roles, Changing Structure*. Boulder, CO: Westview Press.

Hansen, John Mark. 1987a. "Choosing Sides: The Development of an Agriculture Policy Network in Congress, 1919-1932." *Studies in American Political Development* 2: 183-229.

_____. 1987b. "The Ever-decreasing Grandstand: Constraint and Change in an Agricultural Policy Network, 1948-1980." Paper presented at annual meeting of the American Political Science Association, Chicago, IL, August.

_____. 1991. *Gaining Access: Congress and the Farm Lobby, 1919-1981*. Chicago, IL: University of Chicago Press.

Hansen, Niles M. 1990. "Innovative Regional Milieux, Small Firms and Regional Development: Evidence from Mediterranean France." *The Annals of Regional Science* 24(2): 107-123.

_____. 1991. "Endogenous Growth Centers: Small Firms and Flexible Production Systems In Rural Denmark." Department of Economics, University of Texas, Austin, Texas.

Harbin, Gloria L. 1990. "Early Identification: The Challenge to Develop Effective Policies." *Infants and Young Children* 2(1): vi-ix.

Hardin, C. 1952. *The Politics of Agriculture: Soil Conservation and the Struggle for Power in Rural America*. Glencoe, IL: The Free Press.

_____. 1967. *Food and Fiber in the Nation's Politics Vol. III*. Washington, D.C.: National Advisory Committee on Food and Fiber: August.

Harding, Sandra. 1987. "The Instability of the Analytical Categories of Feminist Theory." In Sandra Harding and Jean F. O'Barr (eds.), *Sex and Scientific Inquiry*. Pp. 283-302. Chicago, IL: University of Chicago Press.

Hardy, Donald. F., II. 1983. "Federal Assistance for Rural Development: The Train that Passed in the Night?" *The Rural Sociologist* 3(3): 392-398.

Harris, Chris. 1987. "The Individual and Society: A Processual Approach." In Alan Bryman, Bill Bytheway, Patricia Allatt and Teresa Keil (eds.), *Rethinking the Life Cycle*. Pp. 17-29. London, UK: The Macmillan Press Ltd.

Harrison, Bennett. 1974. "The Theory of the Dual Economy." In Bertram Silverman and Murray Yanowitch (eds.), *The Worker in "Post Industrial" Capitalism: Liberal and Radical Responses*. Pp. 269-287. New York, NY: Free Press.

_____. 1984. "Regional Restructuring and 'Good Business Climates': The Economic Transformation of New England Since World War II." In Larry Sawers and William K. Tabb (eds.), *Sunbelt/Snowbelt: Urban Development and Regional Restructuring*. Pp. 48-98. New York, NY: Oxford University Press.

_____. 1992. "Industrial Districts: Old Wine in New Bottles?" *Regional Studies* (forthcoming).

Hartmann, Heidi. 1976. "Capitalism, Patriarchy, and Job Segregation by Sex." In Martha Blaxall and Barbara Reagan (eds.), *Women and the Workplace*. Pp. 137-169. Chicago, IL: University of Chicago Press.

Harvey, David. 1985. *Urbanization of Capital: Studies in the History and Theory of Capitalist Urbanization*. Baltimore, MD: Johns Hopkins University Press.

_____. 1988. "The Geographical and Geopolitical Consequences of the Transition from Fordist to Flexible Accumulation." In George Sternlieb and James W. Hughes (eds.), *America's New Market Geography: Nation, Region, and Metropolis*. Pp. 101-134. New Brunswick, NJ: Rutgers University Press.

_____. 1989. *The Condition of Postmodernity: An Inquiry Into the Origins of Cultural Changes*. Oxford, UK: Basil Blackwell.

Haskins, Ron. 1989. "Beyond Metaphor: The Efficacy of Early Childhood Education." *American Psychologist* 44(2): 274-282.

Hauser, Robert M. 1991. "What Happens to Youth After High School?" *Focus* 13(3): 1-13.

Havens, A. Eugene. 1986. "Capitalist Development in the United States: State, Accumulation, and Agricultural Production Systems." In A. Eugene Havens, Gregory Hooks, Patrick H. Mooney, and Max J. Pfeffer (eds.), *Studies in the Transformation of U.S. Agriculture*. Boulder, CO: Westview Press.

Hawley, Amos Henry. 1950. *Human Ecology: A Theory of Community Structure*. New York, NY: Ronald Press Co.

_____. 1984. "Human Ecological and Marxian Theories." *American Journal of Sociology*. 89(4): 904-17.

Hays, Samuel P. 1987. *Beauty, Health, and Permanence. Environmental Politics in the United States, 1955-1985*. New York: Cambridge University Press.

Hays, Samuel P. and Barbara D. Jays 1987. *Beauty, Health, and Permanence: Environmental Politics in the United States, 1955-1985*. New York, NY: Cambridge University Press.

Hayslip, Bert, Jr., Mary Lou Ritter, Ruth M. Oltman, and Connie McDonnell. 1980. "Home Care Services and the Rural Elderly," *The Gerontologist* 20(2): 192-199.

Heaton, Tim B. 1991. "Family and Household Structure and Change in Rural America." Discussion paper for the conference on Population Change and the Future of Rural America, Wye Foundation, Maryland.

Hechter, Michael. 1975. *Internal Colonialism: The Celtic Fringe in British National Development - 1536-1866*. Berkeley, CA: University of California Press.

Heclo, Hugh. 1992. "Poverty Politics." Institute for Research on Poverty Conference Paper, mimeo. Madison, WI: Institute for Research on Poverty, University of Wisconsin-Madison.

Heffernan, William D., and Judy B. Heffernan. 1986. "Sociological Needs of Farmers Facing Severe Economic Problems." In Farm Foundation (ed.), *Increasing Understanding of Public Problems and Policies*. Pp. 90-102. Brook, IL: Farm Foundation.

Hendler, Charles I., and J. Norman Reid. 1980. *Federal Outlays in Fiscal 1978: A Comparison of Metropolitan and Nonmetropolitan Areas.* Rural Development Research Report No. 25. Washington, DC: Economics, Statistics, and Cooperatives Service, U.S. Department of Agriculture. U.S Government Printing Office. Washington, DC: U.S. Government Printing Office.

Henretta, John C., and Richard T. Campbell. 1976. "Status Attainment and Status Maintenance: A Study of Stratification in Old Age," *American Sociological Review* 41(6): 981-992.

Henry, Mark S., Mark Drabenstott, and Lynn Gibson. 1986. "A Changing Rural America." *Economic Review* 71: 23-41.

_____. 1987. "Rural Growth Slows Down," *Rural Development Perspectives,* 3(3): 25-30.

Herring, Edward Pendleton. 1936. *Public Administration and the Public Interest.* New York, NY: McGraw Hill.

Hess, Beth B. 1986. "Antidiscrimination Policies Today and the Life Chances of Older Women Tomorrow." *The Gerontologist* 26(2): 132-135.

Hester, Randy. 1985. "Subconscious Places of the Heart." *Places* 2: 10-22.

Hetherington, E. Mavin, Kathleen A. Camara, and David L. Featherman. 1983. "Achievement and Intellectual Functioning: Children in One-Parent Households." In Janet T. Spence, ed., *Achievement and Achievement Motives: Psychological and Sociological Approaches.* Pp. 208-284. San Francisco, CA: W. H. Freeman and Co.

Hickey, JoAnn S. 1992. "Uneven Development in Rural Southern Counties, 1959-1984." Unpublished Ph.D. dissertation. Ithaca, NY: Cornell University.

Hicks, J. R., M. A., and B. Litt. 1932. *The Theory of Wages.* London, UK: Macmillan.

Hildreth, R. J., and Walter J. Armbruster. 1981. "Extension Program Delivery: Past, Present and Future: An Overview." *American Journal of Agricultural Economics* 63:853-858.

Hill, Robert B. 1972. *The Strength of Black Families.* New York, NY: National Urban League.

Hirschl, Thomas A., and Gene F. Summers. 1984. "Shifts in Rural Income: The Implications of Unearned Income for Rural Community Development." *Research in Rural Sociology and Development* 2: 127-141.

Hirst, Stefen. 1985. *Havsuw 'Baaja: People of the Blue Green Water.* Supai, AZ: Havasupai Tribe.

Hobbs, Daryl. 1991. "Rural Education." In Cornelia B. Flora and James A. Christenson, (eds.), *Rural Policies for the 1990s.* Pp. 151-165. Boulder, CO: Westview Press.

Hodge, Robert W., and Barbara A. Laslett. 1980. "Poverty and Status Attainment." In Vincent T. Covello (ed.), *Poverty and Public Policy: An Evaluation of Social Science Research.* Pp. 126-163. Cambridge, MA: Schenkman Publishers, Co.

Hodson, Randy. 1978. "Labor in the Monopoly, Competitive, and State Sectors of Production." *Politics and Society* 8:429-480.

_____. 1983. *Worker's Earnings and Corporate Economic Structure.* New York, NY: Academic Press.

Hofferth, Sandra L. 1987. "Child Care in the U.S." Paper presented before the Select Committee on Children, Youth, and Families, June.

Hoffman, Soul, and John Holmes. 1976. "Husbands, Wives and Divorce." In Gregy Duncan and James Morgan (Eds.), *Five Thousand American Families: Patterns of Economic Progress*. Vol. 4, Pp. 23-75. Ann Arbor, MI: Inst. Soc. Research.

Holden, Karen C. 1989a. "The Transition from Wife to Widow: Data Issues in Measuring First-Period Income Effects in SIPP and the RHS." In Bureau of the Census, *Individuals and Families in Transition: Understanding Change through Longitudinal Data*. Washington, D.C.: U.S. Government Publishing Office.

_____. 1989b. "Women's Economic Status in Old Age and Widowhood." In Martha N. Ozawa (Ed.), *Women's Life Cycle and Economic Insecurity: Problems and Proposals*. Pp. 143-169. Westport, CT: Greenwood Press.

Holden, Karen C., and Richard V. Burkhauser. 1986. "Pensioners' Annuity Choice: Is the Well-Being of Widows Considered?" Discussion Paper no. 802, Institute for Research on Poverty, University of Wisconsin.

Holden, Karen C., Richard V. Burkhauser, and Daniel A. Myers. 1986. "Income Transitions at Older Stages of Life: The Dynamics of Poverty," *The Gerontologist* 26(3): 292-297.

Holden, Karen C., and Timothy Smeeding. 1990. "The Poor, the Rich, and the Insecure Elderly Caught in Between," *The Milbank Quarterly* 68(2): 191-219.

Holmes, John. 1986. "The Organization and Locational Structure of Production Subcontracting." In Allen Scott and Michael Storper (eds.), *Production, Work and Territory: The Geographical Anatomy of Industrial Capitalism*. Pp. 80-105. Boston, MA: Allen and Unwin.

Hooks, Gregory. 1990. "From an Autonomous to a Captured State Agency: The Decline of the New Deal in Agriculture." *American Sociological Review* 55(1): 29-43.

_____. 1991. *Forging the Military-Industry Complex: World War II's Battle of the Potomac*. Urbana, IL: University of Illinois Press.

Hoover, Edgar Malone. 1948. *The Location of Economic Activity*. New York, NY: McGraw-Hill Books Co.

_____. 1971. *An Introduction to Regional Economics*. New York, NY: Alfred A. Knopf.

Hoppe, Robert A. 1979. *Effects of Geographic Cost of Living Adjustments on Welfare Benefits*. Rural Development Research Report 16. U.S. Department of Agriculture: Economics, Statistics, and Cooperatives Services. Washington, D.C.: U.S. Government Printing Office.

_____. 1985. *Economic Structure and Change in Persistently Low-Income Nonmetro Counties*, Rural Development Research Report 50. U.S. Department of Agriculture, Economic Research Service. Washington, D.C.: U.S. Government Printing Office.

_____. 1988. "Appendix--Nonmetro Poverty: Trends and Technicalities," in *Towards Rural Development Policy for the 1990s: Enhancing Income and Employment Opportunities*. S. Prt. 101-50. Proceedings of a symposium sponsored by the Congressional Research Service at the request of the Joint Economic committee. 101st Congress, 1st Session.

_____. 1989. "Poverty in Rural America: The Statistical Evidence," *Outreach to the Rural Disadvantaged: Issues and Strategies for the 21st Century*. Ntam Baharanyi, Robert Zabawa, and Walter Hill (eds.). Proceedings of the 47th Annual Professional Agricultural Workers Conference. Tuskegee, Al: Tuskegee University.

_____. 1991. "Rural Poverty Stabilizes," *Rural Conditions and Trends*, 2(1): 16-17.

_____. 1992. "The Family Support Act, Our Beliefs, and Rural America," *The Family Support Act: Will It Work in Rural Areas?* Robert Hoppe (ed.). Rural Development Research Report. Economic Research Service, U.S. Department of Agriculture (forthcoming).

Hoppe, Robert A., and Donald L. Bellamy. 1989. "Rural Poverty: A Continuing Problem. " Paper presented at a Washington Statistical Society Lecture, Washington, D.C.

Hoppe, Robert A., and Kenneth L. Deavers. 1992. "Beyond the Family Support Act," *The Family Support Act: Will It Work in Rural Areas?* Robert A. Hoppe (ed.). Rural Development Research. Economic Research Service, U.S. Department of Agriculture (forthcoming).

Horan, Patrick M., and Charles M. Tolbert. 1984. *The Organization of Work in Rural and Urban Labor Markets*. Boulder, CO: Westview Press.

Horton, Hayward D. 1992. "A Sociological Approach to Black Community Development: Presentation of the Black Organizational Autonomy Model." *Journal of the Community Development Society* (forthcoming).

Hudson, Roy, and David Sadler. 1988. "Contesting Work Closures in Western Europe's Old Industrial Regions: Defending Place or Betraying Class." In Allen Scott and Michael Storper (eds.), *Production, Work, Territory: The Geographical Anatomy of Industrial Capitalism*. Pp. 172-193. Boston, MA: Allen and Unwin.

Hurd, M., and D. A. Wise. 1989. "The Wealth and Poverty of Widows: Assets Before and After the Husband's Death." In D.A. Wise (Ed.), *The Economics of Aging*. Chicago: Univ. of Chicago Press.

Huston, Aletha C. 1991. *Children in Poverty: Child Development and Public Policy*. Cambridge: Cambridge University Press.

Hynson, Lawrence M. 1976. Rural-Urban Differences in Satisfaction Among the Elderly," *Rural Sociology* 40(1):64-66.

Inglehart, Ronald. 1990. *Culture Shift in Advanced Industrial Society*. Princeton, NJ: Princeton University Press.

Institute for Research on Poverty, University of Wisconsin-Madison. 1980. "On Not Reaching the Rural Poor: Urban Bias in Poverty Policy," *Focus*, 4(2): 5-8.

Jacobs, David. 1982. "Competition, Scale and Political Explanations for Inequality: An Integrated Study of Sectoral Explanations at the Aggregate Level." *American Sociological Review* 47(5): 600-614.

Jacobs, Jerry. 1989. "Long-Term Trends in Occupational Segregation by Sex." *American Journal of Sociology* 95: 160-173.

James, David R. 1986. "Local State Structure and the Transformation of Southern Agriculture." In A. E. Havens, Gregory Hooks, Patrick H. Mooney, and Max J. Pfeffer, (eds.), *Studies in the Transformation of U.S. Agriculture*. Pp. 150-178. Boulder, CO: Westview Press.

Jasper, James M., and Dorothy Nelkin. 1992. *The Animal Rights Crusade: The Growth of a Moral Protest*. New York, NY: Maxwell Macmillan International.

Jencks, Christoper. 1991. "Is the American Underclass Growing?" In Christopher Jencks and Paul E. Peterson (eds.), *The Urban Underclass*. Pp. 28-100. Washington, D.C.: Brookings Institution.

_____. 1992. *Rethinking Social Policy: Race, Poverty, and the Underclass*. Cambridge, MA: Harvard University Press.

Jencks, Christopher, Marshall Smith, Henry Acland, Mary Jo Bane, David cohen, Herbert Gintis, Barbara Heyns, and Stephan Michelson. 1972. *Inequality: A Reassessment of the Effect of Family and Schooling in America*. New York, NY: Basic Books Inc.

Jencks, Christopher, and Paul E. Peterson. 1991. *The Urban Underclass*. Washington, D.C.: Brookings Institution.

Jencks, Christopher, and Susan E. Mayer. 1990. "The Social Consequences of Growing Up in a Poor Neighborhood." In Laurence E. Lynn Jr. and Michael G. H. McGeary (eds.), *Inner-City Poverty in the United States*. Pp. 111-186. Washington, DC: National Academy Press.

Jensen, Helen H. 1982. "Analysis of Fringe Benefits for Nonmetropolitan versus Metropolitan Employee Compensation," *American Jounral of Agricultural Economics* 64(1): 124-128.

_____. 1983. *Farm People's Health Insurance Coverage* RDRR No. 39. Washington, D.C.: Economic Research Service, U.S. Department of Agriculture.

Jensen, Helen, and Priscilla Salant. 1985. "The Role of Fringe Benefits in Operator Off-Farm Labor Supply." *American Journal of Agricultural Economics* 67(5): 1096-1099.

Jensen, Joan M. 1990. "Rural Families in Transition." In *National Rural Studies Committee: A Proceedings*. Pp. 9-19. Cedar Falls, IA: National Rural Studies Committee.

Jensen, Leif. 1989. "Rural-Urban Differences in the Utilization and Ameliorative Effects of Welfare Programs." In Harrell R. Rodgers, Jr. and Gregory Weiher (eds.), *Rural Poverty: Special Causes and Policy Reform*. Pp. 25-39. New York, NY: Greenwood Press.

_____. 1991. "The Doubly Jeopardized: Nonmetropolitan Blacks and Mexicans." In C.B. Flora and J.A. Christenson (eds.), *Rural Policies for the 1990s*. Pp. 181-193. Boulder, CO: Westview Press.

Jensen, Leif, and Diane K. McLaughlin. 1992. "The Family Support Act and Aid to Families with Dependent Children: Implications for Nonmetro Areas," *The Family Support Act: Will It Work in Rural Areas?* Robert A. Hoppe (ed.). Rural Development Research. Economic Research Service, U.S. Department of Agriculture (forthcoming).

Jensen, Leif, and Marta Tienda. 1989. "Nonmetropolitan Minority Families in the United States: Trends in Racial and Ethic Economic Stratification, 1959-1986." *Rural Sociology* 54: 509-532.

Jessop, Bob. 1990. *State Theory: Putting the Capital State in Its Place*. Cambridge, UK. Polity Press.

Jewett, Claudia L. 1978. *Adopting the Older Child*. Harvard, MA.: Harvard Common Press.

Johansen, Harley E., and Glenn V. Fuguitt. 1990. "The Changing Rural Village." *Rural Development Perspectives* 6(2): 2-7.

Johnson, Alice K. 1989. "Measurement and Methodology: Problems and Issues in Research on Homelessness." *Social Work Research and Abstracts* 25(4): 12-20.

Johnson, Glenn L. 1980. "Theoretical Considerations." In Glenn L. Johnson and C. Leroy Quance, (eds.), *The Overproduction Trap in U.S. Agriculture: A Study of Resource Allocation from World War I to the Late 1960's*. Pp. 22-40. Baltimore, MD: The John Hopkins University Press.

Johnson, Harry G. 1965. "Poverty and Unemployment." In B. Weisbrod (ed.), *The Economics of Poverty*. Pp. 166-170. Englewood Cliffs, NJ: Prentice-Hall.

Johnson, Merrill L. 1989. "Industrial Transition and the Location of High-Technology Branch Plants in the Nonmetropolitan Southeast." *Economic Geography* 65(1): 33-47.

Johnson, Thomas G. 1991. "Poverty and Human Capital Investment." Unpublished manuscript presented at the meeting of the Rural Sociological Society, Columbus, OH, August.

Johnson, Thomas G., and David E. Broomhall. 1991. "Perceived Employment Opportunities and Educational Performance in Virginia's Coal Counties." Powell River Project Symposium and Progress Reports, September.

Johnson, Thomas G., David S. Kraybill, and Brady J. Deaton. 1989. "Improvements in Well-being in Virginia's Coal Fields Hampered by Low and Unstable Income." *Rural Development Perspectives* 6:37-41.

Johnston, R. J. 1988. "The State, the Region, and the Division of Labor." In Allen Scott and Michael Storper (eds.), *Production, Work, Territory: The Geographical Anatomy of Industrial Capitalism*. Pp. 265-280. Boston, MA: Allen and Unwin.

Johnston, William. B., and Arnold. E. Packer. 1987. *Workforce 2000: Work and Workers for the 21st Century*. Indianapolis, IN: Hudson Institute.

Jones, Jolin Paul, III. 1987. "Work, Welfare, and Poverty Among Black Female-Headed Families." *Economic Geography* 63(1): 20-34.

Jones, Jolin Paul III, and Janet E. Kodras. 1986. "The Policy Context of the Welfare Debate." *Environmental Planning* 17: 63-92.

_____. 1990. "The State, Social Policy, and Geography." In Janet E. Kodras and Jolin Paul Jones III (eds.), *Geographic Dimensions of United States Social Policy*. Pp. 17-36. London, UK: Edward Arnold.

Kaldor, N. 1972. "The Irrelevance of Equilibrium Economics." *Economic Journal* 82(328): 1237-1255.

Kale, Steven R., and Richard E. Lonsdale. 1979. "Factors Encouraging and Discouraging Plant Location in Nometropolitan Areas." In Richard D. Lonsdale and H. L. Seyler (eds.) *Nometropolitan Industrialization*. Pp. 47-56. New York, NY: John Wiley and Sons.

Kalleberg, Arne L., and Aage B. Sørensen. 1979. "The Sociology of Labor Markets." *Annual Review of Sociology* 5: 351-79.

Kalleberg, Arne L., Michael Wallace, and Robert P. Althauser. 1981. "Economic Segmentation, Worker Power, and Income Inequality." *American Journal of Sociology*. 87(3): 651-83.

Kamerman, Sheila B. 1984. "Women, Children and Poverty: Public Policies and Female-Headed Families in Industrialized Countries." *Signs* 10(2): 249-271.

Kane, Thomas J. 1987. "Giving Back Control: Long-Term Poverty and Motivation." *Social Service Review* 61(3): 405-419.

Katz, Michael B. 1989. *The Undeserving Poor: From the War on Poverty to the War on Welfare*. New York: Pantheon Books.

Kaufman, Robert L., Randy Hodson, and Neil D. Fligstein. 1981. "Defrocking Dualism: A New Approach to Defining Industrial Sectors." *Social Science Research*. 10: 1-31.

Kaufman, Robert L., and Seymour Spilerman. 1982. "The Age of Structures of Occupations and Jobs." *American Journal of Sociology*. 87(4): 827-851.

Kautsky, Karl. 1988. *The Agrarian Question*. Translated by Pete Burgess. Volumes 1 and 2. London, UK: Zwan Publications.

Kenney, Martin, Linda M. Lobão, James Curry, and W. Richard Goe. 1989. "Midwestern Agriculture in U.S. Fordism: From the New Deal to Economic Restructuring." *Sociologia Ruralis* 29(2): 131-148.

Kerr, Clark. 1954. "The Balkanization of Labor Markets." In E. W. Bakke, Philip M. Hauser, Gladys L. Palmer, Charles A. Myer, Dale Yoder and Clark Korn, *Labor Mobility and Economic Opportunity*. Pp. 92-110. New York, NY: Wiley & Sons.

Kickingbird, Kire, and Karen Ducheneaux. 1973. *One Hundred Million Acres*. New York, NY: Macmillan.

Kile, Orville M. 1921. *The Farm Bureau Movement*. New York, NY: Macmillan Co.

Kile, Orville M. 1948. *The Farm Bureau Through Three Decades*. Baltimore, MD: Waverly Press.

Killian, Molly Sizer, and Thomas F. Hady. 1988. "The Economic Performance of Rural Labor Markets." In David L. Brown, J. Norman Reid, Herman Bluestone, David A McGranahan and Sara M. Mazie (eds.), *Rural Economic Development in the 1980's: Prospects for the Future*. Pp. 181-200. Agricultural and Rural Economy Division, Economic Research Service. U.S. Department of Agriculture. Rural Development Research Report no. 69. Washington, D.C.: U.S. Government Printing Office.

King, Desmond. 1989. "Economic Crisis and Welfare State Recommodification: A Comparative Analysis of the United States and Britain," in M. Gottdiener and Nikos Komninos (eds.), *Capitalist Development and Crisis Theory: Accumulation, Regulation and Spatial Restructuring*. New York, NY: St. Martin's Press.

Kling, Rob, Spencer Olin, and Mark Poster. 1991. *Postsuburban California: The Transformation of Orange County Since World War II*. Berkeley, CA: University of California Press.

Knorr-Cetina, Karin, and Aaron V. Cicourel. 1981. *Advances in Social Theory and Methodology: Toward an Integration of Micro- and Macro-Sociologies*. Boston, MA: Routledge and Kegan Paul.

Knowlton, Clark S. 1970. "Violence in New Mexico: A Sociological Perspective." *California Law Review* 58(October): 668-781.

_____. 1972. "Culture Conflict and Natural Resources." In William R. Burch, Jr., Neil J. Cheek, Jr., and Lee Taylor (eds.), *Social Behavior, Natural Resources and the Environment*. Pp. 109-145. New York, NY: Harper & Row, Publishers.

Knox, Hugh. 1987. "The Nonmetropolitan South in the 1990's: Convergence or Stagnation?" *Review of Regional Studies* 17(3): 1-4.

Knox, Paul L., and John Agnew. 1989. *The Geography of the World-Economy*. New York, NY: E. Arnold.

Kodras, Janet E. 1986. "Labor Market and Policy Constraints on the Work Disincentive Effect of Welfare." *Annals of the Association of American Geographers* 76(2): 228-246.

Kolko, Joyce. 1988. *Restructuring the World Economy*. New York, NY: Pantheon Books.

Kominski, Robert. 1991. *Educational Attainment in the United States: March 1989 and 1988*. CPR Series P-20, No. 431. Washington, D.C.: GPO.

Korbin, Jill E. 1992. "Child Poverty in the United States." *American Behavioral Scientist* 35(3): 213-219.

Kort, John R. 1981. "Regional Economic Instability and Industrial Diversification in the U.S." *Land Economics* 57(4): 596-608.

Kotlikoff, Laurence J. 1989. *What Determines Savings?* Cambridge, MA: MIT Press.

Kotlikoff, Laurence J., and Avia Spivalk. 1981. "The Family as an Incomplete Annuities Market," *Journal of Political Economy* 89(2):372-391.

Kraly, Ellen P., and Charles Hirschman. 1990. "Racial and Ethnic Inequality Among Children in the United States: 1940 and 1950." *Social Forces* 69(1): 33-51.

Krugman, Paul. 1991a. *Geography and Trade*. Cambridge, UK: MIT Press.

_____. 1991b. "Increasing Returns and Economic Geography." *Journal of Political Economy* 99(3): 483-499.

Kusel, Jonathan P. 1991a. "A New Approach to the Study of Forest Community Well-Being." Presentation at the meeting of the Rural Sociological Society, Columbus, OH, August.

_____. 1991b. "It's Just Like Baseball: Well-Being in Forest Communities." Unpublished Ph.D. dissertation, University of California at Berkeley.

Lamb, Michael E., and Abraham Sagi. 1983. *Fatherhood and Family Policy*. Hillsdale, NJ: Lawrence Erlbaum Associates.

Land Assistance Fund. n.d. Land Loss Prevention Manual. Atlanta, GA: The Federation of Southern Cooperatives.

Larson, Donald K. 1989. "Transitions of Poverty Amidst Employment Growth: Two Nonmetro Case Studies." *Growth and Change* 20(2): 19-34.

Lash, Scott, and John Urray. 1987. *The End of Organized Capitalism*. Cambridge: Polity Press.

Layzer, Jean L., Barbara D. Goodson, and Christine Delange. 1986. "Children in Shelters." *Response* 9(2): 2-5.

Lee, Courtland C. 1985. "Successful Rural Black Adolescents: A Psychological Profile." *Adolescence* 20(77): 129-142.

Lee, Gary R., and Marie L. Lassey. 1980. "Rural Urban Differences Among the Elderly: Economic, Social and Subjective Factors." *Journal of Social Issues* 36(2): 62-74.

Lee, Robert G. 1990a. "Social and Cultural Implications of Implementing 'A Conservation Strategy for the Northern Spotted Owl.'" Independent paper prepared for Mason, Bruce and Girard, Portland, Oregon.

_____. 1990b. "Sustained Yield and Social Order," in Robert G. Lee, Donald R. Fields, and William R. Burch, Jr. (eds.), *Community and Forestry: Continuities in the Sociology of Natural Resources*. Pp. 83-94. Boulder, CO: Westview Press.

_____. 1991. "Institutional Stability: A Requisite for Sustainable Forestry," in Starker Lectures 1990, Sustainable Forestry: Perspectives for the Pacific Northwest. College of Forestry, Oregon State University, Corvallis.

_____. 1992. "Moral Exclusion and Rural Poverty: Myth Management and Wood Products Workers." Unpublished manuscript prepared for the Working Group on Natural Resources and Poverty, Rural Sociological Society Task Force on Persistent Poverty in Rural America.

Leidner, Robin. 1987. "Homework: A study in the Interaction of Work and Family Organization." In Ida Harper Simpson and Richard L. Simpson (eds.), *Research in the Sociology of Work*. Vol 4. Greenwich, CONN: JAI Press.

Leighton, Alexander H. 1965. "Poverty and Social Change." *Scientific American* 212(5): 21-27.

Lemann, Nicholas. 1991. *The Promised Land: The Great Black Migration and How it Changed America*. New York, NY: Alfred A. Knopf, Inc.

Lerman, D., and J. Mikesell. 1989. "Rural and Urban Poverty: An Income/Net Worth Approach." In Harrel R. Rodgers and Gregory Weiher (eds.), *Rural Poverty: Special Causes and Policy Reform*. Pp. 1-25. New York, NY: Greenwood Press.

Levine, Adeline Gordon. 1982. *Love Canal: Science, Politics, and People*. Boston, MA: Lexington Books.

Levitan, Lois, and Shelley Feldman. 1991. "For Love or Money: Nonmonetary Economic Arrangements Among Rural Households in Central New York." In Daniel C. Clay and Harry K. Schwarzweller (eds.) *Research in Rural Sociology and Development*. Vol. 5, Pp. 149-172. Greenwich, CT: JAI Press, Inc.

Levitan, Sar A. 1985. *Programs in Aid of the Poor*, fifth edition. Baltimore, Ma: The Johns Hopkins University Press.

Levitan, Sar A., Garth L. Mangum, and Ray Marshall. 1981. *Human Resources and Labor Markets: Employment and Training in the American Economy*, 3rd edition. New York, NY: Harper and Row.

Levy, Frank. 1987. *Dollars and Dreams: The Changing American Income Distribution*. New York, NY: Russell Sage Foundation.

Levy, Frank, and Richard C. Michel. 1991. *The Economic Future of American Families: Income and Wealth Trends*. Washington, DC: Urban Institute Press.

Lewis, O. 1966. *La Vida: A Puerto Rican Family in the Culture of Poverty—San Juan and New York*. New York, NY: Random House.

Lewis, Oscar. 1969. "The Culture of Poverty." In Daniel P. Moynihan (ed.), *On Understanding Poverty: Perspectives from the Social Sciences*. Pp. 187-200. New York, NY: Basic Books.

Lichter, Daniel T. 1987. "Measuring Underemployment in Rural Areas." *Rural Development Perspectives* 3(February): 11-14.

_____. 1989. "Race, Employment Hardship, and Inequality in the American Nonmetropolitan South." *American Sociological Review* 54(3): 436-446.

_____. 1992. "Migration, Population Redistribution, and the New Spatial Inequality." In D. L. Brown, J. J. Zuiches, and D. R. Field (eds.), *The Demography of Rural Life*. University Park, MD: Northeast Regional Development Center.

Lichter, Daniel T., and David J. Eggebeen. 1992. "Child Poverty and the Changing Rural Family." *Rural Sociology* 57 (Summer, forthcoming).

Lichter, Daniel T., and David J. Landry. 1991. "Labor Force Transitions and Underemployment: The Stratification of Male and Female Workers." *Research in Social Stratification and Mobility* 10: 63-87.

Lichter, Daniel T., Diane K. McLaughlin, and Gretchen T. Cornwell. 1992. "Migration and the Loss of Human Resources in Rural America." In Lionel J. Beaulieu and David Mulkey (ed.), *Investing in People: The Human Capital Needs of Rural America*. Boulder, CO: Westview Press. Forthcoming.

Lichter, Daniel T., and Janice A. Costanzo. 1987. "Nonmetropolitan Underemployment and Labor-Force Composition." *Rural Sociology* 52(3): 329-344.

Lin, Xiannuan, Terry F. Buss, and Mark Popovich. 1990. "Entrepreneurship Is Alive and Well in Rural America: A Four State Study." *Economic Development Quarterly* 4(3): 254-259.

Lincoln, James R. 1978. "The Urban Distribution of Headquarters and Branch Plants in Manufacturing: Mechanisms of Metropolitan Dominance." *Demography* 15(2): 213-222.

Lipietz, Alain. 1986. "New Tendencies in the International Division of Labor: Regimes of Accumulation and Modes of Regulation." In Allen J. Scott and Michael Stooper (eds.), *Production, Work, Territory: The Geographical Anatomy of Industrial Capitalism*. Pp. 16-40. Boston, MA: Allen and Unwin.

Lippke, Bruce, Keith Gillis, Robert Lee, and Paul Sommers. 1990. "Three-State Impact of Spotted Owl Conservation and Other Timber Harvest Reductions: A Cooperative Evaluation of the Economic and Social Impacts." *Institute of Forest Resources Contribution* No. 69, University of Washington, Seattle, WA.

Lobão, Linda M. 1990. *Locality and Inequality: Farm and Industry Structure and Socioeconomic Conditions*. Albany, NY: State University of New York Press.

Lobão, Linda M., and Michael D. Schulman. 1991. "Farming Patterns, Rural Restructuring, and Poverty: A Comparative Regional Analysis." *Rural Sociology* 56(4): 565-602.

Logan, John R., and Harvey L. Molotch. 1987. *Urban Fortunes: The Political Economy of Place*. Berkeley, CA: University of California Press.

Losch, August. 1954. *The Economics of Location*. Translated by William H. Woglom and Wolfgang F. Stopler. New Haven, NJ: Yale University Press.

Lowi, Theodore J. 1964a. "How the Farmers Get What They Want." *The Reporter*. May 21: 34-37.

_____. 1964b. "American Business, Public Policy, Case-studies, and Political Theory." *World Politics* 16(4): 677-715.

Lowry, Ira S. 1966. *Migration and Metropolitan Growth: Two Analytical Models*. San Francisco, CA: Chandler Publication Company.

Lozier, John, and Ronald Althouse, 1974. "Social Enforcement of Behavior Toward Elders in an Appalachian Mountain Settlement," *The Gerontologist* 14(1): 69-80.

Lozoff, Betsy. 1989. "Nutrition and Behavior." *American Psychologist* 44(2): 231-236.

Lubeck, Sally, and Patricia Garrett. 1988. "Child Care 2000: Policy Options for the Future." *Social Policy* 18(4): 31-37.

Lyon, Larry. 1987. *The Community in Urban Society*. Chicago, IL: The Dorsey Press.

Lyson, Thomas A. 1989. *Two Side to the Sunbelt: The Growing Divergence Between the Rural and Urban South*. New York: Praeger.

_____. 1991. "Economic, Social and Environmental Impact of Economic Development Distribution." In *Economic Productivity and Adaptability, Publication 60*. Pp. 1-28. Northeast Regional Center for Rural Development, Pennsylvania State University.

Lyson, Thomas A., and William W. Falk. 1992. *Forgotten Places: Uneven Development and the Loss of Opportunity in Rural America*. Lawrence, KS: The University Press of Kansas.

Macinko, Seth. 1991. "Gospels of Efficiency, Public Policy and Rural Poverty: The Case of the U.S. Commercial Fishing Industry." Presented at the meeting of the Rural Sociological Society, Columbus, OH, August.

Malecki, Edward J. 1988. "Technological Imperatives and Modern Corporate Strategy." In Allen J. Scott and Michael Storper (eds.), *Production, Work and Territory: The Geographical Anatomy of Industrial Capitalism*. Pp. 67-79. Boston, MA: Allen and Unwin.

Marchak, Patricia M. 1983. *Green Gold: The Forest Industry of British Columbia*. Vancouver, BC: University of British Columbia Press.

Markides, Kyriakos S. 1983. "Minority Aging." In Matilda White Riley, Beth B. Hess and Kathleen Bond (Eds.). *Aging in Society: Selected Reviews of Recent Research*. Pp. 115-137. Hilldale, NJ: Lawrence Earlbaum Associates Publishers.

Markley, Deborah. nd. "Small Business Rural Banks: Assessing and Strengthening the Link." Washington, DC: The Aspen Institute.

Markusen, Ann R. 1985. *Profit Cycles, Oligopoly, and Regional Development*. Cambridge, MA: MIT Press.

_____. 1987. *Regions: The Economics and Politics of Territory*. Totowa, NJ: Rowman & Littlefield.

Marshall, Ray, and Vernon M. Briggs, Jr. 1989. *Labor Economics: Theory, Institutions, and Public Policy*. Howewood, IL: Irwin.

Martin, Teresa Castro, and Larry L. Bumpass. 1989. "Recent Trends in Marital Disruption." *Demography* 26(1): 37-52.

Martinez-Brawley, Emilia E. 1990. *Perspectives on the Small Community: Humanistic Views for Practitioners*. Silver Spring, MD: NASW Press.

Martinez-Brawley, Emilia E., and Joan Blundall. 1989. "Farm Families' Preferences Toward the Personal Social Services." *Social Work* 34(6): 513-522.

Marx, Karl. 1967. *Capital: A Critique of Political Economy*. In Friederich Engles (ed.). Translated by Sammuel Edward Avelin. Vol. 3. New York, NY: International Publishers.

Massey, Doreen. 1984. *Spatial Divisions of Labor: Social Structures and the Geography of Production*. London, UK: Macmillan.

Massey, Douglas S. 1990. "American Apartheid: Segregation and the Making of the Underclass." *American Journal of Sociology* 96(2): 329-57.

Mattera, Philip. 1985. *Off the Books: The Rise of the Underground Economy*. New York, NY: St. Martin's Press.

Mayer, Karl Ulrich, and Urs Schoepflin. 1989. "The State and the Life Course." *Annual Review of Sociology* 15: 187-209.

Mazur, Allan, and Jinling Lee. 1991. "Sounding the Global Alarm: Environmental Issues in the National News." Forthcoming.

McBarnette, Lorna. 1987. "Women and Poverty: The Effects on Reproductive Status." In Cesar A. Pearles and Lauren S. Young (eds.), *Women, Health, and Poverty*. Volumes 3 and 4, Pp. 55-81. New York, NY: The Haworth Press.

McConnell, Grant. 1966. *Private Power & American Democracy*. New York, NY: Alfred A. Knopf.

McCormick, Richard L. 1986. *The Party Period and Public Policy: American Politics from the Age of Jackson to the Progressive Era*. New York, NY: Oxford University Press.

McGranahan, David A. 1983. "Changes in the Social and Spatial Structure of the Rural Community." In Gene F. Summers (ed.), *Technology and Social Change in Rural Areas*. Boulder, Co: Westview Press.

_____. 1988. "Rural Workers in the National Economy." In David L. Brown, J. Norman Reid, Herman Bluestone, David A. McGranahan, and Sara M. Mazie (eds.), *Rural Economic Development in the 1980's: Prospects for the Future*. Pp. 29-47. Agricultural and Rural Economy Division, Economic Research Service. U.S. Department of Agriculture. Rural Development Research Report no. 69. Washington, D.C.: U.S. Government Printing Office.

_____. 1991. "Introduction." In *Education and Rural Economic Development Strategies for the 1990's*. Pp. 1-12. Agriculture and Rural Economy Division, Economic Research Service, U.S. Department of Agriculture. ERS Staff Report No. AGES 9153.

McGranahan, David A., and Linda M. Ghelfi. 1991. "The Education Crisis and Rural Stagnation in the 1980's." In *Education and Rural Economic Development: Strategies for the 1990's*. Pp. 40-92. Agriculture and Rural Economy Division, Economic Research Service, U.S. Department of Agriculture. ERS Staff Report No. AGES 9153.

McLanahan, Sara. 1985. "Family Structure and the Reproduction of Poverty." *American Journal of Sociology* 90: 873-901.

McLanahan, Sara, and Karen Booth. 1989. "Mother-Only Families: Problems, Prospects, and Politics." *Journal of Marriage and the Family* 51(3): 557-580.

McLaughlin, Diane K., and Carolyn Sachs. 1988. "Poverty in Female-Headed Households: Residential Differences." *Rural Sociology* 53(3): 287-306.

McLaughlin, Diane K., and Lauri Perman. 1991a. "Returns vs. Endowments in the Earnings Attainment Process for Metropolitan and Nonmetropolitan Men and Women." *Rural Sociology* 56: 339-365.

_____. 1991b. "The Role of Returns versus Endowments in Explaining the Gender Earnings Gap in Nonmetropolitan America." Paper Presented to the Annual Meeting of the Rural Sociological Society of America, Columbus, OH: August.

McLaughlin, Diane K., and Leif Jensen. 1991. "Poverty Among the Elderly: A Metro-Nonmetro Comparison." Paper Presented to the Annual Meeting of the Rural Sociological Society, Columbus, OH: August.

McLeod, Jay. 1987. *Ain't No Makin' It: Leveled Aspirations in a Low-Income Neighborhood*. Boulder, CO: Westview Press.

McLoyd, Vonnie C. 1989. "Socialization and Development in a Changing Economy: The Effects of Paternal Job and Income Loss on Children." *American Psychologist* 44(2): 293-302.

_____. 1990. "The Impact of Economic Hardship on Black Families and Children: Psychological Distress, Parenting, and Socioemotional Development." *Child Development* 61(2):311-346.

McLoyd, Vonnie C., and Leon Wilson. 1990. "Maternal Behavior, Social Support and Economic Conditions as Predictors of Distress in Children." In Vonnie C. McLoyd and Constance A. Flanagan (eds.), *Economic Stress: Effects on Family Life and Child Development*. Pp. 49-69. San Francisco, CA: Jossey-Bass Inc.

McMichael, Philip, and David Myhre. 1991. "Global Regulation Vs the Nation-State: Agro-Food Systems and the New Politics of Capital." *Capital and Class* 43: 83-106.

McNickle, D. 1975. *They Came Here First: The Epic of the American Indian*. New York, NY: Harper and Row.

Mead, Lawrence M. 1992. *The New Politics of Poverty: The Nonworking Poor in America*. New York: Basic Books.

Mera, Koichi. 1973. "On the Urban Agglomeration and Economic Efficiency." *Economic Development and Cultural Change* 21(2): 309-324.

Meyer, Carol H. 1987. "Direct Practice in Social Work: Overview." In Anne Minahan, Rosina M. Becerra, Scott Briar, Claudia J. Coulton, Leon H Ginsberg, June Gary Hopps, John F Longores, Rino N. Patti, William J. Reid, Tony Tripody and S.D. Khinduka (eds.), *Encyclopedia of Social Work,* 18Th Edition. Vol 1, Pp. 409-422. Silver Spring, MD: National Association of Social Workers.

Miley, James D. 1980. "Critical Dimensions in Human Ecology: Ideology in American Sociology." *Urban Life* 9(2): 163-185.

Milkove, Daniel L., and Patrick J. Sullivan. 1989. "Should Rural Communities Fear Bank Deregulation?" *Rural Development Perspectives* 5(2): 2-7.

Miller, Sandra E. 1990. *The Mountain Association for Community Economic Development*. Morrilton, AR: Winrock International Institute for Agricultural Development.

Mills, C. Wright, and Melville J. Ulmer. 1946. "Small Business and Civic Welfare." *Report to the Smaller War Plants Corporation to the Special Committee to Study Problems of American Small Business*, U.S. Senate, 79th Congress, 2nd Session. Washington, DC: U.S. Government Printing Office.

_____. 1970. "Small Business and Civic Welfare." In M. Aiken and P. Mott (eds.), *The Structure of Community Power*. Pp. 124-154. New York, NY: Random House.

Mincer, Jacob, and Solomon Polachek. 1975. "Family Investments in Human Capital: The Earnings of Women," *Journal of Political Economy* 82: S76-S108.

Mingione, Enzo. 1991. *Fragmented Societies: A Sociology of Economic Life Beyond the Market Paradigm*. Translated by Paul Goodrich. Cambridge, MA: Basil Blackwell Ltd.

Mink, Gwendolyn. 1990. "The Lady and the Tramp: Gender, Race and the Origins of the American Welfare State." Pp. 92-122 in Linda Gordon (ed.), *Women, the State and Welfare*. Madison, WI: University of Wisconsin Press.

Mishel, Lawrence, and Ruy A. Teixeira. 1991. *The Myth of the Coming Labor Shortage: Jobs, Skills, and Incomes of America's Workforce 2000*. Washington, D.C.: Economic Policy Institute.

Mizruchi, Ephraim Harold. 1967. "Aspiration and Poverty: A Meglected Aspect of Merton's Anomie." *Sociological Quarterly* 8(4): 439-46.

Moen, Jon R. 1989. "Poverty in the South." *Economic Review*. Federal Reserve Bank of Atlanta, LXXIV(1): 34-36.

Mollenkopf, John H. 1983. *The Contested City*. Princeton, NJ: Princeton University Press.

Molnar, Joseph J., and Greg Traxler. 1991. "People Left Behind: Transitions of the Rural Poor." *Southern Journal of Agricultural Economics* 23(1): 75-83.

Morrill, Richard L., and Ernest H. Wohlenberg. 1971. *The Geography of Poverty In the United States*. New York, NY: McGraw-Hill.

Morris, Charles, and Mark Drabenstott. 1991. "Rethinking the Rural Credit Gap." *Rural Development Perspectives*, 7(1): 20-25.

Morrison, P. 1972. *The Impact and Significance of Rural-Urban Migration in the United States*. Santa Monica, CA: The Rand Corporation.

Morrissey, Elizabeth S. 1985. Characteristics of Poverty in Nonmetro Counties, *Rural Development Research Report 52*. U.S. Department of Agriculture, Economic Research Service. Washington, D.C.: U.S. Government Printing Office.

_____. 1991a. "Intergenerational Poverty in Metro and Nonmetro Areas." Paper presented at the 16th annual National Institute on Social Work and Human Services in Rural Areas. Nacagdoches, TX. August.

_____. 1991b. *Work and Poverty in Metro and Nonmetro Areas*. Agriculture and Rural Economy Division, Economic Research Service, U.S. Department of Agriculture. Rural Development Research Report No. 81, (June). Washington, DC: U.S. Government Printing Office.

Mott, Frank L., and Sylvia F. Moore. 1978. "The Causes and Consequences of Marital Breakdown." In Frank L. Mott (Ed.), *Women, Work and Family*. Lexington, MA: Lexington Books.

Mulkey, Lynn M., Robert L. Crain, and Alexander J.C. Harrington. 1992. "One-Parent Households and Achievement: Economic and Behavioral Explanations of a Small Effect." *Sociology of Education* 65: 48-65.

Murgatroyd, Linda, Mike Savage, Don Shapiro, John Urry, Sylvia Walby, Alan Warde, and Jane Mark-Lawson. 1985. *Localities, Class, and Gender*. London, UK: Pion.

Murray, Charles. 1984. *Losing Ground: American Social Policy 1950-1980*. New York, NY: Basic Books.

Muth, Robert M. 1990. "Community Stability as Social Structure: The Role of Subsistence Uses of Natural Resources in Southeast Alaska." In Robert G. Lee, Donald R. Field and William R. Burch, Jr. (eds.), *Community and Forestry: Continuities in the Sociology of Natural Resources.* Pp. 211-227. Boulder, CO: Westview Press.

Myrdal, G. 1957. *Economic Theory and Under-Developed Regions.* London, UK: G. Duckorth.

Nardinelli, Clark, Myles S. Wallace, and John T. Warner. 1987. "Explaining Differences in State Growth: Catching Up Versus Olsen," *Public Choice* 52(3): 201-213.

Nash, Roderick Frazin. 1989. *The Rights of Nature: A History of Environment Ethics.* Madison, WI: University of Wisconsin Press.

National Audubon Society. 1989. *Greed and Wildlife: Poaching in America.* (Film) New York, NY: National Audubon Society.

Nelson, Barbara J. 1984. "Women's Poverty and Women's Citizenship: Some Political Consequences of Economic Marginality." *Signs* 10(2): 209-231.

_____. 1990. "The Origins of the Two-Channel Welfare State: Workmen's Compensation and Mother's Aid." In Linda Gordon (ed.), *Women, the State and Welfare.* Pp. 123-151. Madison, WI: University of Wisconsin Press.

Noël, Alain. 1987. Accumulation, Regulation, and Social Change: An Essay on Political Economy." *International Organization* 41(2): 303-333.

Nord, Mark. 1991. "Natural Resources and Persistent Rural Poverty: In Search of the N.nexus." Unpublished manuscript prepared for the Working Group on Natural Resources and Poverty, Rural Sociological Society Task Force on Persistent Poverty in Rural America.

Norman, Abigail. 1985. *Keeping Families Together: The Case for Family Preservation.* New York, NY: Edna McConnell Clark Foundation.

Northrup, Emily M. 1990. "The Feminization of Poverty: The Demographic Factor and The Composition of Economic Growth." *Journal of Economic Issues* 24: 145-160.

O'Connor, Alice. 1992. "Modernization and the Rural Poor: Some Lessons From History." In cynthia M. Dunca (ed.) *Rural Poverty in America.* Pp. 213-233. New York, NY: Auburn House.

O'Connor, James. 1973. *The Fiscal Crisis of the State.* New York, NY: St. Martin's Press.

Offe, Claus. 1985. *Disorganized Capitalism: Contemporary Transformations of Work and Politics.* Cambridge: Polity Press.

Ogbu, John U. 1981. "Origins of Human Competence: A Cultural-Ecological Perspective." *Child Development* 52(2): 413-429.

O'Hare, William P. 1988. *The Rise of Poverty in Rural America.* Number 15 (July). Washington, DC: Population Reference Bureau.

O'Hare, William, and Brenda Curry-White. 1991. "The Rural Underclass: Examination of Multiple-Problem Populations in Urban and Rural Settings." Paper presented at the annual meeting of the Rural Sociological Society, Columbus, OH. August.

Office of Technology Assessment. 1986. *Technology and Structural Unemployment: Re-employing Displaced Adults, OTA-ITE-250.* Washington, DC: U.S. Government Printing Office.

Office of Technology Assessment. 1990. *Critical Connections: Communication for the Future, Summary*. Office of Technology Assessment, OTA-CIT-408. Washington, DC: U.S. Government Printing Office.

Oliver, Robert W. 1971. "Early Plans for a World Bank." *Princeton Studies in International Finance*, No. 29. Princeton, NJ

Olsen, Marvin Elliot, Dora G. Lodwick, and Riley E. Dunlap. 1992. *Viewing the World Ecologically*. Boulder: Westview Press.

Opotow, Susan. 1990. "Moral Exclusion and Injustice: An Introduction." *Journal of Social Issues* 46(1): 1-20.

O'Rand, Angela M., and Richard Landerman. 1984. "Women's and Men's Retirement Income Status: Early Family Role Effects." *Research on Aging* 6(1): 25-44.

Orshansky, Mollie. 1963. "Children of the poor." *Social Security Bulletin* 26(7): 1-13.
_____. 1965. "Counting the Poor: Another Look at the Poverty Profile." Social Security Bulletin 28(1): 2-29.

Osterman, Paul. 1988. *Employment Futures: Reorganization, Dislocation, and Public Policy*. New York, NY: Oxford University Press.

Paar, John B. 1966. "Outmigration and the Depressed Area Problem." *Land Economics* 42: 149-159.

Palerm, Juan Vincente. 1988. "Transformations in Rural California." *UC Mexus News* No. 21/22.

Papanek, Hanna. 1981. "The Differential Impact of Programs and Policies on Women in Development." In Roslyn Dauber and Melinda L. Cain (eds.), *Women and Technological Change in Developing Countries*. Pp. 215-227. Boulder, CO: Westview Press.

Parcel, Toby L., and Charles W. Mueller. 1983. *Ascription and Labor Markets: Race and Sex Differences in Earnings*. New York, NY: Academic Press.

Park, Robert Ezra. 1952. *Human Communities: The City and Human Ecology*. Collected Papers of Ezra Park. In Everet Chenington Hughes, Charles S. Johnson, Jitsuichi Masuoka, Robert Redfield and Louis Wirth (eds.). Vol II. Glencoe, IL: Free Press

Parker, Edwin B., Heather E. Hudson, Don A. Dillman, and Andrew R. Roscoe. 1989. *Rural America in the Information Age: Telecommunications Policy for Rural Development*. Lanham, MD: The Aspen Institute and University Press of America.

Parker, Steven, Steven Greer, and Barry Zuckerman. 1988. "Double Jeopardy: The Impact of Poverty on Early Child Development." *The Pediatric Clinics of North America* 35(6): 1227-1240.

Parker, Tim. 1989. "Nonmetro Employment: Annual Averages, 1988." Press Release (Feb. 27, 1989). Washington, D.C.: Economic Research Service, U.S. Department of Agriculture.

Parr, John B. 1973. "Growth Poles, Regional Development, and Central Place Theory." *Papers of the Regional Science Association*, 31: 173-212.

Payer, Cheryl. 1982. "The World Bank: A Critical Analysis." New York, NY: Monthly Review Press.

Pearce, Diane. 1979. "Women, Work, and Welfare: The Feminization of Poverty." In Karen Wolk Feinstein (ed.), *Working Women and Families*. Pp. 103-124. Beverly Hills, CA: Sage Publications.

_____. 1990. "Welfare is Not for Women: Why the War on Poverty Cannot Conquer the Feminization of Poverty." In Linda Gordon (ed.), *Women, the State and Welfare*. Pp. 265-279. Madison, WI: University of Wisconsin Press.

_____. 1992. "The Feminization of Poverty." In Janet Kourany, James Sterba and Rosemarie Tong (eds.), *Feminist Philosophy: Problems, Theories, and Applications*. Pp. 207-219. Englewood Cliffs, NJ: Prentice Hall.

Pearce, Diane, and Harriette McAdoo. 1981. *Women and Children: Alone and in Poverty*. Washington, DC: National Advisory Council on Economic Opportunity.

Pearles, Cesar A., and Lauren S. Young. 1987. *Women, Health, and Poverty*. New York, NY: The Haworth Press.

Pearson, Jane L., Andrea G. Hunter, Margaret E. Ensminger, and Sheppard G. Kellam. 1990. "Black Grandmothers in Multigenerational Households: Diversity in Family Structure and Parenting Involvement in the Woodlawn Community." *Child Development* 61(2): 434-442.

Pearson, Ruth. 1988. "Female Workers in the First and Third Worlds: The Greening of Women's Labor." In R.E. Pahl (ed.), *On Work: Historical, Comparative and Theoretical Approaches*. Pp. 449-466. Oxford, UK: Basil Blackwell Ltd.

Peck, Jamie A., and Adam Tickell. 1991. *Regulation, Theory, and the Geography of Flexible Accumulation: Transitions in Capitalism, Transitions in Theory*. Spatial Policy Analysis Working Paper 12. Manchester, England: University of Manchester.

Peet, Richard. 1991. *Global Capitalism: Theories of Societal Development*. New York, NY: Routledge.

Peluso, Nancy Lee. 1991. *Rich Forests, Poor People: Forest Assess Control and Resistance in Java*. Berkeley, CA: University of California Press.

Perloff, Harvey S., and Lowdon Wingo, Jr. 1961. "Natural Resource Endowment and Regional Economic Growth." In Joseph J. Spengler (ed.), *Natural Resources and Economic Growth*. Pp. 191-212. Washington, DC: Resources for the Future.

Perman, Lauri, and Beth Stevens. 1989. "Industrial Segregation and the Gender Distribution of Fringe Benefits." *Gender and Society* 3(3): 388-405.

Perroux, Francois. 1955. "Note Sur La Notion De 'Pole De Croissance." *Economie Applique* (January-June): 307-320.

Phillips, Anne. 1977. "The Concept of 'Development'." *Review of African Political Economy* 8: 7-20.

Phillips, Deborah A. 1987. *Quality in Child Care: Does Research Tell Us?* Pp. 23-26, 33-45, 89-95. Washington, DC: National Association for the Education of Young Children.

Philp, Kenneth R. 1977. *John Collier's Crusade for Indian Reform: 1920-1954*. Tucson, AZ: The University of Arizona Press.

Pihlblad, C. T. 1975. "Culture, Lifestyle and Social Environment of the Small Town." In R.C. Atchley and T.O. Byerts (Eds.), *Rural Environments and Aging: Proceedings From a conference Held at the University of Kentucky, Lexington KY, March*. Pp. 47-62. Washington, DC: Gerontological Society.

Piore, Michael J. 1975. "Notes For a Theory of Labor Market Stratification." In Richard C. Edward, Michael Reich, and David M. Gorden (eds.), *Labor Market Segmentation: Conference of Labor Market Segmentation*. Pp. 125-50. Lexington, MA: D.C. Heath.

Piore, Michael J., and Charles F. Sabel. 1984. *The Second Industrial Divide: Possibilities for Prosperity*. New York, NY: Basic Books.

Polanyi, Karl. 1957. *The Great Transformation: The Political and Economic Origins of Our Time*. Boston: Beacon Press.

Portes, Alejandro, and Leif Jensen. 1992. "Disproving the Enclave Hypothesis." *American Sociological Review* 57(3): 418-20.

Portes, Alejandro, Manuel Castells, and Lauren A. Benton. 1989. *The Informal Economy: Studies in Advanced and Less Developed Countries*. Baltimore, MD: The Johns Hopkins University Press.

Portes, Alejandro, and Robert L. Bach. 1985. *Latin Journey: Cuban and Mexican Immigrants in the United States*. Berkeley, CA: University of California Press.

Precourt, Walter. 1983. "The Image of Appalachian Poverty." In Allen Batteau (Ed.), *Appalachia and America: Autonomy and Regional Dependence*. Pp. 86-110. Lexington, KY: University of Kentucky Press.

Pred, Allan R. 1966. *The Spatial Dynamics of U.S. Urban-Industrial Growth, 1800-1914: Interactive and Theoretical Essays*. Cambridge, MA: The M.I.T. Press.

_____. 1973. "Industrialization, Initial Advantage and American Metropolitan Growth." In J. Blunden, C. Brook, G. Edge and A. Hay (eds.), *Regional Analysis and Development*. Pp. 176-193. New York, NY: Harper and Row.

Preston, Samuel H. 1984. "Children and the Elderly: Divergent Paths for America's Dependents." *Demography* 24(4): 435-457.

Price, Daniel O., and Melanie M. Sikes. 1975. *Rural-Urban Migration Research in the United States: Annotated Bibliography and Synthesis*. Department of Health, Education and Welfare, Pub. No. (NIH)75-565. Washington, DC: U.S. Government Printing Office.

Prosser, William R. 1991. "The Underclass: Assessing What We Have Learned." *Focus*, University of Wisconsin-Madison, Institute for Research on Poverty 13: 1-5, 9-18.

Radin, Norma and Graeme Russell. 1983. "Increased Father Participation and Child Development Outcomes." In Michael E. Lamb and Abraham Sagi (eds.), *Fatherhood and Family Policy*. Pp. 191-218. Hillsdale, NJ: Lawrence Erlbaum Associates.

Rank, Mark R., and Thomas A. Hirschl. 1988. "A Rural-Urban Comparison of Welfare Exits: The Importance of Population Density." *Rural Sociology* 53(2): 190-206.

Rasmussen, David, and Thomas Zuehlke. 1988. "Sclerosis, Convergence, and Taxes: Determinants of Growth Among the American States." Paper presented at the 27th annual meetings of the Southern Regional Science Association, Morgantown, WV: April 14-16.

Rasmussen, Wayne D., and Gladys L. Baker. 1972. *The Department of Agriculture*. New York, NY: Praeger.

Redman, John M. 1990. *Metro/Nonmetro Program Performance Under Title II-A, Job Training Partnership Act*. Agriculture and Rural Economy Division, Economic Research Service, U.S. Department of Agriculture. Staff Report No. AGES 9072.

Redmond, Sonjia Parker, and Joan Brackman. 1990. "Homeless Children and Their Caretakers." In Jamshid A. Momeni (ed.), *Homelessness in the United States--Data and Issues*. Pp. 123-132. New York, NY: Praeger.

Rees, Gareth. 1984. "Rural Regions in National and International Economies." In Tony Bradley and Philip Lowe (eds.), *Locality and Rurality: Economy and Society in Rural Regions*. Pp. 27-44. Norwich, UK: Geo Books.

Reich, Robert B. 1988. "The Rural Crisis, and What To Do About It." *Economic Development Quarterly* 2(1):3-8.

Rescoria, Leslie, Ruth Parker, and Paul Stolley. 1991. "Ability, Achievement, and Adjustment in Homeless Children." *American Journal of Orthopsychiatry* 61(2): 210-220.

Reynolds, Lloyd George. 1985. *Economic Growth in the Third World: 1850-1980*. New Haven, CON: Yale University Press.

Riley, Matild White. 1987. "On the Significance of Age in Sociology." *American Sociological Review* 52(1): 1-14.

Ritchey, P. Neal. 1976. "Explanations of Migration." *Annual Review of Sociology* 2: 363-404.

Robinson, Glen O. 1991. *American Bureaucracy: Public Choice and Public Law*. Ann Arbor, MI: University of Michigan Press.

Robinson, Kenneth Lean. 1989. *Farm and Food Policies and Their Consequences*. Englewood Cliffs, NJ: Prentice-Hall.

Rodgers, Harrell R., Jr., and Gregory Weiher. 1989. *Rural Poverty: Special Causes and Policy Reforms*. New York, NY: Greenwood Press.

Rogers, Carolyn C. 1991. "Nonmetro/Metro Children: Similar Families, Different Economic Conditions." *Rural Development Perspectives* 7: 40-41.

Rogers, David L., and Willis J. Goudy. 1981. "Community Structure and Occupational Segregation: 1960 and 1970." *Rural Sociology* 46(2): 263-281.

Romer, Paul M. 1990. "Endogenous Technical Change." *Journal of Political Economy* 98(5-2): S71-S102.

Ropers, Richard H. 1991. *Persistent Poverty: The American Dream Turned Nightmare*. New York, NY: Plenum Press.

Rose, Arnold Marshall. 1967. *The Power Structure: Political Process in American Society*. New York, NY: Oxford University Press.

Rosenberg, Samuel. 1975. "The Dual Labor Market: Its Existence and Consequences." Unpublished PhD. dissertation, University of California, Berkely, CA.

Rosenfeld, Stuart A., Edward M. Bergman, and Sara Rubin. 1985. *After the Factories: Changing Employment Patterns in the Rural South*. Research Triangle Park, NC: Southern Growth Policies Board.

Ross, Peggy J., and Elizabeth S. Morrissey. 1987. "Two Types of Rural Poor Need Different Kinds of Help." *Rural Development Perspectives* 4: 7-10.

_____. 1989. "Rural People in Poverty: Persistent Versus Temporary Poverty." National Rural Studies Committee. Stoneville, MS: May 17-18.

Rossi, Peter H., and James D. Wright. 1987. "The Determinants of Homelessness." *Health Affairs* 6(1): 19-32.

Rovner, Julie. 1988. "Congress Approved Overhaul of Welfare System," *Congressional Quarterly Weekly Report*. pp. 2,825-2,831.

Rowles, Graham D. 1980. "Growing Old Inside: Aging and Attachment to Place in an Appalachian Community." In Nancy Datan and Nancy Lohmann (Eds.), *Transitions of Aging: Proceedings*. Pp. 153-170. New York, NY: Academic Press.

Rowntree, B. S. 1901. *Poverty: A Study of Town Life*. London: Macmillan.

Ruggie, John Gerard. 1982. "International Regimes, Transactions, and Change: Embedded Liberalism in the Postwar Economic Order." *International Organization* 36(2): 379-415.

Ruggles, Patricia. 1990. *Drawing the Line: Alternative Poverty Measures and Their Implications for Public Policy*. Washington, D.C.: The Urban Institute Press.

Ryder, Norman. 1965. "The Cohort as a Concept in the Study of Social Change." *American Sociological Review* 30(6): 843-861.

Sakamoto, Arthur. 1991. "Sample Selection and the Dual Labor Market." *Research in Social Stratification and Mobility* 10: 171-98.

Sakamoto, Arthur, and Meichu D. Chen. 1991. "Further Evidence on Returns to Schooling by Establishment Size." *American Sociological Review* 56: 765-71.

Sameroff, Arnold J. 1986. "Environmental Context of Child Development." *Journal of Pediatrics* 109(1): 192-200.

Sameroff, Arnold J., and Michael J. Chandler. 1975. "Reproductive Risk and the Continuum of Caretaking Casualty." In F. D. Horowitz (ed.), *Review of Child Development Research*. Pp. 187-244. Volume 4. Chicago, IL: University of Chicago Press.

Sampson, Robert J. 1991. "Linking the Micro- and Macrolevel Dimensions of Community Social Organization." *Social Forces* 70(1): 43-64.

Sanders, Jimy M. 1991. "'New' Structural Poverty?" *The Sociological Quarterly* 32(2): 179-299.

Sanders, Jimy M., and Victor Nee. 1987. "Limits of Ethnic Solidarity in the Enclave Economy." *American Sociological Review* 52(6): 745-773.

_____. 1992. "Problems in Resolving the Enclave Economy Debate." *American Sociological Review* 57(4): 415-18.

Saraceno, Chiara. 1992. "Women's Work(s): A Complex, Multifaceted Component in Household Strategies in Times of Economic Crisis." In Lourdes Benéria and Shelley Feldman (eds.), *Unequal Burden: Economic Crises, Persistent Poverty and Women's Work*. Boulder, CO: Westview (forthcoming).

Sassen-Koob, Saskia. 1986. "The Dynamics of Growth in Post-Industrial New York City." Paper presented at the Workshop on the Dual City. New York, NY.

Sawhill, Isabel V. 1988. "Poverty in the U.S.: Why Is It So Persistent?" *Journal of Economic Literature* 26(3): 1073-1119.

_____. 1989. "Povety in the U.S.: Why is it so Persistent?" *Journal of Economic Literature* 26(3): 1973-1119.

Schaefer, Earl S. 1987. "Parental Modernity and Child Academic Competence: Toward a Theory of Individual and Societal Development." *Early Child Development and Care* 27: 373-389.

Schallau, Con H. 1990. "Community Stability: Issues, Institutions, and Instruments." In Robert G. Lee, Donald R. Field and William R. Burch, Jr. (eds.), *Community and Forestry: Continuities in the Sociology of Natural Resources*. Pp. 69-82. Boulder, CO: Westview Press.

Schorr, Alvin L. 1992. "Ending Poverty: The Children's Hour." *American Behavioral Scientist* 35(3): 332-339.

Schorr, Lisbeth B. 1989. *Within Our Reach: Breaking the Cycle of Disadvantage*. New York, NY: Anchor Books Editions.

Schorr, Lisbeth B., and Daniel Schorr. 1988. *Within Our Reach: Breaking the Cycle of Disadvantage*. New York, NY: Doubleday.

Schrag, Judy, Lucretia Swinburne Farago, and Lisa Walker. 1983. "Education for the Handicapped in Rural Areas." In Jerry L. Fletcher (ed.), *Rural Education: A National Perspective*. Pp. 155-182. Davis, CA: International Dialogue Press.

Schulman, Michael D. 1992. "Structural Perspectives on Poverty." Unpublished manuscript prepared for the Working Group on Natural Resources and Poverty, Rural Sociological Task Force on Persistent Poverty in Rural America.

Schultz, Theodore W. 1943. *Redirecting Farm Policy*. New York, NY: Macmillan.

_____. 1945. *Agriculture in an Unstable Economy*. New York, NY: McGraw-Hill Book Co.

_____. 1961. "Investment in Human Capital." *The American Economic Review* LI(1): 1-17.

_____. 1979. "The Economics of Being Poor." Nobel Lecture, Stockholm, Sweden, December.

Schumpeter, Joseph A. 1942. *Capitalism, Socialism, and Democracy*. New York, NY: Harper & Row Publishers.

Schwarzweller, Harry K., Jones S. Brown, and J.J. Mangalam. 1971. *Mountain Families in Transition: A Case of Study of Appalachian Migration*. University Park, PA: Pennsylvania State University Press.

Scott, Allen J., and Michael Storper. 1988. *Production, Work, Territory: The Geographical Anatomy of Industrial Capitalism*. Boston, MA: Allen and Unwin.

Scott, Jean Pearson, and Karen A. Roberto. 1985. "Use of Informal and Formal Support Networks by Rural Elderly Poor," *The Gerontologist* 25(6): 624-630.

Selznick, Phillip. 1966. *TVA and the Grass Roots: A Study in the Sociology of Formal Organization*. New York, NY: Harper and Row.

_____. 1987. "The Idea of a Communitarian Morality." *California Law Review* 75: 445-463.

Seminoyov, Moshe. 1983. "Community Characteristics, Female Employment and Occupational Segregation: Small Towns in a Rural State." *Rural Sociology* 48(1): 104-119.

Sen, Amartya. 1985a. "Well-being, Agency and Freedom: The Dewey Lectures." *Journal of Philosophy* LXXXII(4): 169-221.

_____. 1985b. *Commodities and Capabilities: Professor Dr. P. Hennipman Lectures in Economics* Volume 7. New York, NY: North-Holland.

_____. 1987. *The Standard of Living*. Cambridge, UK: Cambridge University Press.

_____. 1990. "Gender and Co-operative Conflicts." In Irene Tinker (ed.) *Persistent Inequalities: Women and World Development*. Pp. 123-149. New York, NY: Oxford University Press.

Sewell, William H., Archibald O. Haller, and George Ohlendorf. 1970. "The Educational and Early Occupational Status Attainment Process: Replication and Revision." *American Sociological Review* 35(8): 1014-1027.

Shapiro, Isaac. 1989. *Laboring for Less: Working but Poor in Rural America.* Washington, DC: Center on Budget and Policy Priorities.

Shepherd, William G. 1975. *The Treatment of Market Power: Antitrust, Regulation, and Public Enterprise.* New York, NY: Columbia University Press.

Sherman, Arloc. 1992. *Falling by the Wayside: Children in Rural America.* Washington, DC: Children's Defense Fund.

Sherraden, Michael W. 1991. *Assets and the Poor: A New American Welfare Policy.* Armonk, NY: M. E. Sharpe, Inc.

Shkilnyk, Anastasia M. 1985. *A Poison Stronger than Love: The Destruction of an Ojibwa Community.* New Haven, NY: Yale University Press.

Shockey, James W. 1989. "Overeducation and Earnings: A Structural Approach to Differential Attainment in the U.S. Labor Force (1970-1982)." *American Sociological Review* 54: 856-64.

Shonkoff, Jack P., and Samuel J. Meisels. 1990. "Early Childhood Intervention: The Evolution of a Concept." In Samuel J. Meisels and Jack P. Shonkoff (eds.), *Handbook of Early Childhood Intervention.* Pp. 3-31. New York, NY: Cambridge University Press.

Shover, Neal, Donald A. Clelland, and John Lynxwiler. 1986. *Enforcement or Negotiation: Constructing a Regulatory Bureaucracy.* Albany, NY: SUNY Press.

Sidel, Ruth. 1986. *Women and Children Last: The Plight of Poor Women in Affluent America.* New York, NY: Viking.

Sinclair, Barbara. 1991. "Governing Unheroically (and Sometimes Unappetizingly): Bush and the 101st Congress." Pp. 155-184 in Colin Campbell, and Bert A. Rockman (eds.), *The Bush Presidency: First Appraisals.* Chatham, NJ: Chatham House Publishers.

Skees, Jerry R., and Louis E. Swanson. 1986. "Examining Policy and Emerging Technologies Affecting Farm Structure in the South and the Interaction Between Farm Structure and Well-Being of Rural Areas." In *Technology, Public Policy and the Changing Structure of American Agriculture.* Vol 2, Pp. 373-495. Background Papers, Part D: Rural Communities. Washington, D.C.: Office of Technology Assessment.

Slaughter-Defoe, Diana T., Kathryn Nakagawa, Ruby Takanishi, and Deborah J. Johnson. 1990. "Toward Cultural/Ecological Perspectives on Schooling and Achievement in African- and Asian-American Children." *Child Development* 61(2): 363-383.

Slottje, D.J., and K.J. Hayes. 1987. "Income Inequality and Urban/Rural Migration." *Review of Regional Studies* 17(2): 53-56.

Smith, Eldon D. 1988a. "Economic and Social Infrastructure in the Strategy of Regional Economic Development: An Alternative Theoretical Perspective Relevant to Open Economies." Staff Paper 250. Department of Agricultural Economics, University of Kentucky, Lexington, KY.

_____. 1988b. "Reflections on Human Resources in the Strategy of Rural Economic Development." Staff Paper 256. Department of Agricultural Economics, University of Kentucky, Lexington.

Smith, James P. 1989. "Children Among the Poor." *Demography* 26(2): 235-248.

Smith, Joan. 1984. "Nonwage Labor and Subsistence." In Joan Smith, Immanuel Wallerstein and Hans-Dieter Evers (eds.), *Households and the World Economy*. Pp. 64-89. Beverly Hills, CA: Sage.

Smith, Ken R., and Cathleen D. Zick. 1986. "The Indcidence of Poverty among the Recently Widowed: Mediating Factors in the Life Course." *Journal of Marriage and the Family* 48:619-30.

Smith, Ken R., and Phyllis Moen. 1988. "Passage through Midlife: Women's Changing Roles and Economic Well-Being." *Sociological Quarterly* 29:503-524.

Snipp, C. Matthew. 1988. "Public Policy and American Indian Economic Development." In C. Matthew Snipp (ed.), *Public Policy Impacts on American Indian Economic Development*. Pp. 1-22. Albuquerque, NM: Native American Studies, Institute for Native American Development, University of New Mexico.

_____. 1989. *American Indians: The First of this Land*. New York, NY: Russell Sage Foundation.

Snipp, C. Matthew, and Leonard E. Bloomquist. 1989. "Sociology and Labor Market Structure: A Selective Overview." In William W. Falk and Thomas A Lyson (eds.), *Research in Rural Sociology and Development: Focus on Labor Markets*. Vol. 4, Pp. 1-27. Greenwich, CT: JAI Press.

So, Alvin. 1990. *Social Change and Development: Modernization, Dependency and World-System Theories*. Newbury Park, CA: Sage.

Soja, Edward W. 1989. *Postmodern Geographies: The Reassertion of Space in Critical Social Theory*. London, UK: Verso.

Solow, Robert. 1990. "Poverty and Economic Growth." *Focus* 12(3): 4-5.

Sørensen, Aage B. 1977. "The Structure of Inequality and the Process of Attainment." *American Sociological Review* 42(6): 965-978.

Sørensen, Aage B., and Arne L. Kalleberg. 1981. "An Outline of a Theory for the Matching of Persons to Jobs." In Ivar Berg (ed.), *Sociological Perspectives on Labor Markets*. Pp. 49-74. New York, NY: Academic Press.

Sørensen, Annemette, and Sara McLanahan. 1987. "Married Women's Economic Dependency, 1940-1980." *American Journal of Sociology* 93(3): 659-87.

Spenner, Kenneth I., Luther b. Otto, and Vaughn R. A. Call. 1982. *Career Lines and Careers: Etry Into Carrers Series*. Vol. 3. Lexington, MA: Lexington Books.

Spilerman, Seymour. 1977. "Careers, Labor Market Structure, and Socioeconomic Achievement." *American Journal of Sociology* 83(3): 551-593.

Stack, Carol B. 1974. *All Our Kin: Strategy for Survival in a Black Community*. New York, NY: Harper and Row.

Stallmann, Judith I., Ari Mwachofi, Jan L. Flora, and Thomas G. Johnson. 1991. "The labor market and human capital investment." SP 91-17, Department of Agricultural Economics, Virginia Polytechnic Institute and State University, July.

Stanback, Thomas M. Jr., and Richard V. Knight. 1970. *The Metropolitan Economy*. New York, NY: Columbia University Press.

Staub, Erving. 1989. *The Roots of Evil: Origins of Genocide and Other Group Violence*. New York, NY: Cambridge University Press.

Sternlieb, George, and James W. Hughes. 1975. *Post-industrial America, Metropolitan Decline & Inter-regional Job Shifts*. New Brunswick, NJ: Center for Urban Polity, Rutgers University.

Stevenson, Wayne. 1982. "Youth Employment Status and Subsequent Labor Market Experience." *The Social Science Journal* 19:(4) 35-45.

Stichter, Sharon. 1990. "Women, Employment and the Family: Current Debates." In

Stichter, Sharon, and Jame L. Parpart (eds.), *Women, Employment and the Family in the International Division of Labor*. Pp. 11-72. Philadelphia, PEN: Temple University Press

Stockdale, Jerry D. 1982. "Who Will Speak for Agriculture?" In Don A. Dillman and Daryl J. Hobbs (eds.) *Rural Society in the U.S.: Issues for the 1980s*. Pp. 317-327. Boulder, CO: Westview.

Stoltzenberg, Ross M. 1975. "Occupations, Labor Markets, and the Process of Wage Attainment." *American Sociological Review* 40(5): 645-665.

_____. 1978. "Bringing the Boss Back In: Employer Size, Employer Schooling, and Socioeconomic Achievement." *American Sociological Review* 43(6) 813-828.

Storper, Michael, and Richard Walker. 1989. *The Capitalist Imperative: Territory, Technology and Industrial Growth*. New York, NY: Basil Blackwell.

Strange, Marty. 1988. *Family Farming: A New Economic Vision*. Lincoln: University of Nebraska Press.

Suitts, Steve. 1991. "Empowerment and Rural Poverty." Pp. 235-48 in Cynthia M. Duncan (ed.) *Rural Poverty in America*. New York, NY: Auburn House.

_____. 1992. "Empowerment and Rural Poverty." Pp. 235-48 in Cynthia M. Duncan (ed.), *Rural Poverty in America*. New York, NY: Auburn House.

Sum, Andrew M., and W. Neal Fogg. 1991. "The Adolescent Poor and the Transition to Early Adulthood." In Peter Edelman B. and Joyce Ladner A. (eds.), *Adolescence and Poverty: Challenge for the 1990s*. Pp. 37-109. Washington, D.C.: Center for National Policy Press, University Press of America.

Summers, Gene F. 1986. "Rural Community Development." *Annual Review of Sociology* 12:347-371.

_____. 1991. "Minorities in Rural Society." *Rural Sociology* 56: 177-88.

Summers, Gene F., Francine Horton, and Christina Gringeri. 1990. "Rural Labor-Market Changes in the United States." In Terry Marsden, Philip Lowe and Sarh Whatmore (eds.), *Rural Restructuring: Global Processes and Their Responses*. Pp. 129-164. London, UK: Fulton.

Summers, Gene F., and Kristi Branch. 1984. "Economic Development and Community Social Change." *Annual Review of Sociology* 10: 141-166.

Summers, Gene F., Sharon D. Evans, Frank Clemente, E.M. Beck, and Jon Minkoff. 1976. *Industrial Invasion of Nonmetropolitan America: A Quarter Century of Experience*. New York, NY: Praeger Publishers.

Susman, Paul, and Eric Schutz. 1983. "Monopoly and Competitive Firm Relations and Regional Development in Global Capitalism." *Economic Geography* 59(2): 161-177.

Svahn, John A., and Mary Ross. 1983. "Social Security Amendments of 1983: Legislative History and Summary of Provisions." *Social Security Bulletin* 46(1): 3-48.

Swaim, Paul. 1990. "Rural Displaced Workers Fare Poorly." *Rural Development Perspectives* 6(June-September): 8-13.

Swaim, Paul, and Ruy A. Teixeira. 1991. "Education and Training Policy: Skill Upgrading Options for the Rural Workforce." In *Education and Rural Economic Development: Strategies for the 1990's*. Pp. 122-62. Agriculture and Rural Economy Division, Economic Research Service, U.S. Department of Agriculture. ERS Staff Report No. AGES 9153.

Swanson, Linda. 1988. "The Human Dimension of the Rural South in Crisis." Pp. 87-98 in Lionel J. Beaulieu (ed.), *The Rural South in Crisis: Change for the Future*. Boulder, CO: Westview Press.

Swanson, Linda L., and Margaret A. Butler. "Human Resource Base of Rural Economies." In *Rural Economic Development in the 1980's: Preparing for the Future*. Chapter 7, Pp. 7-1 to 7-23. Agriculture and Rural Economy Division, Economic Research Service, U.S. Department of Agriculture. ERS Staff Report No. AGES870724.

Swanson, Louis E. 1989. "The Rural Development Dilemma." *Resources Number* 96: 14-16.

Szasz, Andrew. 1992. *Environmental Protection and the Grass-Roots*. Minneapolis, MN: University of Minnesota Press.

Talbot, Doroty M. 1985. "Assessing the Needs of the Rural Elderly," *Journal of Gerontological Nursing* 11(3): 39-43.

Taylor, Michael, and Nigel Thrift. 1982. *The Geography of Multinationals: Studies in the Spatial Development and Economic Consequences of Multinational Corporations*. London, UK: Croom Helm.

Texidor del Portillo, Carlota. 1987. "Poverty, Self-Concept, and Health: Experience of Latinas." In Cesar A. Perales and Lauren S. Young (eds.), *Women, Health and Poverty*. New York, NY: The Haworth Press.

Teixeira, Ruy A. 1991. "Demographic Change and the Human Capital Endowment of Rural America." Issue briefly presented at the Conference on Population Change and Future of Rural America, Wye Plantation, Maryland.

Teixeira, Ruy A., and Lawrence Mishel. 1991. "Upgrading Workers' Skills Not Sufficient to Jump-Start Rural Economy." *Rural Development Perspectives* 7(June-Sept.): 19-24.

Teixeira, Ruy A., and Paul L. Swaim. 1991. "Skill Demand and Supply in the New Economy: Issues for Rural Areas." In *Education and Rural Economic Development: Strategies for the 1990's*. Pp. 13-39. Agriculture and Rural Economy Division, Economic Research Service, U.S. Department of Agriculture. ERS Staff Report No. AGES 9153.

Texas Department of Human Services. 1988. *The Colonias Factbook*. Mimeo. Austin, TX: Texas State Government.

The Economist. January 4, 1992: 15-18.

Theodorson, George A., and Achilles G. Theodorson. 1969. *A Modern Dictionary of Sociology*. New York, NY: Thomas Y. Crowell Company.

Thieman, Alice A., Robert Fuqua, and Karen Linnan. 1991. "Iowa Family Preservation Three Year Pilot Project: Executive Summary." *The Prevention Report*. The National Resource Center on Family Based Services. Iowa City, IA: The University of Iowa School of Social Work. Fall: 8-9.

Thomas, Robert J., and William J. Friedland. 1982. *The United Farm Workers: From Mobilization to Mechanization?* Working Paper No. 269. Center for Research on Social Organization. Ann Arbor, MI: University of Michigan.

Thurow, Lester C. 1969. *Poverty and Discrimination.* Washington, D.C.: The Brookings Institute.

_____. 1975. *Generating Inequality: Mechanisms of Distribution in the U.S. Economy.* New York, NY: Basic Books.

Tickamyer, Ann R. 1992. "The Working Poor in Rural Labor Markets: The Example of the Southeastern United States." In Cynthia M. Duncan (ed), *Rural Poverty in America.* Pp. 41-61. New York, NY: Auburn House.

Tickamyer, Ann R., and Cecil Tickamyer. 1988. "Gender and Poverty in Central Appalachia." *Social Science Quarterly* 69(4): 874-891.

Tickamyer, Ann R., and Cynthia M. Duncan. 1990. "Poverty and Opportunity Structure in Rural America." *Annual Review of Sociology* 16(1): 67-86.

_____. 1991. "Work and Poverty in Rural America." In Cornelia B. Flora and James A. Christenson (eds.), *Rural Policies for the 1990s.* Pp. 102-13. Boulder, CO: Westview Press.

Tickamyer, Ann R., and Janet Bokemeier. 1988. "Sex Differences in Labor Market Experiences." *Rural Sociology* 53(2): 166-189.

_____. 1989. "Individual and Structural Explanations of Nonmetropolitan Women and Men's Labor Force Experiences." In W. Falk and T. Lyson (eds.), *Research in Rural Sociology and Development.* Volume 4, Greenwich, CON: JAI Press.

Tickamyer, Ann R., and M. Latimer. 1992. "A Multilevel Analysis of Income Sources for the Poor and Near Poor." In J. Singelmann and F. Deseran (eds.), *Inequality in Local Labor Markets* (forthcoming).

Tienda, M. 1986. "Industrial Restructuring in Metropolitan and Nonmetropolitan Labor Markets: Implications for Equity and Efficiency." In M.S. Killian, L.E. Bloomquist, S. Pendleton and D.A. McGranahan (eds.), *Symposium on Rural Labor Markets Research Issues.* Pp. 33-70. Washington, DC: U.S. Department of Agriculture, Economic Research Service.

Tigges, Leann M. 1988. "Age, Earnings, and Change within the Dual Economy." *Social Forces* 66(3): 676-698.

Tilly, Charles. 1984. *Big Structures, Large Processes, Huge Comparisons.* New York, NY: Russell Sage Foundation.

Timberlake, Michael, Bruce B. Williams, Bonnie Thornton Dill, and Darryl Tukufu. 1991. "Race and Economic Development in the Lower Mississippi Delta." Working paper. Memphis, TN: Center for Research on Women.

Tinker, I. 1981. "New Technologies for Food-Related Activities: An Equity Strategy." Pp. 51-88 in Rosalyn Dauber and Malayans L. Cain (eds.) *Women and Technological Change in Developing Countries.* Boulder, CO: Westview Press.

Tippin, George. 1980. "Is Rural Rural or Is Rural Transplanted Urban?" In Joseph Davenport III, Judith A. Davenport and James R. Wiebler (eds.), *Social Work in Rural Areas: Issues and Opportunities.* Pp. 119-121. Laramie, WY: University of Wyoming.

Tolbert, Charles M. II, Patrick M. Horan, and E. M. Beck. 1980. "The Structure of Economic Segmentation: A Dual Economy Approach." *American Journal of Sociology* 85: 1095-1116.

Tolson, Timothy F. J., and Melvin N. Wilson. 1990. "The Impact of Two- and Three-Generational Black Family Structure on Perceived Family Climate." *Child Development* 61(2): 416-428.

Tomaskovic-Devey, Donald. 1988. "The Impact of Industrial Structure, Labor Market Organization, and Income Transfers on Changes in U.S. Poverty, 1959-1979." Paper presented at the annual meetings of the American Sociological Society, Columbus, Ohio, August.

_____. 1990. "Understanding the Structural Sources of Rural Poverty: A Conceptual Position Paper." Raleigh, NC: Department of Sociology, North Carolina State University.

_____. 1991. *Sundown on the Sunbelt? Growth Without Development in the Rural South*. Report to the Ford Foundation. Raleigh, NC: Department of Sociology.

Townsend, Peter. 1979. *Poverty in the United Kingdom: A Survey of Household Resources and Standards of Living*. Berkeley, CA: University of California Press.

True, Alfred C. 1928. *A History of Agricultural Extension Work in the United States: 1785-1923*. Washington, DC: U.S. Government Printing Office.

Truelove, Cynthia. 1989. "Global Industrial Restructuring and the Industrial Informal Sector in Rural Colombia: Importing Paradigms from the Periphery." Paper presented at the annual meetings of the Rural Sociological Society, Seattle, WA. August.

Tweeten, Luther G. 1978. *Foundations of Farm Policy*, second edition revised. Lincoln, NE: University of Nebraska Press.

U.S. Bureau of the Census. n.d. *Current Population Survey*, various years. Washington, D.C.: U.S. Government Printing Office.

_____. 1983. "Money Income and Poverty Status of Families and Persons in the United States: 1982 (Advance Date from the March 1983 Current Population Survey)," *Current Population Reports*, Series P-60, No. 140. Washington, D.C.: U.S. Government Printing Office.

_____. 1988. "Measuring the Effect of Benefits and Taxes on Income and Poverty: 1986," *Current Population Reports*, Series P-60, No. 164-RD-1. Washington, D.C.: U.S. Government Printing Office.

_____. 1989. *Poverty in the United States 1987*. Current Population Reports, Series P-60, No. 163. Washington, D.C.: GPO. U.S. Government Printing Office.

_____. 1990a. *Current Population Survey, March 1990*, Tape Technical Documentation/prepared by Data User Services Division, Data Access and Use Staff. Washington, D.C.: U.S. Department of Commerce.

_____. 1990b. *Current Population Survey, March 1990* [machine readable data file]/conducted by the Breau of the Census for the Bureau of Labor Statistics. Washington, D.C.: U.S. Department of Commerce.

_____. 1990c. "Measuring the Effect of Benefits and Taxes on Income and Poverty: 1987-88," *Current Population Reports*, Series P-60, No. 170-RD. Washington, D.C.: U.S. Government Printing Office.

_____. 1990d. "Measuring the Effect of Benefits and Taxes on Income and Poverty: 1989," *Current Population Reports*, Series P-60, No. 169-RD. Washington, D.C.: U.S. Government Printing Office.

_____. 1990e. "Measuring the Effect of Benefits and Taxes on Income and Poverty: 1990," *Current Population Reports*, P-60, No. 176-RD. Washington, D.C.: U.S. Department of Commerce.

_____. 1991a. "Measuring the Effect of Benefits and Taxes on Income and Poverty: 1990," *Current Population Reports*, Series P-60, No. 176-RD. Washington, D.C.: U.S. Government Printing Office.

_____. 1991b. "Money Income of Households, Families, and Persons in the United States: 1990," *Current Population Reports*, Series P-60, No. 174. Washington, D.C.: U.S. Government Printing Office.

_____. 1991c. "Poverty in the United States: 1990," *Current Population Reports*, Series P-60, No. 175. Washington, D.C.: U.S. Government Printing Office.

U.S. Department of Agriculture. 1976. "Analytical Support for Cost of Living Differentials in the Poverty Thresholds," *The Measure of Poverty*. Technical Paper XV. Prepared by the Economic Research Service of the U.S. Department of Health, Education, and Welfare. Washington, D.C.: U.S. Government Printing Office.

_____. 1987. *Rural Economic Development in the 1980s*. Washington, D.C.: Economic Research Service.

_____. 1990/1991. *Rural Conditions and Trends* 1 (No.4). Economic Research Service. Washington, DC: U.S. Department of Agriculture. U.S. Government Printing Office.

U.S. Department of Commerce, Bureau of the Census. 1991. "Poverty in the United States: 1990." *Current Population Reports: Consumer Income, Series P-60, No.175.* Washington, DC: U.S. Government Printing Office. November.

U.S. Department of Commerce, Bureau of Economic Analysis. 1991a. *Local Area Personal Income 1969-86*. Computer files of metro and nometro personal income date (Machine-readable date file). Washington, D.C.

_____. 1991b. *Local Area Personal Income: 1984-89*, Vol. 1, Summary. Washington, D.C.: U.S. Government Printing Office.

U.S. Department of Education. 1990. *Digest of Educational Statistics*. U.S. Department of Health, Education and Welfare, Office of Education. Washington, D.C.: GPO. U.S. Government Printing Office.

U.S. Department of Health and Human Services. 1978. *Overcoming Barriers to Planning for Children in Foster Care*. Pp. 47-63. Washington, DC: Administration for Children, Youth and Families, Children's Bureau.

U.S. Federal Committee on Standard Metropolitan Statistical Areas. 1979. *The Metropolitan Statistical Area Classification*. Final Standards for Establishing Metropolitan Statistical Areas Following the 1980 Census. Washington, D.C.: U.S. Government Printing Office.

U.S. Senate Special Committee on Aging. 1988. "The Rural Health Challenge." Serial No. 100-N, Senate Report No. 100-145. Washington, DC: U.S. Government Printing Office.

Uhlenberg, Peter. 1973. "Noneconomic Determinants of Nonmigration: Sociological Considerations for Migration Theory." *Rural Sociology* 38: 296-311.

Urry, John. 1981. "Localities, Regions and Social Class." *International Journal of Urban and Regional Research* 5(4): 455-474.

_____. 1984. "Capitalist Restructuring, Recomposition and the Regions." In Tony Bradly and Philip Lowe (eds.), *Locality and Rurality: Economy and Society in Rural Regions*. Pp. 45-64. Norwich, UK: Geo Books.

_____. 1988. "Capitalist Production, Scientific Management and the Service Class." In Allen J. Scott and Michel Storper (eds.), *Production, Work, Territory: The Geographical Anatomy of Industrial Capitalism*. Pp. 43-66. Boston, MA: Allen and Unwin.

Vail, David J. 1989. "How to Tell the Forest from the Trees: a Comparison of Recent Technological Innovations in Logging Systems in Sweden and Maine." *Technology in Society* 11: 347-376.

_____. 1992. "Commentary on 'Poverty and Human Capital Investment'." *Correspondence with the Working Group*, January.

Valentine, Charles A. 1968. *Culture and Poverty: Critique and counter Proposal*. Chicago, IL: University of Chicago Press.

Van Praag, Bernard M. S., Theo Goedhart, and Arie Kapteyn. 1980. "The Poverty Line: A Pilot Survey in Europe." *Review of Economics and Statistics* 62 (3): 461-65.

Van Praag, Bernard M. S., Jan S. Spit, and Huib Van de Stadt. 1982. "A Comparison Between the Food-Ratio Poverty Line and the Leyden Poverty Line." *Review of Economics and Statistics* 64 (4):691-94.

Vinson, E. A., and K. M. Jesberg. 1981. "The Rural Stake in Public Assistance: Summary of Findings and Recommendations." In Emilia E. Martinez-Brawley (ed.), *Seven Decades of Rural Social Work: From Country Life Commission to Rural Caucus*. New York, NY: Praeger.

Voydanoff, Patricia. 1984. "Unemployment: Family Strategies for Adaption." In Patricia Voydanoff (ed.), *Work & Family: Changing Roles of Men and Women*. Pp. 61-72. Palo Alto, CA: Mayfield Publishing Co.

_____. 1990. "Economic Distress and Family Relations: A Review of the Eighties." *Journal of Marriage and the Family* 52(4): 1099-1115.

Voydanoff, Patricia, and Brenda W. Donnelly. 1988. "Economic Distress, Family Coping, and Quality of Family Life." In Patricia Voydanoff and Linda C. Majka (eds.), *Families and Economic Distress: Coping Strategies and Social Policy*. Pp. 97-115. Newbury Park, CA: Sage Publications.

Wachtel, Howard M. 1973. "Looking at Poverty From a Radical Perspective." In David Mermelstein (ed.), *Economics: Mainstream Readings and Radical Critiques* Second Edition Pp. 273-277. New York, NY: Random House.

Wadley, David. 1986. *Restructuring the Regions, Analysis, Policy Model and Prognosis*. Paris, FR: Organization for Economic Co-operation and Development.

Waldinger, Robert, Howard Aldrich, Robin Ward, and Associates. 1990. *Ethnic Entrepreneurs: Immigrant Business in Industrial Societies*. Newbury Park, CA: Sage Publications.

Waltman, Gretchen H. 1986. "Main Street Revisited: Social Work Practice in Rural Areas." *Social Casework: The Journal of Contemporary Social Work* 67(8): 466-474.

Ward, Colin. 1988. *The Child in the Country*. London, UK: Bedfore Square Press.

Ward, Kathryn. 1990. "Introduction and Overview." In Kathryn Ward (ed.), *Women Workers and Global Restructuring*. Ithaca, NY: ILR Press, Cornell University.

Warlick, Jennifer L. 1985. "Why is Poverty After 65 a Woman's Problem?" *Journal of Gerontology* 40(6): 751-757.

Warren, Kristin K., Robert G. Lee, and Matthew S. Carroll. 1991. "Timber-Dependent Communities in Crisis: Assessing the Roles and Reactions of Rural Women." Paper presented at Annual Meetings of Rural Sociological Society, Columbus, OH, August.

Watkins, Julia M., and Dennis A Watkins. 1984. *Social Policy and the Rural Setting*. New York, NY: Springer Publishing Company.

Weaver, Clyde. 1984. *Regional Development and the Local Community: Planning, Politics and Social Context*. New York, NY: Wiley.

Weber, Max. 1968. *Economy and Society: An Outline of Interpretive Sociology*. Edited by Guenther Roth and Claus Wittich. Translated by Guenther Roth. New York, NY: Bedminster Press.

Weeks, Edward C. 1990. "Mill Closures in the Pacific Northwest: The Consequences of Economic Decline in Rural Industrial Communities," in Robert E. Lee, Donald R. Field, and William R. Burch, Jr., eds., *Community and Forestry: Continuities in the Sociology of Natural Resources*. Pp. 125-40. Boulder, CO: Westview Press.

Wehler, Cheryl A., Richard Ira Scott, Jennifer J. Anderson, and Lynn Parker. 1991. *Community Childhood Hunger Identification Project: A Survey of Childhood Hunger in the United States*. Washington, DC: Food Research and Action Center.

Weinstein, Bernard L., Harold T. Gross, and John Rees. 1985. *Regional Growth and Deline in the United States* (second edition). New York, NY: Praeger Publishing.

Weller, Jack E. 1965. *Yesterday's People: Life in Contemporary Appalachia*. Lexington, KY: University of Kentucky Press.

Wellstone, Paul David. 1978. *How the Rural Poor Got Power: Narrative of a Grass Roots Organizer*. Amherst, MA: University of Massachusetts Press.

Wenk, DeeAnn. 1989. "A Residential Comparison of Child Care Arrangements." Unpublished paper.

Wenk, DeeAnn, and Constance L. Hardesty. 1992. "Family and Household Effects on the Educational Attainment of Young Adults." In Lionel J. Beaulieu and David Mulkey, *Investing in People: The Human Capital Needs of Rural America*. Boulder, CO: Westview Press.

Wenk, DeeAnn, and Patricia Garrett. 1992. "Having a Baby: Some Predictions of Maternal Employment Aground Child Birth." *Gender & Society* 6(1): 49-65.

Werner, Emmy E., and Ruth S. Smith. 1982. *Vulnerable But Invincible: A Longitudinal Study of Resilient Children and Youth*. Pp. 120-164, 209-217. New York, NY: McGraw-Hill Book Company.

West, P. C. 1982a. Natural Resource Bureaucracy and Rural Poverty: A Study in the Political Sociology of Natural Resources. Monograph #2. University of Michigan, School of Natural Resources, Natural Resource Sociology Research Lab, Ann Arbor.

_____. 1982b. "Tribal Control and the Identity-Poverty Dilemma." In Charles Geisler, et al. (eds.), *Indian SIA: The Social Impact Assessment of Rapid Resource Development on Native Peoples*. Pp. 80-92. Ann Arbor, MI: University of Michigan, School of Natural Resources, Natural Resource Sociology Research Lab, Monograph No. 3.

_____. 1985. "Fisheries and Social Equity: Provisional Perspectives for a Political Sociology of the Indian Fishing Rights Conflict in the Michigan Great Lakes." In C. Bailey, et al. (eds.), Proceedings of the Workshop on Fisheries Sociology. Pp. 85-98. Marine Policy and Ocean Management Center, Woods Hole Oceanographic Institution.

_____. 1992. "Natural Resources and Rural Poverty: The Role of Power, Domination, and Natural Resource Bureaucracy." Unpublished manuscript prepared for the Working Group on Natural Resources and Poverty, Rural Sociological Task Force on Persistent Poverty in Rural America.

Whatmore, Sarah, Philip Lowe, and Terry Marsden. 1991. *Rural Enterprise: Shifting Perspectives on Small-Scale Production*. London, UK: David Fulton Publishers.

White, Leonard D. 1958. *The Republican Era: A Study in Administrative Management*. New York, NY: Macmillan.

White, Robert H. 1990. *Tribal Assets: The Rebirth of Native American*. New York, NY: Henry Holt and Company.

Whitener, Leslie A. 1991. "The JOBS Program and Rural Areas." *Rural Development Perspectives* 7(February/May): 21-26.

Whitman, Barbara Y., Pasquale Accardo, Mary Boyert, and Rita Kendagor. 1990. "Homelessness and Cognitive Performance in Children: A Possible Link." *Social Work* 35(6): 516-519.

William T. Grant Foundation. 1988. *The Forgotten Half: Pathways to Success for America's Youth and Young Families: Final Report*. Washington, D.C.: William T. Grant Foundation.

Williams, Robert C. 1987. *Fordson, Farmall, and Poppin' Johnny: A History of the Farm Tractor and Its Impact on america*. Urbana, IL: University of Illinois Press.

Williamson, J. G. 1965. "Regional Inequality and the Process of National Development." *Economic Development and Cultural Change* 13(4/II): 3-45.

Williamson, Oliver A. 1975. *Markets and Hierarchies: Analysis and Antitrust Implications: A Study in the Economics of Internal Organization*. New York, NY: Free Press.

Wilson, William Julius. 1980. *The Declining Significance of Race: Blacks and Changing American Institutions*. Chicago, IL: University of Chicago Press.

_____. 1987. *The Truly Disadvantaged: The Inner City, the Underclass, and Social Works*. Chicago, IL: University of Chicago Press.

_____. 1991. "Studying Inner-City Social Dislocations: The Challenge of Public Agenda Research." *American Sociological Review* 56(1): 1-14.

Wood, Phillip J. 1986. *Southern Capitalism: The Political Economy of North Carolina, 1880-1980*. Durham, N.C.: Duke University Press.

Worobey, Jacqueline Lowe, and Ronald J. Angel. 1991. "Poverty and Health: Older Minority Women and the Rise of the Female-Headed Household." *Journal of Health and Social Behavior* 31(3): 370-383.

Ycas, Martynas A., and Susan Grad. 1987. "Income of Retirement-Aged Persons in the United States," *Social Security Bulletin* 50(7): 5-14.

Yetley, Mervin J. 1988. "Rural Labor Underutilization." *Choices* (Fall Quarter): 34-35.

Young, Frank W., and Thomas A. Lyson. forthcoming, 1993. "Branch Plants and Poverty in the American South." *Sociological Forum*.

Young, John A., and Jan M. Newton. 1980. *Capitalism and Human Obsolescence: Corporate Control Versus Individual Survival in Rural America*. Montclair, NJ: Allanheld, Osmun.

Young, Kate Porter. *To Be Somebody: Sisterhood and Self in an African-American South Carolina Community*. Department of Anthropology, University of North Carolina, Chapel Hill, NC. (Forthcoming).

Young, Ruth C., and Joe D. Francis. 1989. "Who Helps Small Manufacturing Firms Get Started?" *Rural Development Perspectives* 6(1): 21-25.

_____. 1991. "Regional and Industrial Structure: A Network Approach," unpublished manuscript, Dept. of Rural Sociology, Cornell University, Ithaca, NY.

Zysman, John. 1983. *Governments, Markets, and Growth: Financial Systems and the Politics of Industrial Change*. Ithaca, NY: Cornell University Press.